Reflections

of a

Troubled
Black Man

A Teacher's Quest, Turning Fear Into Strength, and Pain Into Passion

A Memoir

MORRIS H. ERVIN, JR.

This book is a memoir. It reflects the author's present recollections
of experiences over time. While all persons within are actual individuals,
most names, locations, and identifying characteristics have been changed
to respect their privacy, and dialogue has been recreated.

Print ISBN: 979-8-35094-825-7
eBook ISBN: 979-8-35094-826-4

www.morriservin.com

To all my students.

"Love the life you live and live the life you love,
"Let's continue to reimagine education.

Let's collectively rise...and just be patient,
be persistent, never see defeat.

TABLE OF CONTENTS

ACKNOWLEDGEMENTS

Foremost, I want to thank my wife, Dr. Venaya K. Jones, for loving me unconditionally despite my flaws and insecurities. She is my inspiration and my rock. I am so thankful for how she pushes me to want better, be better, and see better things. I feel the full embodiment of what it means to be present when I am with her. I am thankful that Venaya's persistence and love led me to the people and resources that would transform my memoir into a reality.

I am grateful for my daughter, Naimah, and son, Idris, who graciously have had to share me with the world. My persona has sometimes brought them unwanted attention, but they have always handled it with class and grace. They are my first priority, and I am a better man and leader because of the lessons they both are teaching me.

Heartfelt thanks to my parents for showing me the importance of giving and serving the community. I developed my leadership style and generous heart by watching them open our home and resources to less fortunate family members, people in our neighborhood, and the wider community. I am grateful for my sister, who protected me as a little boy and gave me a sense of style as a teenager. Her insights on social justice have fueled my passion for education and societal change. To my little brother, for looking up to me for guidance. I am thankful for our quality times together and how that time impacted his growth and development.

Jayrod Johnson, my brother from another mother, thank you. Our friendship and nurturing relationship represent presence, empathy, full self-expression, intimacy of healthy masculinity, and compassionate manhood. His love for the spoken and written word has always and will always push me to be a better man and author.

To my friend, brother, and colleague, Steve Hardaway, the principal, who took a chance and allowed me to bring my passion for nonviolent communication into my classes and curriculum. Thank you for letting me encourage students to express their emotions when staff frowned upon and ridiculed such an approach to teaching. Steve championed my work, took some hits for me, and used his structural power as principal to green light the documentary film, premiere night, and all the community/parenting workshops that followed. Our personal and professional bond is unmatched.

Dr. James Brown, my spiritual mentor, is the baddest dude on the planet. He is gentle, brilliant, humble, and uses words with eloquence and care. Together, we move worlds and travel through space and time. Most importantly, he helped me see the beauty, sustainability, and power of the peace within and a peace that withstands all possibilities.

Dr. Virgil Wood, a civil rights pioneer and icon, gracefully taught me the essence of reimaging the Beloved Community in contemporary times. Although 93 years young, when he reached out to me, his soul, confidence, fierceness, and resolve for a better world ignited a new fire in me that will never be extinguished.

To my nonviolent communication (NVC) tribe, and especially Dr. Marshall Rosenberg, thank you. From the first time I witnessed him teaching, I was in awe of how he listened and held space. His presence, playfulness, honesty, and his heart touched me deeply. Within moments of being around him, I knew I would dedicate my life to the consciousness, principles, and practices of his work. I want to thank Catherine Cadden for helping me see the importance of being true to myself while doing the deep work. Catherine inspired me to tap into my fearless side, challenging the status quo from a place of love. I also want to thank Jesse Wiens-Chu for his confidence and faith in me. Jesse understands me on a deeply personal, cultural, and structural level. He holds space for the complexity of inequality, and his skill level has depth and breadth. He is a perfect blend of Zen, nonviolent communication, and social justice.

Additionally, I want to thank Barbra Esher, who has supported my NVC journey from day one. Barbra is always ready to support me. She has played a crucial role in my journey to become a certified trainer and my quest to make my teachings more accessible to the masses. Big kudos to Jim Manske, who read my manuscript later in the process and wrote a beautiful testimony. Jim, I am forever grateful.

To Elizabeth Lesser, a powerful woman, co-founder of the Omega Institute, bestselling author, humanitarian, and so many other wonderful things. To me, she is "Ma Liz." In the infancy of my memoir writing, Ma Liz and her love for our relationship informed me not to send her my manuscript if I wasn't serious about writing. She did not want her critique of my manuscript to damage our close relationship. I understood and appreciated her telling me the truth. It brought us closer together and inspired me to dig deep inside. As a result, Ma Liz was the first to read the first draft of my manuscript outside of my editor. Her feedback and endorsement brought me immense joy and brought me to tears. She said, "Son, you have yourself a memoir!"

Super thanks to Yolanda "Eagle Eye" Asher for tirelessly proofreading every word in the memoir in a short amount of time and catching a few glitches in the memoir that made a huge difference. I also want to thank Ben McCullough, my website developer, for capturing the essence of my memoir through the development of the landing page. Ben and I partnered in many meetings and conversations to create a brand that would appeal to my audience. I also want to profoundly thank the BookBaby cover design team for capturing the look I wanted for my memoir.

Thank you, Anita Khayat, Bob Fedor, and Michael Lawson from SCORE, the nation's largest network of volunteer and expert business mentors who are dedicated to helping small business owners like me succeed. For over two years, Bob and Anita have worked with me to make crucial decisions that have allowed me to mature and see my value/growth potential, which has expanded my scope while providing me with excellent guidance. Thank you, Michael, who recently joined the SCORE Team, for conceptualizing a clear marketing plan that coordinates and organizes our efforts to raise awareness, expand my brand presence, and engage my target audience through various channels.

The overall process of writing *Reflections of a Troubled Black Man* took seven years. It was a journey of discovering my voice and confidence as an author. I love to write. I have been writing all my life. However, the process of becoming an author was intimidating. It was terrifying. Early on, I failed to realize the importance of sharing my writing with the community of other writers.

I want to thank my wife for introducing me to the Reverend Dr. Leah Lewis, Founder and Executive Director of The Great Lakes African American Writers Conference (GLAAWC). Dr. Lewis immediately shared information about her writer's conference and the "Discover the Writer Within" workshop led by Shelley Shockley and Dawn Arrington. The writer's workshop provided a safe space for sharing and offering feedback with writers from various backgrounds. Writers in a variety of genres shared their work. We met every Saturday for two hours at the Martin Luther King Library. We were all strongly encouraged to share excerpts from our writing and critique each other's work. I was scared, but I shared a part of my memoir. The community critiqued it and gave me helpful suggestions. Most importantly, they enjoyed my writing style. Thankfully, my willingness to share opened the door for me and the amazing Michelle Phillips Fay, another writer in the workshop, to be selected to read an excerpt of our writings at GLAAWC. Michelle is a juggernaut. She is fearless. She read first. Her words inspired me. The audience cheered for us.

Afterward, Dr. Leah introduced me to Kim Martin Sadler, the editorial director at The Pilgrim Press. Kim had over 25 years of publishing experience. Kim, now retired, has a mission to help writers who choose to self-publish. Her mantra is to ensure an author's writing is stellar and their published book looks professional.

I decided to hire Kim as my editor. Over four years, through personal adversity and a global pandemic, she has been a beacon of light, faith, fellowship, trust, and sustainability for me. I am blessed beyond measure to know and be mentored by someone as extraordinary as Kim Martin Sadler. She is the real deal. She, by far, is a true professional at her craft. In addition to all the developmental editing, reading, and re-reading of my memoir and bimonthly Zoom meetings, she set up a calendar with deadlines. Kim researched self-publishing companies for me; she met with my business mentors, marketing team members, and website developer. Most of all, her passion for authenticity, speaking truth to power, and love for Black Cultural Excellence has transformed me into the author I had always dreamed of being.

CHAPTER 1

Confronting Anger and Rage

"Holding on to anger is like grasping hot coal
with the intent of throwing it at someone else;
you are the one who gets burned."
Buddha

I am passionate about teaching ninth grade American History. My ninth grade students are full of life, and every day is quite an adventure. I love sharing laughs with my students when we occasionally get off-topic. My goal is to create a safe, loving atmosphere that nourishes learning and personal growth. I am adamant about using reading comprehension techniques such as Think-a-Louds, Reciprocal Teaching, and Think Pair share activities. I yearn for students to be eager about their engagement with the historical text to create a meaningful learning environment. I manage a fun but strict classroom. I don't tolerate disrespectful behavior. If my male students are tardy, they must do push-ups before they are allowed in my room. I tend to let my female students slide because they rarely arrive late. When students use profanity, they must look up long multisyllabic words and alternative ways to speak without being offensive to the class. I am the king of my classroom. Because of this, my students love and respect me. If students go too far, I will not hesitate to raise my voice and let them know I will not tolerate disrespect.

One day, in the teachers' lounge, I heard teachers share frightening stories about a new student named Leon. I learned Leon had been transferred directly from a juvenile detention facility. Likewise, students shared their stories about Leon's intimidating presence and how he had bullied them out of their lunch money. One day, as I stood outside my classroom looking at an empty hallway, I saw one student strolling toward me. He had an intimidating gait, one as if he ruled the school. We lock eyes like two prizefighters. I kept my eyes on his face, never blinking nor looking in another direction. No words were exchanged, but my stance and facial expression sent a message—not today, not ever. Additionally, I wish you would try me if you want to; if you are froggy, then leap!

A week later, as I discussed the causes and consequences of World War I, the door flew open as if it had exploded! Suddenly, a figure with a ski mask ran into my room and stood before me! He shouted a variety of curse words while continually grabbing his private parts. As I watched and listened to this masked bandit, all kinds of thoughts exploded in my head, but I didn't make a sound. The thirty students in my room stared at this person until he turned and rushed out the door. I gave a plastic smile, and then I felt a sudden rush and influx of pain. I bolted for the door, intoxicated by my rage. I stalked the intruder from behind as he jogged from the second floor down to the first. I crept closer to him in full fight mode! My mind was desperate, and my reckless head was spinning. I was in a daze. I watched as he pulled off his mask and pushed the door open.

Leon ran out of the building towards the Board of Education, a short distance away. I forcefully pushed the door open and furiously watched him skip away, happy as he could be. I knew he thought he had gotten the best of me. I dashed after him, thinking this kid had to pay for this! So, I ran full speed ahead in my dress shoes. My tie was flowing in the wind like a kite. He had no idea I was running straight toward him. I grabbed him. He yanked away from my grasp. We squared off in front of each other, fists ready to fight. He said, "Man, get out of here before I swing on you!" I didn't respond. Reason came back into my conscience somewhere between his threats and my silence. I said, "What's your problem, Leon, bursting into my class like you crazy?" He said, "I was just playing around. You have a lot of pretty girls in there!" I uttered, "My class is my kingdom, and I don't like anyone messing with my kingdom! Next time, if you want to come in, knock on the door and ask!" "Okay," he said. We gave each other a quick embrace, and he ran off.

As I stood directly across from the Board of Education, thoughts flooded my mind! You left your class, chased a student out of the building, and almost got into a fistfight! I hurried back into the building with the "I'm about to get fired" expression on my face. Entering the building, I ran upstairs to my classroom, realizing the period had ended. I begrudgingly walked to the principal's office with my heart in total panic. I walked into the office, and the secretary said, "Hey, Morris, was that you outside the school by the Board?" I shook my head with a sheepish grin and said, "Of course not, Ms. Betty."

A few days before that incident, the conflict mediation teacher, Kathy, invited me to attend a three-day workshop called NVC, or Nonviolent Communication, in Columbus, Ohio. Why would she give me this? I don't need this, I thought. I threw the brochure into the recycle bin. Something told me I had to rethink my decision, especially after the Leon incident. Honestly, I knew I had an anger problem. Somehow, throughout my life, I had managed to address it without any tools. I walked into Kathy's office and expressed interest in attending the conference. Her face lit up with excitement. She gave me booklets to read and a tape to listen to before the conference.

The conference introduced me to a world created by Dr. Marshall Rosenberg. Dr. Rosenberg developed the NVC process out of curiosity to understand what caused humans to be hostile toward each other. He wanted to create peaceful alternatives to violence on a personal, social, and political level. Dr. Rosenberg received his Ph.D. in Clinical Psychology and started using his technique to integrate schools in the 1960s. Rosenberg eventually created the Center for Nonviolent Communication, which focused on the art of Compassionate Communication. It contributed to a radical shift or transformation in thinking, speaking, and communicating between people from all walks of life in diverse circumstances. Certified trainers who organize workshops, practice groups, and retreats offer NVC training worldwide. The training provides the tools and skills to help prevent and resolve conflicts in families, schools, businesses, corporations, countries, etc. NVC helps us to focus on the feelings and needs we all have rather than thinking, speaking, and acting by using dehumanizing labels or other habitual patterns that can lead to violence. NVC equips people to engage in creative dialogue to rebuild relationships and make collective decisions for the well-being of all.

I attended Dr. Rosenberg's training. His playful way of using his guitar and puppets to facilitate this communication process provoked my need to learn more about this man and his approach. He had this spiritual energy that engaged the audience. I loved his ability to role-play different conflict scenarios and use the language of feelings and needs to get to the root cause of the dilemma. It sparked a new flame within me. I left the three-day conference with a new outlook on life and a desire to dig deeper into this process.

Filled with new enthusiasm after returning from the NVC retreat, someone knocked on the door during my sixth-period History class. I opened it, and there stood Leon. He humbly asked, "May I come to your class this time." I said, "Of course." Leon quietly walked in and sat down. When we finished the history lesson, he joined our discussion about personal struggles and openly shared his story of pain. We became close after that day, often talking during lunch and competing against each other by racing in the hallways. The three-day NVC conference changed my approach to working with aggressive or defiant students. I continued reading books about Compassionate Communication and incorporated a little of the language into my classroom and personal life.

One day, to my delightful surprise, the mediation specialist asked me if I would be interested in attending an eight-day intensive retreat on NVC. It would take place in Seattle, Washington, during the summer. With a smile as wide as the Atlantic Ocean, I said, "Absolutely!" "Great," she responded. "I will submit your name to the principal."

As an educator, I saw African American youth's suppressed anger and rage. Before becoming a teacher, I worked in a juvenile halfway house. I vividly remembered the explosions the young men displayed, from not getting extra snacks to not receiving visits from loved ones. I recall young men being slow to forgive and quick to lash out, attack staff, or destroy property when things did not go their way. Ironically, working in a juvenile setting prepared me to work in inner-city school districts. I noticed similar outbursts there. I got first-hand experience with this pent-up rage on a Friday after *With* my students threw a baby shower for the birth of my son.

With a smile of gratitude on my face, I gleefully stroll across the third floor, heading towards the staircase. To my surprise, a young man decides to walk with me. As we walk, spiraling down from the third to the second floor, we spark a conversation. As we got to the second-floor landing, two other students leaped out with fists of fury and began punching him. I grabbed one of the students and slung him towards the staircase, stumbling down the stairs behind him. I quickly jumped up and saw a few more young men attack the student as he tried to fight for his life. I tossed and pushed them off again and again.

As this melee continued, a ring of students surrounded this battle royale like a huge crowd watching gladiators in a ring. I grabbed the last kid, who refused to stop throwing punches, and slammed him on the floor. As I secured him, pinning his shoulders to the floor, something told me to look over my shoulder—call it instinct or gut response. I quickly turned to see a heavyset boy with his fist cocked back like a slingshot, ready to sucker punch me from behind. I frantically jumped up and shoved him against the wall. I screamed, "What's your problem?"

Finally, the security team joined the mix and gained control of the situation. Trying to straighten my now wrinkled suit, I stood gasping for air. I gently touched my forehead, rubbing a knot that had developed. I trotted up the stairs to gather all the new diapers and toys my students had purchased for the baby shower. Suddenly, I panicked. I realized I was late for a prenatal appointment with my wife. I jumped in the car and rushed home. I hopped up the steps to the front door. It opened. I looked like I had been in a W.W.F. brawl. As my wife looked me up and down, she said, "You're late! Let's go!" I later learned that the fight was a planned retaliation from neighborhood gang activity. The principal immediately handed out expulsions to all the young men involved. However, I wondered if that would suppress these Black youths' consistent anger and rage.

I am glad my views have shifted concerning punishing youth for fights and disruptive behavior. Initially, my thoughts were very stern and strict regarding the discipline of students for disrespectful behavior. I did not hesitate to yell or get in a kid's face if I felt disrespected. Like some adults, I treated young people as objects that could be ordered around and forced to do things my way. When I was in high school, we had muscular security guards who wouldn't hesitate to body slam a student or rough up anyone who got out of line. Maybe, as I reflect on it, I had conformed to the norms around the demonization and the objectification of Black youth.

So, as a youth, this sanctioned rage from my father and other men with authority was just business as usual. Early in my career, I adopted an aggressive attitude of "It's us versus them." We had to show these kids how to stay in line and obey. A fellow history teacher and colleague had the same mentality. He would quickly pull a kid into the hallway, scream, and berate him past the point of humiliation—and then send him back inside the class. As male teachers, specifically Black male teachers, we celebrated this toxic, dysfunctional rage disguised as discipline. My views changed when I taught at a new school where uniformed security guards were armed with handcuffs and mace.

What a wonderful experience we had at the African American Underground Railroad Museum in Cincinnati, Ohio. We explored our history through simulated activities, artifacts, short documentary films, and observations of historical artifacts preserved by the museum. It brought me so much joy to leave Cleveland with fifteen students, a few volunteers, and staff to experience this culturally enriched field trip together. Unfortunately, however, the school's administrators had scheduled the school dance on the same day as our field trip. Nevertheless, I remained hopeful that we would return in enough time for the students to attend. Eventually, we arrived at the school about fifteen minutes after the dance had begun.

The students were so excited they rushed off the bus directly into the school, eager to see friends, share their experiences, and dance to good music. With excitement, I walked behind them. As I approached the door, I noticed somber and troubled looks on the students' faces. As I walked closer, I came to a table at the entrance with two administrators and two secretaries sitting in chairs behind it. The students were not allowed into the party. One secretary sat firm and resolute in denying the students entry. Her rigid demeanor might have scared teenagers, but not me.

I walked directly to where she was sitting and said, Mrs. Smith, "You and I know we are returning from a school enrichment field trip. Someone decided to move the dance to the same day as our trip. That's cruel and unfair. Please let the students enter the dance. I'll stay as a chaperone." Without even a flinch or blink of an eye, she vehemently shouted, "No!" Her words ruptured a geyser of anger, frustration, disgust, and rage inside my diaphragm. I squinted in disgust and responded, "What is the problem? These are excellent students. They should not be held responsible for being late. This makes no sense!" She replied, "It's against the school policy. Students who arrive fifteen minutes late are not allowed in the dance." I sighed deeply as her words spewed hatred, bias, and shameless bureaucracy throughout the lobby.

We continued to spar a few more rounds with each other while the other adults and administrators sat silently. Finally, one administrator I respected as an elder said, "Mr. Ervin, that's enough!" I staggered back. I was clueless about why he sat quietly and did not try to defend the students. He, however, confidently silenced me. Stunned and dazed, I zipped my lips, conceded my valiant try, and accepted defeat. Soon after, I saw a handcuffed student, Raheem, escorted out of the dance by a police officer. Raheem was a creative, down-to-earth, mature, scholarly student who impulsively decided to take matters into his own hands by sneaking into the dance through another entrance. I dashed toward the officer, who was briskly holding Raheem by his handcuffed arms for everyone to see. As he tried to ignore me, I shouted, "Get those handcuffs off, Raheem! He is not a criminal!" I repeated my words several times as another squad car rolled up. Raheem lowered his head to maneuver into the back of the patrol car.

I was speechless. The fury I felt was too difficult to express. I paced outside on the curb, hoping my steps would turn back the hands of time. I pondered. I wondered. How could such a momentous, memorable, inspirational day turn into a disastrous, tragic evening? How could a young man with a 3.5-grade point average, a star athlete on the football team, and the most popular student in the school be handcuffed and tossed in the back of the squad car like a thug who robbed a liquor store? How could an educator like me be so blind not to see something like this happening? Underneath my rage of blame and guilt, I walked to my car with an unbearable sadness, taking the burden of it all on my broad but slender shoulders. Right there, I started to question my role in education. I gained a new awareness of how to treat Black students.

After this incident with Raheem, the blatant show of police and their obsession with power and control illuminated my sense of racial injustice and its burden on Black people. I questioned the excessive number of security and police officers roaming the hallways looking for miscreants. I moved differently as a teacher. I carefully listened to conversations of White staff in the teacher's lounge. I noticed how teachers quickly kicked kids out of class, hoping those "bad kids" would not return. Sometimes, on my off periods, I walked throughout the building. I noticed that most White kids were safely tucked away in the honors or advanced placement classes with a sprinkling of Black students. I peered into the special education wing of the school only to see all Black males in a classroom. Most of them had their heads down on a desk. Only a few attempted to complete a worksheet, while a non-responsive White teacher sat far away behind a desk.

I wondered why high-performing suburban schools with a majority White student population became underperforming schools with a zero-tolerance discipline policy when an influx of Black students enrolled. The suppression of anger, rage, and despair would consistently manifest into school fights. I remember opening my classroom door and hearing loud thuds and curse words from the hallway. I was highly disturbed to see a girl's entire body on top of another girl, with her knees placed perfectly inside her opponent's armpits. The girl on the bottom lay silent as the girl on top mercilessly punched her in the face as she yelled curse words and insults. I sprinted down the hallway, tackling the girl on top. Wow, with a few more blows, that girl would have died or had severe brain damage.

On multiple occasions in the hallways or stairwells, I would break up neighborhood fights that had spilled into the school. I would lecture the young men before the goofy-ass security guards and officers arrived. Each time they came, they gave me an evil glare as if I had committed a heinous crime. One time, a young, tall, slender man with an extra fresh white tee, Allen Iverson cornrows, and baggy jeans that could fit a Volkswagen walked directly up to me with big, bulging eyes. He said, "Mr. Erv, do you know why we stop fighting whenever you come around? It's because everyone around here has the utmost respect for you. You care, and you give a shit about us!" After his brief but moving speech, he gave me the cool side bro hug and sauntered down the hallway.

Respect. Respect. Aretha Franklin said it best. "R.E.S.P.E.C.T., find out what it means to me." The disrespect felt and experienced in Black neighborhoods and schools is normalized and built into them. It's a life trying to survive, filled with stress. I began seeing this world, this multi-layered complex ecosystem called a school, and I perpetually wondered about my place there. Am I perpetuating the problem, or working towards a solution? The very next day, another young man got into a physical altercation with another young man. It was a typical fistfight. However, when I heard about it, I went to the security office to check on the young man who had been assaulted. I knew him and his twin sister because they were in my ninth grade American History class.

Over the semester, I became fond of David because of his vibrant personality and charismatic attitude. In addition to being in my class, I earned his trust and respect. He often shared his personal life and living situation with me. He expressed rage at his father, who abandoned him, his mom, and his sister to live with another woman and raise her kids. His father's abandonment crushed David as he struggled through adolescence and with his identity and sexuality. David carried this burden of rage. At first glance, he presented himself as a colorful student who *lived happily and freely. However, there was so much pain underneath his false persona.*

So, as I slowly opened the door to the security office, I stared in disgust as David sat in handcuffs like a criminal. Before I could speak about this human atrocity, David had flung and thrust himself onto the worn-out and stained carpet. He was screaming and yelling, "No! No! No! I'm tired, No!" He continued to scream and wail. He then leaped up and threw his body into a security monitor. I stepped forward. Officer Patrick, a sinister man who seemed pleased to watch handcuffed Black boys in pain, tried to steer me away. I sidestepped him and used my soothing voice to reassure David it would be okay. His cries eventually became whimpers and short sighs as his body curled up into a fetal position. With his sinister voice and devilish grin, Officer Patrick coldly said, "Give him a ten-day suspension with a recommendation for expulsion." He turned and sashayed out of the security office like a cowboy in a B-rated Western that went straight to DVD.

This rush of hatred bubbled inside of me like a ginger soda. The injustice was bigger than Patrick's. Patrick's actions were a heinous form of educational lynching. How could a school treat young people with malice, injustice, and sanctioned violence? I put my hand on David's shoulder, reassuring him to stay strong and letting him know I would always be there for him. The intense emotions of hopelessness and helplessness clouded my mind like an overcast day. I knew, however, that I had to leave. I turned and walked away.

So, here I am, struggling between two worlds—the violent and internalized hatred within me and this newfound softer, emotionally intelligent approach. The more I live in this unjust system, the more I feel the flames of rage for all involved. I struggled with all of it. Well, I try to celebrate getting through another day, but there's that little voice saying the day isn't over yet, so be careful. I ignore that voice.

Nevertheless, I find myself heading towards the last leg of a typical school day, as I'm finishing the last part of the lesson in my most challenging ninth grade class. This class has an exciting and dynamic feel to it. The classroom was small and cramped, with little desks. Each student had every type of personality you could imagine. You have the quiet, invisible students, the loud, obnoxious students, the loud, rebellious students, the unmotivated but intelligent students, and the students who enjoy my teaching style.

Although my style is indeed full of energy, life, and creativity, it is also full of insecurity and that hidden rage that surfaces at unpredictable times. There were only a few minutes left in class. Teaching this lesson weighed on me. I struggled, and when I struggled, I was vulnerable. When I'm vulnerable, I am powerless; when I'm powerless, I am sensitive. When I am sensitive, I am confrontational; when I am confrontational, I am argumentative; and when I am argumentative, I lash out. It is unbelievable that I am only aware of this chain of reactions after the explosion. It just sneaks up on me—or does it?

Before the bell rang, my last few words stirred up some combative energy in my students, especially Deon. Deon was a solid kid but a little unmotivated at times; he was intelligent, unstable, and someone who kept to himself. Somehow, for some reason, my antagonistic words landed directly at him. I characterized him as a wounded animal and wounded animals attack. I said, "Deon, your problem is you need to stop acting weird and act like you are in the ninth grade." Deon responded with venom. "You need to act your age! Stop trying to be cool and start acting like you're the teacher!"

The sea of murmuring and laughter shredded my ego like a samurai sword. Deon's words tore me apart in front of the entire class. As my body tightened with tension, I felt my temperature rise like heat in an oven. I was ready for a showdown. I rushed over to Deon, imagining I had heard the three-minute bell ring for round one. I pressed his shoulders down as he attempted to leave while screaming at him. I pushed harder, lowered my face to his, and shouted, "Don't you ever speak to me this way again." Everyone in the room was frozen. Eventually, he cried out, "Let me go. Let me go. Get your hands off of me!" I pressed him down for a few more seconds. He wiggled his way out of my shoulder squeeze and ran out of the room. All of the other students also left.

I stuck my head out my door just in time to hear from a distance, "I'm telling my father!" In my rage, I forgot his father, a strong, brilliant, educated Black man, worked as a guidance counselor at the school. His father is a legend. Needless to say, as the adrenaline faded, the guilt and shame washed their way into the shore of my consciousness. I told myself, I think you're in trouble now. How could you be so stupid? You went crazy on that kid. Most of my lunch period was consumed with the feeling of regret. Then, my classroom phone rang. I let it ring a few times as I felt intense pain in my chest and butterflies in my stomach. I grabbed the phone, closed my eyes, and ground my teeth. I said, "This is Mr. Ervin. How may I help you?" Good afternoon, Mr. Ervin. This is William down in the guidance office. I must speak to you immediately about an incident with my son in your class. I responded, "Okay," and slowly walked to Mr. William's office.

I peeked into the office and saw Deon in the chair, eyes still red and puffy from my tirade. His father is at his desk looking assertive, strong, and professional, something I aspire to be. With a stern voice, Mr. William said, "Have a seat, Mr. Ervin, and let's discuss what happened in your class today." I hesitated, then said, "Mr. William, I apologize. I lost my cool with Deon after I felt he got smart with me. I held him in his seat out of anger, frustration, and embarrassment." Mr. William responded, "Let me keep this simple. You had no right to put your hands on my son. You could have handled it another way, and he could have kept his mouth shut. Mr. Ervin, you are a good young teacher, and your heart is right. Please don't take things personally and let your emotions get the best of you. Again, if Deon steps out of line, don't hesitate to call me. I'm a floor beneath you." I replied, "Yes, Mr. William. What I did will not happen again." I turned, looked at Deon, and said, "I apologize, Deon. I had no business putting my hands on you. Hopefully, we can start over tomorrow."

After finishing my apology, I extended my hand. With his eyes fixated on the floor, Deon reached out his hand and shook mine. Mr.

William walked me out and shared, "I'm not sure if I told you, but I'm raising Deon alone. Being abandoned by his mother has caused him a lot of emotional trouble." I nodded as a sign of genuine respect. I appreciated Mr. William giving me a pass and going easy on me. However, I got his message loud and clear.

We, teachers, bring personal baggage into the classroom. We are complex individuals with complex stories, educating complex kids in a complex system that has existed for hundreds of years. In a few intense incidents, I became aware of my struggles to teach in such a hostile environment. The real struggles came when I started to choose another way of being. The choice came from sitting with the source of my rage, assumptions, and perceptions.

My story and how I have perceived myself continue to shape who I am and how I show up for my students. As I chose to get honest with myself, multiple layers of self-discovery were happening to me. It is difficult to take an honest inventory of the tragedies in my life and how to bring them with me every day as I seek to shape, educate, and mold young, impressionable minds. If I look closely, rage has been an influential part of my life. My race, upbringing, class, family, father, and society have tried to decide for me. The challenge begins when we choose for ourselves and become aware of how we perpetuate a system designed to use rage to propel some while destroying others. I am starting to see that if I want the best from my students, I must allow them to bring the best out of me. An Ethiopian proverb says, "To teach is to learn twice." I am just beginning to learn the lessons from my pain, my students, and society's pain. There's beauty underneath the rage if we only take the time to see it.

As educators and administrators, no matter where we decide to teach, the best place to start is by questioning, challenging, and confronting our biases, perceptions, assumptions, and beliefs. As educators, this is where actual change and effectiveness begin. We need to see the educational system as it is. We see the educational system as we are. We filter this system through our thoughts, experiences, and personal, cultural, and social lenses. This lens determines our decisions and choices, what we see, how we see, and how we interact with our students, parents, staff, and administrators.

The whole premise of the Latin word *educere* is to draw forth from within. Subsequently, if we contemplate, reflect, and think critically about our stories and how they shape our teaching environments, we will uncover the rage we project on ourselves, students, and our environments. Moreover, we can see clearly and shift things in our world. Real change only occurs after first accepting it. The value of being open and honest will free us from living our lives by the dictates and expectations of our caged identities. And what happens to caged animals? They attack, yet they also yearn to be free.

Our students bring diverse beauty and tragic experiences into our classrooms and schools. What do we see? Some, most, maybe all students have deep wounds, and they want to trust that we can create a safe space for those wounds to heal. If we ignore what we see or refuse to see, we will be captives of our rage, unhappiness, and ignorance. This cycle of suppression, repression, and oppression in the schools will continue to perpetuate. The practice of change starts with liberating ourselves. We must be liberated from the ideas, concepts, and negative beliefs we drag into our classrooms. Students either submit to these ideas or rebel against them. Everyone involved in the system has open wounds.

We can continue inflicting pain and suffering on these open wounds or start healing. Together. However, we must critically dig deep within ourselves to see beyond the rage, tapping into our wholeness and beauty. Ultimately, this will naturally liberate the beauty and the brilliance that students have within them. Real change is an inside job. Our gifts sit right next to our wounds. Find your purpose and heal your wounds. When teachers and administrators relinquish fear and lead with love, the resistance fades, and learning begins. There are so many layers to uncover. How about we start with the layer of fear that we place upon ourselves? The fear underneath the rage is where beauty lives. Let's begin our journey by embodying the principles of mindfulness and cultural compassion.

CHAPTER 2

Grief: The Greatest Act of Love

"To deny the act of grief is to deny the act of love,
because grief is the greatest expression of love."
Morris H. Ervin, Jr.

I slowly walked to the pulpit wearing a long black flowing garment and jean jacket with the continent of Africa airbrushed on the back. I slowly turned around, and my eyes set on a sea of family, friends, and classmates waiting for me to speak. I stared hard at the casket as though I was waiting for Emmanuel to do or say something. At first, I felt tense, anxious, and unsure about speaking in front of a large crowd at such a devastating time. I looked at Emmanuel's casket. I could see his body lying in the coffin, but I felt his spirit standing beside me.

Seven days prior, I conversed with my cousins in my aunt's small living room. We laughed and joked when she said, "Musa, your wife is on the phone." I picked up the phone and heard her sobbing and crying. I asked, "What's wrong? What happened?" She said, "Something terrible has happened!" There was an uncomfortable silence between us. My stomach was in a giant knot. I felt helpless with the unknown. I blurted out, "Emmanuel is dead!" "Yes!" She said. "I'm on my way!" I replied, as I slowly hung up the phone in shock and disbelief. I walked back into the living room, and everyone was completely silent. I said, "Emmanuel's dead." I didn't stay to see their sad faces. I jumped in my car with my heart pounding out of my chest. I was speeding, weaving in and out of traffic, and running red lights. When I turned on the street where Emmanuel lived, I slowed down to five miles per hour.

Around forty family members were huddled together under the night sky. The colorful flashes of the police car lights shined brightly in the darkness. Everything seemed to move in slow motion. I saw yellow tape across the front of the house. My eyes watered as I watched my brother-in-law push and scuffle with three officers as he desperately tried to force his way into his home to see his son. He shouted, "Let me see my son! I have to see him!" I scanned the somber crowd, looking for my wife. When we found each other, without saying a word, we wrapped our arms around each other in the bitter cold.

I said, "Emmanuel wanted to go home, escape, and learn the 'Secret of the Flight' like our African ancestors. We live in a world where pain and suffering run wild like a boar. We avoid and suppress unbearable pain with drugs, alcohol, food, etc. We also unleash our pain on others with passive and aggressive acts of violence. We want to go home. We debase and humiliate others because we do not feel good about ourselves. We want to go home. People are extremely weighed down in mind, body, and spirit. We want to go home. Emmanuel had this bright light and amazing gift of putting smiles on everyone's faces with his electric dance moves. He also had a sophisticated way of communicating, especially when something wasn't right. One evening, while he played with his cousins at my house, he assertively shouted to them, 'I want justice.' He was only five years old and felt they had mistreated him. We had talked the night before his life ended. He had begun organizing students to fight against racist treatment at his high school. Emmanuel had a voice and would not be silenced.

"Ultimately, Emmanuel chose to return home. He decided to end his young life to escape the oppression around him. He sacrificed his life for us to realize our place in this world. So where is home? The challenge of finding home is learning that it resides inside your heart. When home is a safe place within you, the world does not seem so scary. You can now invite other people to find their homes. When we all know where home is, we can build communities together. Home is your voice. Home is your purpose. Home is finding a reason to wake up every day. Home is a place that no one can take away from you. When you genuinely know home, you don't put things like drugs, alcohol, or destructive people inside your home." I finished my speech by thanking Emmanuel for showing us where home truly is. I paused before I walked off the pulpit. I saw nothing but radiant smiles and felt connected with everyone in the church. My purpose was solidified in this moment of pain and grief.

My wife recalls that painful day. "I knew something was wrong that day. I should have listened to my gut. Several times earlier in the day, I called Emmanuel. No one answered. Then, I decided to go to Walmart before I stopped by. I got to the door and rang the doorbell several times, and no one responded. I climbed through the window. I eerily rushed upstairs and discovered his body hanging in the closet. I felt him. He was cold. I regret not trusting my gut, even though the coroner said it took place early in the morning. It will take a while for me to forgive myself and get over it. I will have many sleepless nights. I refuse to sleep with the lights off. I should have trusted my gut, but now I do."

Emmanuel had been put on punishment, but he told my sister BK, his stepmom, that he couldn't stay at home. Circumstances, however, prevented her from accommodating his needs. Emmanuel's dad and BK had access to only one car that day. I see Emmanuel's personality in his baby brother Zekhi. Like Emmanuel, Zekhi uniquely expressed himself through song, dance, theater, and music. We let Zekhi be who he wants to be. Zekhi is confident and is free to stand up for his beliefs. Zekhi said, "I don't play football or rap. I'm in the Show Choir! I'm not the stereotypical Black kid. I am me. I love karate, the arts, and choir." Emmanuel sacrificed himself so his little brother, who barely remembered him, could live out his dreams and get the justice he deserved. Emmanuel didn't get the opportunity to live out his dreams. Big Emmanuel did his best to raise Emmanuel. Big Emmanuel raised little Emmanuel under challenging circumstances. Little Emmanuel wanted to live with his birth mom. We learned the signs of mental health and depression after Emmanuel's passing. Emmanuel made our entire family more open to the individual needs of all our children.

Emmanuel's brother Zarell shared his memories and recollections of Emmanuel's impact on him. "I never healed from the situation. I was thirteen. I was with him every day. I remember being with my father in the basement when he got a phone call. My father said Emmanuel was not here anymore. At first, I waited for some answers, and then my dad said, 'Wait in the car.' I sat in the car forever. I was sitting and waiting. I prayed for my brother's spirit to move through me. He was my first business partner. We sold candy and cupcakes together. We cut grass together. Emmanuel went around the neighborhood, posting flyers of our services and prices on trees, telephone poles, signs, and in mailboxes of private homes. We had no social media." Zarell chuckled, "We were ten and eleven-year-old master marketing geniuses. Emmanuel cared. He would find snakes and make homes for them out of milk crates. Emmanuel was creative and artistic. He played the piano, and I played the drums. We created songs together. My mom always made sure we were similar but different. I had a red safe. Emmanuel had a blue safe. We were both crazy kids. We put on gloves and boxed every morning before school. One time, I punched him in his lips. I took the gloves off, and he grabbed a knife and chased me around the house—crazy times. When I got to school, I told my guidance counselor. I held things in. He didn't want to get things out. We rode our mini motorbikes up and down the street, getting into trouble. We walked to school when we were around 9 and 10 years old. We discovered a big hill with trees behind the Rascal House Pizza place. We would sit on the ground and throw rocks at trucks. Super dangerous! Finally, a trucker got out of his truck and chased us. We ran and never did that again. We stole pop guns and noisemakers from stores. When we were a little older, around eighth and ninth grade, we played Ding Dong Ditch." Zarell sighed deeply and said, "It took me a long time to get over his death.

"Fortunately, through Emmanuel's passing, I now understand mental health. And we, as Black people, shrug it off. At the time of Emmanuel's passing, my uncle said, 'That was really selfish of Emmanuel to take his life.' In my head, I thought, 'Uncle, did you just say that?' I realized my brother was hurting. It took me a long time to visit Emmanuel's gravesite. After his death, I struggled a lot, from not feeling good enough, not being open and vulnerable, and having the dire need to be liked and accepted.

Over time, while becoming connected with my deeper purpose and establishing a relationship with God, I learned to accept grief as an ongoing process. I cherished the memories, but after he passed, I felt lonely. I regret being in my pre-teen stage before he passed. He started ninth grade, and I started eighth grade. The last month before he died, we did not talk. We were both trying to find ourselves. I regret that. One morning, he was running late for the bus, and I let the bus leave him. I did not try to stop it. We were going through it, lots of testosterone. I'm not sure what it was. I did not talk after he died. I focused on being closed in. After a while, I realized that Emmanuel taught us about life and death. He was in trouble, but he wasn't a troublemaker."

Big Emmanuel also shared his thoughts about his son. *"I remember my son's 2nd birthday. One Friday evening, his aunt bought him and all his cousin's candy. Little Emmanuel immediately gobbled up all of his candy. Next thing, out of nowhere, Little Emmanuel started singing, 'Baby, I'm begging, baby, I'm begging, begging, baby!' It was so on point and on time that my aunt, cousins, and kids burst out with laughter. Little Emmanuel learned to speak early. He was intelligent and naturally funny. He could make you laugh when you didn't feel like it. He was charismatic. Emmanuel was a brave kid, even when he was terrified. We went to see The Lion King. He said, 'I'm Simba. Dad. You're Mufasa.' He loved family. He made you feel special as if you were family.*

"One summer afternoon, while sitting on my couch, I heard my son say, 'You wait right here.' He continued, 'Dad, you told me to stand up to anyone, and if it was a grown person, come get you.' I think, 'This little kid is big, and his daddy is probably bigger.' Emmanuel shouted, 'Here comes my daddy. I just beat your son. I know my daddy can beat you!' My son shared so many profound things. He had a lot of fights in him. In his last battle, he told me he wanted to fight it by himself. It was a racial incident at his predominantly White suburban school.

"As a freshman, Emmanuel took the initiative to lead upper-level students in speaking out against racial injustices at his school. I worried about him taking my real-life lessons into the world. He uniquely adapted my lessons and principles. I miss him. I talk to myself about him but not

to others. He had the closest relationship with his Auntie Linda. He slept in her bed until the day he passed away. His relationship with his auntie never changed. When Emmanuel was just two years old, many of his aunts were bickering to watch over him. After a while, he interrupted them and said, 'Y'all can just share me.' When Zarell and Emmanuel did karate, the teacher tried to instruct Emmanuel on some moves. Emmanuel started holding such a sophisticated conversation with the karate instructor that the instructor said, 'Do you want to learn karate or be a lawyer?'

"Little Emmanuel loved hard. He had an affinity for everyone and made them feel special. I'm different. The loss of my son made me change my mindset. He was a catalyst for lots of change in our family. On another occasion, Emmanuel fought with a dude twice his size. The bigger dude was on top of Emmanuel. Another relative said, 'Emmanuel, do you need me to jump in and help you?' Emmanuel responded, 'Nah, I got him right where I want him!' The relative screamed, 'Dude, you're on the bottom!' Emmanuel loved to entertain, especially during our big family Thanksgiving dinners. Chris Brown, that was little Emmanuel. He was in his element. One year, I signed him up for summer league basketball. He was the smallest kid on the team with the most energy. During the first game, they put a girl on him. He ran the point guard position and didn't hesitate to hit a jumper in her face. He stared at the girl and said, 'Step back!'

"Emmanuel had to fight a lot, especially in my old neighborhood. Emmanuel's cousin was getting bullied at the playground. Emmanuel and his brother stepped in to serve justice. Emmanuel started fighting a boy, then another boy jumped in to hit Emmanuel, and Emmanuel's brother hit him. Lastly, Emmanuel told the boys, 'If you leave my cousin alone, this won't happen again.' The bullies left his cousin alone, and justice was served. When Little Emmanuel was born, he got the nickname George. He was fat and light. When his cousins saw him, they said he looked like George, a little White man. That neighborhood name stuck with him. Little Emmanuel was a brave soul and poetic. He wrote poetry. I took his art for granted. If I had understood him better, I would have approached him differently. A tender soul. A sensitive person. I've seen and witnessed a lot of Black men lose their sons. The pain we all feel is indescribable. I have a couple of friends who made a 180-degree change in their behavior and mindset after losing their sons. Little Emmanuel called me the 'Grey Wolf,' 'which is the epitome of strength, fearlessness, and bravery.

"When Emmanuel was five years old, he wrote me a letter. I understood the magnitude of what he meant in the letter after he passed. I could have done him justice if I had known how much Emmanuel looked up to me. I never thought I was as strong as he thought I was. I try to remember how he thought of me and try to live up to it. I wonder if I deserve that type of respect. It's humbling and inspiring at the same time. At twelve years old, Emmanuel wanted to be in the family round of 'playing the dozens.' I cracked a corny joke and got roasted. I know I wanted to be a part of it. It bombed, and he took the heat for it. Little Emmanuel loved his mom. She was on drugs. A wise man once said, 'Beautiful flower, but take it out of the swamp; it dies.' I said, 'Fuck that! I wasn't going to let my son live with her.'

"This showed me that nobody could love your child like you. I beg to differ. Somebody can love your child more than the birth parents. His Auntie Linda and his second Cousin Cindy loved him. He wanted to stay with his mom. His mom was okay with him smoking weed and doing other detrimental things. I thought I was protecting him. Did my pride get in the way? Was it the right thing to do? I don't think he committed suicide because he didn't live with his mom. Little Emmanuel watched his stepbrother storm into the room when he got in trouble and said he would kill himself. When Emmanuel's mom and I were together, she told me when she was a teenager, she had tried to commit suicide. At the time, I didn't care. Then, my son followed through with it. It hit me hard. Little Emmanuel was depressed. Little Emmanuel said, 'I'm not you!' I realized that the pressure of a man is too much for a boy.

"The pressure I put on my son was too much. When I was seven, my mom told me I was a Mandingo Warrior. I fought through many trials and struggles placed on me. I hated moving back with my parents after my grandmother had raised my brother and me. Grandma sheltered us.

She called us 'Precious and Dutch.' I never lived with my birth mom for long. In all my 37 years, I've only lived with my mom for two years and not consecutively. All my mom gave me was the title of 'Mandingo Warrior.' I passed the torch to my son by saying, 'You can get through anything.' Little Emmanuel said to me, 'Dad, I'm not you. I'm not that strong.' I was not able to accept what he said. I thought Little Emmanuel was strong enough to live without his mother. Now, I know he wasn't.

"The first time my grandmother told me it was okay to cry was at my son's funeral. She raised my brother and me with no hugs or kisses. Then, in her wheelchair at Emmanuel's funeral, she hugged me and said, 'It's okay to cry.' I wondered, was this a curse or a gift? Why did your wife find my son? It would have broken a lot of people. I believe something great can come from bad things. Little Emmanuel's mom made strides after his death. His grandfather said, 'All those people who came out for fourteen-year-old Little Emmanuel showed the type of impact he had on people.' I know he wasn't just mine. I can't say that no one loved him as I did. They loved him the way they did. His enthusiasm was infectious. I remember his talent show performance. One of his cousins got nervous and put the mic on the floor. Little Emmanuel, the entertainer, said, 'I'll take it. I'll improvise. I'll fill in the gaps because the show must go on.'"

I remember the night before Emmanuel's funeral. I stayed up all night writing and rewriting my speech. The sweat poured from my brow down my face. It traveled down to my sweaty fingertips and clammy palms. I struggled to find a powerful, uplifting message to unite the enormous crowd attending Emmanuel's service. Aha! I jumped up and scattered through the dark, cramped room, scavenging for an old folktale book, *The People Could Fly* by Virginia Hamilton. I rummaged through each book until I found the story about our enslaved ancestors titled "The Secret of the Flight." Suddenly, after digging carefully into the story from beginning to end, my speech magically revealed itself at the turn of each page. The meaning of flight. Emmanuel's death. My ancestors' struggles. Escape and home all fit like integrated pieces to a puzzle. I lay on my stomach with my legs sprawled out, pen and yellow scratch pad activated, and the words sliding from my thoughts to the paper. I crafted the message in fifteen minutes. Of course, the process took a few hours to congeal and manifest inside. However, I discovered a writing and speaking style that would serve me for years.

My mind became flustered when I imagined the massive crowd of mourners, including family, friends, and many students from his high school. I questioned myself. Would I be able to do Emmanuel justice at a time of intense grief and agony for me? Can I deliver and transfer my enthusiasm, wisdom, and inspiration from the page to the church tomorrow? I carried this stress and uncertainty until I drifted off to sleep. The next day at the church, my slippery fingers interlocked between my wife's soothing hands. Our children sat in each of our laps, waiting but unsure of what would occur. I scanned the lower and upper sections of the church; not an empty seat was available. My stomach churned like butter as I noticed bickering and side comments from Emmanuel's maternal side of the family. I saw the stress and worry on Emmanuel's stepmom's face. Big Emmanuel sat in silence, and I wondered about it. Despite my unsettled nerves, jittery leg movements, and butterflies in my belly, I made futile attempts to review my one-page speech that had become a crumpled, yellow piece of paper.

Alas, the pastor introduced me, increasing my body's tightness. I squeezed my wife's hand. I stood up and moved to the narrow aisle, heading toward the pulpit. Standing in that pulpit was the most harrowing moment of my life. With Emmanuel's spirit standing beside me, I let go. I turned fear into strength and pain into passion. Something higher communicated to me through my pain and suffering. As painful as it was to lose Emmanuel physically, he helped me channel my gift of moving people with my words. I noticed my ability to shift the energy in the space and direct the tension into love and solidarity.

After leaving the funeral, I made a promise to myself. I declared I would speak, lead, and encourage youth to understand that suicide is a permanent decision to a temporary problem. My role as an educator expanded into a healer, counselor, motivator, therapist, mentor, father figure, hero, and entertainer. I vowed to be present and validate the experiences of as many youths as possible. I promised to carry Emmanuel's tremendous legacy through my work as an educator and community developer. Grief consumed me in the first few months after Emmanuel's death. Sometimes, sharing his story with audiences, especially young people, would bring me to tears. However, each time I shared my gifts and shared Emmanuel's story, my grief metabolized into the greatest act of love.

CHAPTER 3

Decolonizing My Experience: From Individual to Holistic Education

"The journey of a thousand miles begins with one step."
Lao Tzu

I sluggishly arrived at the airport at 6:45 a.m. I moved through the security checkpoints and walked to my terminal. I looked up and saw Patty, an Art teacher at the school where I worked. Patty said, "Hey, Morris, are you excited about this NVC retreat? I can hardly wait! We will meet Kathy at the retreat because she is on a different flight." Kathy is the conflict mediation specialist who introduced me to the NVC stuff. I wasn't feeling it, or maybe denial ruled my spirit. After the incident with Leon, I knew something about me needed to change.

Our first flight to Phoenix, Arizona, lasted three hours. I had the window seat, which enabled me to look at the clouds. I enjoyed looking at all the geographic wonders of the Southwest. Before boarding our connecting flight to Seattle, Washington, I became sick. My stomach started jumping and twisting like acrobats at the Universal Soul Circus. I felt nauseous. Fortunately, our flight to Seattle went quickly. I became enamored with the gigantic Mt. Rainier as we flew directly over it to land. We were finally in Seattle and decided to grab some fish and chips at the airport before heading to Harmony Hill Retreat Center, where our training would occur.

As we exited the airport and headed to a shuttle bus, oddly, a random guy gave me some books. We boarded a shuttle bus. It took us to the ferry that would take us across Puget Sound to our destination. My headache, frustration, and irritation prevented me from enjoying my first visit to Seattle and the Pacific Northwest. We arrived at the retreat center after hours of air and land travel. Finally, I was able to walk into a nice cozy room. I plopped onto my comfortable bed. But only for a short time. I heard a knock on my door, got up, and opened it. A woman's delightful voice greeted me, saying, "Hey Morris, glad you made it. Now it's time to go to a meeting!" It was Kathy. I grimaced and buried my head in the pillow. With a weak and exasperated voice, I uttered, "Thanks, Kathy."

The Puget Sound formed the perfect backdrop, watching over our time at Harmony Hill. It is a gorgeous body of water that drew me closer each time I stared at it. The mountains that made a fortress around the retreat center were sturdy, silent, and strong. These inanimate structures couldn't say anything, but I could feel their magnanimous presence. We gathered outside in 87-degree weather and made a circle. The weather was unseasonably warm and sunny for that time of the year. After we briefly introduced ourselves, we walked inside to eat dinner. The spread of food was healthy and a bit tasty. I gazed at the potatoes, lasagna, salad, and ice-cold water. We finished our meal and returned outside to play games and engage in icebreakers. The group seemed fun, open, and free-spirited.

Most attendees were older White women, a few White males, and no Black women. I was the only Black male. We began by setting up agreements for safety and trust. As we sat together in a circle, we each had an opportunity to share why we chose to attend the nine-day Teach NVC For Life Retreat. With trepidation, I said, "I want to learn all I can about NVC, take some tools and strategies back to my classroom, and continue to grow and evolve through this work." Everyone shared their motives for coming. Some people got emotional and started crying. I realized the power of folks gathering in a circle. At the end of each long day, some of us continued to laugh and hang out. As a part of my daily ritual, I joined in before going to bed.

The next day, we learned how to put our visions in perspective with the tensions and current reality surrounding them. I was frustrated with this exercise because my vision wasn't crystal clear, and I didn't want to embarrass myself in front of the group. Next, we participated in an inner/outer grief circle. I thought, "Man! What is it with these circles of tears!" I watched people share much pain, heaviness, and grief about their professional struggles. I started by stating, "As you all can see, I'm the only young Black male here." I reluctantly shared my struggles as a misunderstood young Black male teacher. It was refreshing to feel victorious after I shared my pain. It was cool that the circle created empathy and a space where people could sit and live in what they were dealing with.

One of the attendees was a woman named Cat Cadden, who has an NVC school called Temba. I believe she is an NVC rock star trainer. She spoke with boldness, passion, and power. Every time she shared, I sat up because I knew she was about to drop some gems. She talked freely about her past and didn't hide anything. Everything about her being is the real deal. "I want to be like her!" I said. Cat shared about people's constant need for belonging and community. She said, "When I did drugs and partied all the time, I was meeting my need for community and belonging." This statement revolutionized my perspective on NVC. It resonated deeply within me. She is challenging, changing, and shaping lives with her work. She understands human connection and youth development on a profoundly spiritual level. I wanted to learn as much as I could from her.

Everyone at the retreat learned about my sugar craze and thought it was hilarious. I love junk food. I like chips, candy, and chocolate chip cookies! None of my favorite foods were on the reservation. I desperately needed sugar, and we were miles away from civilization, I thought, trying to get to the mainland.

I missed my family and needed a break from the gushy, gooey, cultish atmosphere. On Wednesday, I planned to take the ferry, see downtown Seattle, and return to the reservation later that evening. Suddenly, I had another thought. With an assertive, direct voice, I said, Bro, you are here at this nonviolent communication retreat to stop acting so violently, so take this opportunity to work on it. I shrugged my shoulders as if I was right—or at least my thinking brain was right. I finished the intense escape plan and returned to the workshop.

During this exercise, stations were set up based on the four components of nonviolent communication: observation, feelings, needs, and requests. It was cool to realize other ways to communicate beyond how society conditioned us. In our daily language, I learned that we had more words for labels and judgments of people than we had for expressing what's alive for us in each moment. We are conditioned to communicate from our heads, not our hearts. This conditioning leads us to believe this is a standard communication method. However, we confuse what is habitual with what is natural. The natural way to communicate takes real inner work to connect with people.

After the last exercise of the day, I walked to my room only to have a rush of more epiphanies. This retreat was a chance to cleanse my spirit and have an excellent opportunity for personal renewal. I had suppressed things in my life. I needed to work on my marriage, parenting style, teaching skills, and myself. My anger was not the master. The messenger was sent to help identify my deeper needs and values. I wanted to slow life down and return to Cleveland with a renewed mindset. I struggled with this new process of communication. I, however, wanted to stay with it because something inside of me was being tapped and activated. I was ready to take NVC back to the harsh realities of a school and empower students, parents, and administrators to change.

The following day, I rose at 6:30 a.m. to hike with a cool guy named Eric from Nelson, Canada. He loves Billy Idol, the Denver Broncos, and pop culture. The scenery on our hike was breathtaking, but the pace was grueling. As we ran, I felt the burn in my lungs as I struggled through hills and woods, trying to keep up with Eric. We finally reached the top of a gorgeous hilltop overlooking Harmony Hill. I stood with my hands on my hips, feeling the sweat drip down my face. I took deep breaths, and my chest felt like it would explode. I looked around and saw my hiking partner meditating on the ground. I watched him as he sat in a lotus position without a care in the world. I decided to try it. It didn't work because I had no idea what I was doing. As soon as I sat down, he quickly stood and dashed down the hill. I said, "Oh hell no, I ain't making it down this hill." But I did.

Standing in the shower, I reflected on the new retreat and new world into which I had been initiated. It was weird. However, the freedom for self-expression, radical self-care, and emotional safety nurtured my tormented soul. I was there for a reason. Pain pushes you, and purpose pulls you. My defenses were slowly melting away like butter in a skillet. Each day, I found myself letting my guard down and enjoying the freshness of the retreat. As I continued to reflect on my thoughts, they took a detour into the future. I asked myself, "Will I be able to take this feeling back to my world? Will this work control the angry monster that comes out of me? Will I be able to change?"

The following session explored gratitude. I brainstormed with my partner about things I was grateful for. It was remarkable how the facilitators challenged us to think deeply and profoundly about the people, places, events, and life experiences for which we were grateful. In the circle, we learned how to express appreciation and gratitude using the four-step process of Nonviolent Communication. The four steps are observation, feelings, needs, and a specific request.

I decided to share the appreciation I had for my wife. She was home for nine days with my seven-year-old daughter and five-year-old son. I looked at my journal, read my scribbled notes, and said, "When you spend nine days taking care of the kids without me, I feel appreciative, thankful, and happy that you have met my need for support, respect, and consideration. Would you let me take you out to dinner when I return? Also, would you mind if I participated in more retreats and continued to work on myself?" My partner responded as if she were my wife. She replied, "I would hold off on that second request for a while!" This process was like learning how to ride a bike. It felt like I needed training wheels, to speak.

It seemed robotic, exhausting, and cumbersome. However, it challenged me to speak and listen from an authentic place and listen with my heart.

When the session ended, we all decided to swim in Puget Sound. I am not much of a swimmer, but I love socializing and having a good time. We all walked down a narrow path through the woods and down a slope until it opened to a beautiful body of water. All the folks dropped their towels and started running directly into the water. I walked as slowly as a snail and placed my foot slightly into this frigid cold water. I uttered, "This water is freezing!" It wasn't, but I am a bit dramatic. I watched from afar as everyone swam in the frigid Puget Sound.

Later that evening, some of us gathered for a jam session in the living room area. One guy pulled out this incredibly long musical instrument. It looked strange because I had never seen anything quite like it. He blew into it, and a deep sound came through a hollow tunnel. Everyone sat and listened intently as if he was a human snake charmer. I sheepishly asked a woman, "What's the name of that instrument?" She responded, "A didgeridoo. Indigenous Australians developed it in northern Australia within the last 1,500 years, and now people play it worldwide." He continued to play his instrument, and it sounded like a swarm of bees was buzzing and flying inside. The evening took another remarkable turn when Eric started playing music on his acoustic guitar. We all held hands and sang songs I had never heard of in my entire life. We danced and moved our bodies, reciting folk songs late into the night.

I did something I always wanted to do on the last night after our daily session. Eric pulled out his guitar and started to play. Another guy began to make the best tribal sounds on a Djembe drum while the didgeridoo undergirded the trio of talented musicians. I gazed around at everyone as we danced and chanted in the circle. My smile was as wide as the Grand Canyon. However, I felt nervous. I uttered some words and attempted to rhyme and flow with the sounds created by the trio. No one could hear what I was mumbling. So, I slowly let the tension leave my body and allowed my words to flow. I got louder and more confident with each rhyme I constructed in that blissful moment. Now, all eyes were on me, and the music continued to support my impromptu freestyle rapping skills. In addition to my freestyle rap, we all started singing, "There are no bad people, just people who feel bad. No bad people, just people who feel bad!" I thought to myself, never in a million years would I sing folk songs with White people in a place called Harmony Hill! My Black inner hippie was fully activated!

Soon after the party calmed down, Grant, another NVC participant, said, "Hey, Mo. Do you want to go outside and watch the stars?" My face tightened up, and a rush of thoughts flooded my amygdala. I thought, man, I ain't star gazing with a guy. However, Grant saw this world in a way that opened to possibilities, not closed them. Unlike other men, he moved through the world boldly, outside of this man box that protected us and simultaneously destroyed our ability to feel. Grant moved freely through society like a gypsy, exploring, expressing, learning, and growing. I secretly admired him. He is a hybrid between Mr. Rogers, James Dean, and Jim Carrey. Grant is the embodiment of what it means to be free. In his bold request to watch stars with me, he permitted me to step outside my man box for good. I courageously strolled behind him outside. There was not a cloud in the clear night sky. Stars shined like gold-clad earrings hanging from the night sky just out of our reach. We stayed silent as we looked up at the collection of stars that spoke to the wonders of our souls—time stood still as we gazed at the stars together.

The final day arrived. We finished our last session and walked into the dining hall to eat lunch for the last time together. I suddenly jumped up from the table and stared intently at a woman who wheeled in a cart of cookies. I shouted, "Yes, cookies!" It was my first time spending nine days without eating sugar. Everyone in the dining hall began clapping like the feel-good 80s movie, *The Bad News Bears*. I took a bite of the gooey cookie. It was slightly different from the cookies I liked, but I was happy to have it.

After lunch, we talked about how we would spend the rest of our summer. I was thrilled about the new school year. I had new tools, a renewed spirit, and a new and fresh, innovative framework to work from.

Before anyone shared, a woman named Carrie turned to me. She said, "Morris, we spent a lot of time thinking about this, and we want to know if you would be interested in us filming you teaching your kids the art of nonviolent communication in Cleveland." My mind went blank. The room was spinning. I felt flustered, nervous, and rattled. I wanted to get up from the table and leave, never to return. I uttered, "Me, nah. That would be hard to do. I am new at this, and you want me to teach this for a film?" "Exactly," Carrie said. "This is a process that you love, you're authentic, you care, and those kids would benefit from learning and practicing NVC in their lives," she tried to convince me. I looked around the table at everyone staring at me. I paused. I thought quickly, feeling pressured, knowing that saying yes would mean taking a deep-sea dive into unchartered waters. Then Gary, another cool guy who produced documentaries, said, "Yes, Morris. It would be a great opportunity to showcase your talents and expose the kids to this great communication process. Cat and I will be there to support and assist." I paused to think. I definitely would love to learn and watch Cat teach my students NVC. I gulped and said, "Yes," before the flood of negative thoughts drowned me in self-doubt.

When I returned to my room, I sat on the bed and reflected on the last nine days at Harmony Hill Teach For Life NVC Retreat. I felt a swirl of emotions as I thought about the friendships and lifelong bonds, I had created in such a short time. I knew the social intimacy and deep vulnerability I and others shared as a group would profoundly impact my legacy as a man and educator. I let my guard down each day and resisted the urge to play it safe or cool. Each day, I did not allow the difference between my youth and color to hinder the pure joy, wisdom, healing, and forgiveness that Harmony Hill Teach For Life provided me. I am genuinely thankful for being seen by a new community of compassionate human beings. We were all struggling to find our way in a fast-paced world where we all needed to step back and notice how we felt and what we needed.

Still deep in thought, I realized it was time to say farewell. I immediately felt my tear ducts open, and my eyes became moisturized. My head felt as if it were as heavy as a cinder block. It forced me to look downward while walking out of my cabin for the last time. "Suck it up.

Hold it in! You bet' not break down and cry!" I said to myself. I took one more step and saw Grant, my star-gazing Mr. Rogers, James Dean, and Jim Carry friend, heading straight to me. I scrambled to think of something to say. However, speechless, I was engulfed in tears as Grant held me in his arms. It was my first time experiencing the power and presence of empathy without saying a single word. We released our brotherly hug, and I continued down the stairs with saggy red eyes, hugging everyone for the last time.

I climbed into the shuttle with four other folks. We engaged in more profound and intimate conversations while heading to the ferry. When we arrived in downtown Seattle, I walked with Gigi, one of the participants, and helped her find her hotel. As we walked, she chose to share with me the pain of being in a verbally abusive marriage for over thirty years. We walked, and she talked. As we strolled up and down sidewalks, passing museums, fancy shops, and restaurants, my heart, mind, and spirit were intertwined with her.

At the beginning of our conversation, she seemed meek, hesitant, and reluctant. Now, she was fully expressive in sharing her story. I realized she had decided to let go. She realized she was no longer responsible for the years of oppression that made her feel worthless and invisible. I said, "What are you feeling and needing?" She triumphantly stated, "I feel relieved and scared because I need to be free. I want my life back! I'm tired of being mistreated," she asserted. "He holds me hostage because of his wealth. I need independence and a way to care for myself like I did before I married him," she said. We reached her destination. We embraced. She said, "Thank you, Morris."

I skipped away, looking for the first corner store to treat myself to junk food! It was a monumental trip indeed. I basked at the moment before I made the long trek from the Pacific Northwest back to Cleveland, Ohio. In a matter of nine days, I experienced a radical change. Will my change, however, be enough to teach and transform the hearts and minds of students and a system that is going through change itself?

CHAPTER 4

To Teach Is to Learn Twice

"When you want something,
all the universe conspires in helping you to achieve it."
Paulo Coelho

August 28, 2006, First Full Week of School

I arrived at school all week by 6:45 a.m. or earlier, but that is less important than the need to establish a cooperative learning environment. I am in a different mode of thinking, acting, and living. This change is my song, and I will sing it the only way I can. Loud and proud. I am feeling more comfortable each minute of every classroom day. I will hold my first classroom council at the end of the week. On Friday, I will set all my classes up in a circle. The kids will select a sacred talking piece. While music plays in the background, each student will share a celebration or frustration or hold the talking piece in silence. Every day, I use the language of feelings and needs. I translated an incident between a student and her gym teacher during 7th period. I tried conversing with my sister, and I got some clarity on her deeper values. I hope to continue this approach and take it one day at a time until I am proficient. My biggest obstacle is remaining connected to my heart when interacting with my children. If I master this, everything else will be as natural as the flowing of waters and the depths of oceans.

Physical activity is important to me. I live a very active lifestyle. Teaching five classes with twenty-five students or more drains my battery. I sit like a statue in my chair when the bell rings after my last class. Thoughts swim through my mind, but I can't comprehend anything. I unloosen my tie as I slump further down into my chair. I struggle to walk to the light switch and turn it off. I barely made it to my chair to sit in the dark. I think. I need an energy boost before I head home to my family. Aha! I remember a brilliant young math teacher who teaches downstairs below me. We organized some basketball tournaments with the students last year. I am sure he will be interested in working out with me.

It's a new year. Aha! I think of this plan to assemble the perfect team of male educators to lift weights a few days a week after school. I stroll down to the principal's office. Steve Hardaway is the new principal of our small school. He is tall and sharply dressed with a strong, serene presence. His speech is mellow, and each word is articulated with calculated confidence. I remembered our first encounter over the summer.

I recall seeing a man sitting quietly, far from the sobbing, sad teachers who expressed shock and dismay at our principal's abrupt departure. I eased away from the grief session because I was curious about the African American male sitting on the side. I slowly moved toward him. I thought this brother could be a new teacher. I slid directly before him and said, "I'm Morris, the History teacher. What's your name?" In one smooth motion, without flinching, he extended his hand, reaching up to shake my hand. He said, "What's going on? I'm the new principal, Steve Hardaway." He continued, "I just got word about receiving this position a few days ago, and now I am here at this sad retreat. Man, those teachers are having a rough time over there." I chuckled as we both gazed back across the room, watching a room full of teachers vent, complain, panic, and cry all at once. "People hate change. People abhor sudden change. The old principal was solid, and I had a gut feeling he was leaving us," I said. We both strolled into the antique-looking dining room where all the teachers sat close together around the table like at a campfire. I returned to my seat, smiling like a kid who just had the best cotton candy at the carnival. Cool as a cucumber, Steve introduced himself as the new principal of the School of Academic and Interpersonal Development.

The brilliant math teacher, Phil Williams, is slender with an athletic build and a chiseled face. He confidently and quietly navigated around the congested hallways of our small school. Math is his passion. Phil loves to teach. Phil is a few years younger than me, so I assumed the responsibility of his mentor. I sparked conversations with him before and after staff meetings. We chatted about education, relationships, sports, and hobbies. Phil shared his obsession with riding motorcycles. We related on many levels, including the desire to have constructive activities for students after school. Phil is also a skilled basketball player who occasionally referees. I play flag football. Somehow, we both decided to organize a big after-school basketball tournament.

The day finally arrives for the big basketball tournament. The excitement fills the air with the aroma of inter-school athletic competition. Which small school will prevail? This small school initiative, thanks to Bill and Melinda Gates, is a movement sweeping the nation. This power couple created a plan to correct the problems in the American public school system. It started in the early 2000s. Bill and Melinda Gates envisioned a plan to break up large high schools and transform them into small learning communities of 400 or fewer students. In theory, this seemed amazing. In practice, it invoked stress on teachers who don't do well with change. The resistance level from a large percentage of teachers created quite the spectacle at all the planning meetings leading up to this revolutionary change. I watched many heated arguments as teachers, particularly seasoned teachers, scratched and clawed to maintain the current system. For an entire school year, the infighting drained everyone.

As a new teacher, I embraced anything innovative as an opportunity to support the students. It felt like a war where sides had to be picked. The culture pitted the teachers against the administrators. The teachers' battle lines were divided between the tenured senior staff and everyone else fighting for respect and stability. My political stance consisted of being an outspoken militant voice protecting student rights. Everything was a mess and complete with turmoil. Eventually, the small school project became a reality. We divided the school into five separate small schools within the high school. I vividly remember the defeat and despair at the last faculty meeting. A veteran English teacher stood and read a well-crafted speech about the dangers of tampering with tradition. He received a standing ovation. It was interesting to see how administrators used one's tenure and years of experience to set up the small schools.

The experienced, tenured teachers exclusively set themselves up with the best students. As a result, younger teachers were paired with new administrators and more challenging students. All the schools had names that supposedly spoke to the collective identity of each school. As the new year began, students found it challenging to stay in their part of the building, thus only being allowed to interact with members of their small school. The students did not have any input in the naming or identity of the school, which troubled my soul. Students quickly realized the hierarchy established between the elite small schools versus the "bad" small schools. Phil and I, the two new African American male teachers who were solely invested in the learning and socialization of the entire school culture, decided to unify the school with an after-school basketball tournament.

The Williams/Ervin Basketball Tournament took place on May 19, 2006. It had a hectic start. Teams signed up from all the schools. You could feel the pure adrenaline from the kids, who were grateful to be united again. Phil and I had to referee all the games while managing the crowd in the stands. Security guards could not help us with this event. However, several security guards periodically peeked their heads into the gym. Mr. Albert Firestone, the bulky, no-nonsense guidance counselor, volunteered his much-needed services. To expedite the process, we divided the gym in half so we could referee both games simultaneously. Everyone in the stands watched, cheered, clapped, screamed, and genuinely enjoyed themselves. We even had Thelonious Gilbert, a star football player from Ohio State who graduated the previous year, participate. He strolled in, shirtless, tattoos everywhere, with fresh corn rolls and muscles for days. Before the championship game between the Arts school and Business school, we organized a slam dunk contest.

Finally, it was time for the championship game, and it did not disappoint. The Arts school escaped with a narrow victory over the Business school–Charles Terry, who played point guard for the varsity squad, put on a show. Charles electrified the crowd with his superior ball-handling skills and precise passes to lead his team to victory. Equally important, the players showed excellent sportsmanship, and the students displayed exceptional school spirit. We pulled off an outstanding event with basically no support from the school. Phil and I embraced after we cleaned up the gym, challenging each other to brainstorm ways to make the event bigger and better the following year. I limped to my little orange car and struggled to get inside. I felt every ache in every muscle, everywhere in my small frame. The pain and exhaustion were worth it because providing memorable moments for students is a big part of being an educator. Kids have to come to school. They don't have to engage. Our job is to make education real, relevant, engaging, meaningful, and fun.

Having African American male educators dedicate themselves to brotherhood and bonding through weightlifting is a joy. I know that Steve and Phil are in. My goal was to recruit Albert Firestone, the bulky, no-nonsense guidance counselor. Firestone was tough on the students in our small school. He rarely shared his story. However, I was confident he had had a rough upbringing. Firestone embodied a man who made decisions not to be a product of his environment. He used sports as a way out of his neighborhood. Firestone played football throughout college and got an opportunity to play in the NFL. He valued family, showing how he raised his two children and adopted nephew. We debated like two Supreme Court justices on how to engage students and address student misbehavior. He advocated strict, consistent rules to keep them on the straight and narrow. My approach was a connection before correction. Firestone and I wanted the same things for the students. We just had different approaches.

I loved his sense of humor. His animated storytelling abilities and colorful facial expressions kept me laughing constantly. Firestone respected my militant stance on issues as he often affectionately called me

"Mighty!" I considered Firestone my big brother. I appreciated his love and valued our friendship, even though we butted heads like two stubborn rams. Lastly, with the occasional addition of Firestone joining our workout crew, the mission was now complete.

Steve is the planner/organizer of the crew. The plan was to meet in his office fifteen minutes after school. First, we decided to lift weights every weekday for an hour after school. Second, we decided to take before and after shirtless pictures to motivate ourselves to transform our bodies in twelve weeks. Eventually, we began. We strolled to the dim, stuffy, humid weight room. I scanned the room and noticed athletes from other sports teams working out. The screeching and clunking sound from the weights filled the rusty, damp air. We worked out a three-person superset rotation. One man completed a set with another man spotting him with the weights, while the odd man completed a less intense exercise. We switched. We rotated. Some exercises put too much stress on my muscles, but I kept quiet and never showed my inner agony. In addition to lifting heavy weights, we occasionally cracked jokes and told stories about our days at school. They made fun of me because I was rarely on time to lift, so Steve would call me over the P.A. system. Yes, it was well known that I was usually somewhere exercising my right to free speech. However, we always remember it was a competition to see who would come out with the best body.

One day, the fellas and I trudged to Steve Hardaway's office after a brutal yet fun workout. We all sat and felt the aches from our tired muscles. We barely mustered up enough energy to laugh at the usual round of jokes I always came up with. Suddenly, a husky security guard and an administrator barged into Steve's office, carrying an aura of panic, shock, and judgment. They shouted in tandem, "Hardaway, where were you? We've been trying to reach you for the last ten minutes!" Their tone did not rattle Steve. With his low baritone voice, he calmly responded, "What's the problem? My radio has been on my hip the whole time." "A security guard found a student's dead body in the pool. He drowned!" shouted the administrator. All eyes were on us! We jumped like frogs to our feet! Emotions rushed through my body like a tidal wave. I didn't know what to feel. I reluctantly asked, "Who was it?" "Levelle Smith," uttered the security guard. "Every day, his mom waited in the parking lot for him, but he did not come out today. Hardaway, she frantically tried to call you, but you did not pick up," he continued. The gloom and doom of Levelle's name made me sit back down. Levelle, who was in my History class last year, was a bright-eyed, cheerful student! This young man wore a smile like a permanent tattoo on his face. He brought joy and life to everyone around him. I was speechless. Eventually, Steve leaves with the security guard and administrator. Phil and I were left to loiter in pain, shock, denial, and disbelief. So many questions flooded my mind. How? How could someone die in the school's swimming pool? Why was he left by himself in the pool? I wanted answers!

The next day, students crowded the counselor's offices and came to my room to get comfort from me. Students from my previous ninth grade class organized chairs in a circle. They, along with my current students, cried and hugged. We all tried to make sense of this senseless tragedy. Levelle was the third student who had died that month. One student was murdered on the corner in his neighborhood, and another student died from a drug overdose at a grunge party. I continued giving hugs as I listened to kids share memories of Levelle throughout the day. I worried about his family. The thought of a parent burying their child was unbearable. Sadly, it happens pretty often. The pain, hurt, and raw emotions that the funeral of a young person imparts can cause an indelible void in everyone in attendance. It is a permanent, unpleasant stain that no one can wash away.

I walked into Levelle's funeral and looked around. It was filled to capacity. Fortunately, I found a seat in a tight space between two students. We immediately wrapped our arms around each other. I stared out at a sea of Black bodies. The organ played a raucous tune. The scent of tension filled my nostrils as something felt explosive in this church. People formed a line to view his body. I stood at the end of the line as it stretched outside the sanctuary into the hallway. We slowly moved in line, waiting for our turn to view the body. I finally got to the front by the casket. I stared at Levelle in the silk-lined casket. I gently touched his hand. He looked different. I maneuvered my way back through the crowd and found a space on a wall.

I noticed moisture on my hands as we waited for the family to view the body. I was becoming impatient for the service to start. Unexpectedly, I heard sounds and moans of someone chanting "water, water, no, not the water!" I looked around and saw Levelle's mom, grandma, and other family members holding hands as they walked toward the casket. The "water" moans from his grandma incited more wails and yells from other family members and friends. The cries turned into screams. The screaming continued until the family finished viewing Levelle for the last time before taking their seats in the front row.

As the preacher was about to begin, I observed a man with four youths boldly making their way to the casket. The man boldly asserted, "I'm going to see my son, and no one is going to stop me. Come on, kids." The man motioned his hands, telling the young people to follow behind him. You could hear people begin to grumble and mumble. Then, it was total silence. He turned around in front of Levelle's casket with his kids and said, "This is the first time my kids are seeing their brother!" The kids slowly walked to their brother's casket while their dad stood watchfully, daring anyone to interrupt the moment. The tension was thicker than a milkshake. Then, without a word, the dad and his children turned and left the church. I caught a glimpse of one of the kids. My eyes grew large. I realized he was a former student who attended my old school. The preacher finally started the service. A long line of people formed who wanted to reflect on Levelle's life. Students shared. I shared. Near the end of the service and before the casket was closed, I slipped out of the church and went home. Levelle will be missed.

It is so easy for me to drift back into the past. I lived there for intense periods of my life. I'm so grateful to my wife for purchasing two books that helped me take a deeper look at my inner world and set me on my unique path in life. The books were *Emotional Resilience* and *The Alchemist*. In *Emotional Resilience,* I learned about the many crucial moments and memories I had suppressed deep within my subconsciousness and how toxic nostalgia intrusions had interrupted my days. These moments and memories shaped my life in positive and negative ways. The mental intrusions from the past were hurtful, and I had to become receptive to them to heal. While reading, I assessed my patterns, habits, personality type, and defense mechanisms.

The more I read, the deeper the exploration of my past interested me. I took a deep-sea dive into my inner space to find valuable treasures from within. I combined my love of expressing my feelings and needs through journaling with the new knowledge acquired from *Emotional Resilience*. *The Alchemist*, the story of learning how to gather wisdom while pursuing one's dreams, is a book that changed my perspective on life. While reading *The Alchemist*, I traveled along this great adventure with Santiago, the story's main protagonist. I realized that life is an adventure and the key to life is to follow your heart. Alchemy is the ancient practice of converting lead into gold. After reading this book, I became aware of and identified my seemingly magical powers to transform lives. Like Santiago, I placed myself at the center as I searched to discover the soul and meaning of life and uncovered more of my gifts and powers. My purpose began to reveal itself as I became more confident and driven to pursue a path of self-development and social transformation.

I became confident in my ability to infuse the language of feelings and needs into my ninth grade American History class and my twelfth grade African American History Course. I knew I had a month to teach my students the process and consciousness of NVC before the trainer, Cat, arrived with the film crew. When away from home, I felt most at home in my classroom.

I started my first day bright and early. I strutted into the building wearing a light pink/salmon shirt, matching tie, dress slacks, and stylish dress boots. First, I stopped for a delightful conversation with the custodial crew about politics, vacation, and family. I always enjoyed our fun chats. I then went up three flights of stairs to the third floor. The hallway was lit but empty. As I made my brisk walk to my classroom, I could hear the clicks of my shoe heels on the floor and felt the rubbing of my briefcase against my shoulder. I clicked the lights on in my classroom while looking at the papers, folders, and notes splattered around my tiny wooden desk. I sat in my chair, ensuring my feet were firmly planted on the floor. I sat tall in a dignified posture and softly let my eyes close. I felt the sensations in my body while taking the time to breathe deeply and slowly.

Next, I played instrumental hip-hop and calmly arranged my class chairs into the sacred circle. Friday was known as Council Day. Council Day is a practice rooted in Native, Eastern, and African traditions. It is heavily used in nonviolent communication seminars, training, workshops, and retreats. I had plenty of time to learn about the importance of circles while participating in nine consecutive days at the Teach for Life NVC intensive retreat. The circle represented respect, solidarity, unity, and trust. It fosters a sense of deep inclusion and belonging. As I sat behind a student desk along the rim of the circle, I continued to reflect on the risks and rewards of teaching students this new revolutionary concept of communication as ancient as the Pyramids. As old as the approach is, it is foreign to this typical authoritarian and punitive school system. This will shake things up, and I like it. I decided to make relationships and social agreements the center of this class.

Finally, the morning bell rang. I leaped up like a bolt of lightning had struck me. I delightfully strolled towards my door as I gleefully anticipated the entrance of my ninth grade World Studies class. I stood in the hallway right outside the door like a kid waiting to see the ice cream truck on a sunny day. I waved, hugged, and gave cool handshakes and high-fives to students who begrudgingly walked past my room into their other classes. My students, however, swooped into my room, hearts heavy and minds ready for our Friday council session. We all stood in the circle, with music gently playing in the background. I watched delightfully as students energetically tossed a colorful designer Nerf-style football inside the circle. I scanned the circle in awe and pure delight before we sat down. In a cheerful voice, I said, "Happy Friday, and welcome to our sacred council. Jamar, please recite the purpose and procedures for this ritual." Jamar stood, breathed, and smiled, showing his pearly whites. He shrugged his shoulders and patiently waited until everyone's eyes were on his small frame. Jamar spoke with the tone of an experienced lawyer. "The purpose of the sacred council is to take our time to think, feel, listen, and be heard. As we learn to speak from the heart, we change habits for a lifetime. We focus on a slower pace to create space and slow down. These are the guidelines for the sacred council: 1. We open class with silence, music, a poem, or a game. 2. We pass a ball around the room in one direction, letting each person talk or be silent. Each person receives one minute to talk if needed. The class is focused on feelings, needs, and how to make life wonderful. 3. When the ball is passed to the next person, that person must paraphrase or validate the previous person's words. When the person is satisfied with the paraphrase, the next person takes two full breaths and speaks. Students may choose to share a celebration or a loss."

We would begin with students sharing personal frustrations at home and in their family life. I watched in awe as each student slowly but assertively took time to examine the words that expressed the feelings and needs posted around the room. One student, Dominique, snatched the ball from Michael. With fire in her eyes, she shouted with trepidation, "These feelings and needs are so stupid and worthless! I can't go back into my neighborhood or even outside this class talking like this! People at this school try you. They test you. We don't talk. We fight!" My pupils dilated. My heart rate increased while looking at the students, who nodded and clapped in agreement. "Yeah, pass me that ball," I hear someone from the opposite side of the circle shout. Stephanie's hands were flailing like an air traffic controller. "You can't use no 'I feel' because 'I need.' That makes you look soft."

The temperature rose in the room. My ears crackle from side rumbles, mutters, and chatter. As the collective rant spread like wildfire, I struggled to put my feelings aside as the rage of their helplessness and powerlessness echoed around the circle like dominoes. I would be a fool to stop this. Yet, like a girl playing Double Dutch, I patiently waited for my turn to hop in. Eventually, I calmly yet assertively said, "Please toss me the spirit ball." It landed in my hands. I squeezed it as tightly as I could. If I could have made a wish to the teacher gods, I would have asked them for wisdom, insight, and guidance to capture the rage, despair, and fear hurled around the sacred circle. I prayed that with my presence, gentleness, and compassion, I could hold the validity of their pain like a mother holding a newborn child. "This pain has been brewing inside of everyone," I gasped. "The cycle of violence that circles you at home, in your neighborhood, and this school is a heavy burden to bear. Violence is so prevalent that it has become natural and normal. I want everyone to remember that despite your circumstances, you always have the right to choose." Suddenly, while speaking, I was interrupted. Mikey, another student, said, "But Mr. Ervin, what if someone is about to hit you in the face? What will you use to protect yourself—words?" Again, the class buzzed, cackled, and let out cheers and jeers like an audience at the Jerry Springer Show. "Listen, everyone."

I paused to assert my courage and my compassion in one full breath. "I am nonviolent, but that doesn't mean I will not protect or defend myself. My physical safety and well-being are important, especially because I need to be here for you and my family. However, at all costs, my first priority is to use my communication skills to de-escalate conflict between me and another human being—especially one who looks like me. This is called self-restraint, and it takes real strength." I stood up like Gandhi leading his people against the British, and said, "Violence begets more violence. Everyone who has the privilege of taking my class has the unique opportunity of being part of a new culture at Winston High School. I can't lead this fight alone. We don't fight with our fists. We fight with our intellect." There was nothing left to say. The class was silent. I scanned all the faces around the circle. They sparkled like stars in the night sky. I felt my chest lighten, and a surge of positive energy emanated throughout my entire being. I thought of the word "education," which comes from the Latin root *educere*, which means to draw forth from within.

Later that afternoon, a few minutes before my African American History class, I took three humongous bites of a crisp green apple. I love African American History. My mind wandered back to my college days when I wrote a 20-page paper on the Back-to-Africa movement with Marcus Garvey. I continued to drift back to my childhood when my entire family and I watched the history of Motown snuggled together on the old, dusty, worn-out sofa in our dense living room. I remembered the confusion I had watching Western movies sitting beside my dad. I always asked, "Where are all the Black people? Were we alive back then?" I recalled my favorite movies, such as *Glory, The Wiz*, and *The Learning Tree*. I relished every opportunity to see anything that expressed the essence of Black culture—one last stop. As I continued today's dream, it took me to a Stevie Wonder concert.

I could see his colorful beads twirl on the dark stage as he created magic on his Steinway piano. Alas! My seniors strolled in. Many wore oversized white T-shirts that looked like nightgowns. The girls slowly and confidently sashayed into my stuffy room wearing jersey dresses and high-heeled sneakers. I blinked a few times to ensure I wasn't seeing a mirage. The chatter was abrasively loud. It was so loud that my *Black Star* album with Mos Def and Talib Kweli was barely a whisper compared to the thunderous rants, epithets, and long-winded soliloquies being hurled around the circle. I rubbed my arms and took a few deep breaths.

The random conversations continued. I wanted to see if the students would stop and acknowledge my presence. I strolled to the computer and clicked the pause button to remind myself to take it easy. "Nigga chill out! You know I get more hoes than you!" "Nigga you must be out of your mind. I get way more hoes than you!" Two young men went back and forth like a tennis match, hurling the most oppressive word in the history of this country. The chatter mellowed, and the class prepared to decide how to weigh in on the hotly contested debate. Surprisingly, the word "nigga," was a perfect place to start.

I strutted into the center of the circle, and with the pride of an African chief, I recited this quote, "Words can bring death or life! Talk too much, and you eat everything you say!" I followed this and said, "This will be the greatest learning experience in your high school career that's sadly ending in one semester. It saddens me to say that I was the first to create an African American History course in this school district. When I first submitted the curriculum, it was rejected by the school board. I, however, made a decision not to be discouraged. I revised and reconstructed my ideas and refused to take no for an answer. I had made history. Now, I want each of you to also make history with me. In my course, we will explore the history of African Americans, beginning with Mother Africa and around the globe. I want you to think until it hurts. You will read books and engage in critical thinking until it hurts. You will feel my pain, and I will feel yours. We all shall build this community together."

I triumphantly asked, "Any questions?" The silence was piercing. I basked in the glory of waiting for a response, any response. They looked spooked. Then, a young man playfully murmured, "I thought this class was gonna be fun." My eyebrows raised, and a sheepish grin overshadowed my face like a brisk sunset. I declared, "Let the fun begin!" After I had concluded my intro, my attention and focus returned to the word "nigga." I asked, "Does anyone know what 'nigga' means?" I waited patiently for any response from the room filled with puzzled students. "Well, why don't you just tell us?" You're the famous Mr. Ervin with the dreads, the reputation, and the charming good looks!" someone said. I turned to identify the student who had arrogance, confidence, and an insolent voice. To my surprise, it was Ari Rose. Ari was a young lady known for making teachers earn every dollar of their paychecks. I had heard stories about Ari that could be screenplays for a horror movie.

She was the urban legend at the high school. I locked in on Ari's small petite frame and innocent girlish looks. On the surface, she was delightful as a beautiful rose, but if you got too close, you would get pricked by her thorns. I thought to myself. "How did I miss her name on the roster? Why would she take my class?" The only exchanges we had had in four years were scowls and witty remarks as she passed by my class. Once, I had to help remove her from a teacher's room because she was sitting on the teacher's desk like the Native American legend Sitting Bull and refused to leave.

Her hostile words cut through everyone like a machete. When she exploded, everyone ran for cover. Her middle name should be Ari "Righteous Trepidation" Rose. As I attempted to respond, I felt my belly burn, and my lips curl slightly. "Well!" She howled as she widened her eyes and tilted her head. Then, the bell rang. "Listen. Tomorrow, we will finish the conversation about the word 'nigga.'" I quickly noticed two gentlemen trying to slither out of the room. "Hold it!" I shouted and smiled. "Fellas, I hope you have strong arms. Give me forty pushups straight." They sighed and dropped to do the pushups. I said, "Listen. We will study three African empires this semester. Mansa Musa, Askia Muhammed, and Sundiata. I want y'all to tell me which name we will use to address each other. We are regal, royal, and resilient. The English language is so colorful, and so are other world languages. You are with me to expand your knowledge, consciousness, attitudes, and skills while learning about our history and culture. With that being said, work together, and don't take too much time to select the name. See y'all tomorrow." They skated out of my room.

The next day, before my African American studies class, I strategically played a new artist's slam poetry piece. I was confident his verbal acrobatics and in-depth knowledge of history, sung over pulsating beats, could surely set the right ambiance. His name was Future. His poetry enlightens, educates, uplifts, and inspires. I stood relaxed by my door as my students hurriedly filed in to hear the deep booming voice coming from the speakers. Future's words were like magnets, pulling them in. They plopped down in their seats, mesmerized by his complex rhyme schemes, metaphors, and hyperboles. Eventually, I let his song saunter them into cheers and jeers as they bounced in their seats, pleased with this enlightening experience. I slid over to the speaker and lowered the sound.

I asserted with pride, "Welcome to African American studies. Would Reginald and Michael please come to the front of the class and share the title that will be used to address me and other male students?" They stood looking at each other with the etiquette of statesmen and walked forward. "We chose the word *Mansa* because we like how it sounds. He was the richest king to ever live on this earth!" they said. I nodded and said, "I like the sound of that." I smiled and watched the young men proudly walk back to their seats. "Does anyone know the history of the word 'nigga'?" I asked. I loved waiting. I waited and waited. Okay. "What do you feel about the word 'nigga'?" I asked. A student responded, "It's cool. We use it all the time. I don't know why adults get all bent out of shape."

Another student energetically replied, "Yeah, we, as Black kids, can say it all we want, but we bet not hear that word come out of a White person's mouth." This response received lots of praise and applause as the majority, if not all of the African American students, agreed. He continued. "We are allowed to use this word. Yeah, I get it came from slavery, but we took it back from White people." I purposely waited as the students glared at me with wild anticipation, salivating for a response. I gazed around the circle with silent curiosity, using the power of delay to create tension, conflict, and excitement. I said, "Does anyone else have any opposing opinions, comments, or perspectives on the 'nigga' word?"

Suddenly, a hand was raised. It was the hand of a young lady with a long torso and a bright smile. Her name was Raven. She stated, "I don't think anyone should say the word regardless of color. Also, the word means ignorant, so ignorant people use that word, not me." The callousness from her words sent an echo of stillness through the room. I heard no cackles, jeers, or cheers. There were only stares and smacking of lips as an unmistakable expression of disapproval. I calmly said, "Words have meanings and histories attached to them. Words and language create narratives and stories that empower or enslave people. Specifically, the word 'nigga' was derived from the Spanish word, *Negro*, meaning Black, and the Greek for *Necro* meaning dead or corpse. Now, it is true that words take on different meanings throughout different periods. It is also true that marginalized or oppressed groups can take the word as an attempt to regain a sense of power."

This word has so much history and controversy that the debate is ephemeral. However, my obligation and mission were to enlighten everyone on the history and the causes of events and circumstances that had directly impacted our people for centuries. I stated, "As we continue to research, learn, and grow as a community, my charge is for you to begin to critically challenge many of the norms that have been passed down to you, in an attempt to keep you from learning the rich legacies that are within you and beyond you.

"Raven dared to speak her truth despite the negative response it received. That was true power. There is a thread that connects the past to where we stand today. What you decide to do or say outside this class is your business, but when you step into my arena, it's an opportunity to be transformed. Words create worlds. I see nothing but royalty and unlimited potential in every person in this class. My question to you is, 'What do you see?'"

Each day, the poetry radiated from the computer into the beautiful souls sitting in the circle. Students used their composition books and pens to journal their feelings and needs juxtaposed with the world and ancient civilizations of Africa. After journaling their experiences of the previous evening, they closed their books like they were in a vault. I said, "Take a look at this quote. Look around the room and decide how this quote makes you feel and what needs it inspires and provokes within you. Lastly, decide what action you want to take regarding the quote. When you finish, partner up and discuss your perspectives. When we gather in the circle, I will put students in the 'hot seat.' We will see who will be seen and heard through the most persuasive spoken word." The "hot seat" was a gritty exercise that embodied ways students enjoyed learning. It incorporated drama, movement, music, and dialogue. The premise of the exercise was based on the Ethiopian quote, "To teach is to learn twice."

I was honored to provide a safe space where students could freely express the art and practice of the spoken word. This was rooted in ancient African civilizations. The twenty-first century educational needs and skills it provides are critical/creative thinking, collaboration, communication, problem-solving, and global citizenship. It is a fascinating process to apply and refine students' voices as they/we continue to make meaning in our world. Two chairs were placed in the circle's center, and a question was asked with a yes or no response. Each student chose a perspective to defend in a hotly contested battle of presence, compassion, and reasoning. The beauty of this practice enabled the outer circle of students to pick a side while intently listening to the fight that interpreted, evaluated, and analyzed the whole process. If a student decided they had enough, they could gracefully tag another student to join them or escape to the outer circle. The level of energy and community created was incredible as the content crystallized in their minds and spirits. Everyone was motivated to study and research to prepare for the next battle. Intrinsically, motivation was built by tapping into my students' needs, values, and wishes. This enhanced the need for learning, personal growth, and community.

Suddenly, like a gentle whisper in the wind, Ari Love softly said, "Let me try this." I shook like a tambourine with delight as she slid her slender body into the hot seat while waiting for her opponent. "I'll go too. This sounds like fun," shouted Samantha. Her smile emanated as she strutted to the middle of the circle across from Ari to take a seat. Samantha was pure Black girl magic. From head to toe, she wore a color-coordinated outfit. Her fashion sense was style meets an internship. She puts the C in class. Samantha woke up with a purpose. She strived for perfection and sought to squeeze every morsel of learning from her high school experience.

Her smile was deadly because her intellect and wit were her weapons of choice. I melted with joy and became giddy as a child, realizing when she chose to take my elective course. Samantha traveled a long way from the honors wing of the school to participate in this experience of history and culture. She probably was lonely. Often, high-achieving Black girls in honor classes are like rare gems surrounded by a sea of whiteness. Samantha yearned for culture. She desired something real, innovative, and nourishing to her spirit.

Before the marquee matchup began, I shared a few thoughts. "Archeologists found fossilized skeletal remains curled up like a fetus in the semi-arid region of Ethiopia. Equally important, scientists compared DNA material from fossils found in Africa to DNA taken from people in various parts of the world. Scientists concluded that all humans descended from one common female. Carbon tests on bones and stone tools dated them 3.2 million years ago in present-day Ethiopia. Ultimately, all our journeys began on the continent of Africa, the birthplace of all humankind. Despite current races and cultures, all humans share the same origin. This bond would be tested by injustice and inhumanity, which seems to go hand in hand with human development." I continued, "Here is the question to debate, and you must connect your responses to feelings and needs. Is it important to learn that humans are more alike than different?"

Samantha dove in first. She said, "Yes, because humans have traveled, migrated, and adapted to all parts of the globe. However, this meets their need for adventure and discovery by knowing that our DNA/ genetics stayed the same despite our physical differences. It meets the need for connectedness and closeness. Ari leaned back in her chair, then leaned forward, clasping her fingers together. She looked into Samantha's eyes and said, "No, people are content with their differences. This meets the need for creativity and originality. No one wants to be alike. That's boring. Also, racism and other inequalities thrive on our differences, so one group stays on top at the expense of the other." This dazzling debate pulled everyone in as they were deeply engaged in the question. Some students hesitated, then summoned the courage to step inside the circle like a game of Double Dutch. They flipped knowledge. They twisted knowledge, all while making meaning and prior connections. "Time!" I shouted, "Please read chapters one and two tonight. Also, please write a journal entry on any observations from today's debate, feelings, needs that were met, and any ideas on how to change the debate next time."

"How about we create teams of boys against girls?" Ari said with a sparkle in her eyes. I noticed my heart smiling from within as the class ended for the day. Before I turned the ignition key, I sat in my car, perplexed, and pleased at Ari Love's transformation. She brought a sassy force and optimism that pushed us all forward. As I continued to daydream, my mind wandered to another special girl I admired, much like Ari Love

CHAPTER 5

The Power of Relationships

"When you fully trust someone without any doubt,
you finally get one of two results: a person
for life or a lesson for life. Love recognizes no barriers.
It jumps hurdles, leaps fences, penetrates walls
to arrive at its destination full of hope."
Maya Angelou

I stare incessantly at the skinny Christmas tree leaning to the side like a hangover. I salivate at the shiny packages with neatly tied green and red bows. I creep into the kitchen, and my nose is tickled by the smell of the fresh chocolate chip cookies baking in the oven. I sneak up to the mixing bowl and stand on my tippy toes in my transformer pajamas. With the tip of my index finger, I swipe it along the bowl for a quick sugar fix. "Morris, get out of that kitchen and keep your fingers off the batter!" My mother playfully screams, as I dash back into the living room. Standing close to the old leaning Christmas tree, I gaze straight into a bulb to see my distorted reflection.

There is an echo and a scratch before I hear "Rudolph the Red-Nosed Reindeer" playing soulfully from my father's record player. He only plays Best of the Temptations album. Their soulful singing comforts and soothes me. I feel my chest jumping around from the excitement and anticipation of Christmas Day. I sprint upstairs to my sister's room. I don't knock. I hurry in and plop on her bed. "Ma!" she screams, sounding like a siren on a red fire truck. I hop off the bed and say, "Maya, you got some Bubblicious?" I'm always in awe when I go to the store, and Mom lets us get a pack of gum. I always get grape or purple flavor. I usually devour my gum within thirty minutes. Maya savors her pieces like they are gold or titanium or something. She goes to her secret stash and gives me a piece. My eyes are as big as a Martian as I put a piece of that sugar into my mouth. Before I leave, I ask, "Can I sleep here with you tonight? You know it's Christmas Eve, and we always do our ritual." No response from my big sister is a yes, so I skip back down the stairs, eager to eat my mom's fried pork chops, corn, and mashed potatoes. Dinner ends. We eat a few delicious cookies, and my excitement grows like an avalanche because I know the faster I fall asleep, the sooner Christmas day will be here! "Remember, if you come downstairs too early, Santa will throw ashes in your eyes," my dad added with a strange, stern expression. I don't want to make Santa angry and ruin my Christmas. Then Mom cheerfully says, "Aren't you guys forgetting to leave the cookies and milk for Santa?" My sister and I turn around and race into the kitchen to get the milk and delicious cookies for Santa.

Later that night, lying on my back, I look across the room to my sister's bed. Time is torture. It is nighttime, and I have no clue what time it is. I toss and turn, trying to keep my eyes closed. Ugh, it doesn't work. The more I fight sleep, the more I lose. My sister also can't sleep. We tell jokes and laugh. When the roar from our laughter echoes down the hallway, we hear, "Maya and Morris go to sleep!" As a result, we whisper, laugh, and joke, barely enough to listen to each other but enough to elicit more giggles and chuckles. Next, Maya says, "You ready?" I respond, "Yup!" We both count to three and rapidly flail our arms and legs relentlessly as we make snow angels in our beds. We squeal, scream, and make screeching sounds like little chipmunks until we become exhausted from the erratic movement. We eventually both settle down, becoming still as we notice the rise and fall of our tummies. Lastly, the natural heaviness from my eyes closes like a rusty garage door. I have no fight left in me as I drift from my excitement to sleep.

"Pshhh, Pshhhh, Morris! Wake up! Wake up!" I'm startled by my sister's cheerful whispers. I slowly raise my torso as my legs stay planted in the bed. "What will we do?" longing for my big sister to tell me. "You go down first, and I'll be right behind you!" She reassures me, although

I don't believe her. "Okay," I whisper as I climb out of the bed. I creep towards the stairs like a ninja, unsure if ashes will be thrown in my face. Finally, I make my way to the stairs. I sit softly, sliding down each one. Finally, I stand straight up before the last stair, grinning, laughing, and screaming uncontrollably. "Maya, Mommy, Daddy!!!! Santa was here! Santa was here!" I look around the tree, mesmerized by bikes, portable stereos, action figures, an Easy Bake oven, board games, and much more. I continue screaming, jumping up and down until my big sister, mom, and dad join me.

I giggle about those old Christmas rituals my sister and I once enjoyed. I owe her big time for protecting me when Mom dropped us off at the daycare. She held me and my hand tightly every day before the mean staff pried us apart and forced us into separate rooms. I also recall the talent show she participated in in the sixth grade. Maya and two of her close friends lip-synced a routine by the Pointer Sisters. I remember the daily rehearsals held after school. I delightfully watched as they wiggled, shook, and shimmied to the song "Neutron Dance." They looked like true professionals. The Hawaiian-themed outfits, colorful hair clips, and glowing bracelets captured the essence of the 1980s. They electrified the crowd at the talent show. Unfortunately, they lost. The first-place winners were a brother and sister duo who tore the stage up with "I Feel for You" by Chaka Khan. My sister and her cute friends were disappointed with a third-place victory.

Growing up with my big sister had its challenges, too. She used her words like a Samurai and was known to slice anyone up with them. Being young and exceptionally small, I took on the daunting task of defending her honor. I often looked up to a bigger foe who, with rage in his eyes and licking his wounds, hunted my sister after enduring a scolding in front of everyone. On one occasion, with shaking knees and a foreign object between my sweaty palms, I stood my ground and taunted her adversary to make my day. We binged on 80s movies such as *16 Candles, Breaking, The Last Dragon, Adventures in Babysitting, Wildcats, Lucas*, and many more. We memorized lines from each movie and would recite them at will.

We often spent Saturdays at the best mall on the planet, Randall Park Mall, or we found ourselves skating at the South Gate rink.

Eventually, we moved into our high school years. We argued and fought over the telephone, or I was nosy when her boyfriend visited. Although we constantly argued, we both honored the no-snitch rule and never blabbed incriminating secrets to our parents. Although she buzzed past me in our high school's large hallways without looking my way, she always had my back when I needed her. She would be right there for her little bro if I got into potential scuffles. I loved her brazen style of dress. She had a knack for putting outfits together. In the 90s, she had this Toni Braxton, Anita Baker, and Halle Berry asymmetrical hairstyle that drove the neighborhood boys bananas. A lot of ashy boys had crushes on my sister. They gave me money, gifts, and all types of offerings to put in a good word for them. When I became interested in girls, they had to be bold, creative, and fearless like my sister.

I had a haunting memory. I was always fond of my sister's attention and admired her adorable friends. One day, a couple of my friends were at my house. They all tried to win the attention of my sister's friends. Somehow, the afternoon turned into a bizarre fashion show where the boys wore bathing suits, heels, makeup, and colorful hair clips. My sister and her friends clapped, judged, and laughed at us. After the girls made up our faces with blush, eye shadow, and foundation, we modeled the bathing suits. I became contestant number one. I hurriedly put on a hot, sizzling, pink one-piece swimsuit with heels. I strolled down the stairs, swaying exaggeratedly to loud applause, cheers, whistles, and gut-wrenching laughter. My friends tumbled down the stairs behind me. They strutted and pranced along with plastic smiles, salivating for the same level of admiration from the girls. Finally, we stood shoulder to shoulder, waiting for the announcement of the ridiculous winner. Unfortunately, suddenly, without notice, the girls sprang forth from the living room couches, leaving us standing, ashy knees and all.

October 5, 2006

Relaxed and at ease, I capture recent moments of my life at my favorite spot, Borders Bookstore. I snuggle in at a table directly facing the self-help books. I pause before opening my stylish journal with a picture of an antiquated globe on the front cover. I sink into my chair, letting my thoughts and recollections slowly surface to the top of my mind. There's much running around to do before my weekend football trip to Chicago. I'm still fasting during the month of Ramadan. It feels good. My prayers, however, are inconsistent. Before the trip, I requested to miss a day of work. I decided to spruce up my room. The NVC documentary will be filmed a few days after I return from my football trip. The drive to Chicago went well. My team members and I had a fascinating conversation about race. I, being the only Black man in the car, listened to my White teammates express their desire to be with Black women.

The trip usually went as planned. We would arrive at the hotel and go to a bar, and everyone except me would get drunk. We woke up early, barely making it to the flag football tournament. Fasting while playing football takes my game to the next level. I feel refreshed and energized, and my mind is super clear from distracting thoughts and impulses. My self-control game is dialed up to a high vibration. In this tournament, we decided to play in the A division. The A division is the highest and most competitive division in flag football. The talent is bigger, faster, stronger, and contains elite athletes who played college or professional ball.

My limited football experience never discourages me in big moments. I rise to the occasion because I'm "Mighty!" We played strong throughout the entire tournament. I am blown away at my first opportunity to play at night under the lights. Not surprisingly, I almost ran a huge punt return for a touchdown. I played tough defense. Sadly, we got eliminated in a very close game. I want to get better. I got exposed a few times because this competition has little room for error. However, I'm a small warrior who will be prepared for the state tournament next month. We drove home and arrived at my house at 12:30 a.m. After a short night's sleep, I barely made it out of bed. I had a sore body and a curious mind, eager to experience a week of inspiration, excitement, and significance.

Monday evening after school, I met Cat, the dynamic NVC trainer, Hillary, a filmmaker, and George, another filmmaker who would film the footage of my classes for five straight days. We went to Wild Oats and sat down at long wooden tables. I wasted no time sharing my experience teaching the language of feelings and needs to my high school students in a little over thirty days. "Man, initially, I felt so much pressure to do it right, then I just trusted my instincts and let my natural creativity take over." As they calmly listened while munching on organic pita chips, I continued, "Using games, music, and the sacred council created a robust sense of safety for the students. It was refreshing to see all my classes blossom and form tight-knit communities outside of the chaos that dictated their lives. NVC helped establish a refuge where learning thrived, and young minds had the opportunity to soar," I said. We spent another forty-five minutes going over details and paperwork for the week. I described my daily teaching schedule and the flow of my day. Before we concluded, Cat and I agreed to meet an hour before school every day to carve out a plan for team teaching using NVC and history. As I steered the wheel on the drive home, I noticed tiny chill bumps spreading along my forearms. I stopped at a red light to look at my palms. They were as moist as chocolate cake. I tried to ignore what I believed was imminent. I arrived home and parked my car. I moved as slow as a snail. I attempted to avoid seeing my family and up to my bed. Soon after, my head was congested, my throat became scratchy, and my nose poured like a faucet. I was too exhausted to be angry about coming down with the flu.

The morning quickly arrived. I convinced myself the flu would not stop me from this delightful, fulfilling, and momentous week ahead. I fervently said, "I will persist and get through this!" While ignoring my symptoms, this affirmation helped me throw on a jazzy shirt and tie combination. I quickly and quietly left home and headed to school. Arriving early before the sun peeked through the clouds, Cat and I created a plan for the day. We spread our feelings and needs cards on two tables. We were clear on the most sacred needs for the week, what we hoped to accomplish, and how we planned to work together and take care of ourselves throughout the process.

I gazed at the clock with relief. I had at least twenty minutes before showtime. At first, I hesitated. I looked at Cat and asked, "Why were you at that Teach for Life NVC training?" You seemed very different from the other trainers. You stuck out like a sore thumb. What I admired about you was your ability to connect beyond the words of NVC and the safe process of the language. Every time you spoke, it was from your soul. I sensed a deep level of pain and a deep level of freedom, liberation, and self-expression. I needed you to be there." "Wow, Morris! I appreciate you seeing my bigness in this way. I resonated with the bigness and spark of creativity and authenticity that lived within you," Cat said with a huge grin. She continued, "It was my first time leading a session on my safety, trust, and respect game.

"I'm not sure if you remember, but I disagreed with one of the lead trainers when I introduced the idea that sometimes you have to do a round where kids name, 'I felt disrespected when,' as a feeling. I went toe-to-toe with her in front of the group, but then later, big time, in a meeting. She thought it was not teaching NVC. I countered it was because we don't need to get so hung up on the language or the phrasing. I worked with kids who had never been asked what respect looks like to them. So, they needed a chance to express and discover their need for respect. I remember you thanking me for bringing that point up." I paused before I gleefully shouted, "Oh yeah! That's right. I love that you like to shake things up! I can't do anything in a formal, cookie-cutter way.

"My edge is about using platforms like NVC to dismantle the status quo while getting the kids to see the beauty and brilliance in themselves." I jumped out of my chair, "We got to be able to shimmy. It's all about the shimmy and the courage to shake things up!" I continued. Cat said, "Well, there's gonna be a lot of shaking going on this week!" And I truly believe that teachers are the most creative humans on the planet, but the dominant systems at play keep us from our play!" Surprisingly, I felt my chest expanding from the wisdom and energy cultivated from this conversation. I signaled George and Hillary, who were testing their equipment. They both give me a thumbs up. The first bell rang. I trotted to the door to take my position so I could greet the kids with Cat standing beside me.

My first-period, ninth grade American History students sluggishly sat in their seats with blank faces and stares. The silence in the room spoke loudly as I tuned into a few faint mumbles and whispers that traveled around the circle. I spotted a few female students who nervously touched and patted their freshly styled hairdos for the big day. The two cameras added an element of caution. The filming, at least for the moment, was smothering the freedom, safety, spontaneity, and trust we had built for the last thirty days. I took a moment, sensing my anxious thoughts that this may be too much. Did I adequately prepare them? Will the students open up? Will this be a disaster? I pulled myself together, took a deep, slow breath from my abdomen, and exhaled.

Then, with a big smile, I said, "Greetings, class. Welcome to the filming of the NVC documentary. Can all of you believe that it's finally happening? I am so proud of our progress with speaking, learning, and playing with the language of feelings and needs as we learn American History. Before I let this amazing trainer, who will co-teach with me, introduce herself, let's play a game." I motioned for all the students to stand up. Standing up can break the tension and silence in the room. Next, I picked up a green Nerf football and tossed it to a random student in the circle. Then, they tossed it to another student in the circle. I let the tossing continue for a few minutes. Some students caught the ball. Some students dropped the ball, and others refused to toss or catch. Pleasantly, with each toss, more laughter, movement, warmth, and playfulness entered the space. "Now," I said. "Let's do our council check-in using observations, feelings, and needs. The first person with the ball will share an observation, then toss the ball to the next person who will say a feeling. They will then toss the ball to another person, expressing a need. The last person will share an action, step, or specific strategy. The goals are not to overthink, share from your heart, listen from your heart, and have fun." Immediately following the game, students delightfully plopped back into their seats with the joyful noise and cheerfulness essential to the learning process.

Cat wasted no time skillfully asking, "Greetings, class. I'm Cat, and I created an NVC school. What would a school be like that has absolutely zero punishments?" Mostly, all students look stunned and intrigued at the same time. Cat calmly continued, "This is the radical education Mr. Ervin taught you. This is the essence of transformative education that you all get the privilege of experiencing. However, this is not a privilege. This is a human need. We all need to be free and connect on a deeper level. This education creates opportunities for everyone to be seen and to be heard. This education creates the capacity for us all to give from the heart naturally. With NVC, the guilt, shame, force, demand, and expectations we are conditioned to survive under can be transformed into compassionate giving. This is my calling, so Mr. Ervin invited me to join him in teaching and facilitating this week." Cat's words reverberated deeply within me. Her authentic wisdom immediately captured the hearts and minds of each student.

It was fascinating to see, at least on the surface, a White woman who had nothing in common with these predominantly African American students engage with them and build trust so quickly and intimately. Throughout the rest of the day, she knew exactly what to say and what not to say. Her ease and flow with the students on the first day amazed me. I guessed wrong. Beneath the surface, Cat had one major thing in common with the students: struggle. Cat knew struggle. She knew pain. She knew suffering. Cat is a survivor. My students survived daily. The beauty is that she made herself so vulnerable and open to the kids without pushing too far. She wasn't patronizing or seemingly phony. She embodied the work. Eventually, the first day came to an end. The last class shuffled out, and I immediately sank into my chair and unloosened my tie. Cat and I debriefed for an hour about the wonderful day. We spent another forty-five minutes being interviewed by our documentary team. When we finished, I sluggishly climbed into my car and drove home.

The next day, during homeroom, the principal made an announcement over the PA system that sent shock waves of aggravation and antagonization through my classroom. In an autocratic tone, he announced, "The things of this nature will not occur. You will be suspended if you enter any door or let anyone in any room other than the A-room." This message was a perfect segue into Cat's words of wisdom as she eloquently shed light on systems of domination. She spoke in a soothing tone. "As long as we have a system where someone has power over another individual, we're going to remain a suppressed group of people who want to rebel." I added, "Remember that we are in a school that authorizes the security guards to mace and handcuff students at will. We are in a school where a teacher or administrator can freely walk into your personal space, grab your identification necklace, and demand you tell them where you're supposed to be. As we reflect on our education and government systems, what is this school? Is it an autocracy, oligarchy, or democracy?"

Our provocative statements captured the frustration and powerlessness of the students and helped frame their experience in the larger context of World and American History. Additionally, I asked questions such as, "What is human nature? What is our role as citizens? What is the role of the government?" I proudly watched as students pondered these questions as they pertained to their lives as young adults. Our reflections evolved into a lively debate around the school's zero-tolerance policy versus the no-punishment and judgment zone that had been nourished in my classroom environment. "In a way," a student said with a sheepish grin, "This class is like the revolution in France. I heard people talk about you and your style, Mr. Ervin. They think we are not learning. They think all we do is cry, complain, and share our feelings. However, they judge you because they need to understand and let go of their fear." I listened intently as other students built on this point and showed the parallels of how history is being made.

Before we closed, I instructed the students to read the two opposing philosophies of Thomas Hobbes and John Locke. I said, "Read these two men and write in your journal about your role in your family, school, and community. Tomorrow, we will continue the debate on the role of government. Is it to compel order or obedience, or protect the people's natural rights? Does the government and your school have an obligation to the people and students it governs? As you read and write in your journal, think not from the limited perspective of right versus wrong, but from the expanding field of feelings and needs."

Eventually, the day ended. I was as grateful and equally drained. I felt the heaviness of my body and the dryness in my throat. I attempted to sit up, but my body naturally sank into the wooden chair. I squinted at the camera team while waiting for them to add a new film cartridge in preparation for the upcoming hour-long interview after a thrilling, exciting, and thought-provoking day. Simultaneously, George, our cameraman, with a sparkle in his eye, sent me a thumbs up as the camera started to film. I heard the question, "Can you speak more about your teaching philosophy and how NVC compliments it?" "Sure," I said with unflinching confidence. "NVC allows me to remain in joyous power and still be clear about matters of concern or importance, and I switch my empathy to my students, even when I need empathy. Empathy is such a precious need because, in this environment, I have no support. So, I constantly choose to create ways to care for myself while supporting my students because the main priority is learning. We play. We learn. We interact. We learn again, and we play some more."

"I integrate timeless ancient cultural practices from indigenous African and Native American cultures. I embed the natural techniques of games, storytelling, movement, dialogue, and drama to activate and stimulate the frontal lobe of a student's brain, which regulates cognitive skills such as emotional expression, problem-solving, and memory. Last, we establish safety and trust, building strong relationships and community." The cameras stopped taping. We were done, and the day had ended.

During my afternoon ninth grade History class the next day, I strolled around the room as students worked in collaborative groups on an assignment. Usually, I allowed time for students to read, discuss, and establish roles before we moved to the Socratic Seminar. My Socratic Seminar brought history to life through lively formal discussions based on the text in which a student facilitator asked open-ended questions. In my class, the student facilitator who owns this role is Sherry. Sherry is a feisty, intelligent, witty, confident young lady who walks and talks purposefully. Every day, she arrived in class with a zeal to learn and a fire that extinguished students who attempted to disrupt the learning process.

I adored Sherry. We have had countless conversations before school, during lunch, and after school. She is a sweet young lady, and I admire her. Surprisingly, Sherry had her head down as I approached her table, and her feet were tapping incessantly on the floor. "Sherry, Sherry," I uttered lightly, "Are you ok? I need you to get ready to lead the seminar." Her head stayed planted in her arms. She didn't budge, and her feet continued to tap the floor. I attempted to get her to speak to me a few more times as I became concerned about this drastic change in her behavior. Finally, she snapped her head from under her arms and shouted, "Get away from me! I don't want to speak to you!" A rush of embarrassment, shock, and distress filled my body. I took a few steps back. I tried to gather myself. I gently walked towards her and tried to whisper to her. She lashed out again, "Get away from me!" Instantly, Cat rushed over to the table, and Sherry bolted out the door. I nodded, signaling some of her closest friends to follow her. My tear ducts were opening, so I quickly approached my desk to gather myself.

The class was silent and aware that something was terribly wrong with Sherry. At that moment, I was speechless. I had no empathy or wisdom to share. I briefly acknowledged my ability to be skilled enough to recognize that her explosion was not about me. My heart still pounded rapidly. I took short breaths to settle my mind and re-engage with the class. A few minutes went by. I decided to move on with the lesson. Soon after that, the door cracked open. With her head down, a melancholy Sherry walked in my direction. She stopped and remained silent. She uncrumpled a short newspaper article between her palms and placed it in my hand. Finally, she turned in complete silence and walked back to her seat. I stood and read the caption, "William Henry to receive ninety-nine years to life for rape and kidnapping."

CHAPTER 6

The Power of Vulnerability

"It's room for everybody's pain. But I fear my pain
won't be seen, recognized, or validated."
Morris H. Ervin, Jr.

My jaw tightened as I read the crumpled caption about the tragic fate of Sherry's father. A rush of emotions swirled throughout my mind. I felt relieved that I did not consciously cause the pain and confusion. I felt devastated for Sherry and all Black girls who felt rejected, abandoned, and dismissed by Black fathers, strangled by a system, and caught in a web of hopelessness and despair, disconnected from their pain and oblivious to the deep cycle of destruction left in their absence. I stuttered, searching for the right words to soothe her in this stressful moment. She paused and looked at me with puffy red eyes. With a shaky voice, she said, "I get a criminal as a father, some low life who was abusive to my mother and abandoned me. However, I walk into this class every day and see a strong, Black, positive male role model who loves so much and is loved by everyone. And today, when I got the news, I was overwhelmed with jealousy, anger, and rage. It's not fair! Why can't you be my dad!" I received her pain. I welcomed her rage. I did not need to say or do anything. She was safe. She was loved. She could express her unconditional grief in that delicate moment of vulnerability and anger. Cat and her close friends cared for her outside my classroom. They allowed her most tender, broken, and fragile parts to be exposed but again held her with compassion. A celebration of what it means to educate children who face a crisis. Children who continue to survive despite tremendous amounts of trauma, grief, and loss. We all were present in her most significant moment of need.

On that day in class, Cat began with an inquiry question about puppets. With utter delight and joy, watching my students scrutinize every word from Cat's mouth was riveting. In full mode, Cat sat comfortably in her chair, flung her purple shawl effortlessly over her left shoulder, and asked, "What's a symbol? A symbol is something that represents something else." She nodded at me. I said, "This class is a giraffe classroom, which means no matter how someone approaches you, you still have power. You still have control, understand that?"

Immediately after sharing our brief intro of the lesson, I motioned for one of my students, Tim, who craved attention like bees crave honey, to put on a pair of giraffe ears. Cat attempted to speak but patiently waited for Tim to stop giggling. She said, "This has stopped more fights, so just buy, and wear them around the school. The visual of having giraffe ears is a strong reminder of how you can listen for tragic ways people communicate in an attempt to express feelings and meet needs. You always have a choice to wear giraffe ears, or jackal ears that respond with self-blame or attack with self-rage. Tim, you are in the most challenging seat. That is why you are giggling. It's called the hot seat. When someone challenges you with a hard-to-hear message, the challenging part is to hear what's alive in that person. What is the person feeling and needing? Cat scanned a sea of vulnerable faces and asked, "What messages do family, friends, and teachers say are hard for you to hear?"

The bell rang earlier than expected, and my class hurried out while the others hurried in. This class had chosen to step outside the classroom dynamic by moving the desks and using carpet pieces to sit in a circle on the floor. While this quick transition happened, I decided to go over a few ideas with Cat. Suddenly I heard a thundering voice shout, "Bitch, I'll slap you!" I quickly pivoted with dilated pupils. I stared at Ebony, who had positioned her body directly over Ivory. Ivory sprang up and fired back, "Bitch, slap me then!" I quickly navigated my body between them as a barrier to avoid a potential slug match! Cat drifted over as well. The entire class gasped and, with apprehension, wondered what would happen. "I'm getting tired of her fat ass!" Ivory shouted directly to Ebony over my broad shoulders. "She's tired of me? She's tired of me? She ain't going to talk to me like that!" Ebony shouted while trying to push her way through me with her head down in embarrassment.

I stood tall. Firmly and calmly, I said, "Ladies, sit down and have a seat before I choose to use protective force." The protective use of force is only used to protect people or stop any harm that could occur. It is different from punitive force. The punitive force is used to make people suffer. Finally, I took Ivory outside to the empty hallway. We slowly walked towards a hall window. Her body was rigid, shaking, and intense as she let out a few more wails and yells. "Ivory, take all the time you need and breathe slowly and deeply. Focus on the trees, the grass, the sunlight, or whatever you see that's outside." I told her, "We stand together." I waited patiently as she began to take slower and deeper breaths. I noticed the ease and relief on her face, and the tightness and tension started to leave her body as she returned to herself. Ivory firmly said, "Mr. Ervin, every day, Ebony comes for me, making little comments about my hair and clothes. Today, I wasn't having any of it!" I responded, "Ivory, it sounds like you tried to be patient and ignored her, but today, you felt outraged from holding all those emotions inside. You wanted to defend yourself and get respect." "Yes, there's a lot of pressure from girls at this school. It's hard to stay away from the drama. I'm usually quiet and keep to myself, but you can only take so much," Ivory continued with a relaxed and stressful tone.

I listened and offered a few more rounds of empathy and active listening. Lastly, I asked if Ivory would be willing to discuss things with Ebony tomorrow when things cooled down. With a smile, Ivory agreed, and we walked back into my classroom. As we entered the room, I saw Cat and Ebony sitting close to each other while the class listened intently to the dialogue. Cat explained, "Ebony, this is the system you're in that gives punishments and rewards. What happens after you choose to start a fight to meet your need for respect?" In a low voice, Ebony responded, "I get a ten-day suspension." Cat replied with an assertive grin. "How does that meet your need for respect? However, ten days away from school might meet your need for freedom!" Cat continued as she opened her message to the class. "NVC breaks down the meaning of love and fear in this system with an acronym." Cat stood and wrote both words vertically on the chalkboard to define each letter with another clarifying word.

"L is Listening, O is for Observation, V is for Validation, and E is for Empathy. This is what real love looks like. A love that breaks down barriers and opens hearts. A love that challenges and a love that thinks critically. A love that questions and suspends harsh judgment. A love that builds, cleanses, and purifies, never a love that tears down." I scanned the room to see which students appeared planted as we sat on the sacred circle carpet. The atmosphere of healing sent chills through my body. Cat continued, "FEAR is Force, Enemy images, Authority, and Reward or punishment. Fear limits what is possible. Fear creates silence, and silence perpetuates violence. Fear destroys bodies, minds, and futures. Fear is a mental prison. Fear is safe. Fear is survival. Fear is holding on to hateful, shameful, and self-loathing labels about self and others, leading to cruelty, inhumanity, and despicable acts of violence."

As Cat spoke her truth, her last sentence hit me in my gut. My body became tense, tight, and constricted. My world became small. I tightened my jaw and squeezed my fists tightly. I am held hostage by so many memories of the passive and physical violence to which I have been victimized, just like so many others. My belly felt hot, and my legs shook. I became overwhelmed with rage that was couched in immense heartbreak. Without a blink and with a stoic face, I said, "You just heard Ebony. Before the fight, she called Ivory a bitch." As I spoke, my hands moved with each word.

I continued speaking and said, "So when I call someone a bitch, then I don't see them as a human being. I can beat the hell out of them and feel good about it." To my irritation and disgust, the class nervously laughed and giggled. "No, I'm not laughing," I asserted. "This isn't funny." At that moment, I did not need humor. I was totally frustrated. I needed to show and receive consideration and kindness from people. "You have been indoctrinated in a world of violence for so long that you think it's funny, so you laugh nervously when you hear me, your teacher, use profanity," I said in a stern voice. "I am only using those words to drive home my point,"

I continued. "You are so young and pure. But you are living in a system that will take that purity and innocence from you if you let it. It can turn you into an animal. You are a human being. Don't you think it's inhumane to want to beat someone down over a space on this carpet? Or are you dealing with issues that are not being addressed? If so, why aren't they being addressed? I preach this every day in this class! This is so petty!" I retorted, pounding my fist on my desk three times.

I noticed the uncomfortable silence that permeated the room because of my righteously indignant rage. I felt my chest cavity erratically rise and fall in my shirt. At the same time, Cat's touching words allowed me to release the tension that had built up in my body. Cat said, "This is a great opportunity to sit and hear what's alive in your teacher. It's real. It's total honesty. Mr. Ervin, are you feeling desperate because of how hard you have been working and how you have tried to make peace, at least in this one classroom? You wanted to give your students the experience of having freedom and choice. You wanted a paradigm shift. You wanted a system that can be built on love, where someone listens to another human being, and someone who validates another human being; a place where there's actually an empathetic connection."

Cat beautifully highlighted my pain. Underneath my rant, my heart was broken, and my heart ached. I felt my chest expand. I felt the air freely moving in and out of my lungs. My belly felt soft. Concurrently, as this awakening experience happened within me, it spread throughout the circle and room. Students proudly sat up. There was a sweet presence in the room. Amber triumphantly spoke, "Until we took this class, most of us were reactionary in our actions. We fought and exhibited violent communication. We didn't think to use what you taught us—evaluation versus observation. We lived based on what we were taught throughout our life." A few more students spoke about the violence that encapsulated their lives and how my class gave them the tools and a new perspective on relating to history, themselves, and the world around them.

Similarly, when the last group of students left my room, I slumped in my chair, loosening my tie as my thoughts bounced inside my head.

My legs felt like concrete, and my feet and toes ached. I was exhausted because I was fasting, had extremely long workdays, and the interviews and filming weighed on my small but strong frame. Amid my pain, however, I reminded myself that it was Thursday and tomorrow would be the last day of filming. I smiled.

Steve Hardaway, my principal, was also interviewed. Our relationship was refreshing because we had the same love and vision for students, especially our desire for marginalized students to succeed. Steve strolled into the room, fresh as a crisp dollar bill. He was always ready to spit wisdom using his calm, optimistic tone, and poised presence. The cameras rolled. With his platinum smile, Steve cheerfully said, "My hope, through Mr. Ervin's work, is for more teachers to use this program. It should be open to all the staff, and hopefully, our district can become a pilot district."

Friday finally came. My students were always ecstatic about council day. They worked tirelessly throughout the week for the opportunity to freely express themselves and jointly use their problem-solving skills. Ironically, after my day of councils, one of the principals visited me during my break. Standing in the doorway, her large eyes surveyed the room as if she were waiting for something bizarre to happen. Or maybe she wanted me to do a magic trick, I thought. "Geno Bailey, you have him in your class, correct?" she asked. Surprised by the random question, I nodded and said, "Yes, I have Geno in my second-period class." She made a scowling face as she invited herself into my classroom. She paused and plopped down in a student's chair. She said, "He is a very disrespectful young man who never takes his baseball cap off. He strolls up and down the hallways like he owns this school. He needs a swift attitude adjustment." Rambling on, she continued, "One day, however, he came to my office before I could give him his detention, and he calmly said, 'Principal, I know you're getting frustrated with your repeated attempts to get me to take off my cap. I understand that you need to be respected in your role of authority and as a principal of this school. Would you mind giving me my detention because I don't want to be late for Mr. Ervin's history class?'" She chuckled and said sarcastically, "Geno articulately spoke to me with class and as a complete gentleman. What are you doing with these kids?" I said, "We create a community where everyone's voice is heard. I seek to understand the students, get to know them, and gain their trust. I also believe my job is to inspire and motivate them to be an integral part of my class. Geno has a real disdain for authority. However, he loves to express himself philosophically. I incorporate what he loves into my curriculum." I returned her shady look as she stood speechless. She turned and disappeared.

A few months earlier, Geno had joined my class. He is a handsome young man with a magnetic smile, personality, and charisma. On his first day, he was unafraid to talk and be himself. Geno is an aspiring hip-hop artist who loves to write music. School was not his thing. He, however, was quite gifted, but he needed to apply himself to his classes. During the first week of school, Geno needed help arriving on time. I stayed on him about this. He lived with his grandfather. He, however, never mentioned a mother or father. I had a strong sense that he took care of himself. On council day, we had a powerful exchange in front of the cameras, leaving me with a lifelong indelible impression. During our council session, the sharing became more profound and quite emotional when we discussed family and support systems. Geno, who always expressed himself in the council, hesitated when he received the spirit ball; it was his turn to share. Geno said, "It would be nice to have a male figure in my life because I go through many tough situations outside of school." I paused and let the words settle into my spirit. The class looked stunned because Geno was a young man who appeared to have it all together. He wore the most expensive clothes. Every day, he showed up with a swagger and confidence that his peers adored.

I motioned for the spirit ball, and Geno tossed it across the circle to me. I caught it and said affectionately, "I hear the sadness of one of my students who needs guidance and direction. I am willing to support him in his time of need." Geno motioned for the ball, and I tossed it back to him. He replied, "I request that Mr. Ervin become my mentor so we can talk and hang out sometimes."

Later that day, in my senior African American History class, the council session revealed a deeper truth about Amina. Amina was a witty young lady with a charismatic personality. She had a small circle of friends and loved to debate about Philosophy, Theology, Astrology, and Ancient History. It's obvious that school is not her thing, but she is inspired to learn. Amina also struggled to arrive at school on time and accumulated many tardies and unexcused absences. Her chances of graduating were as thin as the air in the Colorado mountains. However, Amina appreciated a teacher like me who challenged her mind, enjoyed her individuality, and wanted her to succeed. Surprisingly, during the council discussion, she called for the spirit ball. All the students quietly, yet swiftly, whipped their heads towards her as if they were watching an intense tennis match.

Amina rarely spoke in council, so the students were eager as a beaver to hear what she wanted to express. She caught the ball with one hand. Amina slowly inspected it like she was looking at a rare gem. She said, "At first, I did not see the relevance of what Mr. Ervin was teaching with these feelings and needs. I usually would say whatever was on my brain and deal with the consequences." She paused and continued, "I'm not the type to share my business. I'm a private person. However, everyone knows my sexuality and my sexual preference." The room was still like blades of grass on a hot, humid Cleveland day. Everyone leaned their bodies into the center of the circle, pretending as if by doing so, they could hear better. Amina's voice, however, was quite clear and deep as the Caribbean Ocean. They were just being dramatic. Amina went on to say, "My mother hates that I'm gay. She is sickened by my lifestyle. We argue so much and so often that there is no love, respect, or peace between us. She refuses to accept me for who I am. I'm disgusted with our relationship." While Amina hesitated before she continued, I looked around the circle. The power and depth of their empathic expressions and desire to listen were earth-shattering. "One evening," Amina continued, "I remembered something Mr. Ervin said about making observations, not evaluations. I remembered how he talked about hearing someone's feelings and needs and connecting with their heart, not their head. So, I decided to try observing and hearing my mother's feelings and needs. With each comment she made, I took a deep breath and reflected on what was underneath her feelings and deeper needs in her evaluations and assumptions about my lifestyle. In doing this, she stopped with her assumptions and asked me how I felt and what I needed from her. We continued this deeply meaningful, affectionate conversation for two hours to help us find ways and strategies to meet our needs." Without hesitation, the class let out a thunderous applause in complete support and solidarity with Amina. The class ended.

This was the last day of filming an extraordinary documentary highlighting the work of two educators who sought to bring the best out of students who had been through the worst. I gasped. My eyes were blurry and heavy from an invigorating yet exhausting week. I was invited to share closing words before completely slumping into a student's desk. I straightened up like a ruler and felt a burst of energy. I saw an imaginary clock with the hand counting down. Three, two, one. In that small amount of time, I was confident I could connect with my spirit to discover some inspirational words to end with. "On any given day, who knows what they might face when they're not in school? Be it physical abuse, sexual abuse, poverty, despair, or just perpetual sadness," I said. "Besides the toxic stress surrounding them, students are greeted at school with more force and control. It's tough to have the space and time to figure out who they are now and who they want to become in the future." I continued, "You must sit somewhere and critically reflect on your actions and decisions. Ask yourself, 'Am I living the life I want?' When you have more reflection, you will have more peace. The beauty is finding a sacred place with an open community where people can be honest and supportive. That's my hope."

CHAPTER 7

Choose Your Love, Love Your Choice

"Love takes off the masks we fear we cannot live
without and know we cannot live within."
James Baldwin

October 13, 2006, A Special Bond

Venaya and I worked tirelessly on writing the essay she needs to apply to veterinary school. She hates writing essays, while on the other hand, it gives me great joy to write them! Our emotions flow like the movement of a seesaw high as Mt. Everest and low as Death Valley. On our small sunken couch, we sit shoulder to shoulder like sardines in a can as we search her past experiences for inspiration to write. I gaze into her big brown eyes and see the reflection of pain and agony as I try to cheer her through this tumultuous process. I assure her that we will succeed. We were able to write four essays together, and then one day, we hit a wall like a car going 100 mph. Venaya boiled with rage when I tried to teach her about the writing process. We argued. Our voices raised, and Venaya shut down. After that, I wanted to quit. Despite these intense moments of butting heads like two rams on a narrow mountain ledge, we accomplished our goal. The next day, she cried, and I ranted. We argued again, and somehow, we pushed through and reached the other side of the rainbow.

October 26, 2006, Eid Celebration

The Muslim celebration of Eid had ended, and so did our fasting. We took our kids to visit their aunts, Chuck E. Cheese, Red Lobster, and my parents' house. Naimah, our daughter, received her "Baby Alive" doll, and Idris, our son, received his "Game Boy." Venaya and I exchanged gifts, too. I bought her two workout outfits and a pair of pajamas. She bought me a jean jacket with the continent of Africa airbrushed on the back. As I reflected on my holy month of fasting, I began strong. I prayed daily, woke up early, and read the Holy Quran. I, however, was inconsistent with my daily prayers. My intense stomach pains made it difficult to fast daily, but I completed the month. My motivation to practice my faith was low. I was curious about Venaya's commitment to me, knowing that I had struggled to practice Islam for a few years. She, nevertheless, was patient with me—but how long will this last?

November 2, 2006, Deep Clarification

Venaya needs clarification and understanding about where I stand in our marriage and religion. She said frustratedly, "This is a never-ending, drawn-out conversation that's not even close to closure." She became increasingly angry and upset from our conversation. Fortunately, the discussion helped me. I was living out the unfinished business of my early and late adolescence. My impulse to relive my childhood and teenage years had hijacked my present and seduced me into doing irresponsible things. I was trapped in a cycle of selfishness. It wasn't very pleasant to name it, but it was so true. I purposely disappeared from my wife's radar. I checked out. I was not honest about where I went and what I was doing. This caused Venaya to confront me with a stream of screams and yells that hit me like tides gushing and crashing on a rocky coastline. I reacted by shutting down like a garage door. I am not in high school, and she is not my parent. She is my partner. Surprisingly, I wrote down her last heartfelt question after her tears and rage had subsided. She asked, "Do you see me as a true friend? A friend that you can hang out with and bring around your other friends?" She left me speechless. I was stuck. She knew I had confided in other women, which crossed the line—and

I still do it. I walked away from the conversation, my nostrils flaring and eyes wide open. One thought. One question. My past is my present. I had put my unresolved past in my actions.

The following evening, I dilly-dallied inside my home. First, I stopped in the kitchen to assess the number of pots, pans, and cups piled up in the sink. After a short pause, I pushed my hand through the murky water filled with gook and pulled out the stopper. I removed all the filthy dishes from the sink and ran warm, clean water into it as I poured in some dish liquid. The warm suds refreshed my thoughts that had aimlessly wandered from past to present to future. In the distance, I heard a faint but strong call of my name. Feeling troubled, I abruptly stopped, turned around, wiped my hands, and ran up the stairs. With a foolish look, I stood against the narrow bedroom door facing Venaya. I felt pressure in my stomach. I couldn't understand why I had tension in my body. "The quieter and more silent you get creates more distance and space between us. I see you're perfectly happy with the way things are." Venaya's words stung like wasps attacking me.

I gripped and squeezed the narrow door frame like it was my favorite blanket. Internally, my brain was overwhelmed, and my body had become as tight as a crowded bus heading slowly downtown. In my mind, Venaya's tongue-lashing lasted another fifteen minutes. I rarely tried to provide her with a response because I was speechless. The conversation or scolding ended, and I released my hold on the door frame and scampered back to my appointment with the dishes. "UGHHH," I said with frustration, looking into a sink filled with cold water and duds instead of suds.

Nevertheless, I drained the cold water again and poured more dish liquid and hot water into the sink. I gently placed both hands in the sink, filled with fresh sparkly suds, until my wrists were submerged in water. Suddenly, my mind was clear, and rational thoughts returned. I gave myself a full explanation of my current unexplainable behavior. I thought, "I'm troubled because my current work schedule does not make enough time for my wife and children. It does not meet their needs for closeness and connection. I had expended all of my energy meeting the needs of my students. When school ended, I was exhausted."

Nonetheless, I overcame exhaustion by meeting my needs for fun, exercise, fitness, and connection with my colleagues and friends after work. Upon arriving home, I had nothing left to offer my family, who loved me the most. I usually isolated myself in the kitchen or went into my office to escape by writing in my journal. Eventually, I resurfaced after a few shouts and calls from my wife, who attempted to make me address my children's basic needs. Sadly, my wife felt as if she was forcing me to have dinner. I wanted to understand this vicious pattern of not being accessible and present for my loved ones. I was clueless about why I needed so many reminders to be intimately connected and attentive to my wife's needs. I felt regretful and confused because I had put her last. I was hopeful, however, that I could move past her frustration and my disappointment to a place of mutual progress, understanding, and companionship. This is what I needed. I wanted to reassure my wife that I am here to support and treat her with grace and compassion. I wanted to be intentional about making quality time with my wife and children. I wondered how to restructure my week and evening routine to make that happen.

I asked myself, "Who am I? Why did I choose marriage at such a young age?" I didn't believe I was capable of meeting my wife's needs. My wife, with eyes so big and beautiful, smooth caramel skin, and full lips, demanded that I provide her with love, attention, care, and closeness. When she talks to me, I feel rattled, guarded, and reluctant to say anything beyond, "I don't know." I think that I'm being verbally assaulted for something to which I am clueless. I cringe inside when we argue because I am afraid to tell her the truth.

In an argument we were having, Venaya, with the venom of a snake, shouts, "You show love to everyone in the world except me. You act phony out in public. I want you to be the real you so I can experience the joy you spread to the world." She continued to share her sadness and other frustrations about her career. She continued, "My personality is tough because I constantly question my goodness and self-worth from my accomplishments or perceived failures." The beauty of this woman is that she is as real as it gets. When the tension from the argument subsided, I shared that I would like to look at us as friends. I want to work on our friendship, and I need to be honest and truthful. When I say something, Venaya takes me at my word. She despises a liar who can't stand behind their words with actions. Venaya responded, "I can't let go of my anger towards you for not loving me unconditionally. I feel like I'm the one always chasing you around!"

What is it about turning 30 that deeply troubles my soul? I constantly fight demons that cause me to be depressed about this milestone age. Unfortunately, my wife and two young children pay the price with my mood swings, temper tantrums, and anxiety attacks. I am either obsessed and anxious about the future or swept away with regretting my past.

One day, my wife wanted me to ride with her to pick up our daughter from a friend's house. I know my wife is fearful of driving long distances alone. I did not care. I refused to drive. She continued to plead with me. Reluctantly, I agreed. I decided to drive her by displaying a crappy mood and then giving her the silent treatment. We arrived at the home of our dear friends, the Abu-Khaled family. This family is like a second family to me and my wife. They have cared for us from the earliest stages of our young marriage by providing us with support and guidance. Usually, under normal circumstances, the love and comfort from this family would have changed my mood. Nope. I sat with a fake smile while cringing on the inside. The maternal elder of the Abu-Khaled family has a gift of clairvoyance. Well, she could see the internal struggles weighing on my mind. She could cheer me up with delicious food, then cleverly drop her infinite wisdom on me. As I sat, I thought, Venaya has set me up. She has told this woman about my struggles with my faith and depression. Umm Walled, I call her. She looked at me and smiled. Her smile was as big and bright as the Grand Canyon. And without asking, she shared the importance of keeping God close through prayer and being careful of the devil's trickery. I listened to her lecture but attempted to shield her wisdom from piercing my soul. Did I want to be miserable and alone? Our visit soon ended, and we drove an hour back home with our daughter in tow. I rode utterly silent.

Despite my internal struggles, I continued to accept unconditional love from my wife and children. On Father's Day, I awoke and was given two beautiful homemade cards from Naimah and Idris. My children also placed two pairs of much-needed Old Navy jeans across the bed. Then, my lovely wife showed me a paid receipt for 16 sessions with a personal trainer, Mike Harris. I said with enthusiasm, "Venaya is a bad woman!" She is more in tune with my wants and needs than I am! I love football. I play flag football all year and travel to tournaments nationwide. It is truly my dream and passion. If this flag football career works out, I might have a chance at semi-pro ball, then Arena Football. I tried on my new jeans and looked at myself in the closet mirror. "Happy Father's Day to Me!" There are days in my life when I crave freedom and adventure.

One day, I rose early on a clear, muggy summer morning. I carefully and methodically picked my Incredible Hulk cut-off shorts, sleeveless shirt, and netted baseball cap to cover up my braided hair. Then, I slipped downstairs out of our apartment. I grabbed my bike and headed out in search of what life had to offer. I spent a few hours exploring different parts of my apartment complex. I watched in awe as young girls jumped Double Dutch rope while singing nursery rhymes. I found other hills and makeshift ramps to jump up and over. The thrill of being in midair and full flight was exhilarating. I parked my bike on the ground and eagerly joined a creative football game called "Down a Man." The goal is to catch the ball and run for your life in the opposite direction for a touchdown. Then, dare to run out of the end zone, with the speed of a cheetah, hoping to avoid being tackled by bigger dudes. Pure adrenaline! What a game! I scored! Even though the game ended, I will safely stash away the memories in my mind. I continued my journey to a friend's house. He invited me inside for a game of Pac-Man, Space Invaders, and Pitfall! We finished some games and dashed outside to chase the neighborhood ice cream truck! Aww! Yes! Two red, white, and blue Bomb Pops!

We savored every bite and flavor of this sweet treat. After the Bomb Pops, my friend announced he had to return home for dinner. I said, "Dinner!" The sun was fading into the distance. I quickly hopped on my bike and pedaled as fast as the speed of light. I was hoping to make it home before nighttime! No one can be out at night because the Green Lady might snatch you! I finally reached my apartment at 4925 Banbury Court! My mom's face was stern when she said, "I almost called the police. Where have you been all day?" I stared at her, frozen with fear. I shrugged my shoulders as I attempted to tell her about my day. When I finished, she said the words that tore me up every time. "Wait until your father gets home," and "You're staying inside the house tomorrow!" The pain of a belt wears off. However, being forced to miss one day of fun during a miraculous summer is torture.

As an adult, my thoughts would occasionally slip back to my childhood. I tend to disappear into my world purposely. I love going out during the summer. On any given day, I would run sprints up and down a hill and do drills with a friend from work. After my intense workout, I randomly drove to my cousins' neighborhood to work out. Jab and Fence are street heroes to me. They were the first people in my family to have muscular physiques. They taught me how to walk with my hands. I never learned how to do a backflip. However, watching them do backflips was like watching pure magic. It was cool to hang with them as adults. I loved working out with them, lifting weights, and reminiscing about growing up. We finished the routine. Next, I would stop at my mom's house to shower and eat some of her delicious food. As a married man, my mom loves for her son to stop by and eat her food.

My next stop was the public library. I spent a few hours prepping for my upcoming African American History course, which I was thrilled to teach for the first time. I then went to the mall to purchase some cool Puma sneakers. I enjoyed the sights and sounds of the mall and bumped into people I knew or grew up with. Sometimes, I saw students I had taught. I enjoyed catching up on what they were doing. Finally, I would drive home at sunset, smiling from ear to ear. It seemed that my wife took offense to my random days of freedom. It's frustrating for her because I would disappear. Well, that sounds familiar. I realized I needed days like that to revitalize my spirit. As I grow as a person, husband, and father, I know my needs matter. However, the challenge is making sure I check in with my wife. And honestly, I am not too fond of that. Well, at least I don't get punished anymore. On second thought, I still pay for it.

Parenting is a journey where only the strong survive. In my mind, parenting seemed easy. My wife and I often saw couples struggling with their kids in public. We did not have children then, so it was easy to criticize and pass judgment. However, on June 7, 1999, everything changed. Naimah came into this world on a hot, muggy day. I remember holding her tiny, wrinkly body in my arms. I felt grateful that she was healthy and proud to be a father. I did not expect the following days to be difficult, but having our first child turned our world inside out.

Our daughter had colic. There was no peace in our house until she was seven months old. Colic results from an allergy to milk protein or lactose intolerance in formula-fed babies. In Naimah's case, she negatively reacted to specific foods in Venaya's diet that passed through her breast milk. Naimah did not just cry; she screamed for hours at a time. I recall coming home from work to Venaya, who was speechless. She immediately placed our screaming daughter in my arms and walked upstairs. I turned around and, with my colicky child, walked for an hour on a sunny, muggy evening through our townhome complex. I walked with my daughter hoisted over my shoulder, gently rubbing, and massaging her back until she begrudgingly fell asleep. With my clothes drenched in sweat, I gingerly walked back home. My only goal was to get Naimah inside without waking her. Another successful strategy to soothe my daughter's intense crying was dancing to Otis Redding's Greatest Hits compilation with her on my shoulder. Otis Redding's soulful, upbeat tunes and classic ballads worked like a charm. We started with "Satisfaction," "Mr. Pitiful," and ended with "Sitting On the Dock of the Bay." Thanks, Otis!

The intense crying took a heavy toll on Venaya because we agreed she would be a stay-at-home mom. My wife never had a break because I was taking classes during the day and working the second shift in the evenings. Naimah refused to let anyone console or hold her except Venaya and me. Her grandparents, aunts, uncles, and close friends could only observe our little screaming machine from afar. Eventually, the intense crying episodes faded, and then my daughter's absolute fear of being in public and around people began. If we went to birthday parties or other social gatherings, Naimah stayed attached to my wife. We slowly encouraged Naimah to socialize by attending play dates at local community libraries and activities such as ice skating, gymnastics, and ballet. We were initiated quickly, fast, and in a hurry to the whirlwind of sacrifices that come with parenting.

At that time, Naimah was a shy, timid seven-year-old who loved to play house with her baby dolls. She struggled with anxiety. Playing mommy to her dolls was a safe place where she felt free. She loved to read Junie B. Jones books. Her small athletic frame was perfect when swinging on the monkey bars at the playground. A playground is a place where she competed against little boys running sprints. She often displayed a sheepish grin after she claimed her victory. I would laugh as I watched disgruntled fathers console shocked and disappointed sons after their crushing defeat. My Naimah would imitate me when I worked out in the garage by doing pushups, crunches, and mountain climbers. Naimah is most joyful when she helps her mom nurture wild kittens back to health. She is eager to hold and caress these small furry creatures with barely open gooey eyes. She feeds them with a baby bottle and unselfishly divides her time equally between them. Naimah protects her younger brother Idris like a lioness protects her cubs. She would force him to hold her hand when we went places. Watching Naimah translate what Idris said when he got frustrated was so cute when they were toddlers. I adore Naimah's gentle, caring spirit, and I hope she will continue to grow and find her way through life's many rainbows and hardships.

My son entered this world on March 1, 2001. At the time, I lived in the isolated world of a first-year teacher at Paul Robeson High, an inner-city school. I spent my evenings and weekends coaching varsity girls' track. At the tender age of 23, my stubbornness prevented me from seeing that my wife needed me. I was non-existent. I would joke by saying, "How did Idris get here?" We did not plan on having a second child. He just arrived. I vividly remember the two hours and forty minutes it took for Venaya to birth him into this world. When it seemed she had nothing left, the nurses pulled out a bar for her to hold onto. She gave her last push. Boom! He arrived! I, however, freaked out because they used forceps to pull him out of her womb. I shouted, "Oh my god, what is wrong with his head!" He looked like a little alien. Everyone reassured me that massaging his head would return it to a normal shape.

Idris was an easy baby. He stayed as quiet as the morning dew. Idris rarely cried for anything. He let us hold him and feed him. He just slept. As an infant, my son looked like a Michelin baby. His round belly and jovial laugh like Santa Claus became lively conversations amongst our family and friends. Eventually, our son's heaviness made us worry when he developed Respiratory Syncytial Virus Infection, commonly known as RSV. This infection caused inflammation of the small airways in his lungs, leading to Idris using a breathing machine at night. Idris's heavy wheezing and pauses in his breathing kept us on guard. One night, we thought Idris had stopped breathing. We panicked and quickly rushed him to the emergency room. He recovered well, and the infection gradually went away.

When Idris was five years old, he was obsessed with Spiderman. My wife hated it. When we went places, I allowed him to wear his Spiderman costume, including the mask! Idris loved wrestling, and every time he visited his cousin's house, he would fall out on the kitchen floor, exhausted from all the rough house play for the rest of the night. Idris is sweet. However, when things didn't go his way, he exploded like a volcano. His explosive fits sometimes triggered my explosive volcano, which often left him feeling scared and me feeling regretful and sad. One day, I had to go to his school after I received a call from his teacher to pick him up early. When his teacher saw me approaching her room, she rushed towards me with eyes as bright as the moon. She said, "Come quickly to my room. There's been an incident involving your son." I felt butterflies in my stomach, tightness in my chest, and shortness of breath.

As I hurriedly strolled toward her, I wondered what could have happened. She opened the door. The room was empty. It looked like everyone had evacuated because an earthquake had occurred. To my shock, I saw chairs on the floor, desks flipped upside down, and papers and crayons covering the floor like a blanket. Then I heard a tiny angelic voice say, "Hi, Daddy!" I fixed my eyes on my son sitting on the floor with his pants off, revealing his ashy legs. He was playing with blocks like the sweetest kid on the planet Earth. The teacher noticed my eyes turning red, my erratic breathing, and my vengeful glare. She calmly grabbed my hand and walked me to the principal's office. His volcano and my volcano would erupt many more times throughout his childhood.

Summer nights are the best. The days are hot and humid. However, the summer nights in Cleveland are a perfect blend of warm temperatures and cool breezes. One particular night, I had the pleasure of meeting some college friends for an old-school hip-hop concert at the Grog Shop. I arrived early and walked into a large, barely lit room. I stood in the crowd facing the stage, patiently waiting for my friends to enter and for the concert to begin. My friends arrived. We immediately embraced each other with smiles and began sharing stories from our college days. The concert started, and I focused on Buckshot Shorty, Boot Camp Clique, and Smith and Wesson. They stood on stage performing classic hit after classic hit as the crowd screamed, hands in the air, and recited every word. When the concert ended, I trotted up a hill to my car, thinking about the styles and fashions of my college days.

My first year in college was clouded with controversy and conflict as I searched for my identity. My parents pulled into the parking lot in a shiny forest-green Jeep Cherokee. I opened the trunk and got my belongings. I kissed my mom, hugged my four-year-old brother, and gave my dad a firm handshake. My brother screamed like he was on a rollercoaster as I stood blankly watching my family drive back to Cleveland. I was in complete shock. I thought, "Well, this freedom thing is what you wanted so badly, and now you have it." I felt disconnected from my body as I walked into my dorm room. It was quiet, and I was lonely. I took a nap to ease my mind. When I woke up, I decided to walk down the narrow hallway to see what or who I could find. I peeked into a room and saw a skinny African American male wearing an LA Dodgers jersey with African beads around his neck. I walked inside, and we talked for two hours. I guess this was now my home.

I am small in stature, standing only five foot seven inches tall. My presence, however, is strong. My style is bold. I sport an afro and wear fatigued pants with big, unlaced Timberland boots. My favorite T-shirt says, "Islam is Dominant." I accepted Islam in my senior year of high school. I did not change my name but chose the Muslim name of Musa, which means Moses in Arabic. This decision caused a lot of friction and tension in my Christian household. My favorite music genre is hip-hop. I love playing basketball, lifting weights, and shooting pool. I always kept my prayer rug across my shoulder and my machete in my backpack with my books. I love to learn, and I get a thrill sitting in the front row in all my classes, just waiting to challenge the professor or argue with my classmates about a particular topic.

I struggle in math class, which weighs on my mind. Sitting in class, I try to understand the professor as he scribbles sample problems for us to write in our notebooks. Twice a week, I attend his tutoring sessions. When that did not work, I asked an intelligent student in class to tutor me. One day, as I sat in class, anxiously watching the professor pass out our exam scores, I felt my heart pulsate. I felt a rush of energy as he placed the exam face-down on my desk. I hesitantly turned it over and glanced at the F written across it!

In frustration, I mumble words aloud, feeling disgust for my teacher and the entire class. Behind me, I could hear laughing and joking. I jump out of my chair like a killer whale in the ocean. I move my desk out of the way to be nose-to-nose with the person I thought was laughing. I shout, "Don't you ever call me stupid or disrespect me in your life!" The student staring at me froze in terror. In the distance, I heard my professor yell for us to sit down. I ignore him! I scream profanity and rush for the door, slamming it as hard as possible, trying to tear it off the hinges. I race down the hallway, and as I approach the second set of glass doors, I pull my leg up to my chest. Kicking the glass door with my Timberland boots, I shatter the glass. In panic, I turn around and run back upstairs to the second floor. I quickly found two African American men in an office *to whom I could vent my anger and fear. They listened, consoled me, and reassured me everything would work out. I stayed in their office until the smoke cleared. I finally returned to my dorm room, knowing my action would get me arrested and kicked out of college. I waited and waited and waited. I looked out my window for an hour straight, waiting for the police to enter my dorm and arrest me. The cops did not come. It was a miracle or mystery that the whole class, including the professor, did not report me to the authorities.*

July arrived. I was frightened at the thought of turning 30. I could not believe my twenties would soon be a thing of the past. I was uneasy and unsettled about the big 3, 0. I love my wife, and we will celebrate nine years of marriage on July 19, 2006. I loved my children. I loved teaching. However, episodes of sadness continued to haunt me day and night. These episodes quickly turned into childlike tantrums and rage at any moment. I often said, "Be happy with the life you have chosen or the life that has been chosen for you." I yearned for the freedom to go places and do things just for me. I shrugged my shoulders and wondered if I was being selfish.

Flag football is my thing! I have played it for a couple of years. I enjoy physical exertion, intense competition, traveling, and meeting players from around the country. My greatest gifts in this sport are speed, quickness, instincts, and toughness. I secretly imagine that I can live my dreams whenever I score a touchdown, run a kickoff, or punt return into the end zone. Yes. I play defensive back. I am fearless! How I play football reflects how I live my life. My ultimate mission is to neutralize the opposing team's most gifted, talented, and fastest wide receiver. My cheerful, energetic, and positive attitude motivates my team and entertains the crowd. What I love the most about myself is that I never give up on a play. During one game, I recall a receiver catching a pass on the other side of the field. As I ran and locked my eyes on my target, I thought, no way am I going to let him score. With every gallop, I made up lots of ground until I removed his flag right before he attempted to score the touchdown.

On July 23, 2006, I turned 30 and intentionally planned a perfect day of football, family, food, and fun. I dashed out of the house, going to the second day of an intense football tournament. We won the first game. During the second game, as I ran toward a guy to pull his flags, I suddenly saw a beam of white. B-Rush, one of the players, hit me so hard that I returned to my 20th birthday. I felt the full force of this two-hundred-fifty-pound ex-NFL linebacker. I hit the ground. However, I sprung up, accelerated, and pulled the receiver's flag in one motion. Unfortunately, we lost. Before we left the field, I gathered my teammates in a circle and screamed at them about our lack of toughness and how I almost lost my life!

I limped to my car in the hot sun, thinking it might be time to call this flag/weekend warrior thing quits! I arrived home and walked inside, holding my neck. I was pleasantly surprised to see baked chicken, vegetables, pot roast, and banana pudding on the table. I love it when Venaya's mom cooks for me. Her food is delicious. I finished my meal, showered, and visited my parents with my children and nephews. When I pulled into the driveway, my father had the little red wagon out with a grin, ready to play with his grandchildren. I skipped up the front stairs, passed the kitchen, and headed directly into the living room to chat with my mom. She felt my sadness. My mother usually knew when her firstborn was sad. I shared my depression about letting go of my twenties. She responded, "I gave up my life so early that turning 30 was not a big deal. I married your father around the same time you married your wife. It's tough, but you learn to live with it." I listened intently, and when our conversation ended, I decided to walk in my old neighborhood.

As I slowly walked, many childhood memories flooded my mind. The sights, sounds, and smells quickly took me back to a simpler time. I stopped by to see a childhood friend. Her birthday was a day before mine. We had known each other since the sixth grade. "When we were in middle school, do you remember when I kicked you in your balls?" she asked. "You fell to the ground screaming, and the French teacher kicked you out of class!" I sigh, saying, "Yes! I painfully recall that!" We continued sharing old stories, and we shared stories about our children. She is a classroom teacher and wants to leave Cleveland and move to North Carolina. Our conversation ended, and I returned to my parents' home to gather the kids and head home. Lastly, I entered my home and sat on the couch. My wife and children handed me a box with a shiny silver chain and bracelet inside.

On Monday afternoon, I waited outside the community college before entering the classroom to pick up my children. The teacher stared hard at me. We would begin the conversation about my son at any moment. "Idris had a horrible day today. He keeps distracting the class, and he will not respect my authority," she said, looking at me with a 'You better fix your child' attitude. She continued, "This is a summer enrichment program. I don't have to let him stay." "My apologies for my son's behavior. Hopefully, after we talk, you will see his improved behavior," I responded, simultaneously feeling the usual self-blame pains rising in my stomach. I managed to end the conversation and walked back to my car with my children.

"Naimah, get in the car, baby girl," I said. She climbed inside. Standing outside the car, I bent down to look at my son. I was now face-to-face with my nemesis. "What happened today?" I asked as I watched Idris fold his arms tightly like he wanted to hug himself. He squinted his eyebrows close together and refused to respond. I tried to react. However, I realized that connecting with my son was more important than getting in his face to confront him. I waited. I asked, "Do you think she mistreats you?" "Yes!" He screamed. "She did not help me when I needed her!" At that moment, I realized the power of creating a quality connection when my needs and my son's needs are equal.

Normally, I would react negatively to my son's antics, not realizing that hurt and frustration stimulated his tantrums. This time, I allowed him to talk. He finished. I said, "Idris, I understand you are upset with your teacher. However, not listening to your teacher adds to your problem. It also made it difficult for her to teach the class. Can we both consider getting help and cooperating with the teacher's directions? I know you like the program, but you will be asked to leave if you get in trouble again." He nodded affirmatively. I celebrated what seemed to be a successful conversation. Phew! This NVC talk is a lot of work!

The next day, I dropped my children at the local community college to attend the NASA summer camp. Before Idris went inside, we hugged and high-fived each other. I shared positive words and made him laugh, hoping he would have a great day. I drove back to the Peaceful Inn. There is something about this place I adore. The Peaceful Inn Settlement provides various social services for families throughout the greater Cleveland area. They provide after-school educational programs, summer enrichment programs, daycare services, a food pantry, and many other community services. The Women's Temperance Union League founded this settlement center in the late 1800s. In the past, I worked in the Summer Achievement program with second to fifth-grade students who lived in the housing projects where the center is located. My partner, Ms. Bonita, teamed up with me to provide daily instruction in reading and math, weekly enrichment activities, cultural arts, and health and fitness field trips. Ms. Bonita's loving smile fueled the kids. She nurtured them while attending to their social and emotional needs. She complimented my wild, raucous, energetic style. She was the Ying to my Yang! We made the best out of that summer. The second graders arrived every morning filled with enthusiasm, zest, curiosity, and a delightful yearning to be seen. We visited museums, science centers, metro parks, and other cultural institutions. We infused music, movement, and storytelling to enrich their minds and feed their robust spirits. We sang songs on bus rides. The kids taught us new dances. However, one day, my intense, unlimited appetite for adventure went too far.

Three staff members, including an intern and about twenty second graders, took a hike along one of my familiar trails. I was grinning cheek to cheek while leading everyone through the shrubbery and hilly terrain throughout Cleveland's Metro Parks. We sang songs! "This is the way we roll, we roll, this is the way we roll! We march! We march with pride." I spotted a large structure across a creek. I stood in awe at the beauty of this historic landscape as it called me. It said, "I have been waiting for you to conquer me as I have been sitting here lonely for generations. Briskly make your way through the slippery pond and conquer me."

"Let's do this!" I yelled. My eyes expanded, and my heart pulsated. Without hesitation, I asked everyone, "Who wants to climb that hill?" The little kids responded as one fierce choir, "Me!" I gave the signal, and like troops following Washington across the Delaware River, we set out on this journey. I was completely unaware of what the other staff members thought about my suggestion. They just better keep up with us, I thought. We strategically stepped across rocks as we watched the stream of water flow on the sultry, hot summer day. For a second, I thought my decision to climb a hill was crazy. I, however, completely ignored my conscience. I stood in the middle of the creek to ensure all the kids got safely across. We made it. We stood breathing heavily, our clothes slightly damp, as we looked at the mammoth steep hill.

I proudly said, "We are going to conquer this steep hill. Staff, take the kids around that winding pathway until you reach the top. I am climbing straight up!" They gathered the children and took them through the winding path. To my delight, the young male intern with the summer camp decided to climb with me. We started together, finding cracks, crevices, and twigs to pull ourselves up. My fingers tightly grabbed small stones as I used all the muscles in my abdomen to pull my lean frame up the cliff. As we ascended higher, the ground and creek became smaller. The air smelled clear as the sun directly hit my dark skin. I simultaneously climbed as I kept my eyes locked on the young man just inches underneath me. I shouted, "You good?" He uttered, "Yeah, I'm good!" I clambered to the top, pulling one leg up at a time. I stood feeling victorious. Without my assistance, the young intern pulled himself up the last ledge and stood next to me.

We heard the high-pitched voices and steps made by the kids who trotted directly toward us. Ms. Bonita looked spooked as she ran and approached us, shouting, "Where is Irene? We can't find Irene!" Fearing the worst, I looked down the cliff. We saw Irene climbing up with this sparkle in her eyes. My heart dropped past my stomach and then beneath my feet. I felt sick. I dashed back over the cliff, twisting my body towards Irene. I yelled, "Irene, don't move!" She completely ignored my plea, determined to reach the top like her idiotic camp counselor. Finally, I decided to wait for her and prayed that she would not fall backward. Trying to grab her and climb back up might be the end for both of us. So, I decided to stretch my body, keeping my legs on the cliff, encouraging Irene to keep going. Finally, I could grasp her tiny hands and pull her to the top. Phew!

I gathered everyone in a circle. We all took a deep breath. I impulsively buried this near-death experience in the back of my mind. I shouted, "Are you ready to go back down?" They screamed in one voice, "Yes!" I walked around the cliff to find a part that was not as steep and with less debris. Without any hesitation, I started sprinting down the hill. The kids galloped, tripped, stumbled, and rumbled down the hill as we headed back toward the creek. I stopped and looked back to ensure everyone was safe and had made their way down. Many kids struggled, so I suggested they slide down on their bottoms. They slid down. We were now all safely on the ground. We continued our journey along the creek. I decided to make a detour deep into the forest. I glanced at a small entry point off the beaten path and approached it. Everyone followed me. We squeezed through the narrow pathway that led us to an isolated part of the forest. The shrubbery was thick, and the trees were very tall. The area had cold dampness and a slight breeze with little sunlight. I was in the front, daring and pushing myself to venture further into the unknown. The kids were equally curious and intrigued by this new adventure.

We marched through nature, trampling over dead leaves that made crunchy sounds under our feet. Suddenly, I heard multiple screams. I quickly whipped my head around and watched the children swatting a swarm of bees surrounding them like Kamikaze pilots. My intern dashed away like Jesse Owens, heading back towards the creek. I attempted to knock bees off the kids while trying to usher them safely out of harm's way. As numerous bees attacked me, I felt multiple pinchings, throbbings, and stings. Finally, I moved the kids away from the ambush. The children were screaming, crying, and yelling at the top of their lungs. If looks could kill, I would have been dead on the spot. We moved slowly along a road we found as we aimlessly walked, hoping to find our bus. On the bus, we checked to see the damage—twenty kids had bee stings, some with multiple bee stings. I examined the children as they walked to their seats.

Many had swollen eyes, lips, red ears, and lumpy arms. Eventually, the children settled down, and I looked at the eight stings up and down my arms and on top of my head. As I drifted off to sleep on the ride back, I thought about the waiting parents who would be angry and how I would lose my job.

Saturday, August 12, 2006

Venaya struggled today. She was irritated, frustrated, and angry. She needs much respect, consideration, and appreciation for her motherly roles and duties. I tried to use the language of feelings and needs. She was not trying to hear it today. I am working with my older sister and younger brother to plan a get-together for my parents' 35th anniversary. We secretly invite family and friends to our parents' home on Sunday at 5 p.m. In the present moment, I am overwhelmed with joyful emotions. I live an open, honest life without blame, shame, guilt, or punitive thoughts. I have never felt this way. I hope I will always feel alive from the inside out.

The thrill of winning the biggest flag football tournament of the summer gives me a simple rush of happiness. I stand in the middle of my teammates, dirty cleats and stinky jerseys filled with dirt and grass stains. We all rejoice with high fives and hugs. This is a brutal weekend tournament with teams from Cleveland and other cities throughout the East Coast competing for the Referees Trophy. We did it! Despite being 5'7 and 145 pounds soaking wet, my desire to dominate at the cornerback position keeps me playing with an edge. I love football. I regret not playing in high school or college. My motivation is to completely shut down bigger, stronger, and more experienced receivers than me. Self-confidence is the key. It also helps to have blazing speed and pure football instincts. As I cheerfully strut to my Trailblazer following the game, my mind quickly shifts into planning mode.

I rushed to the grocery store to grab some last-minute items. I hurried home and walked inside, thankful to Venaya for ironing my jeans and burnt orange shirt. I was thrilled when my wife suggested I wear

Uncle Tommy's colorful tie. I concurred. I arrived at my parents' home and convinced them to let me chauffeur them to a movie. I dropped them off at a lackluster movie and took a lovely cruise in my dad's shiny black Escalade. I drove with the windows down, and the radio completely turned up. It felt good. I rode towards home, beaming from cheek to cheek as I reflected on my parents' life together. I vaguely remembered the story of how they met. Suddenly, as I sat at a red light, the story hit me like a Mike Tyson punch. I recalled my mom sharing the following story. I, however, am unsure if it was real or fake.

Your dad and I met during the summer of 1966. I was playing softball at the recreation center, assigned to second base. During the game, an unknown young man literally picked up an infield base and hit me in the back of the head. The dirt and dust from the ground settled inside my big afro. After my initial shock, as the young man ran off the softball field, I scanned the entire field to find him. He was grinning, and he was cute. Soon after the game ended, I asked one of my teammates about the handsome young culprit. She identified the man as Morris Ervin. She became my intermediary to pass messages back and forth. We were very bashful. Morris was 17, and I was 16. Eventually, to my disgust, I realized my teammate also liked Morris and did not intend for us to be together.

We resolved the dilemma and finally had our first date at Angela Mia's Pizza joint. We spent most of the date in awkward silence, munching on tasty pizza. Finally, before he took me home, we both opened up about being with other people and decided to cut them off to be with each other. Shortly after our first date, we made it official. However, later in the week, I heard through the grapevine that Morris was in a car accident and was hit head-on by another car crossing a median. He was in a coma. I rushed to the hospital. When I entered the lobby, a sea of females were all waiting to see Morris. I managed to enter the room with his mom and older brother. I had never met them, so I quietly stood by the door away from his family. To everyone's surprise, Morris suddenly opened his eyes *and shouted, "Pat!" His brother sat up in his chair and vehemently stared a hole through me, asking, "Who the hell are you?"*

I rushed inside my home. My little brother Elias and his friends eagerly waited for me to give them orders. We quickly wiped tables, vacuumed rooms, hung banners, and decorated the living and dining room areas. Shortly after, my aunts and cousins arrived with delicious meals ready to be devoured. My sister also came with a big pot of spaghetti and garlic bread. I am not much of a planner. However, I felt proud of myself for helping my siblings plan the party on such short notice. Finally, I jumped back in the Escalade, realizing that the movie was probably over, and picked up my parents. As I drove, I pondered all the memories of my childhood.

On a cold, blustery day, my dad took everyone in the neighborhood who could fit in his powder blue Buick sledding. We sled until our fingers became itchy, our toes froze, and our faces felt as hard as peanut brittle. I remember the holiday parties where we invited our whole family over to eat, sing Motown songs until early in the morning and spend the night. I thought about my mother's delicious fried chicken that she packed on our road trips. I smiled when I thought about the times we impatiently waited for Friday night board games, popcorn, and a movie. It was magical when my folks took us to the drive-in theater on starry summer nights. And who could forget the night we gathered around our floor model television to watch Michael Jackson moonwalk on the Motown 25 special? The anticipation of Christmas, especially Christmas Eve, when my big sister and I slept in the same room, agonizing over Christmas Day finally arriving. And the thrill of my screams on Christmas morning when I discovered the tightly wrapped gifts with toys, clothes, and everything we asked for. In those moments, I instilled the value of family deeply within me.

As we pulled up to our street, my mom and dad slowly examined each familiar car parked close to their home. They both exclaimed, "We aren't expecting anyone over. What could be the occasion?" I turned in the driveway, making sure not to give any eye contact with either of my unsuspecting parents. We walked up the stairs; I opened the screen door, and everyone screamed, "Happy Anniversary!" Family and friends entered the kitchen to greet my parents with hugs and handshakes. My parents, still bashful after thirty-five years of marriage, stood close together to pose for pictures. My mom looked at me and said, "You pulled one over on us." Before we began eating, I invited everyone to join me outside. I gathered everyone in a circle and asked them to share their gratitude and appreciation for my parents. We all felt the gentle silence as everyone stood around with smiles and grins. I began, "I am most grateful to my parents for deciding to stay committed to each other through the trials and tribulations that marriage, work, and raising a family can bring. I am sure it can be rough at times. However, this is a celebration of the power of love." Before I finished, a rush of emotions came over me, and I began weeping in front of everyone. My mom, cousins, and aunt wrapped their arms around me.

I gathered myself and wiped my red eyes. I felt a deep cleansing from the emotional episode. I decided to take a stroll around the block. I call it the walk to release my inner joy and enthusiasm. I returned about ten minutes later and found everyone eating and conversing with one another. Before I reached the end of the yard, my sister Erica said, "Morris, you are so dramatic!" My mom looked at me and said, "And all you did was call people and tell them what you needed?" "Yes!" I responded with a nod of affirmation.

Gas prices are soaring. Unfortunately, I was still paying the lease on my 2004 Chevy Trailblazer. Finally, I decided to go to the dealer to see what other options were available. As a result, I left the dealership with a burnt orange Chevy Aveo. The car looked as if you wind it up, and it would go. It had a weird shape and small wheels! The color left little to the imagination. I loved my little tangerine. When I arrived home and my family saw the car, they thought my tangerine was disgusting! They refused to see the beauty and the economic sustainability of having such a car as this.

At that time, my appetite for nightlife was a newly found interest mainly because of traveling the country playing competitive flag football. Occasionally, I tended to find reasons not to disclose that I had escaped to this newly discovered world—in my tangerine wheels.

We anxiously arrived in the city on Friday night after a long drive. Like clockwork, we freshened up, threw on our best button-down shirts, and drove directly to a bar or nightclub without hesitation. We strutted in the club to the pulsating sounds of hip-hop, Top 40, and dance hall music. The music thumped as I studied the club's atmosphere. I chuckled as most of my teammates strolled towards the bar in preparation to drink themselves into a stupor. I don't drink. However, the music created a tension inside of me that I needed to release. I hopped, skipped, and bounced directly onto the dance floor. It's on! I pumped my arms in the air while spinning, sliding, and performing wild dance moves to the crowd's delight. I pointed in the direction of the DJ, giving him a confirmation to keep the jams coming.

Time stood still as sweat dripped down my forehead, burning my eyes. There was little to no space on this dance floor. Bodies were everywhere as I continued slithering around the floor with dance fever. On the dance floor, I reconnected with a burning desire to dance like a kid from the 1980s. I danced in groups. I dance with females. I danced all night long. The DJ finally said, "Close out your tabs because this is the last song for the night." I gathered my intoxicated teammates, grabbed the keys, and helped them navigate through the club to the parking lot. I drove back to the hotel. We woke at dawn, rushed to the football field, and balled out! The trip had ended. I returned to family life, yearning to experience another weekend.

Traveling, dancing, clubbing, football, and freedom on weekends became the focus of my life. This made absolutely no sense because when I was in college, clubbing of any kind was off-limits. While in college, society tells a young person to be wild and free. I did not drink, smoke, or have casual sexual relationships with females. When I met my wife in college, she had just begun her pledge process to become a member of

Sigma Gamma Rho. I was completely against it. I constantly expressed my disappointment in her choice to be a follower and join a sorority. I criticized everything. My militant, underdeveloped, limited view of life resulted from my acceptance of Islam at a mosque with a Black power vibe. At the tender age of seventeen, I had no idea of the cultural and social context that juxtaposed my innocent decision to join a religion in search of brotherhood.

CHAPTER 8

Victims and Survivors
of Our Education

"You must find your own unique pathway in the world;
the masses, or majority, never do. Until you set
the tone for your existence. You will follow others
who are, in turn, following you."
T.S. Eliot

Each day during lunch, I noticed about twelve young men sitting on the stage in the social room, apart from the rest of the school. Each day, like clockwork, I would cautiously meander past them with a quick head nod or fist pump, eager to receive a nod or a fist pump in return. They possessed an energy, a royal aura, that resonates with me. Eventually, after eating my lunch, I found the courage to go over and chat with them. The conversation went well. I realized these young men are Muslims. I had little knowledge of Muslims or what they believe. Later that evening, I asked my mom about Muslims. She said, "Islam is a jail religion where Black men discipline themselves. They don't eat pork, and they dislike White people. You are already Black. If you think about becoming a Muslim, that's two strikes against you." I listened to her, but I felt confused. Shortly after this new revelation, my close friend Corey took a sacred oath called Shahada to become a Muslim. On Friday, Corey asks if I want to see the temple or mosque. I said, "When are we going?" He chuckled and said, "Right now!" I felt a familiar heaviness move over me—the lump that returns every time I receive a brief visit from my number one nemesis, fear. I said, "Bro, we will have to cut school to go. If my pops finds out, it's over for me!" Corey said, "Jumu'ah or Friday prayer is on Fridays at 1 p.m. Jumu'ah is held at this time every week." All we need to do is sneak past the main hallway, quickly jog out the back entrance, and get to my parked car on the side street." He turned and strutted away, giving me no opportunity to defend my case. I follow him, and we jump in his rusty Oldsmobile, heading to the Friday prayer. We pull up to an unfamiliar driveway next to a huge house with a small, congested parking lot. Corey places a small colorful cap or kufi on his head. I was wearing my red baseball cap. We entered a small area outside the entrance, where we remove and leave our shoes. The place looks like cardboard and smells like mildew. We walk further into the house, which I learn is a mosque, and we follow the direction of an older brother who motions for me to sit on a bench in the waiting area. He greets Corey, whom he calls Kareem, with the greeting, "As-salamu Alaykum." They both disappear into another part of the mosque. I sat uncomfortably in silence. However, my inner thoughts were deafening. The round brother at the security desk says, "Your red hat is cool. Is that a picture of a little Black boy on your brim?" "Yes. It is," I slowly replied. "Pro Model hats are the thing now. I, however, took a character from a board game and stuck him on my hat for cultural self-expression and attention."

Time was moving as slowly as a snail. I anxiously continued to sit on the wooden bench, examining each individual who strolled past me into the secret room. I observed men wearing colorful kufis, thick beads, long flowing tops resembling dresses, and African dashikis. They all went into the private room. Most brothers greet me with a smile. Some rush right past me into the room. Suddenly, I hear a thundering voice on a loudspeaker reciting something in a foreign language. When the powerful voice spoke in English, his words, and every point he made hit me like grenades and missiles detonating. One part of me feels apprehensive about being at the mosque, while another is intrigued to learn more about this new culture. The sermon ended. I heard the strange foreign language again. The brothers filed out of the small room into the congested parking lot. Many brothers asked me if I wanted to be a Muslim. I stuttered. I desperately searched for the right words to *say. However, I froze like a Bomb Pop. Corey, aka Kareem, looks happy as he shakes hands and embraces his younger and older brothers. Before we left, I recognized some of the young men from school. We locked eyes, smiled, and exchanged handshakes. Finally, Corey and I hop into his rusty Oldsmobile and drive back to my neighborhood.*

The only thing I know about Islam is they don't eat pork. They don't consume alcohol, and they don't have sex before marriage. I know the word will eventually spread around the school about my conversion. And it did. Every day, Muslim brothers assertively approached me in the hallway, wondering when I would take my Shahada. My non-Muslim friends also approached me and asked, "Are you crazy?" "Those Muslims are crazy!" "Why would you want to be a Muslim?" "You are a cool, positive dude, Morris, don't do it." Each day at school, the same thing occurred. It was a tug-of-war between old friends and associates against my new way of life. My friend Corey spends almost every day and most weekends at the mosque. He wants to move into the mosque.

Unfortunately, another dilemma I have is the current tension between Muslims and a neighborhood group called the "Kinfolk." Minor skirmishes have been between these individuals in and outside school and in the neighborhood. I had to remember that I was Morris. I am a cool, positive, expressive, creative young man who enjoys History class, hip-hop music, gym class, Timberland boots, and Girbaud jeans. I'm an average student but a profound thinker. I love to play sandlot football, especially against rival streets. My father rules with an iron fist, and my mother and I share our feelings. I also irritate and admire my older sister.

Finally, the day arrives. I lace up my colorful, comfortable Adidas sneakers, open my screen door, and embark on my journey into Islam. I am not sure if I am walking in the right direction. However, I continue walking. It is a bright sunny day, about sixty-five degrees. My mind is clear during the walk. The journey to the mosque consists of two humongous streets, Jordan Road, and Mecca Boulevard. Jordan Road has average suburban houses with small manicured lawns. As I approach Mecca Boulevard, I quickly recognize the Mecca Rapid, the city's above-ground train system. I continue along the journey that seems impossible and possible simultaneously. I AM EXCITED when I eventually reach Mecca Square Plaza because the mosque is now less than twenty minutes away. In the distance, right before I jog across the street, I can see the big striped house sitting on the corner. Surprisingly, my nerves are settled, and my mind is as clear as this sunny day. I surmise that I have walked for nearly two hours. The long journey gave me a sense of fulfillment, independence, and accomplishment.

As I expeditiously walk up the small rocky parking lot, I spot a young man staring at me through the door screen. I continue to walk up the pathway while I watch him quickly put on his shoes and dash out the door, running directly toward me. I am clueless. He stops before me and breathes fiery, forceful words into my face. "Nigga, if I ever catch you running through here again, I'm gonna kill you!" he said. I stare at him with a puzzled look and an alarmed mind. I ask myself, am I in the right place? But I know I am in the right place. Seven seconds pass, and we begin to square off like two prize fighters. In the distance, someone says, "That's Maya Ervin's little brother. Chill, man." The brother slowly backs away without a word and returns to the mosque. I hesitantly follow behind him, still shaken from this verbal altercation.

Finally, with full permission, I drift past the security desk into the forbidden room. The carpet is lush green. The room is open with a wooden pulpit at the front, similar to a church. I gaze around and see a few brothers reading holy books while others move back and forth on the carpet in prostate positions. In my mind, I envisioned experiencing a grandiose initiation into Islam. Finally, a brother said "Kalima Shahada." Everyone stopped their activities and formed a semicircle around me. As instructed by a brother, I dropped to my knees and placed my index finger in the air. I repeated after him in the Arabic language. "There is no God but Allah, and Mohammed is his messenger." The ritual ended before I had the opportunity to be nervous. Finally, all the brothers embraced me with a three-in-one hug. They threw me over their shoulders three consecutive times before releasing me to the next brother waiting in line. I lined up to make my first prayer as a Muslim, called Isha. I mimic the movement of the brothers praying to my left and right. The prayer ended.

Fortunately, a brother gave me a ride back to my house, which was quite a distance away in the suburbs.

When I arrived home, I spoke to my family and trotted straight upstairs to my room. Along with my anxious thoughts, I crawled into my twin-size bed and wondered when or how I would tell my family the news of my Islamic conversion.

I entered the back door, heading straight into our bedroom. The light was still on, which made me cringe, knowing that a conversation with Venaya was about to happen. "How was your trip? Did you guys win the tournament?" she asked. "It was cool," I responded. "Well, come sit down. I have some thoughts to share with you." I'm glad she couldn't see the expression of pure torture on my face. I tightened my fist and took a swipe at the air before sitting on the couch next to my beloved. "What?" I asked with no intention of talking. She said, "I'm unsure how this NVC thing goes. However, I want to share my feelings about using this approach." The sheer fact of her wanting to use this language lit me up inside like it was fireworks on Independence Day. She stated, "When I hear you talk on and on about NVC, I feel frustrated and irritated because I want you to equally consider your role in practicing the religion of Islam." My heart sank through the floor. My face tightened up and turned hard as a stone. I want so badly to escape or jump out the window if necessary.

I mustered a response, "I am not inspired to practice Islam. I am not feeling it like I feel NVC." Venaya asked, "Have you tried to meet new Muslims or find new ways or resources to support you?" I answered, "No!" "That's unfortunate because I remember when Islam was the center of your universe. You surrounded yourself with good Muslim brothers and spent every free moment at the mosque. I vividly remember how you put Islam over our relationship in college by setting firm boundaries. What happened to you?" Her words resonated deeply within me. I saw the beauty in her round eyes of rage. Her words pierced my soul. I frustrate her. She still sees so much potential in me. My thoughts swiftly wandered back to the Kent State University campus to a time when "The One" entered my universe.

It's Thursday night on campus, and I am alone as I stroll inside to buy a greasy hamburger and a thick milkshake at Easthaven, the campus's nightly food and recreation hangout. My roommate, Big Jeremy, aka Big J, who would have been with me, is probably listening to music in our small, stuffy dorm room. I finish eating my burger and head directly toward the billiards area. I am the King of Billiards. I win competitive games against much older college students without breaking a sweat or taking off my backpack. But before I can take another step, a ray of quiet beauty suddenly catches my attention. A young lady with smooth caramel skin and a sleek Toni Braxton hairstyle is standing by the napkin dispenser with her food to go.

Time stands still. I see no one else but her. I stare and stare and stare. Finally, before she moves, I anticipate her exit and swiftly position myself in her path. As she approaches where I am standing, I hope my D'Angelo-style cornrows will be enough to attract her attention. We lock eyes, and with a smile as bright as the Milky Way, I say, "Hey." She flashes a smile and continues to walk past me and right out of my Thursday night. After seeing this beautiful sister, I had no interest in playing pool. I stood helplessly, thinking about when and where I would see "The One" again. I jog across campus to my dorm and burst into my room like the FBI. "Big J, Big J! I saw 'The One!'" I shout. Big J says, "For real, man? That is awesome. Did you have a conversation with her?" he asked. "Nope, but I smiled and said hello," I answered enthusiastically. Occasionally, "The One" would cross my path on the bus or as I walked across the campus yard.

The school year ended, and all summer, I thought about her. At the beginning of the next school year, I chopped off my D'Angelo braids for the new and improved brush wave look. Unfortunately, after a devastating knee injury from a brutal sandlot football game, I added a pair of crutches to my look. My injury caused me to take a special bus to my classes—which I hated. One night, as I waited in the library parking lot for the bus, I saw "The One" walking towards me. Tension built up in my chest as she glided closer to me. All types of questions flooded my mind.

"What should I say? Will she stop and talk to me? What if I stutter or sound like a fool?" I tried to calm the butterflies swirling in my gut as she approached me with my crutches propped up against the building. Similar to our first encounter, I didn't know what to say. Somehow, I could muster up the courage to say, "Hey, how are you tonight?" "The One," answered, "I'm good," as she continued to walk past me. I couldn't believe she was getting away again! I shouted, "What's your name?" She turned around with a grin and said, "Venaya," as she disappeared.

One uneventful day, as I went to pick up dinner, I saw her in line at the cafeteria. As I walked up behind her, strangely, nearly every part of my body reacted. My ears crackled, my knees shook like dice, and my heart beat like a song from a Sony Walkman. As I thought about what I would say to "The One," the aroma of the mystery meat tickled my nostrils. As I stared at the lifeless food options under the bright, heated lamps, I casually said to her, "This food is disgusting. I am not sure how I can digest this every day." "I know," she responded. "It is pretty bad. Are you planning to eat here or take it to your room?" she asked. At the time, my mind could not process that she had just invited me to eat. I say, "Naw, I'm heading to my room." What! The woman of my dreams just asked me to join her for dinner, and I declined! She smiled and walked towards a table where she sat with a friend. I quickly regained my senses and followed her. I saw my big, cuddly roommate, Big J. I motioned for him to join us.

Big J is a nice, sweet, gentle giant. He loves to blast his music, wear designer sneakers, oversized flannel shirts, and lift heavy weights in the gym. His pride and joy are his two master blaster gigantic speakers that sit like royalty in our tiny dorm room. What I love the most about Big J is his stand-up comedy routine. It puts me in stitches every time I see it. Big J pulled up a seat within inches of "The One's" friend. With a twinkle in his eye, he rests his head between his massive hands and stares at "The One's" friend. We eat and talk briefly until "The One" says, "We are getting ready to return to our room. Here's my number. Call me," as I intently watch her write her number on a napkin. As they walked away, I punched Big J, saying, "Bro, you stared at her girl the whole time without blinking!" Big J laughed and said, "I know Musa. She was so fine!" We laughed as we left the cafeteria and returned to our loft-style dorm room. "Big J, play some of that Outcast, 'Get Up, Get Out, and Get Something,' I say, feeling good. He nods and turns up the amplifier. We crank my favorite hit as I carve Venaya's name and the title, "The One," in my underwear drawer.

This conversation was holding me hostage, and my mind wanted to escape. I sank deeper into the old couch until it felt like I was falling into quicksand. The rumble of Venaya's words agitated me. They provoked me as I murmured between her pauses, searching for the right words. I was speechless. I was hopeless, and this was getting old, I thought, as I let out another murmur. I breathed. My stoic posture infuriated her. She wanted answers. She shouted, "Did you really want to marry me?!" I still couldn't find the right words to express myself. I was lost. Something truthful, however, needed to come roaring out of my mouth. I hesitated. Finally, I said, "I'm not sure what I wanted back then. I am different now." She stared at me with a foggy gaze as tears welled up in her eyes. My stomach made a deep gurgling sound as I swallowed vomit. My belly, face, and body felt tight and hot. The silence felt like a violent act but without a single word being exchanged. Venaya screamed at the top of her lungs, "You are such a coward! You can't even answer the question. I chose you. I wanted to marry you because of pure love. I was over playing games and dating other men. Marriage was the right thing to do. However, it is obvious to you that it was a mistake!" She stormed out of the room and slammed the frail door. I sat frozen in my thoughts, not moving. I closed my eyes and fell asleep.

September 28, 2006

Today is an in-service day for schoolteachers. I have been trying to keep up with my daily prayers. I called my friend, Hasan-Mumin, to support his first fast during Ramadan. Venaya is finishing up her applications to veterinary schools. I'm confident about her essays because I worked with her to complete them. I love writing personal essays. My son Idris continues having problems at school because of his fierce temper. The other day, he punched the same kid three times. He also had an episode with his teacher where he got angry and tried to bite her. My daughter Naimah is struggling with school, and working with her at home is a complete and utter disaster. I get so impatient, and I'm quick to yell at her. There is so much tension during homework time. It stresses everyone out. The good news is that Naimah's tutor told us she could read fine. She craves one-on-one attention. My little teenage brother Elias received his driver's license this week. He stayed cool as a cucumber as he passed both parts of the test. My Mom and Pop were there with him for support. Of course, he wants to drive to a haunted house with his boys. My workout routine is going well with Steve, Phil, and Albert. I am starting to notice a positive change in my physique.

My little brother and I are fourteen years apart. This age gap put a strain on my social life for a while. I reluctantly picked him up from daycare, and we walked home together. Every day after school, he would plop close to me in our living room to watch *The Mighty Morphin Power Rangers* and *Barney*, the purple dinosaur. He hated to see me leave for college. However, I let him stay with me for my little sibling's weekend. My marriage put more distance between us when I chose to start a family of my own. As I grew as a husband and a father, I still made time to visit and support him when he played sports. I am sure he wanted me to be around a lot more. I remember that fateful day when I stood in my parents' kitchen. I laugh as I reflect on my angry middle school tantrum.

I hear my mom calling me from the kitchen, unsure why she wanted to talk with me. I slowly start walking towards the kitchen table with the orange paint reflecting off the walls—my family members are die-hard Cleveland Browns fans. She whispers in a low tone, "You know I had that fender bender car accident a few days ago, and I received a physical exam. However, from the physical exam, they told me that I am pregnant." "Pregnant!" I scream. The words echo and bounce off the bright orange paint throughout our cozy home.

"How did this happen? How could this happen?" I asked in a piercing shrieking tone. My mother sits in silence with a blank stare. I

am surprised I don't get smacked for such an aggressive tone with her. I assume she is letting me vent from the shock and awe of this news. "Well, you still know Dad and me still——," I fiercely finished her statement, "Have sex! Why didn't y'all use protection?" This is bizarre because I am only thirteen, and I am taking full liberty to reprimand my mom, who is forty-one like she is the child. I continue to stand as my mother calmly remains seated. Suddenly, tears gush from my eyes down my face. My mother speaks to me. However, all I can hear is the word "pregnant." I turn, stomp out of the kitchen, and run upstairs to my room.

Eventually, Elias Romare Ervin entered this world on May 6, 1990. He had squinty eyes and a head full of thick, curly hair. There are so many stories to share as Elias grows older. The time he walked down the block to the local corner store. He slipped away without me knowing. Imagine a four-year-old walking alone to the corner store. I remember watching his first daycare concert. My folks had to work, so I had to sit in the audience that afternoon. The other kids belted out tunes while my brother stood frozen the whole time with a blank look. He loved the opportunity to tag along with me and my future wife on our lovely dates. My brother slid between the concrete and grass when we walked. We both chuckled hard as he shouted, "Don't laugh!" He and my future wife competed for my attention like two prize fighters in the ring. I remember the call I received right before I headed out to chaperone my high school's prom.

I could barely hear my mother's trembling words as she said, "Morris, about fifteen boys, jumped Elias and Brian on our street." "I'll be right there!" I say fiercely, slamming the phone down on the table. "Naaya!" I called my wife. "Hurry up and get in the car. My brother got jumped by some dudes on the street!" I strip off my suit and throw on sweats, a tank top, and some sneakers.

I'm fantasizing about the brutal assault of my little brother while trying to focus on driving safely. The butterflies are twirling in my stomach as I absorb each speed bump to my parents' house. I hit the corner of my street, slightly turning my Charcoal Grey Chevy Trailblazer on two wheels like General Lee from The Dukes of Hazzard or K.I.T.T. in Knight Rider. I barely pull into the driveway, dash from my car, and leap up the stairs into the dimly lit kitchen. My parents, brother, and friend quietly stand in the kitchen, waiting for my revelation. "Elias, come here, bro. Let me see your face," I say. He walks over as I gently touch his face, positioning it in the light to examine the damage. I can see slight puffiness on the right side of his face below his right eye.

I'm relieved it is not nearly as bad as I imagined. I'm furious that anyone would put their hands on my brother. I turned towards my brother's friend. I am slightly puzzled and concerned that my brother's gargantuan-sized friend, built like an offensive lineman, allowed this pummeling. He stands silent and quiet. Suddenly, his friend's mom burst into the kitchen screaming hysterically, wanting answers. At this point, I asked, "What happened?" "Big Pun and some of his dudes just picked a fight with us for no reason." A scowl covers my face. "Big who?" I ask. Elias responds, "Big Pun. He's always bullying kids and picking fights with kids. He and his thugs also love hanging out at the park and smoking weed. He comes on our street to sit on the porch at that dusty house on the corner where everyone hangs out." Without a word, I trot towards the front of the house, pass the etagere, and open the front door that leads to our small front yard. The weather is pleasant with no wind, no sun, just an average May day. I pace around the front yard like a K-9, looking for clues. Aha! I see a small black mobile device lying in between blades of grass.

I hold the phone in my hands as if I had discovered gold! Next, I gaze to my left. Two young males, one chunky like Campbell Soup, walk directly toward the house. As I stand with anticipation, I notice my anger, excitement, and eagerness stirring inside me like a human tornado. I shout, "Yes, these fools are dumb enough to return to the crime scene!" At the sound of my voice, my parents, brother, his friend, his mom, and my wife were all a short distance behind me on the porch. I went blank. I blocked out all outside noise because I saw my target and was ready to detonate. Like Lance Armstrong holding his arm high as he victoriously crosses the finish line at the Tour De France, I hold the phone high. The two fools walk with a swagger until they see my small yet determined frame. They stop by the curb. I stroll closer to them and say, "Is this what y'all looking for?" I know I have a sinister scowl on my smooth chocolate skin. They respond, "Yeah, that's our phone," one said. I exclaim, "Man! Y'all dumb for jumping my brother and his friend in front of my house and then returning for this stupid phone!" As I hear myself, I realize the slight possibility that I might assault these minors. It's unbelievable that in a fit of rage, some sense has entered my deranged mind. I ask, looking past the fat pun and directly at the older one. "How old are you?" He responds, "Nineteen." I boldly say, "Perfect, you want this phone, come and get it." I toss the phone gently on the grass, pull my sweatshirt over my head, and walk right toward them. They freeze like museum statues. I faintly hear screams from my mom. I stop because she is directly in front of me, pushing me away from a potential fight. Just as I sidestepped her, the police arrived. Surprisingly, the officers calmly escort me away from the two young men. They question everyone and eventually take the young men away in the squad car. Before walking back inside, my wife says sensually, "You looked sexy, taking off your shirt all angry and heroic." I sheepishly grinned for a moment as we entered my parents' home.

After all that had occurred, something within me was not satisfied. So, I decided to walk to the dusty house on the corner and talk with all the dudes causing trouble on the block. I motion with my arms for my dad and little brother to follow me. Together, we walked to the notorious corner house. As we approached the house, we saw toys, bikes, food wrappers, and other debris lying on uncut grass. I proudly strutted closer to the home with my dad and brother close behind. I approached five guys crowded together on the front porch and, without hesitation, walked up to them and stared until their meaningless conversation abruptly stopped. "Listen and listen well. Mess with my brother and his friends again, and I'll be back. I'm not concerned about who did what, but if something goes down, the next time I return, I won't be talking. Try me," I say with a sinister yet confident tone. There is complete silence and five blank stares. I let the threat simmer and marinate like a fat, juicy steak grilling on hot coals. Then, as smooth, and cool as a summer day, I returned to my house with my beloved father and brother.

The lion in me will roar to protect my family. What I loved most about that incident with my brother was how I appreciated my dad for allowing me to handle the situation. We did not exchange many words after returning home. My dad is not a great communicator. I believe, however, that he passed the torch to me. One thing for sure: throughout my childhood, my dad protected me, my sister, my brother, and my mom. In my opinion, as I got older, it seemed excessive. He was quick to defend his family from anyone. Like the lyrics of Drake's song, my dad could go from zero to one hundred quickly.

As a teenager, it was a challenge to see how his overprotective ways were an act of unconditional love. In his entire life, he never spoke of his father. Unfortunately, if you asked him anything about his dad, he would respond with an attitude or ignore you. This mystery ate away at me. I wanted to know who my father looked up to when he was growing up. I wanted to know who he admired. The only answer I got from him was soul singer David Ruffin from the legendary Temptations. He adored this famous Black entertainer. He forced us to watch every documentary on David Ruffin and the Temptations. He wore an afro like David Ruffin and also those big gazelle glasses.

Eventually, as a teenager, I wanted to find my identity, stretch my wings, and find my voice. However, my attempts were futile with a father who always had his sights on me. Even hanging out with my friends was a problem. He did not want me to be in the streets. One time, I tried out for the track team. After a month of practice, I said I would travel to different states for the indoor track season. He had a fit. There was so much resistance and drama I quit the team. Eventually, I became interested in Islam. I, however, kept this interest a secret.

Finally, when I did share my passion for Islam, I received negative comments such as "You already have a strike against you being a young Black man, why do you want another strike?" As mentioned, I became a Muslim without sharing the decision with my family. I needed my own religious identity. Ironically, my favorite meal was fried pork chops, corn, and mashed potatoes. Muslims can't eat pork. So, my first big test was resisting my mom's delicious pork chop meal. She just knew I would break when I smelled those pork chops. I religiously practiced my faith by spending most of my time at the mosque. Unfortunately, one evening at the mosque, I experienced a life-changing event.

I was invited to attend the mosque's Saturday evening cookout, Holoqa. Of course, I did not tell my parents. Excitedly, I jumped on my green mountain bike and embarked on my adventure to the mosque. With each turn of my pedal, I could feel the burn in my quadriceps and thighs—probably because of the friction the front brakes put on my front tire rim. I pedaled past grandiose mansions with circular driveways to single-family or two-story dilapidated units. I was in awe at how the environment changed from the beautiful Mecca Lakes to the hard-core smell of urban decay on Winston Willis Blvd. Finally, I pedaled up the steep hill and entered the mosque's pothole-filled driveway.

I parked my bike, walked to the door, and rang the doorbell. A brother with a funny voice and pot belly ushered me inside. I neatly placed my shoes next to two rows of sneakers, sandals, and boots. I passed the security desk and turned left into a small bathroom to make wudu (ablution) before prayer. I arrive just in time to make the evening prayer (Maghrib). I tiptoed into the prayer room like a cat burglar on the freshly vacuumed carpet. Some brothers were prostrate on the carpet, while others quietly talked to each other in the small, dark room. I look directly ahead and see a wooden pulpit. Suddenly, a tall, imposing figure swiftly walks straight toward the front of the room. He prepares everyone for prayer. We all jumped in lines and rows, standing shoulder to shoulder, to listen to Imam Mustafa recite the Holy Quran.

At the end of the prayer, the Imam returned to his upstairs chambers while others headed straight to the parking lot for the cookout. I followed another group of brothers upstairs into a room with an oval table. I nervously waited for something to happen. To my astonishment, we learn about the life of Prophet Muhammed (May Peace and Blessings Be Bestowed on him) through ancient stories narrated by scholars called hadith. I also observed spirited discussions on how to apply the lessons *of the Prophet's life today. As a newcomer, I smile and quietly follow all the heated and inspiring conversations. "I'm enjoying this," I thought. However, as the night progresses, something is gnawing at my spirit. Something doesn't feel right. I ignore it. Earlier in the evening, I had made a futile attempt to call my parents to inform them of my whereabouts, but the pay phone was out of order. It was getting very late. "Where is Musa," someone says, bursting into the room. I acknowledged that I was Musa. "Come with me now!" an unknown brother demanded.*

My legs were wobbly, and my head spun as I rushed down the steep, narrow stairs, past the prayer room, and out the screen door into a crowded parking lot. At this point, I'm out of breath as I weave in and out of my brothers, trying to make my way to a side street. As I approached the street, I heard a commotion. Someone was screaming and shouting. I finally could maneuver past the last few brothers to see a tall, slender brother with cornrows pointing a handgun at my mom, who desperately tried to pull my father back to the car. Time stood still. I immediately realized it was very late, and they came to the mosque looking for me.

I quickly ran towards the brother and shouted, "That is my father!" Without hesitation, I pushed his arm towards the grassy hill, then turned to wrap my arms around my father, who was still lunging and attempting to confront the brother with the pistol. Eventually, I managed to pull him backward. He finally decided to listen to my mom, screaming, "Moe, get in the car, and let's go!" I got in the car, and we sped off down the street. We arrived home and rushed inside. I stood in the vortex of my mom, dad, and sister, screaming at me about how I had joined a dangerous cult. They all took turns shouting at me, pointing, pleading, and threatening me to leave the religion. Eventually, I just placed my hands over my face and burst into tears. My dad almost lost his life tonight.

As I sit on the bed, all I can see is the image of the brother's extended arms aiming a gun at my father. It repeated itself in my head into the early morning. I did not fall asleep. Monday morning before school, my dad pulls me close into his personal space with fire in his eyes and says, "Don't let me catch you down at that temple with those Mooslems, do you understand?" I replied, "Yes sir," and we jumped into his Silver Buick Park Avenue so he could drop me off at school. I stared at the clock like an eagle. I was desperately waiting for the lunch bell to ring so I could confront my Muslim brothers. I walked with precision to the area reserved for Muslims at lunch. I position myself directly before them like a drum major leading a band.

Before my rant, I paused to see if anyone was going to acknowledge the near murder of my pops and the worst weekend of my seventeen-year-old life. I wait, and I wait. With each passing second, the blood vessels in my head constricted. I could feel the thunder and lightning rumble in my belly. I finally yelled, "All y'all sat outside Saturday night, and nobody said that's Musa's father! That's whack. Y'all went over to my house and played basketball with him. Nobody! Y'all was gonna let my father get his head blown off!" When I finished screaming, my chest cavity rose and fell like a ship tossed at sea. I paced back and forth, studying and staring directly into everyone's face. Silence. I storm away.

I entered the small library with my backpack, pen, and book, *The Compassionate Classroom.* I eagerly walked to an empty table, salivating, and anticipating the valuable gems I would find in this incredible book. As I perused the pages and sections, I was struck with wonder and delight as I read the many insightful quotes about the philosophy of nonviolence, meditation, and spirituality. *The Compassionate Classroom,* written by Surah Hart and Victoria Kindle Hodson, states in its premise, *"Compassion is not a static state, nor is it a destination to be reached. Compassion is not a subject that can be taught. Compassion is a way of being in a relationship, acting, and interacting. At the same time, certain practices can help cultivate this way of being. In our experience, Non-Violent Communication is the most practical and powerful of these practices."*

As I continued reading and preparing to implement the practices of Non-Violent Communication, I realized the power lies within me. The mood, aura, and ambiance that flow within me will connect and engage on a deeper level with students. I set the temperature. I determine the weather and the climate of my classroom, my household, and my entire life. Boom! I am mesmerized by quote after quote, each allowing me to tap into something, a side of me that never had an opportunity to flourish.

I put down *The Compassionate Classroom* and decided to stroll through the library. I needed to walk off the intense emotions I had experienced. "I can't! It is not that easy," I thought aloud and planted my body and thoughts in the Black History section. Before I selected a book, I asked myself, "Why didn't I tell my mom? Why didn't I tell anybody? What did she do to me? Why am I suffering if that was over 13 years ago? The past is over. Isn't it?" I found a book titled *Without Sanctuary: Lynching Photography in America* by James Allen. The cover displays a lifeless African American male hanging from a tree with a crowd of White spectators standing and smiling beneath him. With each turn of the page, my heart pounds and shudders as I scrutinize each picture. The images evoke a deep emotional charge and profound despair within me. Eventually, before I decided to close the book, my eyes became fixated on a picture of a Black woman in a dress hanging from a bridge. The shock. The rage. The sadness. I need to honor and remember my ancestors and the daily terror and brutality they endured. Equally important, I am curious about the psychology and fear that hate breeds. What do White folks think they need? What are they subconsciously thinking and feeling when they systematically desire to oppress others? The author states, "Through all this terror and carnage, someone—many times a professional photographer—carried a camera and took pictures of the events. These lynching photographs were often made into postcards and sold to crowds in attendance as souvenirs. Historians have also detailed the carnival atmosphere and the social ritual of lynching, which was often announced in advance and drew thousands of people from the surrounding area." The beauty and tragedy of my experience at the library helped me discover similarities between my childhood and the harsh experiences of my people. I am identifying and learning tools that will enable me to feel and possibly help me heal. Hopefully, I will also gain the necessary strength to help families, communities, and society heal.

CHAPTER 9

Making Sense Out of Intergenerational Pain

"Peace—it does not mean to be in a place where
there is no noise, trouble, or hard work. It means to be
in the midst of those things and still be calm in your heart."
Tatah Mentah

Most mornings, with the precision of an acrobat and the stealth of a panther, I leap from underneath my covers and quietly spring onto the floor. I trot into the bathroom and click on the light. Aha! Legacy! As I walk into my closet, fresh from the shower with steam oozing from my head, I can feel the enormous smile that stretches from my chin to my upper cheeks. "It is time to introduce the Legacy Project to my African American History class," I shout. "I have the perfect attire to wear," I say to myself. I select my lime green polo shirt and pair it with a green plaid blazer, complete with black, green, and yellow sneakers. Green is an excellent color that symbolizes nature and the natural world. Green represents tranquility, good luck, health, and prosperity. Immediately after getting dressed, I wink at myself in the mirror before grabbing a granola bar and hopping into my orange car. Education is about selling yourself, your product, and your service. It's about your aura, your magnetism, and if you don't know the secret of selling, they will never buy in. This is what I think as I fortify myself for the day ahead.

Later that morning, as I stood proud in my green attire, ready to address my African American History class, I began with the popular quote, "'There is a thread that connects the past to the present.' I am eager, excited, and enthusiastic about exploring the personal thread of history that connects your families. Please pull out your journals and reflect deeply and intensely on the word 'legacy.'" I slowly slide behind my desk. In awe, I scrutinize the room, noticing the stillness, intensity, and wonder of contemplative journal writing. To contemplate means "to connect with your temple or the place of your divinity." As the students continue to write, I use the time to do a self-evaluation. I gather my thoughts and note any tightness, discomfort, or tension in my body. Now, I can casually, yet energetically, share the project that has the potential to reveal, uncover, hurt, and heal. Immediately after the timer rang, each student wrote a few more thoughts and closed their journals so that their attention was focused on my green plaid jacket!

I ask, "Has anyone ever thought about what your life means? Have you ever considered what has been passed down to you by your ancestors and family? Has anyone ever thought about what you will pass down to your children and loved ones who will come after you? In other words, a legacy can be property, money, a will, or anything handed down from the past, as from an ancestor or predecessor." I ask, "Is that clear?" I glance up and down the rows, watching silent, uncomfortable nods and head shakes. Then, someone says, "I thought legacy is your reputation or something that you're notorious for, not something that happened way back in the day. I know guys in my family and neighborhood with untouchable legacies. In other words, no one messed with them!" I felt playful and relaxed as this comment released the tension in the room, and students came alive. I received a few more comments about the legacy of being rich, famous, and a movie star.

Students freely and openly identified legacy as something badass or entirely outside of themselves. I thought, "Glorifying this celebrity and entertainment culture is thicker than a tropical rainforest in South America or the Congo." I let the noise and excitement simmer, and I continued. "Earlier, I mentioned legacy as something passed down throughout your family, like an inheritance, property, money, land, etc. That's the legal aspect of a legacy. Equally important, a family legacy is the accomplishments, beliefs, actions, and guidance passed down to future generations. Thus, those family members can adopt and adapt those lessons, teachings, and wisdom to make their lives meaningful and fruitful." Now, I feel delighted to see the students' conversations and reflections turn inward on themselves. The room is still. I continue, "By interviewing your oldest relatives, you will discover if you have a legacy to carry forward or will create your legacy and pass it down. As you prepare to interview your oldest relative, I have a list of open-ended questions to help you delve deeper into their lives and extract memorable moments, hard times, celebrations, traditions, and wisdom. It would help to ask for a family artifact with real sacred value.

"Artifacts can include vessels and personal objects of adornment, such as buttons, jewelry, and clothing. Finally, after completing the interview, you will all answer the ultimate question of a legacy when you share your findings and artifacts." Immediately following the conversation, I basked in the moment and stood proudly. Knowing my students eagerly awaited the opportunity to take ownership of their narrative. It was beautiful. Suddenly, a voice from the back of the classroom asks, "Mr. Ervin, what about your oldest relative? Who are you going to interview?" My eyes widened as my stomach tightened. I could feel the tension in my chest. I had an urge to retreat and a strong sensation to avoid the conversation, but I was stuck. Then, a ripple effect occurred across the room as more students felt the urge to chime in. "Yeah, we want to know about your family too!" I unleashed an awkward smile while warm sensations tingled through my spine.

My mind quickly detours to the news of my grandfather, Carver Youngblood, who was recently released from state prison for murdering my grandmother when I was ten. Briefly, I feel uneasy, uncomfortable, and out on a limb. I'm torn about revealing this family secret, as it has been locked away in my spirit for over two decades. I inhale deeply and slowly. I desperately try to protect myself against the assault of thoughts now taking over my mind.

Finally, I ended the questioning, saying, "Of course, I'm in!" despite the extreme complications surrounding my oldest family member. Without caution, I share, "My grandfather was released about a month ago. He served almost twenty years for the brutal murder of my grandmother." I continued, "This is not an easy choice. It's risky because my grandfather is a heinous, callous murderer in the eyes of my family, especially my mom, who will be furious and heartbroken if she finds out I visited him."

Ironically, my grandfather wanted to talk with me for some strange reason. I am one of the first family members he was excited to speak to. Above all, old skeletons will surely dance out of the closet if I go through with this interview. Surprisingly, lightness and ease came over my body. The heaviness and tension had subsided. I realized this was the first time I had shared my embarrassment, pain, mystery, and misery around this family tragedy. The silent curse that no one spoke about.

Similarly, without even a glimmer of doubt and poised as ever, my students enthusiastically shouted, "You have to live your life." "We can tell that this is important to you." "We got your back." "We're in this together." Later that evening, as I drove home, I swerved left onto a haunted-looking narrow street. I drove slowly down a deserted street with empty grass fields, dilapidated buildings, rusted cars, and closed mechanic shops. My speedometer showed I was going below 20 mph, as my heart rate accelerated with anticipation. My mind buzzed. I wondered, "Will this be a disaster?"

"How will he look?" and "What will he say?" I wondered. Eventually, the journey ended as my car pulled up to a two-story apartment building. Before I exited my vehicle, I took a deep breath and grabbed my yellow scratch notebook and a pen. "Morris, Morris!" I heard a faint, scratchy voice that penetrated through my car window. I rolled down the window and looked in the direction where I heard the voice. "Morris, I'm up here," the scratchy voice said. I looked up and saw a small head protruding out of a narrow window. I quickly jumped out of my car to get a clear view. "Come right in and up the stairs," my grandfather said. I smiled on the brisk, cold night, sensing a yearning to reconnect in his frail tone. I hopped and skipped up the stairs that spoke in the language of squeaks, creaks, grumbles, and thuds—like grumpy old men. When I reached the top floor, a door opened. I looked into the eyes of a frail but stubborn man who was once mighty in stature. His head was clean-shaven. He had wrinkles, but not many. He motioned me to follow him into his tiny, one-room, cluttered apartment. "Take a seat, Morris. Let me grab you a glass of water," he said. I watched his crooked frame limp into the kitchen and return with some water. I plopped down on an old couch with loose, saggy cushions and worn-out coils. I sank so low into the couch that I felt like I had fallen into a black hole. I struggled to sit up and tried to move forward to feel my feet touch the dusty floor. After a short pause and exchange of surface greetings, I abruptly asked, "Grandad, did you kill grandma?" He quickly responded confidently yet deliberately, "No, I did not kill my wife. I spent almost 20 years in the joint for something I didn't do. They put me in that stinking place to rot. They took my life from me and never tried to find the criminal who did it. Morris, they set me up!" After this intense moment, I paused before speaking again. I had to gather my thoughts. I was confused because I expected him to admit it. I exhaled and then inhaled an aura of peace. I was curious and wanted to go deep beneath the layers of his statement. I wanted to learn about the beginning of his journey. I wanted to understand how we got to this place as a family. I snapped back and assertively asked, "Grandad, if you say you didn't murder grandma, then what did you do? I'm heartbroken about our family's misery and suffering," I said. "You are the patriarch of our family. It all begins with you, so I want to know about the choices and mistakes you made along this path to get us to where we are today," I continued. Grandad said, "Morris, I made it out. I'm a new man. I learned a lot in the joint. I had years to think about what they did to me. I kept my mind sharp by working out and staying in shape. Look! You see my arms. I was doing pull-ups with them young niggas! I still got it! Morris, the police turned my family against me. Do you hear what I'm saying? They had no real evidence to convict me."

"Your momma and her sisters turned on me on that stand in court. I worked on myself, and I forgave them. My wife was a drinker, and she ran the streets. She wasn't a saint. She would get drunk and leave. Somebody killed her, and it wasn't me." I was enamored at how he spoke with so much energy and life. I'm unsure if he's running a game, but he was very animated. I wondered if I got my characteristics from him. I said passionately, "Grandad, Grandma did not start out drinking and running the streets. I assume this happened over time and from the cheating and verbal and physical abuse throughout your relationship. Did you beat Grandma? Did you verbally, physically, and sexually abuse your family?" I asked. "Yes, I got physical with my family," he replied. "My wife let the kids run around and do whatever they wanted," he continued. "Granddad, do you realize all the harm you caused this family?" I asked, looking intently into his face. "Are you willing to take responsibility for something that you did? Your children, my aunts, uncles, and mom, suffered a lot under your roof, negatively impacting their lives and relationships with their families. My cousins and I are the third generation in your legacy, and we still bear the burden of drugs, violence, abuse, pain, and suffering from you." "When will it end?" I asked. "You can take the first step by admitting the wrong and harm you've caused to the people you were supposed to protect and love. So, if you're not ready to apologize now, that's on you. Today, however, I came here as your grandson to get the bigger picture of our family history. My ultimate question to you is, what is your legacy? What is the legacy of this family? What are you passing down? And what are you leaving behind?"

"Let's begin. I'm going to ask you questions about your life. Just relax and tell me as much as you can recall," I said. "Well, Morris," he said, leaning forward in his dusty old reclining chair. "I was born on December 2, 1926, in Montgomery, Alabama, Lawrence County. My momma's name was Wilma Lee Youngblood. She was born in December of 1885, and my daddy's name was Charlie Tucker. I don't know when he was born. My parents and grandparents were free sharecroppers who did not have the right to vote. We did hard labor, plowing the field with horses and mules and planting crops such as sweet potatoes, corn, cotton, and peanuts. I grew up with three brothers and three sisters, and we cooked, washed, sewed, ironed, and got the wood together at night to make a fire for the house to be warm. Our parents ruled us with fear and harsh punishments. We grew up scared a lot. My dad was a heavy drinker, and my mom was very religious. She dragged us to church every Sunday while instilling in us the value of a positive work ethic. We wore our Sunday best. We received a new pair of shoes every five years. We wore Tom McCanns, Roy Logas, or the boots with the pocketknife. We had fun playing football and baseball in the neighborhood. We idolized lots of Black baseball players who played in the Negro Leagues. My baby brother was great at baseball and basketball. We called him 'Shot Crazy.' My older brother, Gerry B. Youngblood, graduated high school and joined the army. My other older brother, Cyprus, named after my grandfather, was also a heavy drinker and died in prison. We did enjoy cookouts in the summer and celebrated Christmas in the winter. We believed in ol' Saint Nick. My dad died when I was thirteen, leaving my mom alone to raise seven children. Unfortunately, I dropped out of middle school to help around the house. I now regret that because I believe there is no progress without education. Struggling to survive with no education and living in the South was tough. We, Black people, were still enslaved, in a sense, fighting against Mr. Charlie. We had no trust for the White man. A few years later, on December 7, 1941, Pearl Harbor happened."

"At 15 years old, I lied about my age and signed up for the physical to join the army during World War II. I remember they took a busload of Black men to Georgia for the physical examination. I failed the physical and was not allowed to fight in the war. Next, I migrated out of the South, looking for opportunities like many Blacks. This departure was called the Great Migration. I ended up in Niagara Falls working in a steel mill. It was harsh labor, and I did not stay long. Then, in May 1945, I went to Cleveland, Ohio. I was unemployed when I met your grandmother. I wasn't sure if she graduated high school or not. We had our first child before marriage and eventually married in 1948. I was 20, and she was 17. When our second child was born, that's when the problems started. I had issues with her mother, grandfather, sister, and brother interfering in our marriage. I knocked her grandaddy down and beat up her sister and brother. Meanwhile, the babies kept coming, seven children. We continued to argue with each other and fight. My wife let the kids do anything they wanted, making me very angry."

My grandfather's words created a world of time, history, and space I had always yearned for. Throughout his story, I closed my eyes and let my imagination wander with him into his past. Surprisingly, I did not expect my granddad to open up. I'm thankful he did. On the other hand, I feel torn because none of this will change the brutal death of my grandmother. In my eyes, there is still a heavy curse over the family, and he is the perpetrator. "Granddad," I said with a stern face. "I want to know your legacy, and what are you leaving behind?" He paused, stuttered, and surrendered to silence. I could tell he was hoping and praying that this question would evaporate. So, I sat back and sank deeper into the worn-out sofa's black hole. I let it simmer like a pot of yams; like a pot of lamb curry, I let it marinate in his spirit. "I don't know, Morris," he said, looking like a frustrated child. "I can't answer that question." At first, his response stimulated pain and resentment in me. Flashes of the words "an epic failure" and "my granddad is worthless" streaked across my mind.

Albeit, after a few moments, those thoughts faded away, and my sense of purpose, compassion, and understanding landed safely in my heart. I surmised my grandfather was a lonely man. A prideful man. A man with an ocean full of regret, misery, heartbreak, and agony buried deep within him. Here was a man who probably never had someone who just took the time to listen to him. Here was a man who, despite the circumstances, felt alone, betrayed, and abandoned by his family. I intend to be patient as I guide him through a journey of peace and reconciliation with himself and his family. There are more questions about the murder, the other family, and the woman he secretly supported outside his family. Despite it all, I must take it slow and celebrate this moment. I said, "Okay, Granddad. You're not getting off that easy. I'll be back again with the same question, and I want you to think about it before I return." He giggled with a sigh of relief that, at least for the moment, I made him feel he was now off the hot seat. Knowing it was time for me to leave, he attempted to hop up before me like a competition and said scratchily, "Morris, you promise that you will come back to visit me now." I nodded as we shook hands and embraced. I left his apartment with a sense of happiness and sadness. As I reached for my car door, I turned and looked up towards my grandfather's building. I smiled. His bald head was protruding from the small, narrow window. I waved, got into my car, and drove off into the night.

The Legacy Project presentations helped the students uncover meaningful stories and insights about their family history. One student revealed that her roots went back to the Virgin Islands. Her grandmother had openly discussed their culture and roots from the island and their journey to America. One young man discovered that his grandfather had twenty-seven children. Another young lady received a valuable bracelet passed down through her family for generations. I watched in awe as each student proudly stood before their peers to share the valuable history and lessons they had learned by interviewing their oldest relative. Likewise, I also bravely spoke about my interview with my grandfather and how he had not provided me with an answer about his legacy. Deep within, however, I had a sense of a legacy brewing inside of me.

December 20, 2006, Winter Break

It was a fun and stressful day before winter break. All day long, I had holiday music playing in my room. My students and I improvised old and new dance moves. We had a colossal sing-along to the best Christmas song ever, "Silent Night," by the Temptations. Between the singing and dancing, on my lunch break, a few girls came to talk to me. One expressed that she might be pregnant. Also, I had to mediate some girl drama in one of my ninth grade classes. Unfortunately, I felt the tension and received evil looks from teachers because students scrambled to stay in my class all day for food, music, and fun.

Today, some students even cut their boring classes to be with me. I love providing joy and freedom of self-expression, especially before any holiday break. This form of entertainment and community building catches on quickly. I realize that students find ways to entertain themselves. Regretfully, it usually involves alcohol, drugs, or sexual activity. My role is to initiate a healthy, fun experience connecting youth with adults. Wow! During fourth-period class, a few young women and men were in my room listening to music. Eventually, we created dance routines for each song. Suddenly, the room filled with students. I should have charged admission! Amid laughing and singing, I felt the pure joy, fun, excitement, and closeness we shared before the winter break.

January 10, 2007, Teacher's Lounge

Keegan, the only White student in my class, said, "Mr. Ervin, that was the best speech I've ever heard." After fifth-period class, I answered questions about "have to" and "should" language and how those words can lead to violence. Students were grateful for my class because it provided lots of freedom and autonomy, something they didn't receive as teenagers. However, I noticed that my students are getting frustrated because they want a family night so I can help their parents understand the fundamentals of the NVC language. One student said, "I'm feeling disappointed because I wanted a family night sooner, and it seems like it's not going to happen." Other students echoed, "Yeah, could you talk with my parents, too? They never understand us!" After hearing my students' concerns, I expressed my thoughts of not being their savior or rescuer because they would make me responsible for fixing situations and people. It takes time to heal. I empathize with my students' longing to see a transformation inside my class and within their families and communities.

I reassured them if they continued getting better, things would change. I explained how tough it is to show compassion to the people you love the most. The students agreed with my statement. Next, I gave them clear examples of how to slow down and not rush when they talk to avoid regretting the harsh words that can pour out of their mouths. Unexpectedly, the bell rang, and as usual, it interrupted my flow. Sixth-period students blew into my classroom with their chaos and craziness. Amid this storm, a student named Cherelle and I had a twelve-minute heartfelt conversation. During this conversation, I listened to her feelings of guilt and shame as she danced around the details of her dilemma.

I understood her need for privacy and support. I gently reassured her of her bravery and self-worth. Phew! Finally, Keegan slid back into my room to finish expressing his delight and was moved by my inspirational teaching style. Keegan said, "This class, as you put it, contributes to my joyful power. You listen to me and my classmates. Now, I'm much more aware of my habits and thoughts and how they impact my decisions within the different environments I find myself in. I reflect on my most important needs in these different situations." I extended my hand for a handshake, and he pulled me in for a hug. Keegan continued, "I want to cry at this moment." I responded, "Me too!" Keegan let me go, and before he strolled out of my class, he said, "If I have no choice, I have no voice in life."

January 11, 2007, National Flag Weekend

As I organized my room in preparation for my absence, I felt sad, uneasy, awkward, and guilty. I didn't want to leave my students for four days. Although it's the National Flag Football Tournament, I still need reassurance that everything will work in my absence. Before leaving, I had a brief, intense, and passionate exchange with Firestone, the no-nonsense guidance counselor. He was like my big brother. We constantly challenge each other about our opposing views on education and discipline. In short, his style demands accountability and respect from youth, while my style builds trust through mutual respect, inspiration, and choice. When the word "counselor" comes to mind, I envision someone who seeks to learn what the students need most while helping them connect to why school can help them succeed.

Our conversation ended, and I drove home thinking about how fun this trip would be because Venaya was joining me this year. Venaya has decided to take this trip with me as a much-needed getaway and a way to prepare for her interview with West Central University in Los Verdes, California. Venaya's sister picked us up and dropped us off at the airport. Eventually, we arrived in sunny Orlando, Florida, where Venaya's cheerful aunt picked us up. We arrived at their gorgeous and spacious house. She guided us into a private area with a bed, a living room, and many snacks. We ate, and we slept. The following day, we cooked a delicious breakfast on the patio. I read a book to relax. We also reviewed questions to help prepare Venaya for her interview at West Central University. The weather was perfect and pleasant, making it easy for us to relax. After studying, we shopped.

I finally dressed and played in the National Flag Football Tournament. On the first night, I received a pass interference call that set the opposing team up to score a touchdown. The receiver, who I guarded, had swift feet, and he hit me with a few double moves to find an open. I made the adjustments. We scored on offense and were only down by three points with two minutes left. The opposing team had the ball on offense, and I used my instincts and quickness to jump in front of the pass to make a diving interception. We scored, and we won. When we woke up the following day, Venaya studied for the interview again, and I asked her questions to prepare her for the interview process. I also finished reading another book about NVC. I aim to complete the practice book, draft a letter, and send it to the parents for Parent Night.

On day two of the tournament, we beat a team called the Vipers, and we beat our rivals, the Titans, a team from Cleveland, Ohio. The receiver, B.J., got the best of me again, but we still prevailed with the victory. On Sunday, we ate breakfast, worked on the interview process, and headed out for the last day of the tournament. We lost a close game to a team called Aftermath. Next, we played our rivals, the Titans, again, blowing them out 20-0, which put us in the B Division National Championship game. We battled our opponent, and the game went into overtime. They prevailed. The tall, fast receiver I chased around the field gave me my props. He tried out for the Detroit Lions and said, "I don't ever want to see you again." We dapped each other up, and he celebrated with his team. I had two interceptions in the tournament and played solid, tough defense. I improved in turning around and defending deep passes down the field. Venaya and I had a relaxing weekend in Florida with sunny, 80-degree weather. She hinted that she wanted a creative proposal for our tenth anniversary. My team is 2nd place National Champions, and I completed my parent letter for Family Night!

February 11, 2007, Border's Book Store

Venaya arrived home from her interview at West Central University. She said it was different and felt uncomfortable with the four questions. We also plan to discuss our needs, specifically our sadness, her need for closeness, and my need for space and understanding. After many years, my side of the family had its first get-together at my cousin Beaver's house. It was refreshing to see all my cousins, uncles, and aunties. Venaya gave me some advice. She said, "It takes time. Go slow, and don't try to heal everyone all at once." I sigh. I still haven't found the courage to speak honestly about my mom's comments and guilt trips.

Similarly, I feel no connection with my sister. Right before Venaya and I left, my mom leaned over to me and said, "You always have to leave early. You should learn to say no!" Due to this dysfunction, I plan to conduct a family meeting using the language of feelings and needs. My friend Aquib and I had a very open, honest, and heartfelt talk. It was refreshing. I want to tell my family that I've met my grandfather. I guess I can use my classroom history assignment to introduce this topic.

February 12, 2007

Barack Obama announced his bid for the Democratic Presidential Nomination. The "Idris War" continues, and I'm on edge. I'm angry, hurt, sad, and frustrated because I yearn to do things differently with him, but it's challenging. I have crazy thoughts like, "I could beat the hell out of this little kid!" Sometimes, he cries and dives at my legs, refusing to let me go. Other times, he throws a tantrum by repeating "No" and "No" while crossing his arms, making noises, stomping his feet, and then sitting down. I took him and my daughter to an indoor track meet last weekend. He refused to leave. He sat down on the track while taking off his shoes and socks. It was a real forty-five-minute struggle to encourage him to cooperate without violence. I did appreciate the support from a compassionate stranger who helped me through this embarrassing situation. I need to focus. I have abandoned my workout routine, and my life is out of order. I have lost my flow at work, too. I need to get my rhythm back.

CHAPTER 10

The Secret of the Flight

"If you want to go fast, go alone.
If you want to go far, go together."
African Proverb

With its aura of excitement, February brings me joy, meaning, and deep connection when celebrating Black History Month. It's concerning that some Black people are unaware of how Black History Month was established. Some believe that the "White man" or the government conspired against us by granting the shortest month of the year to honor the contributions of people of the Diaspora. Wrong! My ancestor and historian, Dr. Carter G. Woodson, "The Father of Black History," created Negro History Week in February 1926 to honor the birth of President Abraham Lincoln and abolitionist Frederick Douglass, whose birthdates were February 12 and 14, respectively. As a brilliant historian, he was also aware of the many contributions Black people had made and needed to highlight our heritage and achievements. Since 1976, every U.S. president has officially designated the entire month of February as Black History Month. Here is a list of significant events in February: On February 1, 1865, President Abraham Lincoln approved the Joint Resolution of Congress, submitting the proposed 13th Amendment to state legislatures. Ratified on February 3, 1870, the 15th Amendment guaranteed voting privileges to Black men. The Montgomery Bus Boycott arrests took place on February 20, 1956. On February 1, 1960, four Black college students staged a sit-in at a Woolworth lunch counter in Greensboro, North Carolina.

Malcolm X was assassinated on February 21, 1965, and Nelson Mandela was released from prison on February 11, 1990. Anchored with this information, my students and I began February by weaving a beautiful thread of knowledge, discovery, and creativity together as we explored the significant contributions of African Americans, past, present, and future. In addition to the magic created in the classroom, we decided to share our learning through a chant with the entire school. Each day during February, my students rehearsed the "African American History Rap," written by Sharon Jordan Holley. This rap has a chant that says, "A, B, C, D, E F, G African American History, H, I, J, K, L, M, N, O, P African American History, Q, R, S, T, U, V African American History W, X, Y, and Z, this is a story all about me." Subsequently, from A to Z, the song highlights individuals, principles, and values that make Black people proud and strong.

Despite the pain and pure exhaustion, I felt eager to tackle a full day of performances and presentations on the last day of Black History Month. I was asked to be the speaker who would close the Flash Through Time event, showcasing a flash of African American History, music, fashion, and activism from past to present. I arrived at work before sunrise to plan a day that would end long after sunset. I pulled out my speech, "The Secret of the Flight," and looked at the vibrant words that jumped off the dingy yellow notepaper. Filled with anxiety and panic, I studied each line in preparation for two speeches and an evening performance for our families. However, I felt relieved when I remembered I was only teaching half the day. I delegated a pair of my mature students, Marsha, and Jackie, to co-teach lessons throughout the day on topics such as Rosa Parks, the Civil Rights Movement, and the history of the word "nigger." This gave me time and space to practice my speech and prepare my students to sing the "African American History Rap" during lunch.

When it was time to perform our song, I strolled from my class to the noisy cafeteria. I skipped up the steps and reached for the silver microphone with my back toward the crowd of students, principals, and security guards. I felt tightness in my chest, fearful I would be alone, struggling to steal the students' attention from greasy pizza, gossip, flirtation, and drama. Hopefully, my students will join me. I turned around to face the massive crowd and the voluminous noise that had the power to swallow my voice.

Hoping not to get tangled in the long microphone cord, I checked the mic and switched on the power. I nervously pulled the microphone close to my mouth and lips and began to make a deep-sounding percussion rhythm from my diaphragm. In between this rhythmic flow, I chanted, "African American History, African American History, African American History." This recitation of words warmed my soul and invoked unity in students sitting in the cafeteria. Suddenly, all my students sprang up from their seats and stood behind me like a choir. I continued the beatbox and began clapping. My students clapped, and so did everyone in the cafeteria. The chant was strong, powerful, harmonic, and vibrant.

My students chanted with me with a force of self-confidence, solidarity, pride, and self-love. At that moment, I surmised that the insecurities and struggles of being a teenager had vanished into the greasy cafeteria air. With the nod and sway of my head and hands, I shouted, "Y'all ready?" The crowd roared back, "Yeah!" My students prepared to sing our song, some holding the lyrics while others gladly memorized the lyrics. In the corner of my eye, a student named Willie, carrying a pair of drumsticks, joined us and caught the beat! Then another student, Ari Rose, stood shoulder to shoulder with me, so I tossed her the mic! Equally important, a few of my tough, cool Black young men, like Mario, Devin, and Ken Ball, slid in next to us with half smiles, waving their hands in the air.

We said, "A, B, C, D, E, F, G!" The choir shouted, "African American History!" I eloquently delivered each rap line with a joyful, vibrant, and enthusiastic tone! Boom! We closed out and shouted, "This is a story all about me. This is a story all about me. This is a story all about me!" I barely had time to catch my breath and bask in the glory of the experience, not just for my students but also for over two hundred students who sat attentively in the cafeteria. Our ancestors' struggle, sacrifice, resilience, creativity, and flow moved through me, my students, and the cafeteria.

After a short rest, I could barely catch my breath in time for the afternoon performance! I hurried down the hallway towards the teacher's lounge. I went inside and changed into my ceremonial black flowing garment and my jean jacket with the continent of Africa airbrushed on the back. After making a necessary self-care stop, I jogged down the stairs to escort my beautiful, supportive wife into the theatre. I scanned the audience as I released her hand, letting her walk in alone. It was filled with students arriving with restless jubilation, anticipation of the show, and my closing words. I went behind the stage and nervously attempted to read my notes, hoping, and wishing I had more time to prepare. I stopped. I stood silent as my legs twitched up into my torso. I calmed myself and attempted to forget about the speech while enjoying the fashion show and the interactive scenes of the event. Soon after, Ms. Riley said, "Give your attention and respect to Mr. Ervin, as he will close us out with motivational storytelling." I jogged straight up to the podium and looked all around the auditorium. I said, "Do you know the secret of the flight?" I saw a sea of heads nodding yes and other puzzled faces waiting for the question to be answered. As I tell the story, I notice a shift in the energy and focus of those in the room.

Using my classic call-response techniques and a dash of humor, I shared the importance of knowing what the secret of the flight meant for our lives. After an extremely long and exhausting day, my speech and the program ended. I stood in the center of the stage and soaked in applause and warmth. Immediately after the afternoon performance assembly for students, my muscles ached, my eyes were red and sore, and I needed nourishment. I grabbed a piece of fruit and a bottle of water. I sat in a dark, quiet space until the night performance. Again, I waited patiently behind the stage. Surprisingly, I was less nervous this time and more settled. Ms. Riley called my name to share my closing words for the night. An overflow of families gathered in solidarity with intense anticipation and waited patiently for inspiration and profound wisdom. I trotted onto the stage, and this time, I immediately ran towards the center of the stage, taking a deep breath, and delivered. Initially, I extended the story about our ancestors' journey from America back to Africa. I said, "We lost the secret of the flight when we were snatched from our homeland. We lost our wings, but the secret of the flight remains within us." At the end of the program, I sat on the empty stage and gathered my thoughts. No one was in the auditorium, so I could sit alone and connect and reflect on that monumental day.

The outpouring of love and admiration I received was overwhelming. I thought aloud, a motivational speaker had been born.

The story of flying Africans is a myth that has been passed down from generation to generation since slavery. It is a secret and a gift from our ancestors. While this myth has evolved over hundreds of years, it remains the source of imagination that depicts freedom, new futures, and the return to Africa. Rooted in the history of Igbo Landing—a site on St. Simon's Island in Georgia, where enslaved people brought from Nigeria revolted and walked together into the marshy waters rather than be sold into slavery. These oral stories became truth to enslaved Africans and enabled them to use flight as a secret language for enslaved runaways. Today, it continues to represent Black mobility toward liberation.

I believe these stories of flight are rooted in truth. As Toni Morrison said, "The one thing you say about a myth is that there's some truth in there, no matter how bizarre they may seem." Virginia Hamilton imagined the story of enslaved Africans who remembered and reclaimed their ability to fly and escape their imprisoned lives in her celebrated children's book The People Could Fly. Hamilton believes that "come fly away" and similar phrases are part of the coded language used by enslaved Africans in organizing their escape. In her story, one by one, enslaved people embrace their spiritual truth and return to their native form as their weightless bodies ascend from the plantation field into the sky towards Africa: "They say the people could fly. Say that long ago in Africa, some people knew magic. And they would walk up in the air like climbing up on a gate. And they flew like blackbirds over the fields. Black, shiny wings flapping against the blue up there."

March 11, 2007

Venaya is extremely angry at me and the kids for all her sacrifices to accommodate us for the last few years. She expressed frustration about passing on the job of her choice to accommodate our schedules. She is upset with her current job, its environment, the hours, and the work ethic of her coworkers. She's mad because she had to take a job that coordinated with the kid's school schedule and my work schedule. She feels she is constantly getting sabotaged because she has put her needs on hold and suffered in silence—until it is finally overflowing on us. This is where her hostility comes from. Venaya needs autonomy, choice, and freedom about where she will work. She needs support, encouragement, and cooperation from us.

Most importantly, I can create space and give her emotional safety and empathy when she expresses her frustration about her career. I can also listen, validate her experiences, and empathize with her concerns. I am responsible for keeping communication open and ensuring everyone's needs are met in the family. Last week, Venaya told me that Idris is still concerned about my abusive fits of violence. He shared that he remembers the time I screamed in his face and other moments of my rage. Idris does not believe I have changed. He uses his anger as a means of getting power. People react and listen to him when he hits other kids his age. Otherwise, my son believes people will always tell him what to do, which frustrates him. Idris said, "Even Zekhi, who is younger than me, doesn't listen to me." Since this heavy conversation with my wife, I felt deeply hurt, sad, and guilty. I translated these feelings into a need for love and patience. I will commit more to nonviolence in my home and everywhere else. Before any part of my song can be sung, I must first conquer the violence towards my family. There is no flight when your words and actions oppress your family. The real flight is uplifting yourself first, then family and community. This takes a lot of powerful self-love, compassion, understanding, and respect.

It was excruciatingly painful as I picked up my phone to call my mom. I constantly worry about her approval. I stared at the digits on the phone and struggled to stay in the moment and not remember all the times I did not measure up. This time, I forgot I had planned something for my son's birthday, and at the same time, I promised my mother I would visit her sick brother. I dialed her number and held my breath. My entire body constricted, tightened, and contracted like a boa constrictor wrapping his body around me. "Hey Ma, how are you?" I asked. Silence was her best weapon. It was the first act of her disapproval and guilt performance. She waited and waited, then responded, "Fine." I stuttered, "I, I'm sorry that I can't see Charles today because I forgot I had planned something for Idris." More silence filled the air like carbon monoxide choking life from me. Finally, with an irritable tone, she said, "You need to be more considerate. Why don't you write things down?" I paused. I hesitated before speaking. Then, before I could talk, she continued, "It's typical. I am used to you spending more time with her family and not mine. Bye, Morris." The conversation ended. I stood motionless with the phone in my hand. The pain and emptiness swirling inside me were indescribable. I felt desperate and helpless. How did we get here? I wondered. I know my occasional inconsideration, absent-mindedness, and immaturity are the least of my mother's painful dilemmas. Something was missing from her life, so she projected her pain onto her children, mostly me. I ordered the book, *Emotional Resilience*, to help her identify her needs and the voids in her life. I also wanted to express my feelings to her in a letter. As I sat alone with pen and paper, more intrusive thoughts seduced me into remembering my past.

I take Venaya's hand as we rush upstairs into the room where my parents are lounging. We enter the room and sit on the carpet. Before I begin to talk, I sense an air of confusion as my father removes both hands from his beloved bag of Ruffles potato chips. I feel worried and apprehension wrap around my mother's shoulders like a warm blanket. I swallowed some water and said, "Venaya and I have been together. We love each other deeply and have decided to get married!" My heightened senses felt the room fill with unexpected grief, bereavement, and shock. My mom mustered up some words in an attempt to recover from her devastation and said, "You are both so young. Your father and I got married young, too." I felt sadness and heaviness pour over me like a summer thunderstorm. Sadly, I felt a disconnect I could not process. Unfortunately, a steady forecast of thunder, lightning, and dark clouds lingered.

I sit alone and in silence on my couch. I am thrilled for my special day to arrive. I surf through a few television and sports channels as I attempt to entertain myself and ease the apprehension and discomfort that brew inside of me like hot tea. I pretend I am good. However, I deny I am heavyhearted and sad. I call my fiancé, and the loud chatter that blasts through the phone confirms she is having fun without me! I need her. I need a connection. I quickly end my call with her and call my friend. He does not answer. Finally, I nestle in with my loneliness and drift off to sleep, anticipating my important day tomorrow.

Today is my wedding day. I woke up early. I did my pre-wedding ceremonial workout, then dashed out of the house for my haircut. I returned home to the wonderful aroma of fried chicken. I ran upstairs to put on my fly black wedding suit. After getting dressed, the scent of fried chicken tickles my nose. I gallop downstairs to the kitchen. Mesmerized, my eyes sparkle like diamonds looking at the pan of chicken. My mouth waters with anticipation for that first delicious bite. Then, my sister appears in the kitchen looking like Roshumba, the Black supermodel. Her short haircut accents her dimples and perfectly positioned eyes. She wears a cute, simple, elegant white dress highlighting her petite frame. With an anxious smile, my mom says, "You all go into the living room so I can take a picture." The front doorbell rings. I opened it. At the door is Venaya's brother, complete with designer sunglasses and a stylish suit vest with no shirt underneath—just his protruding biceps. I smirk and invite him inside for chicken. After eating, we get into the car and drive to the Cleveland Museum of Art. The car slowly moves into a parking spot on a busy road directly across from the museum. I carefully step out of the car onto the grass with my shiny black dress shoes. The weather on my wedding day is perfect. The bright, sunny day has an overcast of clouds and a nice strong breeze. The wind forcefully attempts to push me away from the wedding location. I, however, remain determined to make it to my destination. Nonchalantly, I stroll closer to where a few women are laying the bright green carpet in front of the stately museum. The wind is fierce as it attempts to blow the flower arrangements, decorations, and ornaments down several steps into the duck pond. I walked to the museum's front entrance and stood frozen in time. In silence, I anxiously waited for my big moment.

As I waited, I heard the chatter of voices behind me. I turned around and fixed my eyes on a beautiful orchestra of family, friends, and loved ones standing in a half-crescent moon on the green carpet. Immediately, I experienced earthquake trembling sensations throughout my small frame. I gasped for air. My stomach became tight. The butterflies fluttering in my belly started as I watched my father and best friend sit comfortably on the green carpet. I slowly walked towards them, took my shoes off, and sat beside my father. As we sat on the carpet, we could hear voices growing louder and the wind howling around us. The Imam, carrying his Quran and wearing an illustrious garment fit for a king, joined us. He took his shoes off and sat at the top of the rug. I stood up and saw an image of pure delight walking with a convoy of men and women surrounding her. I heaved a sigh of relief and said to myself, my soulmate is here! My muscular mentor walked beside Venaya, holding the gown's train to ensure it didn't drag on the sidewalk. He led her and her dad, who was dressed in full African attire, onto the rug. The ceremony was quick. Sitting on the carpet, we recited words from the Holy Quran. Following the recitations, we stood and placed a sweet date in each other's mouths to signify the end of the ceremony and the beginning of our lives as one.

We arrived at the local YMCA, where our reception was held. Venaya and I walked through the empty kitchen to reach the reception hall. Entering the hall, we sat at our table in front of the small, outdated, undecorated room. Venaya was furious! The caterer and her team were running late. Needless to say, Venaya was livid when the head caterer finally arrived. Wearing a pink sweatsuit, she hurriedly rushed past us into the kitchen. We walked into the kitchen to share our disappointment and frustration with the Pink Panther caterer. Calmly, Venaya said, "This is very unprofessional. I'm disappointed because the food is not ready, your staff is not here, and our guests are arriving." Pink Panther's eyebrows pulled closer together, and her eyes bulged as she snapped, "I don't need this!" Without hesitation, I lunged toward her like a mountain lion. My wife tapped my arm and said, "This is our day." Like Stevie Wonder, we were "hotter than July," but we turned and walked back into the hall. At that moment, I realized my wife's strong and supportive team of sisters would handle everything. So, my wife and I waited for her sisters and other family members to ramble, scramble, and work their magic with the Pink Panther and her reluctant staff to salvage our reception meal.

As the momentous day moved on, I took time to slowly gaze at everyone to savor this moment of a new beginning in my young life. A twinkle settled in the corner of my eye as I watched family, close friends, and members of my Muslim community laugh, talk, and celebrate our special occasion. I sighed and thought to myself, You're just twenty years old. "Venaya's aunt, who wore a beautiful Egyptian crown, stood up and began singing Regina Belle's song, "If I Could," acapella. Her strong voice soothed the room and created a wave of tears that overflowed and spilled down the cheeks of women, especially my bride and new mother-in-law. This song captures the essence of deep mourning, sadness, and a celebration of life. It evokes so many powerful feelings that are moving in the room. At that moment, I could sense that some deep wounds had healed. As she finished, I was deeply moved and honored to join a strong family. After the song had long been over, sitting with my dad, sister, and little brother, I noticed that my mom was still sobbing uncontrollably. I gently clasped her hand in mine and led her outside. I asked her a few questions, hoping she would express herself. Wrong. The tears pour out with more force, and her breathing intensifies as she gasps for air. I stop trying to do anything. I squeeze her hands while rubbing her back, wishing she would feel better. Confusion and helplessness brew inside my belly like a tropical hurricane. Something in her tears seemed less joyful and more painful. Eventually, we turn around and walk back into the building.

CHAPTER 11

Discovering Voice

Ubuntu: "I am what I am because of who we all are."
(From a definition offered by Liberian peace activist
Leymah Gbowee.)

Standing outside my class one day, I was shocked as I watched my scholarly student, Samantha, jump out of character. She is shouting obscenities and hurls a water bottle at a young lady. I quickly go over to her to calm her. As she feels my warm presence, I ask, "Sam, you good?" "You almost hit her, and that would have caused a fight. You don't want to get suspended. You have a flawless school record," I said. My words of wisdom slowly bring her back into the moment and out of her rage. She snaps back and says, "How could he talk to her right in front of my face? What a loser!" I wait patiently. I am holding more space for her to express herself until her words lose their venom. "Go ahead and get to class," I say with a tone of encouragement. "You're too classy to throw bottles at girls over a guy like you're at the club. Come back during your lunch break and let me know what's really bothering you."

She smirks and giggles as she slowly turns and walks down the hall. Later, Samantha returns to my classroom, expressing her deep frustration, sadness, pain, and hostility toward her mom. Initially, I appear shocked, not expecting the conversation to segue from boy trouble to mom trouble. Surprisingly, I assumed Samantha had the perfect relationship with her mom. Samantha immediately gets right to the point by wasting no words or time. "My Mom does not listen to me. She never understands where I'm coming from. Maybe you can talk with her. Maybe we can talk together?" she anxiously belts out. I nod, realizing the desperate plea from Samantha is real. I feel a sense of connection and deep respect because I know Samantha believes I can help her repair the situation with her mom. In other words, it's time for the work in my classroom to extend into the households where my students come from.

March 15, 2007

I'm incredibly anxious about Premiere Night and the release of our NVC video. I'm also finding peace and ease in my personal life. I feel at home when I can inspire souls and touch hearts. It's thrilling when I hear students talk about coming to support my vision. I'm creating opportunities to live and grasp the meaning of life, which feeds my soul. Yesterday, I moved forward with Idris, but still, much work needs to be done. It was about him wanting his own choices. I let him express his frustrations with a few murmurs and yells, some running on the couch and diving on the floor. I notice my frustration and give him space, allowing him to finish his mini outburst. I then empathize with him and connected with humor. He opens up, and we compromise on a request that meets our needs. Overall, Venaya thinks I do all the work for the kids. I call it support. Maybe I'll let them wash up, scoop the cat litter, and clean rooms without my help. Venaya is also stressed by the kid's lack of appreciation despite all of her efforts. She needs space.

Premiere Night finally arrived. I have had an exhausting day at school. It's impossible to slow down as my thoughts race through my mind. I pace incessantly back and forth, then meander until I settle into a game plan. First, I found a large ice tub, filled it with ice, and put all the drinks in. Then, I started to aimlessly pace up and down the stairs, back and forth, thinking I had so much time before the event began. Next, Venaya arrived, and we ate Subway sandwiches with my friend, Principal Steve. After we ate, I realized the time had swiftly moved, and it was now 7:10 p.m. I am slightly panicked. I scampered up to my classroom to finish my notecards. However, to my delight and distraction, a few of my students popped in to fulfill their volunteer positions for the evening. Each student, expressing nervousness, had positive energy and lots of enthusiasm. I stood up and took a deep breath of happiness and joy. I looked into the eyes of Makayla, Mitchell, Tracy, Courtney, and Layla and saw the freedom and true purpose of what it means to teach and inspire youth. The real meaning of education is to draw forth from within, and students who aren't athletes or scholars will have an opportunity to serve their community while showcasing their talent.

Each student decided what they would contribute and how they would help make the night memorable. We had emcees, ushers, set up crew, poets, and a cleanup crew. I attempted to finish my note cards. However, I was too stimulated to focus, so I dashed downstairs to the theater. My colleagues were setting up and greeting parents and community members who had arrived. I quickly ran to my car and grabbed my black suit and colorful tie. Then, I made my way backstage. I pulled the curtains back to get a peak. My eyes widened as more parents, community members, teachers, students, and the superintendent joyfully entered the theater. In retrospect, my students insisted I showcase the documentary in a public forum so I could show the radical transformation that was happening in my class. The event could be a springboard to teach adults how to use nonviolent language to express feelings and needs—pure genius.

Unfortunately, the collective response from most teachers was, "None of the parents will show up. They never show up to school events." I brushed off the negative responses and promoted the event. I made lots of phone calls and left lots of messages. I also did a creative public service announcement that the school recorded and sent to parents. Voila! I had imagined a full house, and the theater was packed with curious minds and open hearts. The energy in the theater was sweet! So now I was ready to peel back the curtain and slide through. I stepped out, stood behind the microphone, and said, "Welcome to the premiere night of *Keeping It Reel*. *Keeping It Reel* is a short documentary that showcases students in my ninth grade History and twelfth grade African American Studies class who learned the consciousness and language of speaking their feelings and needs through nonviolent communication. After viewing the documentary, we will have questions from the audience and two poetry readings from my students. Also, if anyone is interested in learning about nonviolent communication, you can sign up for some community workshops at the end of our program."

I turned and hopped down from the stage and gave my student the cue to start the documentary. He tapped on the laptop keys and tapped and tapped again. Nothing happened. My chest tightened. I felt tension throughout my whole body. Suddenly, an unlikely person stepped up to assist me. It was the mean secretary who had kept students from entering the dance. I watched as she calmly touched a few keys on the laptop, and without much effort, the documentary began. Suddenly, I realized that the lights weren't out. I struggled to handle the task until the superintendent assisted me. The lights went out. Although the documentary was only ten minutes, it seemed like a full-length movie. I was delighted with what I saw as I scanned between the crowd and the screen. Eventually, the documentary ended. The lights came back on, and the audience enthusiastically applauded.

I shared a few words. "I'm proud of all of my students because we learned a new way of being together. It took a lot of risks and vulnerability. We then had a camera crew film us as we practiced this new way to communicate, learn, and deal with the everyday pressures of life." I continued, "As a community of adults, we rarely get the opportunity to step back and allow our students the freedom, space, and emotional safety to take risks. Students are resilient. They rise to the standards we set if we lead by example and set limits with love. We all worked hard. We all took risks and created something that nobody could take away." I open the floor for questions about the documentary. To my delight, parents stood up and poured their hearts out about the struggle of raising children and how difficult it was to communicate. I received each question and held space for each parent while offering empathy that addressed their concerns. The level of transparency and safe energy in the auditorium touched and moved me deeply. Each of my students boldly shared how learning this communication style has impacted their lives and schoolwork. It was truly an overwhelming feeling of joy as the kids spoke their truth before a hundred teachers, parents, administrators, and community members.

Lastly, two students shared their beautiful poems. I asked if anyone was interested in follow-up workshops to sign up. People came down and enthusiastically signed up for the workshops. As I proceeded to leave, I shook hands, gave out hugs, and talked with people. Kathy, the conflict mediation teacher who introduced me to NVC, motioned me to sit beside an older woman wearing vibrant purple glasses. She had a subtle, powerful presence that I couldn't ignore. Kathy said, "Hey, Morris, this is Rita Herzog. She is one of the founding organizers of Nonviolent Communication. Rita did a lot of the groundwork with Marshall Rosenberg in the early days to share his message with others. She lives in Cleveland." I listened to Rita, whose words of wisdom poured life into me. I knew we would reconnect. I also received a few offers to speak at churches and organizations. The next day, the buzz around school was about students who had effectively used nonviolent communication with their parents—who listened. I received cards and positive emails from teachers and administrators. On that night, we were unified. I will continue to use nonviolent communication to confront issues in schools and communities.

March 18, 2007

I have so much pain, blame, and criticism from my mom and sister that I can no longer handle it. I refuse to let them talk down to me about my daughter and wife. I explode and punch a hole in the basement wall. I let my fury loose, and today, I refused to be treated like a little brother and a momma's boy. I spoke up. Unfortunately, my daughter had to witness my rage. Surprisingly, this made me open up and have a difficult conversation about my past. For the first time, I revealed the sexual abuse I had endured from a teenage babysitter when I was five years old. Surprisingly, my sister also shared a few unfortunate memories from her childhood. I continued and even told everyone about the secret meeting with my granddad, the man my mother had forbidden us to talk with. My mom listened and absorbed the story of my hurt the best she could. I saw the shame and guilt rise in her eyes. I began to give her a perspective about her dad that she never knew or refused to know because of her pain and suffering. I am unsure if something shifted in them, but it shifted in me. I had just confronted the two women who have caused me a lot of pain, and yet two women who I love the most. I don't want this conversation to end. I want it to lead to healing and forgiveness for our family. I could hear my father pacing back and forth upstairs. He yelled at us a few times but didn't come downstairs to join or interfere in our conversation. Right now, I feel nothing but sadness. Hopefully, one day, he will let down his guard and open up.

A few days later, during my lunch period at school, I received a call from my wife. She unleashed more of her pain and reopened wounds that had been inflicted upon me by my mom and sister's venom. She said with a deafening tone, "At this point, I can't let go or forgive them! I want to move away. That was my fucking day, and they ruined it. Do you remember the baby shower when I came home in tears? I'm so frustrated with your inability to support me in confronting your mother and sister about their lack of respect and consideration for my feelings. You chose not to be involved because you were scared. It's common sense to defend your wife when someone disrespects her." I gulped and threw back a response, "It ain't easy. People have different challenges and understand differently if they understand at all." She barked back, "All these years, I was ignored by you and disrespected by them. And also, why aren't you spending time writing me love notes, taking me on dates, or cuddling at night? You started, and yet again, you stopped!" The conversation ended, and I sat with all of Venaya's words. I felt frustration and disappointment with myself. I realized my wife needs to grieve and mourn as well as express what she would have liked to have happened. Maybe I am stuck because she demands these acts of kindness from me.

April 6, 2007

It's a week before Spring break. I feel alive, and I have more energy at this point than I have ever had. My fifth-period African American Studies class enjoyed our self-care day. We hold hands, dance to reggae/ dance hall music, and break bread together while eating delicious food and desserts. We become closer through this feel-good potluck.

143

Unfortunately, I played in my last all-school faculty versus student-basketball game. Bore-ring. It was unlike the game a few weeks before that was held in our small school. Mr. Hardaway invited a DJ to keep our students pumped while we played against the students. The atmosphere is electric.

Students have signs. We have a halftime performance, and my ability to play basketball while antagonizing students in the stands always keeps things fresh and entertaining. Unlike the all-school game, which ended in a tie 63-63, our small school game ended with Mr. Hardaway's smooth and silky last-second buzzer beater to win the game for us. The kids rush on the floor to celebrate while we transition students out of the gym and back to class. It is so sad that the students were rushed out of the game after the all-school game, even though it was a tie score. Our small school knows how to respect kids while allowing them to have fun. The all-school game felt like a prison. The administration and security team treat students like criminals, just itching for something terrible to happen. Our small school sees the best in our students, and they rise to the occasion every time.

Later that night, I lost it with my kids. I let my angry thoughts hijack my mind. I allowed them to enjoy extra snacks and television time to watch cartoons in exchange for perfect compliance at bedtime. However, bedtime isn't going as I planned. Idris refuses to settle down. As I turn out the lights, I continue to hear giggles and chuckles from them. Distraught, I stand and listen outside their bedroom as the chatter continues. I did not give myself any room or space to settle down. Then, like a time bomb, I burst into the room, screaming at the top of my lungs! I shook their bunk beds until they were destroyed. My daughter let out an awkward laugh, which caused me to do more damage to the beds. Finally, the dust settled. I walked out of their room feeling humiliated and embarrassed by my fit of rage.

The day arrived for our Parent Practice Night. I quickly ended an exhausting and exhilarating day of teaching and ran downstairs to the library to set up. I pulled all the chairs from the wooden tables and made a sacred circle. I left space at the back of the library for folks to sign in and sit down. Initially, I was apprehensive about who would show up. At the Premiere Night, over fifty parents signed up for the Parent Night session. Next, while waiting for people to join my first parent nonviolent communication workshop, I sat and ground myself with deep breathing. I finished the meditation just in time to greet the security guards, my first participants. Then, a few teachers hesitantly walked in. Likewise, I greeted them with a warm smile. Another ten to fifteen minutes passed without anyone coming through the door. Suddenly, several parents and students rushed into the library with a roar of energy. I immediately filled my chest cavity like a hot air balloon. My excitement level and gratitude were unprecedented at that moment.

Finally, a few secretaries, Mr. Hardaway, and a few more parents came in at the last minute. I strolled to the front of the room and gazed at all the tables and seats filled to capacity. I thought, now this is how you engage the many systems inside and outside a school. Parents, teachers, administrators, staff assistants, and community members were all in the same place to receive information on effectively engaging with youth. We were together in this specific place and space of our own volition. There was no coercion, and no force was needed, just a genuine desire to choose. I said, "Greetings, everyone. Welcome to our first Parent Night Nonviolent Communication (NVC) Workshop. Tonight is an opportunity to learn the basic process of NVC, and for you to learn how to open up by sharing yourself in a manner you might not have shared elsewhere.

"Here's my first exercise for everyone. Think about a time when you did something from the heart. You did not do it out of fear, obligation, guilt, or shame. You did it to contribute to your life or to make someone's day enjoyable. When you have your story, please stand, and wait for more instructions." A silence draped over the space like a cape as parents and other adults paused to think. Students thought quicker than counting to five and sprung to their feet. I waited and said, "Please follow me to the sacred circle." I turned and walked over to the sacred circle, hoping my community would follow. I felt the shock emanating from the audience. I giggled to myself because most people remained in their seats. They felt safe sitting behind a table. The distance between them, each other, and the speaker was comfortable. I shared that the circle is just a space where everyone is present.

It's easier to connect with others and express yourself. A circle represents natural trust, respect, and risk-taking. I used circles to honor the indigenous tribes of the Americas, Africa, and Asia. "Please remain standing, and when the music comes on, everyone will work together to put themselves in chronological order based on the month and day of your birthday. Go!" The music, "Ain't no mountain high enough. Ain't no valley low enough. Ain't no river wide enough to keep me from getting to you," played. We smiled, we laughed, and we moved around.

All ages. Different backgrounds. One purpose. Music and movement are my go-to strategies in a designated space that evoke positive emotions and create immediate safety, trust, and respect. After each person shared their name and birthday, I asked if anyone would share stories about giving without expecting anything in return. I was delighted as adults and students shared stories of giving to strangers and homeless people, volunteering, consoling friends, visiting the sick or elderly in the hospital, baking sweets, etc. After several people had shared, I interrupted and said, "This is the essence of what you're here to learn tonight. This is the essence of nonviolent communication. We can live in a world where we intend to do things from a place of choice, not obligation. We can live in a world where we contribute solely to making each other's lives extraordinary.

"This giving can manifest in acts of service and how we communicate. I see lots of families in this circle. I know it's hard to communicate with your children, especially when they are misbehaving or irresponsible or if you're exhausted because you have to repeat the same demands repeatedly. I see many security guards, teachers, and administrators in this circle. I know the challenges of educating and maintaining a safe environment for a school with many kids are daunting. The fundamental aspect of NVC communication is a connection before correction. I often ask myself questions that help align me with my intention before interacting with anyone. Do I want to connect, or do I want to get my way? We should contemplate these questions. We live in such a fast-paced world. Some of us have to get through lessons, do home chores, help with homework, cook dinner, or pay bills. Because of this, we often want people to comply and do what we say. Making such demands removes the gift of seeing each person's humanity.

"As parents and school personnel, it's easier not to see our children and students through a neutral lens and, thus, not relate to them as human beings with needs. So, the power in this work is first to step back and ask yourself those two questions, and secondly pause to clarify how you feel and what you need. Then, we can create space and make room to acknowledge the feelings and needs of those with whom we interact. Therefore, before we get into the specific four-step process of NVC, which is to make observations about what is happening, describe how you feel, say what you need, and say what you're requesting from someone. I wish you would first understand that the core of this work is to give without expecting anything in return. We are giving up the dominant system that is based on force, fear, and power. In return, we seek to understand, validate experiences, and work together."

Then, Chance, a young student with short braids, crystal blue eyes, a thuggish demeanor, and a soft heart, stood up and said, "I have a gift to give." He pointed to a young lady in the back of the library and motioned for her to stand by him in the circle. Everyone was quiet. The anticipation was brewing like a fresh pot of Folgers coffee. She timidly stood next to Chance without uttering a sound. She was afraid, yet brave. Chance continued, "Mr. Erv, you know I have mad respect for what you're doing with this peaceful communication thing. I see how you inspire all of us, and basically, I want to do my part. I want to be like you. So, I make myself available to all the hood kids who y'all teachers and principals don't care about." In silence, the young lady looked at the faces of everyone who sat around the circle. Chance continued, "She shared with me that she's been having many family, relationship, and self-worth problems. She told me she wanted to take her life because she felt worthless. And I did what Mr. Erv taught us to do. I stepped back and, without judgment, listened to her needs. I offered her empathy and asked her if she needed care and support from a safe community. She agreed, so I asked if she would join me in the circle tonight. She also wants to take it all in and not speak. And for the record, she ain't my girlfriend."

The tension evaporated, and Chance, with his unrelenting charm, lightened the mood. I responded, "Chance, what a courageous act. I appreciate you taking the risk and asking your friend to join us." I turned and looked at Chance's friend and said, "When you are ready, I have a female counselor you can talk with. She can get you started with the support you need." I finished the session by saying, "Everyone, please take some time this week to slow down and consider how you have communicated with your colleagues, friends, family, children, partners, spouses, and especially those you have trouble communicating with. Remember to step back, pause, identify your feelings and needs, then guess the person's feelings and needs or ask them. You can grab a list of feelings and needs on your way out, and make sure you come back in two weeks with any scenarios you want to role-play."

The session had ended. People socialized for a while and enjoyed refreshments before leaving. Then, Samantha, a scholar in my African American History class, waved her hand and guided me to the computers. She introduced me to her Mom, Sadie, and her little sister, Sophie. Her mother was sharply dressed and well put together. She, however, had a slightly distrustful look but a curious glare. She said, "Mr. Ervin, my daughter can't stop talking about you and your African American History class." I replied, "Samantha is extraordinary. She takes her academics and extra-curricular life seriously. She is truly a delight to have in my class." Sadie responded, "Well, Sam thinks that we don't talk and have issues. This girl is so spoiled." Sam interrupted, saying, "Mom, we never spend time together, and you're always at work." Sadie quickly responded, "Girl, look at you. You are always dressed nicely. Look at the car I drive. Look at the house we live in. We wouldn't have this lifestyle if I did not go to work! And your little sister needs me, but you don't! I'm so tired of you being entitled. I give you everything, Samantha!" Samantha's eyes got puffy. She crossed her arms, leaned against a chair, and incessantly tapped her feet. Sadie continued, "You, young lady, are clueless about what I must do to maintain this lavish lifestyle! I need you to be more grateful!" I softly interrupted and skillfully said, "Miss Sadie, I want to acknowledge your struggle as a single mom and how hard it is to care for your daughters and provide a stable life for them. It also sounds like you're frustrated and would like some appreciation and consideration from Sam. You are exhausted and would love peace of mind and rest."

I turned and said to Samantha, "It sounds like you're sad and miss spending time with your mom. You want to connect with her." Sadie had a blank but warm expression on her face. She mumbled, "Samantha, are you really lonely and missing spending time with me?" Sadie's soft and caring tone softened the tension inside Sam's body. She uncrossed her arms, and a sense of relief covered her face as the tension left the space. Crying, Sam said, "Yes, Mom, I have a 4.0 GPA. I'm active at school. I will get a full academic scholarship to a university, and I appreciate the life you have provided for Sophie and me. However, I miss you. I'm still that little girl who needs to be nurtured and comforted. I'm an emotional being. I love to express myself, and you expected me to be independent when I got older. I'm great at it, but I just need my mom!" Sadie paused and attempted to take it all in. She moved closer to Samantha, grabbed her hand, interlocked her fingers with Sam's, and said, "I didn't know you still needed me in this way. I guess I was so caught up in work and taking care of your little sister I thought you were strong and able to take care of yourself." Sadie turns and gently says to me, "Thanks, Mr. Ervin, we needed this, and I see why she loves your class so much. We will be back."

Saturday was always a shopping day. So, it's my adventure to the grocery store. This particular Saturday morning was different. I felt groggy and tired from a long night at the emergency room with Idris. Last night, Venaya and I dropped Idris and Naimah off at their Auntie Koko's house while we planned to visit a veterinarian program in Chicago. Venaya was considering Ross Veterinary School in the Caribbean Islands. I could only imagine how much fun it would be to spend a few years in the Caribbean while Venaya attended vet school. Just as we were heading to our car, we got a call from Koko. Her voice was shaking as she screamed, "Idris had an accident on the treadmill in the basement!

"He flew off the treadmill, hit his head, and his finger had some skin missing. He's also bleeding from his scalp." We immediately drove to Koko's house and rushed Idris to the emergency room. We were uncertain if his head injury was severe. It was now after midnight, and it was challenging to keep Idris awake. Finally, a nurse called Idris' name. Idris was in my lap as Venaya explained what happened. Idris' neck was rolling around in my lap, and his eyes fluttered open and shut. The doctor examined him and told us Idris was exhausted. He had a gash on his head and some skin missing from his fingers. Idris would need two stitches, and we would be free to go. Venaya and I looked at each other and sighed in relief. We drove home, put Idris in bed, and canceled our trip to Ross.

The next day at the grocery store, I was not my usual gregarious self. Usually, I smiled and made light, yet enlightening, conversations with strangers. Instead, I pulled out the list, walked up and down the narrow, unorganized aisles, grabbed my items, and walked to the checkout line. As I was placing my groceries on the conveyor belt, Venaya called. Upon answering, all I heard was shouting. She screamed, "I got in! I got in! I'm going to vet school in California! I can't believe it!" I immediately jumped up and down like a winning contestant on *The Price is Right*, shouting, "My wife got accepted into veterinary school! She can't believe it! We're moving to California!" I high fived the cashier. I high fived all of the strangers in line behind me. Everyone in line said, "Tell her we said congratulations." As I drove home, I was filled with exuberance and glee. When I arrived, I dashed upstairs and wrapped my arms around Venaya. We danced in a circle. I could feel her heart beating. All I could do was think about her persistence and determination to get accepted into a school. Venaya said, "I opened the mail with Western University on it. I scrolled through the letter, and when I jumped up, I stubbed my toe when I realized I had been accepted." "Wow, that is exceptional. I'm so proud of you," I said as I read the letter. "This is one step closer to fulfilling your childhood dream."

Monday arrived, and I crept into Principal Hardaway's office. I was slightly nervous and shaking in anticipation of telling him I would have to resign at the end of the year. Actually, expecting we might move to California, I sent my resume to schools before Venaya received her acceptance letter. I had a strong feeling that California was where she needed to be. I had visions that if I moved to California, I would teach in South Los Angeles.

Mr. Hardaway, wearing a fresh suit—his usual attire—glided past me in the lobby. Manipulating a ring full of keys, he opened his office door and said, "Mr. Ervin, come in. I have great news to share with you." I smiled at him as I walked into his office and quickly sat in a chair. My entire body was tense. He said, "This nonviolent communication has been a successful pilot project you started in your class. The kids love it. The parents love it. Teachers are trying to get there, and the superintendent is excited and wants more. So, I've decided to lessen your teaching load from five to two history classes next year. The rest of your schedule will be free for you to teach NVC. You can start with our in-school suspension students. This would be a great opportunity to use that time with the kids to teach them about their emotions, communication, and what's getting in their way. You will also be free to continue leading workshops for staff, administration, and parents. What do you think?" I took a big gulp. I attempted to speak, but no words flowed from my lips. He smiled at me and gestured with his hands for me to say something.

I begrudgingly said, "Mr. Hardaway, that would be a dream come true because I've been connecting my students' social, emotional, and cultural lives outside my classroom and into the larger school complex. I've done parent workshops, student-led workshops on peace and nonviolence, and, more recently, more historical workshops connecting students to their heritage and culture. I've done all this deep enrichment work outside of teaching a full load of classes from history to government. Dedicating my teaching style to improving the school's culture and climate while also building a bridge between students, teachers, parents, and administrators would be sweet. Unfortunately, it saddens me to say I'm resigning at the end of this school year. Venaya has been accepted to a veterinarian school in California." Mr. Hardaway quickly responded, "Erv, that's fantastic for Venaya. How about she attend school out West, and you and the kids stay here?" "Brother, that will not work," I replied. "We are a family. We are going with her. I know this sucks because we had so much more innovation to bring to this small school. This was only your first year as principal and our first year working together." "I'm devastated," he said. "However, I understand and respect your choice. I'm sure it will be a rough day letting the students know. I support you here, and anywhere you go. We will keep in touch." He extended his arms across the table, and we clasped hands, leaning into a hug. I walked out of his office with a heaviness unlike any other day. I prepared myself to make it through an entire day by sharing the bittersweet news.

Later that evening, I drove to my parents' small and cozy house. I hoped they would be proud of my decision to move my family across the country to pursue my wife's lifelong dream of becoming a veterinarian. As I drove slowly down the street we moved on in 1986, I soaked up the nostalgic thoughts like a sponge. I gazed at each house I passed until I reached my parents' house. I exited my car and hopped up the front steps, and my dad opened the door like clockwork. I followed him through the kitchen, bearing remnants of the baked chicken they had for dinner, which teased my nostrils. I made a sharp right past the antique clock and phone and onto the stairs, keeping a close pace behind my dad. I continued walking behind him into my parents' room.

Seeing the old bedroom dresser with the large mirror attached felt so comforting. The huge king-size bed took up seventy-five percent of the room. I dropped to my knees and leaned on the bottom of my parents' bed. My dad's side of the bed was disorganized, with a pile of clothes on it. My mom's side of the bed was neat, tidy, and clean, with an air of freshness. The glare of the television illuminated the room, along with the light from the sunset moving down the wall. My little brother was glued to the TV watching Lebron James and the Cleveland Cavaliers face off against Tim Duncan and the well-coached San Antonio Spurs. My parents lay at the head of their bed, eyes locked on game one of the NBA Finals. Typically, I feel tightness and tension in my body before I share something important. My heart would race back and forth, and my thoughts would collide like molecules. And, of course, I would have butterflies in my belly. I waited patiently, cheering, and rooting for the outmatched Cavaliers as they struggled to compete with the superior Spurs. It was exciting and frustrating to watch Lebron put on a one-person show.

I'm sure he yearned for someone, any of his teammates, to give him help. The tension I had anticipating their response to my news was transferred to the stress of wanting the Cavaliers to win the first game in the series. Watching the game as a family was a ritual we had always enjoyed since childhood. This gave me time to build up the courage to share the news. Phew! It was now halftime. I took the opportunity to turn the volume down on the television. I said, "Ma, Dad, Eric. Venaya got accepted into a veterinary school in California. We knew it would be possible, so we've been looking for a place to live. I've also sent my resume out to a few schools. We will be moving in a few weeks." There was a deafening silence, a stillness, that filled the room. I reached out and playfully tapped my brother on his head, saying, "Isn't this exciting? We're moving to California."

He just gave me a blank stare. In a dry tone, my mother said, "This is what she wanted. We are happy for her. California is really far away to move the whole family for school." I nodded my head, not daring to respond. "Hey, Dad," I said as he lunged from under the covers and told my little brother, "Go get their going away gift." As heartbroken as my family was, they knew the day would come when it would be time for me to leave. My brother brought in a banner with the words. "Good luck in California. We will miss you all, and we love you all." My whole family stood up. I hugged my brother, and I hugged my mom. Before I could hug my dad, I stopped.

I was in total disbelief. My dad, a man not big on sharing emotions, was rubbing the corner of his left eye. If I wasn't mistaken, I believe moisture or tears were developing in the corner of his eyes. He tried to act as if he was okay but couldn't hide his emotions. My pops, super strong, super manly, was wiping tears away from his eyes. I was beyond shocked. Nevertheless, I was touched and moved by this tender expression of emotion. Halftime was now over. The third quarter started. The Cavs were getting beaten mercilessly by the Spurs. My dad and I went into the basement to play a few grueling pool games and listen to the Temptations. One of his favorite songs blasted through the stereo, "Sorry is a Sorry Word for All that I've Done for You." He won seven games to my six. I left and went to an old-school 80s and 90s party.

May 22, 2007, Surprise

For the past few days, I have had a horrible headache, sore throat, cough, and stuffy nose. I returned to school after taking a few days off without time to prepare a lesson plan. I am struggling through the fourth period. Now, Timika Barnes wants to walk and talk about her family situation. She walks to Ms. Billingsley's room, and as I walk in, the lights come on. I hear a thunderous roar of students and teachers all over the room. Shouts of "Congratulations" and "We will miss you" ring out. I am extremely touched, thankful, and overwhelmed by this surprise party, which I learned was planned by my student, India. She made invitations, bought pizza and snacks, and was able to keep it a secret from me. When you spread love, everyone is encouraged to spread it by your example, and it continues on and on. This event inspired me to press on. Likewise, I am sure India's life will forever be changed by planning this event.

May 25, 2007, Bittersweet

Today started early, and it has become increasingly irritating and frustrating. It is the last day for our seniors. Unfortunately, a small army of seniors collectively led a coup d'état through the school by trashing it and screaming throughout the halls. They did their very best to wreak havoc and piss off as many adults as possible. Then, on the other hand, other seniors wanted to spend their last day talking with their favorite teachers, socializing with other seniors and first- and second-year students, getting yearbooks signed, and just having a fun free last day to remember their high school. However, the coup d'état was so damaging that the principal announced over the loudspeaker that all seniors leave the building within ten minutes or be prosecuted for trespassing. Simultaneously, I felt rage and sadness. The lack of self-regard and respect from students and administrators epitomizes the need for a new construct for high school. *Submitting to authority or rebelling against authority are the only two choices in the organizational and institutional structure of the system called school. The system of authority does not allow many options and freedom for teenagers. Therefore, teenagers react and rebel with destructive behaviors. Too much energy and resources go into punishment and control.*

Going Away Picnic

I feel very happy, joyful, tearful, and thankful as family, friends, coworkers, and students gathered to wish us well on our journey. We enjoyed poetry, watched praise dancing, and heard people speak about how we touched their lives. One poet recited an amazing poem about the commitment my wife and I shared to create a better world. Venaya's sister rented an ice cream truck. Venaya's aunt cried and struggled to sing "If I Could." I gave a speech about the importance of discovering the courage to sing your song in your own voice.

My sister yearns to be open and vulnerable. Her defenses, however, hold her captive. She pulled me aside to say she wanted to say a few words, but that she didn't because I had asked her. My cousin Glenn gave me words of encouragement. "You're a mentor to so many at thirty. That's special." My cousin Sheila said, "You have that special glow and are comfortable with yourself. You have the touch. The light." I had an extremely valuable talk with my Uncle Jesse, my dad's brother, about the past and his relationship with my father. My uncle revealed that he was born in Tennessee. He and my dad had different fathers, and they were never close due to the age difference. My uncle waited for this special moment to share this information. I never knew much about my father's past, so I sat and absorbed all the information my uncle could provide. He said my dad played basketball and stayed in the streets. With no positive male influences, my father was alone.

I guessed right. My father never addresses the pain of being fatherless. When my Uncle Jesse finished, his daughter, Nikki, expressed her frustration with her dad's controlling ways, which are similar to my father's character. Uncle Jesse's wife, Aunt Theresa, ended the conversation with, "If you want to know your family's history, talk with my Aunt Nancy." This thirty-minute conversation was so rich, deep, meaningful, and eye-opening.

Finally, with me by her side, Venaya tearfully expressed her appreciation for all the love and support from everyone. My teenage friend Aquib and I had a few nostalgic conversations about our high school days. It warmed my soul that he brought his family to our event. A dozen high school students showed love and appreciation for my family. Marvin Mayweather, one of my dearest students, slam poet, and Hip Hop artist, ended the event with an original piece dedicated to my legacy at Winston Willis High School. He received a standing ovation. The celebration ended one chapter in our lives and opened another. Regretfully, after everyone left, we felt outraged that someone stole money and checks from our gift box.

CHAPTER 12

Adapting To Change/ Trust Instincts

"The real man smiles in trouble, gathers strength
from distress, and grows brave by reflection."
Thomas Paine

I finished packing my small orange Chevy Aveo with my wife and five cats. I found a quote often repeated by many that inspired me before my drive to California. "Appreciate the past, contemplate the future, and enjoy the gift of the present." In other words, the past is a memory, the future is a mystery, and the present is a gift. We pulled onto the driveway at 10:30 a.m. on June 27, 2007. We drove thirty-six hours across the country to a new place and world filled with challenges and opportunities in preparation for our greatness. This new journey will make or break us. On the first night of our trip, I drove straight from Ohio to Iowa. There was no scenery. I wanted to drive longer. However, we stopped at a cheap, dirty motel with our five cats. The next day, we were up around 6 a.m. We ate breakfast, and I pushed through Nebraska until we discovered Colorado's beautiful, scary, and adventurous terrain. We drove nine hours through the twisting, turning, narrow ledges and enormous, gigantic mountains.

My little Aveo sputtered, screamed, and hollered as it reluctantly climbed each mountain. We made it through Colorado into Utah. Venaya drove two hours, and we settled into a better hotel with the five cats. That night, we went out for dessert, watched a movie, and fell asleep. The following day, we ate breakfast and headed back on the road. We drove past the beautiful ancient petroglyphs and pictographs in Utah. A few times, we stopped to get closer to the amazing structures covered with red dirt. Venaya snapped a few photos of me at the top of a mountain. We were in awe as we drove past the natural landscapes and viewed beautiful sunsets. Next, we went through Arizona and Nevada. We stopped in Nevada to get gas. The heat strangled and choked the life out of me. It felt like I was inside an oven. This type of heat was a new experience for us. We then drove through Nevada and continued on a straight incline to the higher elevations toward California. In California, the smothering heat continued as we drove past the desert in Palm Springs, heading towards our destination.

Cars and trucks zoomed by like a NASCAR race as we approached civilization. The speeding vehicles and multitudes of people were stressful and overwhelming for me—not to mention the 100-degree plus heat. Finally, we arrived at our destination at 6 p.m. The cross-country trek was now complete. Our townhouse was small, cozy, and neat. Our kids had the luxury of flying to California with their beloved aunt, Kaya. We watched a movie on the first night in our new home and ate questionable Chinese food.

I tossed and turned in bed all night, which felt like a sauna. In the distance, I could hear my wife calling my name from downstairs. She was wailing, "Musa, Musa, are you ok? All you do is sleep!" I rolled over again and again, not sleeping and not being awake. I was stuck. This was my first week in a new state, and I was hibernating like a bear. I had made a suffocatingly hot bed my safe space from sadness, confusion, and deep despair. I felt scared, paranoid, and unsettled. My energy level was pointing towards emptiness. However, a bright side of the week was hanging out with Venaya's youngest brother, Troy. Troy had been in Southern California for over a decade. He left the Marines and made California his permanent home. Troy is among the most dapper, gifted, and charismatic people I have ever met. He is a creative being searching for that higher spiritual awareness and guidance by studying Taoism. His wit and sense of humor can light up the room. Troy is an excellent cook. He tears it up in the kitchen and is an inspiring actor. Troy brings fun and excitement to all. He wants to grow and elevate his abilities and leadership to a broader audience. Troy and I resonate with each other as, like me, he was born under the fire sign of Leo. We both say, "Y'all can hate us, but y'all can't break us."

Troy invited us to Venice Beach with his girlfriend. When we arrived, my heart was beating rapidly. I held my children's little hands in anticipation of seeing the Pacific Ocean. We strolled on the boardwalk. My eyeballs moved around like a pinball machine. I saw people rollerblading, riding bikes, jogging, and performing. We continued to walk beyond the boardwalk, passing volleyball nets, picnic tables, and basketball courts until we reached the beach's sand. I looked out at the vast ocean. The sound was terrifying yet soothing. We looked further down the beach and saw a shirtless figure waving enthusiastically to get our attention. My kids shouted, "Uncle Troy!" They ran towards his chiseled physique. He scooped them up and yelled, "Wuzz up!!!!!!" He heightened his voice like a pirate and spun the kids senselessly until they looked like they wanted to vomit. He led us to a special area on the beach for our picnic. Troy introduced us to his girlfriend, Coconut. We ate delicious snacks and watched the kids run around the sand for an hour. I was grateful to have a family member in California. Venaya told her brother, "I'm so happy we are together. I know you're busy, and I'll start vet school soon. However, let's make sure we spend time together."

Our next adventure was meeting Venaya's father's childhood friend Alvin, who lives in the Inland Empire on the outskirts of Los Angeles. He drives a trailer for Hollywood movies. He has an incredible home tucked far from the city's madness and smog. Venaya's family was visiting California. A cookout was planned for them before they flew back to Cleveland. Venaya's oldest sister is the best aunt. While we drove across the country, she flew our kids to Disney World. We relaxed at Alvin's house, ate good food, and watched our kids and their cousins swim in the pool. I couldn't stop thinking about the emptiness and loneliness that would befall us once our family had left. We all felt but did not express this collective sadness as the night progressed. The wonderful day we had, had come to an end. We bunched together for one last picture. Under the shiny, bright stars, we hugged each other tightly. Venaya shared tears as we said our goodbyes. My children were sad and became uncooperative because they did not want to be separated from their cousins and aunts by three thousand miles.

After arriving home, Naimah and Venaya cuddled in bed and watched our favorite dance documentary, *Rize*, until they drifted off to sleep. I could not fall asleep. The apprehension and tension flowing through my body kept me up. The next day, however, I awakened with a charge of energy. This was the first time I did not sleep the entire day. I went to the library, scrolled through teacher sites, and uploaded my resume and cover letter. With each click of the mouse and submission of my resume, something deep within me strained for expression. I had another itching outside of teaching. I sent my last resume with a huge sigh of relief and anticipation of how I wanted to spend my time tomorrow.

The next day, I woke up at 6:30 a.m. I shuffled to the kitchen, shoved tart pineapples in my mouth, then tiptoed upstairs to shower. My heart fluttered as I stood in the shower, anticipating my destination today. I wore my old polyester dark blue suit with small polka dots and a butterfly collar shirt. I threw some oil in my locks that I tied in a bun. I slid out of the house, jumped in my car, and towards the 10 West highway. The traffic moved slowly as I struggled to focus while heading to my destination. I had driven an hour when I exited the highway towards downtown Los Angeles. The massive buildings, crowds of people, smog, and abject poverty stimulated my senses beyond control. Driving in downtown LA, I could feel the thrill and euphoric pulse of the city. I hit a hard left on Third Street and went through skid row. My spirit, heightened as I left home, was lowered as I saw hundreds of people who were homeless. The swift change of scenery from poverty-stricken communities into prosperous ones baffled my senses. I continued on Third Street and wondered if I was heading in the right direction. I remembered that Troy lived on La Brea Avenue, and if I continued west on La Brea, I would reach my destination. I pulled out the address I had written on a sheet of paper and looked up at the numbers on the street. I didn't see the address I was looking for. Confused yet determined, I spotted a parking space and impulsively parked my car there. It was only a few blocks from Third Street. I hopped out of my car and headed to Third Street to find Q Modeling Agency.

In college, I shaved my head and got attention for my dark chocolate skin and high cheekbones. It didn't hurt that it was the 90s when Ralph Lauren had opened the door for Black male models after christening Tyson Beckford, the first Black male supermodel. I loved wearing Polo, Tommy Hilfiger, J Crew, and Benetton. In addition to those brands, I had a creative urban grunge style that attracted attention. I shopped at thrift stores and adored wearing retro designs from the 70s and 80s. I had quite the eccentric style in college, plus Black men were in.

The passion to become a model never left me. Since I was now living in Southern California, I thought, why not try to model professionally even if I am only five feet seven inches tall! Walking down Third Street, I finally saw the words "Q Modeling Agency of Los Angeles." Unfortunately, it was not open. I was an hour early and had time to explore the city. I walked back to my car and was disgusted to see I had a ticket on my window. I spot the ticket person placing a ticket on the vehicle in front of mine. "Geesh," I belted. "Fifty dollars!" I said, looking at the small yellow paper. I got in my car and slammed the door. I continued driving west until I saw the Beverly Hills sign, the sign I had seen in so many movies.

I cheered and smiled, knowing I was actually in Beverly Hills. This time, I found a legitimate parking spot before I continued on my new adventure. I kept driving. I looked up at the street sign. My eyes widened as I saw Melrose Avenue. I was excited with each step I took. I absorbed fancy cars, picturesque women, and designer stores. Curiosity inspired me to walk inside a designer store. Nothing was great about the clothes, but the price tags were astronomical. The store bored me, so I continued walking and stumbled upon Rodeo Drive. My jaw hung low as I gazed upon several Bentleys, a Maserati, exotic BMWs, and a limited-edition Mercedes Benz. I walked up to an all-black Mercedes Benz sports coupe with a lion design on the hood. I laughed as I spotted the paparazzi following someone across the street.

The hour quickly went by. I hopped back into my car and drove back to the modeling agency. I confidently slipped inside the narrow door and jogged up the steep stairs leading to a small office door. I walked inside and saw two women, two desks, and a few bulletin boards bearing the headshots of models. I happily and hesitantly made my way to one of the desks. The woman calmly said, "Are you here for the open call?" Before I could say anything, with minimal eye contact, she fired two more questions in a robotic tone, "How tall are you? And do you have any pictures?" I handed her my headshots and shyly stepped back as she scanned them. I hoped for some positive feedback. She asked again, "How tall are you?" I lied and said, "I'm five feet nine inches tall. I mustered a kernel of courage and asked, "What about my pictures? What do you think?" Alas, she made eye contact with me. She responded with a small smile and semi-pleasant tone, "You're a beautiful man." I quickly responded, "I know I'm photogenic, with the perfect physique." She swiftly cut me off and said, "Do you want me to be honest?" My body tensed up as my teeth grinded together. "Sure," I said, "Sure." So, she said, "It's a smaller market for males. It's a small market for Black males and an even smaller market for Black males with locks. Most men cut them off. Are you willing to sacrifice that? You have a specific look, and we want versatility in our male models. All male models need to be at least six feet tall. Here is a list of other agencies in the area." She finished. I slowly walked away as another woman whizzed past me and stood exactly in my spot. I heard the receptionist say, "You're not what we're looking for."

I left the office absorbing the sting of defeat and the hope for success with different agencies. I sat in my car and pulled out the list of other agencies. I called each one and inquired about the requirements for open calls. I returned home feeling confident even after being rejected by the agency. I was as giddy as a little boy in a toy store after my epic experience in LA and Beverly Hills. I was eager as a beaver to persist in the modeling and entertainment business. My happiness abruptly ended when Venaya said, "What did you do today? Did you have any luck finding a teaching job yet?" For some reason, a question from my wife naturally evoked a defensive stance in me.

I firmly stated, "Finding a teaching job out here is tough. It's all about who you know. I went to a modeling agency today and received a kind rejection." Venaya snarled and said, "You spent your entire day at a modeling agency when you could have used that time to search for a teaching job?" I squinted my eyes and stuttered a response, "I've been stressed lately. I needed a day to get away, plus modeling, acting, and entertainment have always been my dream. I know we are here to follow your dreams, but I see nothing wrong in exploring my dreams as well." She fired back, "Are you in a fantasy world? Can you tell the difference between fantasy and reality? We have young kids and bills to pay, and the cost of living is so high. I will start school soon, and you wasted time today trying to be a model? I can't be with you. You are such a child!" She exited the cozy living room, leaving me to marinate in anger, despair, and helplessness.

July 15, 2007,

California Mosque, Strategies to Cleanse the Heart from Within

Friday is a holy day for Muslims around the world. We attend the Friday Jumuah prayer. This Friday message always comes when I need a potent reminder of how important my faith and spiritual practices are to my well-being. It's cool because this is my first Friday prayer in California. I walked into the mosque. It's crowded from front to back and side to side. Brothers are shoulder to shoulder, all representing continents and countries from around the globe. Watching brothers dress in bright, colorful garments to honor this day is enjoyable. Many have left work to attend the weekly Khutbah or sermon. In Cleveland, I usually arrive late.

Arriving late here, I am squeezed into the middle of the back row. For some reason, I enjoy the clamped closeness of the mosque. I sit, feeling the warm air circulated by a few ceiling fans. The imam or spiritual leader takes his place on a wooden raised platform and delivers his message. He begins by reciting verses from the Holy Quran. He gives the sermon in Arabic, the language in which the Quran was revealed. It's tough to focus during the Arabic part as one whose language is English. Thankfully, I can recognize a few words from studying the language.

Nevertheless, I rely on the imam's influx of tone of voice to stay focused. After he completes reading in Arabic, he translates his Khutbah into English, saying, "Strategies to cleanse the heart from within. Don't be a slave to your desires. Don't worship yourself. Ask for forgiveness, and repent. Pray. Remember Allah through Ibadah (acts of worship), reciting the Quran, and learning and understanding the meaning of the Quran. Lastly, remember death as it knows no boundaries, color, age, ethnicity, or status. The real jihad (inner struggle) is to conquer your inner self; then, you can conquer injustice, calamity, and falsehoods and spread the truth. You will be held accountable for who and what you worship besides Allah. Allah forgives all sins, big and small, fornication and adultery. We can all follow this example and forgive each other."

The imam finishes with another supplication called a dua as we raise our hands in unison. We then line up shoulder to shoulder in perfect symmetry for the jummah prayer. Our prayer was now over. I hug brother after brother, embracing each hug as a symbol of brotherhood, unity, and worldwide community. As I returned to my car, I reflected on what the imam shared concerning conquering or confronting your inner struggle (jihad). Once this is done, you can conquer systems of hatred and injustice. I thought I had many internal struggles to conquer.

I feel like such a fool. My ego, however, will not let me express this vulnerability to the one who has been there for me and with whom I share my life. I realize the distance of resentment between us has grown like the huge ancestral vines of an oak tree. Our relationship feels meaningless, cold, and detached. I think we both want out. I have built up tension from moving 3,000 miles away from a thriving teaching career and a budding motivational speaking business. Venaya hates how selfish I am and how I continue to prioritize my needs over our family's needs. I have been searching for a teaching job I am not invested in, nor do I give a shit about. I am all about myself right now, but I am afraid to admit it. I am scared to leave the relationship and afraid to admit that I am confused. Our bed is cold at night. My wife stated she needed me to babysit the kids while she studies for her veterinary degree, then she would ghost my selfish, childish ass. Am I only worth watching our children while my brilliant wife presses forth toward her dream? Venaya is independent. She is focused. Is she better off without me? My thoughts were twisting me around like a contortionist at the circus, even though I was in no mood to express my true feelings and needs. I want to ignore, distract, avoid, and pretend. It seems like I am in a perfect place to pretend. I want to act, entertain, and model. I want to be a Hollywood star while my marriage crumbles like a dry blueberry muffin. Venaya has checked my ass, and I have lost my will and care to fight.

This is my rant as I sit in the living room watching our children play outside. Suddenly, I realized I had not read a book in quite a while. I contemplated several books I could read and selected *The Isis Papers: The Keys to the Colors* by Dr. Francis Cress Welsing. At that point, I had nothing to lose. Thankfully, I loved digging into a great book. So, I decided to read after the children were asleep. Since Venaya and I weren't really on speaking terms. I got comfortable in my cozy living room, grabbed refreshments, and opened the book. I briefly read the introduction and prologue, which piqued my interest. I stopped and skimmed through the headings of each chapter. I read the chapters on symbols and the symbolism of Christ. I wanted to stop in the middle of the chapter on the symbolism of Christ, but as tired as I was, I continued searching for an answer. I finished scanning other chapters and was ecstatic to read more, hoping to find an arsenal for my intellectual weaponry.

Maybe I was reading out of desperation as I faced the bleak reality that the only relationship, I had known in my young adulthood was ending. Or perhaps I was an imposter pretending to be something in my relationship I am not. With every turn of the page, my palms and brow sweat as if misty phlegm had covered my entire body. It felt like a mouse trapped in a maze, hoping for a way out or a way to stay in. Surprisingly, my weary eyes stumbled upon chapter 23, "The Crises in Black Male/Black Female Relationship: Is it a False Problem?" I resisted, thinking the chapter could not help my situation. Anyway, I decided to read on since the title was provocative. I became intrigued after reading the first two pages. I was especially interested in the statement, "We keep talking about the problem without identifying the problem beneath." I drooled. I wanted more. The words "problem beneath" piqued my senses and awakened my spirit. Dr. Welsing stated, "When the underlying dynamic is exposed, analyzed, and understood, it is possible to remedy the symptom (false problem)."

"The short and long-term tactics will be developed when the underlying cause is discovered, addressed, and neutralized, then the false problem will wither away. If we find the real cause, then Black male/Black female alienation will yield true harmony." Wow! I wiggled and shook my knees erratically back and forth while making a high-pitched sound of pure jubilation. I said, "Dr. Welsing, I am all yours! Tell me. Show me and guide me to the real cause." Dr. Welsing touched on how Apartheid (white supremacy) put a social and economic strain on the Black male/female relationship in South Africa. I thought, yes, historically, slavery forcibly separated males from their families and forbade them to marry. Warmer. Warmer! Dr. Welsing continued, "We fail to realize the fundamental dynamic of white supremacy has been untouched. We need an in-depth analysis of the global behavioral phenomenon of white supremacy. Most non-White people are victimized in all areas of their life: economics, education, entertainment, labor, law, politics, religion, sex, and war." Warmer! Warmer! "Failure to analyze the white supremacy dynamic deeply is a tragedy because this dynamic is the fundamental cause of the failed relationships between Black males and Black females," Dr. Welsing wrote.

During slavery, enslavers separated Black couples for eleven months out of the year. The past is the present. Today, there are more African American female-headed households. Dr. Jawanza Kunjufu states, "Black single moms love their sons and raise their daughters." This creates strong women and weak men. Likewise, this creates a destructive, self-fulfilling cycle of relationships between the two. If Black boys are typically spoiled, they grow up ill-equipped to deal with society and the institutions that oppress Black men more harshly than Black females. Black males are victimized severely by the racist system of policing and the racist policies of the education system. This excessive and disproportionate pressure on Black males by global white supremacy produces a grave imbalance between the Black king and queen, who were both victimized. Suddenly, I thought about my victimization. My mind traveled back through some intense moments of my life.

We say goodbye to all our friends. I pick up my infant daughter and grab my wife's hand, and we walk down the dark street to get into our car. Before we pull off, my daughter fusses, cries, and falls asleep in the car seat. I drive down the street and stop at a red light. Feeling tired from a long night, I slowly pull off as the light changes from red to green. I look in my rearview mirror, and I notice something strange." Venaya, baby, something isn't right. A car is following closely behind us with the headlights off." Before she could respond, bright police lights began flashing. I pull over to the side of the poorly lit road. My heart is racing, and a lump develops in my throat. I look at my wife and say, "Bay, this always happens to me. Just stay calm." Two officers slowly walk up to the car. One officer shines a bright flashlight directly into the car on the passenger side. The other officer approaches my side. I roll my window halfway down. The officer says, "You ran that red light." I responded, "No, officer, I did not run that red light." "Show me your license," he retorts. I reach into my jacket, and to my surprise, I have no wallet or license. I sigh deeply, realizing I left my wallet in my other jacket at school. With deep regret, I reply, "Officer, I don't have my license on me." "Well, give me your full name, number, address, date of birth, social security number, work address, and work phone!" he demanded. As I gave him the information he requested, I could feel the bright light shining on the innocent faces of my wife and daughter. The officer says, "We will be right back." We sat in the car for ten, twenty, thirty minutes.

My whole body is tight, and my mind is racing. What's about to happen next? My wife seems nervous and uneasy as she waits. Our infant daughter is still asleep. After about forty-five minutes, both officers return to the car. One flashed the flashlight on Venaya again, and the other came to my window. The officer says, "I need you to take a fingerprint test." I watch him pull a black fingerprint pad out of his pocket. I paused. Taking a deep breath, I say, "Excuse me, officer, I'm not sure I've ever heard of such a test. Would you please explain it to me in more detail?" Silence. I could feel the heavy tension. My heart began to pound in my chest like a drum. The officer shouts with an angry tone, "Are you going to do it or not!" I did not respond. Seven to ten seconds pass, and then the officer reaches into my vehicle and attempts to pull me out through the window! His hands are on my jacket, pulling and tugging on me. My neck gets caught around my seatbelt. My wife screams in terror, "His seatbelt is choking him! His seat belt is choking him!" The officer holding the flashlight pulls out pepper spray and screams at Venaya, saying, "Shut up before I spray you with it!" He then comes around the car to help his partner pull me through the window.

Fortunately, my wife could reach across the seat and managed to unbuckle my seatbelt. The officers yank my body through the window and slam me on the concrete street. They pick me up and slam me on the hood three more times. Then, one officer puts both hands around my throat, choking me. I am gasping for air as spit flies from my mouth. The officer yells, "You spit on me. You spit on me. That's assaulting a police officer!" One officer keeps his hands locked around my throat, and the other officer yanks and pulls both of my arms behind me, trying to cuff me. He yanks my arms with such force that I experience a sharp pain, grinding, and popping of my right shoulder. The strength of his pull made me hit the ground again. I brace my body without any resistance and keep it tense through the assault. They finally scoop me off the ground and cuff me. As they shove me in the back of the patrol car,

I could hear Venaya shouting in panic, "I don't know where I'm at. Where is the police station? Where do I go?" I could hear the officer scream, "Shut up before I arrest you too!" I am squirming in the back seat as it pulls away, leaving my wife and daughter on a dark, empty road late at night. I was overcome with anger and rage. I started shouting curse words! I slid down in the back seat, propping my feet against the window, dividing them from me. I begin to kick the window like a mule repeatedly. I tried to shatter it! Laughing, one officer placed a 2 x 4 board between us to neutralize the force from my kicks while the other turned on a country music song at full blast! They laugh! They giggle! Suddenly, the car stops.

The officers pull me out of the car. I look around, and it's black, completely dark. One officer takes the cuffs off of my wrists. I freeze with terror. We stare at each other for what seems like an eternity. They are silent, and I freeze like a statue. I tell myself, "If you move, blink, sneeze, or stumble, you will die!" Then, the officer makes the cuffs tighter around my wrists and places me back into the squad car.

Finally, we arrived at the police station. They placed me in a small police van. I sit in that tiny, cramped box for twenty minutes with pain and blood-stained wrists from the tight cuffs. Finally, they took me to the station and booked me. I asked the booking officer, "What am I being charged with?" He says, "Obstructing official police business." I was taken to a jail cell, where I slowly limped inside. My body is sore with intense pain in my shoulder, and my clothes are torn and wrinkled. Sitting on the rusty bench in the dark cell, all I could think about was the safety of my wife and daughter. I got down on the dirty floor and pushed my body weight up and down until my body was limp.

I dropped to the floor like the weight of a steel frame. I do 100 pushups to ease my mind and pass some time. After a few hours, I and all the inmates went to a common area to watch television. I shared my story with other inmates. Our conversations were eye-opening, but I am still in shock because I am in jail! Eventually, our television time ends, and an officer escorts me to my cell. I could hear a man screaming a deadly horrific scream from a distance. He did this for hours. His screams echoed throughout the entire jail.

As I continue to sit in my cell, I hear the secretary saying with an attitude each time she picks up and slams the phone back on the receiver. She scowled, "Morris Ervin is here. Yes, he is here. Morris Ervin is here!" I get one phone call and use it to contact my teacher, for whom I'm a student teacher. I am embarrassed to tell her I am locked up and will not be at school the following day. The next morning, my bail was posted. I cautiously walk towards the front of the police station, where over twenty people are waiting anxiously to see me. My wife rushes towards me and wraps her arms around me. My mom, dad, sister, and brother all hug me, along with my friends and Muslim community members. Standing in this sea of support, I realize I am loved.

CHAPTER 13

Coming of Age, Confronting Racial Tension

"Perhaps the turning point in one's life
is realizing that to be treated like a victim
is not necessarily to become one."
James Baldwin

It is the day of the pre-trial, and I am pretty nervous. I spent the entire morning thinking about it. I met with my lawyer, and we went over the case details. However, during our conversation about my documents, I realized he has no experience trying cases like mine. He is a Muslim brother who is offering his services for free. Despite all this, it makes me cringe and deflate inside like a flat tire. Later, I head to the court and wait for it to open. It opens, and I walk inside. Then, to my shock and disgust, both officers casually walk into the elevator, standing right across from me. I stare directly at them. Looking at them makes my blood boil. Alarms go off, and fireworks of rage explode inside of me. They give an evil smirk of victory. I imagine myself pouncing on them like a mountain lion on its prey.

Ding. The doors open, and we walk out. I stand and listen to what sounds like gibberish as the judge spouts details of that uneventful night. Standing, I notice that my body is becoming tense and tight. My tear ducts fill with tears. I stand frozen. I stand helpless. My good brother, the lawyer, prepares his case, and when he is summoned to speak, he speaks briefly and articulately. I need clarification as to what's about to happen. Then, the judge vehemently says, "I have listened to both sides of the story. I will drop all charges if you are willing to do a few days down at a diversion program. Or, if you choose to fight this and take it to trial and lose, you will face dire consequences." I turn to my lawyer and ask, "Will I be able to have my wife testify on my behalf?" My lawyer shares my question with the judge. The judge responds, "Although your wife was there that night, she is impartial, and her witness testimony will not count." I sink. My lawyer says, "Judge, please give us a moment." My lawyer looks at me and says, "Brother, I would take the diversion class. They're willing to drop all of the charges."

"Listen," he continues, "You are in school and teaching. This will put a lot of stress and strain on you. And, if you don't win the case, there's a lot to lose and a lot at stake." I shake my head. I was speechless. My mind, spirit, body, and heart ached for all the men who have been harassed, taken advantage of, or brutally murdered by cops. Inside I scream, "Fight this shit! This ain't right!" Fear and reason, however, have wrapped their sensible arms around me. It is suffocating the activist in me. I realize that my good brother and lawyer is ill-equipped for this. So, despite everything my inner being is saying and everything I stand for, I accept the shitty deal. After I took the deal, something in me died.

There is a constant tension between Black youth and the police in Greater Cleveland, Ohio. The green and white patrol cars closely monitor us, especially Black male youth. The police in the gray uniforms, with matching hats and shining shoes, are sworn enemies. My friends and I have had no positive interactions with police officers. Maybe this poor relationship is because I have witnessed many unnecessary stops and frisks. I have seen so many young Black men being pulled over and having their car or person illegally searched that I wear this hatred against the cops as a badge of honor.

Police only enforce laws. They tell us what we can and cannot do in the streets. They confiscate our bicycles because they have no registration stickers on them. And, of course, they strategically position themselves all around the front entrance of our high schools at dismissal. Each week, Cleveland Commons High School dismisses over three thousand students. Some ride the school bus, some walk home, and some want to *do what teenagers do—hang out. The front steps of our school are the perfect place to socialize, laugh, joke, talk with friends, and flirt with girls. The school steps serve as a meeting place for kids trying desperately to be accepted and fit in. For Black students, relationships are built and destroyed, as the latest fashion trends are fully expressed during this free, un-sanctioned time. Reputations are made or destroyed, and urban legends are born on those stairs. Additionally, two fast food restaurants, Wendy's, and Pizza Hut, are directly across the street. Unfortunately, the cop's nefarious daily presence creates an unseen tension that is undoubtedly felt.*

So, one day after school, I was wearing my usual dapper attire: a tie-dyed shirt, Girbaud Jeans, and Puma Disc sneakers. I decided to go outside. I opened the door to the blare of ear-piercing sirens. Directly in front of me was a massive group of young Black boys fighting in the street. There were large crowds of spectators watching every second of the melee. The atmosphere is charged and lively as pockets of primarily Black students loiter, linger, socialize, jeer, and cheer as this protest disguised as rebellious teenage behavior continues. Despite all the chaos, I walk across the street to Wendy's to grab a hamburger and fries. As I walk up the driveway towards the restaurant, I lock eyes with the most racist cop on the force. We call him "Pacman." His empty blue eyes communicate hatred and animosity, especially toward young Black men. Pacman has a dirty track record of beating Black boys with batons and billy clubs just for jaywalking or trespassing. He will make you pay. As we continued the stare-down, something in me, pride, dignity, or self-respect, could not look away nor back down. As he sits comfortably on the passenger side of the squad car, Pacman lowers his window and says with disdain, "Keep it moving, boy!" Without hesitation, I shout deep from the pit of my diaphragm, "Fuck you, you racist bitch!"

The car immediately stops. The hazards flash on as both officers leave the vehicle and come directly toward me. My feet feel like cement. As I sink in the cement, my only option is to stand tall. Both officers approach me. Pacman coldly says, "What did you say?" His words were a code to humble myself, save face, back down, and bow down. I stalled a bit, noticing a crowd of students forming a human gladiator ring around the cops and me. I say, "Fuck both of y'all punk asses!" Without a word, Pacman removes his hat and suit jacket and tosses them on the hood of his cruiser. I pull my shirt off, put my fists up, and braced my weight on my back leg. I hear the crowd say in unison, "Ahh shit!" Both cops dash toward me. Suddenly, someone grabs me from behind and pulls me away from the cops and the crowd to safety.

When I was released, I turned around, panting, and holding my jugular, to see a Black police officer. He calmly says, "Are you crazy? Do you know what was about to happen to you? They would have put you in the hospital or worse! I'm Brendon's older brother. I just joined the force. I know who you are. You're a good kid. Run away from here and get home because Pacman and his boys know who you are. In a few minutes, they will be on your ass." He places his hands on my shoulder and nods while nudging me ahead. I backpedaled for a few strides, overwhelmed with gratitude and emotion, as I put my Pumas to work, turning, then sprinting all the way home through the back streets to avoid more cops.

One hot, humid summer night, friends on my street were hanging out in front of our mutual friend Jerome's home. It was late, around eleven in the evening, and we were noisy. Out of nowhere, a police car suddenly pulls up on us. Surprised and shocked, we all stopped what we were doing. With eyes as wide as the moon's light, we froze like deer in headlights. We were as stiff as mannequins in a storefront window. The cop steps out of the vehicle and approaches us. Suddenly, Devontae leaps for the bushes, and in an instant reflex, the cop draws his weapon and points it in our faces. "Freeze! Don't move a goddamn muscle!" he says. Jerome and I slowly raised our hands into the night sky as Devontae lay in Jerome's pricker bushes. The cop runs towards the bushes and motions for Devontae to get up. With his hands raised towards the night sky, the cop shoves him toward us. He pats us down like petty criminals and thugs, only finding Now and Later, and bubble gum wrappers. Finishing the stop and frisk, without a word, he retreats into his squad car, driving off into the night. We all kept our hands pointed to the night sky long after the officer disappeared. Feeling relief, Jerome and

I shoved Davontae back into the pricker bushes! It was easier to blame Davontae for his stupidity than to wrap our pre-teenage minds around being racially profiled and potentially gunned down on our street, in our neighborhood, and in front of our parents' houses.

I didn't know I was Black until I moved into a predominantly White suburban neighborhood. After unpacking some boxes when we moved into our new home, I ventured outside to survey my new community. It was the weekend before I would start fifth grade. Surprisingly, I met a new friend named Bobby Kay on one of my new neighborhood adventures. Bobby and I bonded over Gi Joe and Thundercat action figures. One day, we decided to race our bikes around our block. After finishing our race, we sat down on the sidewalk around the corner from our street to eat some Lemonheads. The sidewalk temperature was just right, with no clouds in the sky, and the breeze made me feel at ease. Then, just as we were about to get our bikes and go for a ride, a bigger White kid approached us. His big frame provided an eclipse of the sun. The day immediately became less bright. Hey Bobby, "What are you doing playing with that nigger!" I didn't understand what was happening as that word was new. However, something in my body told me something was wrong with me. I sat frozen as Bobby quickly gathered his things and left with the eclipse boy.

The first week of school was a disaster. I vomited all over the carpet while waiting in line at recess. I spent the rest of the day in the nurse's office because neither my mom nor dad could pick me up. On the second day, I redeemed myself during recess. I stepped outside on the gigantic playground. I was amazed as kids ecstatically ran wildly towards the swings and the jungle gym. Other kids formed lines to race each other on the mini track marked by four separate white lines. I made my way over to the uproar and chaos happening by the big oak tree. Each boy was wrestling to determine who was the "King of the Battle Royale." I eased my way into the line as I watched Demond Stinkley destroy and toss each competitor aside like a feather. Ever since WrestleMania 1985, featuring Sergeant Slaughter, Mr. T, Hulk Hogan, and Andre the Giant, became popular, wrestling for young boys determined one's fate and hierarchy on the playground.

Demond looked strong and unbeatable as I continued to witness his absolute dominance. I squared off against Demond, whose initial bullrush did not work against my quickness, lateral movements, and outstanding balance. He tried. I slid around him. He used his brute strength. As each second passed, I used my leverage and instincts as more kids came to see this spectacular match. Internally, I knew I could tire him with speed, quickness, and endurance. We locked horns like rams on his last attempt to slam me, and we began to spin around like gymnasts. "A tie! It's a tie." I heard voices shout in unison! Demond was crushed. As far as Demond was concerned, a tie meant a chink in his armor. On the other hand, I moved up the ladder and was recognized as one of the toughest but smallest kids in fifth grade.

As we returned from recess to class, I failed to realize my fifth-grade tyranny and alienation. Mrs. Crabapple was my White, chubby, bland, fifth-grade teacher who enjoyed her power status over her ten-year-old students. Her attire was drab, and her facial expressions were crude. She only came alive when she delivered bad news. Whenever I was in the hallway, I would observe other fifth-grade teachers. They had lively personas and enthusiastic personalities. They motivated their students. I yearned to be in their classes.

On the contrary, Mrs. Crabapple carried an attitude of callous indifference. Teaching was not a career to her. It was just a job. On the first Friday of my fifth grade, Mrs. Crabapple placed a notice on my desk and the desk of Cindy Taylor, another new Black girl in the class. The message read, "Report to room zero below the library for speech classes." Before I could finish reading the notice, a strange woman stood in the doorway and called for Cindy and me to join her. I reluctantly rose from my seat, suspicious and worried about this new situation. We followed the teacher into a desolate part of the school. Cindy and I sat down. The teacher made us read words that I quickly understood. We sounded out consonants and vowels as the teacher spoke to us in this silly, immature voice. I wouldn't say I liked the experience. Upon completing the tasks, the teacher said we would be pulled out of class every Tuesday for this mess. It left me with an empty feeling. The same feeling I felt when the eclipse boy called me a nigger. Sadly, I never told my parents. A few years earlier, I had a similar experience with another teacher.

Each morning on the noisy school bus, I would gently press my face against the window as I watched my mom get smaller and smaller. As my mother disappeared from my sight, I would keep my now puffy, teary red eyes plastered against the window, made foggy by the early morning dew. I carefully step off the bus and stand in single file, heading into the building. Ambling to my classroom, I notice that the building smells like mildew and cardboard. Before I walk in, I hear a voice that makes my heart sink towards my Velcro Nike sneakers. Mrs. Tatertot screams, "Grab a folder and sit two at a desk, and absolutely no talking!" I scramble to my seat with my backpack thudding against my small body and sit. I examine this woman from head to toe. Her Afro is short, dark, and tight to her head like a chia pet. She wears all black, and her glasses sit slightly off her round face. When she stands, the classroom gets a bit darker. I am afraid of her.

One morning, a few weeks later, as I sat at my desk humming, I felt the force of the chalk eraser hit me directly on the side of my head. "Get over here now. What is wrong with you?" she shouts. I did not realize what had happened as I scrambled to join the children on the floor in a circle. Other times, she grabbed my ear until the pain went from a sharp sensation to a burning sensation for not following instructions on time. Lastly, one day, while reading the alphabet as a class, I reluctantly raised my hand to ask to go to the restroom. I wait. I wait. I wait. She saw me and continued to move along with her lesson. Eventually, tears formed in my eyes as the moistness and odor emanated from my corduroy pants. Finally, she dallies my way and points to the door. I moved slowly out of the classroom and into the bathroom, attempting to clean myself up. It is a complete disaster. Somehow, I removed my underwear and tried cleaning them at the sink.

I have a tragic memory that makes it incredibly challenging to speak up. The event spiraled into a world of confusion and robbed me of my innocence way before racist police and teachers ever did. This silencing of my spirit led me to rage and self-violence. I remember the pure disgust of her mouth and hands on my petite body, leaving permanent stains that bleach couldn't erase. She placed my fingers inside of her. I wanted to close my eyes. I tried to get out of bed, play, or do anything that would rescue me from this strange experience. My victimization started when I was five at the hands of a sixteen-year-old predator.

Being exposed to sexually lewd acts as a child can alter the development of your brain and distort your reality. Feelings of shame, disgust, rage, and anger can form before you know what the emotions mean. Feeling alone and isolated from my family at such a tender age caused me to remain silent. After these early sexual experiences, I had weird fantasies, images, and daydreams. Mentally, I lived in a fantasy world. No one could enter that world. And, of course, I did not know what awaited me as a young Black male. I entered preschool and kindergarten raw, vulnerable, and wounded. I tried my best to protect myself from the layers of oppression at school that I could not understand, so I stayed quiet. The silence was a way to survive and protect myself from the trauma I endured. It all made sense. I was scared to open my mouth. The pain was unbearable, and I could no longer handle it. I lived in silent rage until my senior year of high school.

One Saturday afternoon, I sat in my neighborhood barbershop, waiting for my haircut. The barbershop was an incredible experience of a distinctive culture. At the barbershop, I witness fly Black male barbers wearing the latest fashions, driving expensive cars, and wearing the latest, trendiest haircuts. It was like walking into a Hip Hop video every Saturday. Every Black boy aspires to be like the young Black barbers. Sometimes, my wait was two hours. However, I knew it would be worth the wait to walk out looking like Big Daddy Kane. On one Saturday, as I was next to get my cut, another young man popped up and sat in my barber's chair.

Rather than speak up, I said nothing. I silenced myself. When the barber finished with the young man, he squinted his eyes and looked my way. He assertively said," Little Morris, you were before him." He motioned me over to him. With butterflies forming in my stomach, I slowly walked *over to him. He continued, "I was so busy I didn't realize it. Listen, you need to speak up, or life and many opportunities will pass you by. Don't hide out anymore. It's time to stand up." After that short but powerful speech, I received more than a fresh cut that day. A kernel of my truth and purpose was revealed to me.*

I snapped out of the trance. My entire body was damp with sweat. I looked at my phone. It was three in the morning. I was amazed at how I transported myself back to my early 20s, then my teenage years, to adolescence, early childhood, then back to my elementary school. The sense of clarity had awakened parts of me that were dormant. These crucial memories of victimization and criminalization have tremendously affected my identity and how I have chosen to live my life. I realize that my internal personal struggles fit a larger struggle for Black liberation. I know that digging deeply into my past helps me to experience the freedom I yearn for. My freedom is an internal process. For many years, I had associated freedom with an external process. I now realize I had allowed institutions, family members, and others to condition and define my thoughts and feelings.

Today, I create the space and time to deprogram myself. I intend to let go of this victim persona and embrace full autonomy over my life. I understand my development has been delayed, thus the selfish need to relive my teenage years. I have a better understanding of my future with the wisdom of Dr. Welsing. I now have the presence of mind to search deeply within. Today, the false perception that freedom and pursuing the American dream are external processes that will help me fulfill my whims, desires, and impulses has been challenged. I was aligned with a bigger mission brewing inside me before my family moved to that White suburban neighborhood. I have been chosen to fight for the freedom of other oppressed people. However, I am still on the journey to free myself from the destruction of my oppression.

In Dr. Welsing's The Isis Papers, she contends that Black couples should only define their joint success in terms of achieving education, housing, jobs, and money rather than explicitly countering the global and local dynamic for White genetic survival (white supremacy). We attempt to function with the wrong game manual and wrong rules. As victims of White supremacy, we spend most of our time disputing, struggling, and fighting one another. Thus, relationships go from bad to worse. We do not know how the white supremacy dynamic drives Black couples apart. If we understood white supremacy, the first priority for each Black male and female would be to master specific patterns of perception, logic, speech, action, and emotional responses that would counter white supremacy scientifically.

Further, Dr. Welsing suggests that Black couples should focus on love, marriage, and lust. Then, Black men and women would work together as a team, building and growing together. We would look outward beyond ourselves to counter the fundamental problem of eradicating the Black collective. People grow close together as long as they remain focused on the prize. By fighting White supremacy, they prevent the force of injustice from tearing them apart. This fight will ensure they stay united while expressing strong love and respect for themselves.

The grind is real. I remember spending five hours on career websites daily, emailing my resume, calling jobs, and visiting school districts. I underestimated the challenges of finding a teaching position in the large Southern California market. Despair almost filled my lungs until I remembered the Coalition of Essential Schools network from my friend Kathy. Coalition schools fit my style and creativity in teaching, as some schools are grounded in the principles of NVC. Inspired, I researched a few schools and spent the entire day applying to various Coalition schools for any mentor, teacher, or tutor opening. Exhausted from a long day of calls and voice messages, I contacted one last school called the Wildwood School.

Surprisingly, an administrator returned my call after a few days, letting me know they had no openings. I, however, was referred to a principal who was opening up a new school in Los Angeles called Creative Life Charter. I immediately called the school to set up an interview. I met with Theodore, the new school's principal. I felt comfortable sharing my experiences, especially around creating communities of nonviolence. He was delighted to hear that our missions aligned. The next day, Theodore invited me back for a second interview with the director of the school and his board members. From all directions, I received a volley of questions. It fulfilled my need for total self-expression. The energy between the administrators, the board, and me symbolized the beginning of a relationship that propelled me into my first opportunity to teach in a new and innovative school. It seemed risky, but I trusted my instincts. The board offered me a position, and I accepted it. My first assignment was to attend an all-expense paid teacher's conference in San Diego, California.

My kids and I crowded in the back of a regal, antiquated auditorium. We patiently waited for Venaya and her classmates to walk across the stage in their white coats. I sat mesmerized at the rite of passage ceremony that powerfully displayed my wife and other first-year students. In front of family, school administrators, and friends, each student swore to announce their obligation and commitment to the healthcare practice publicly. The presentation of the white coat ceremony symbolically transformed Venaya and her first-year colleagues from ordinary students to health professionals. Finally, my wife's name was called, and she enthusiastically strolled off the stage in her white coat. I felt the significance of beginning any goal with the end in mind. We anxiously waited for her outside with the other proud families. As soon as she found us, Venaya rushed over, and we all embraced under the bright California sun. Later that night, Venaya reflected on the beginning of her veterinary school journey. She said, "After a week of team building and orientation, our week concluded with a white coat ceremony. The whole week seemed surreal. We were a group of 118 people who had achieved their dreams. We had made it after years of hard work. We made it where others didn't. The ceremony made my education more purposeful. After reciting my oath, I knew I was no longer studying to pass an exam. I was studying to save lives. The feeling of accomplishment filled the room. You could hear the pride as we recited our oath."

I woke up early the following day and had breakfast with my wife. The smiles and laughter between us felt natural as I discussed my excitement about attending an open call for the Essence Festival Runway Show. We finished breakfast. I walked upstairs, and after a quick warm shower, Venaya oiled my scalp, placed my locks in a nice man bun, and suggested the perfect outfit. Of course, my selections were tasteless and terrible, so I surrendered to her fashion expertise. I let her pick out a vibrant green collar shirt with a matching tie, jeans, and my fashionable black, yellow, and green sneakers. I accessorized it with my stylish belt with the silver buckle. We embraced. She laughed before sending me out the door and said, "Now, you're ready. You look good. Have fun and good luck."

I left with a lot of appreciation and gratitude for the support she gave me. After about an hour's drive on the expressway, I pulled up to this massive dome cylindrical structure in Inglewood, California, called the Forum. I remembered the image of the historic building as the place where Magic Johnson, Kareem Abdul-Jabbar, James Worthy, and the rest of the showtime Lakers dominated professional basketball. I parked, feeling puzzled and stressed about finding a way to get in. Fortunately, a woman in a security vehicle pulled up and drove me to the main entrance. Next, I walked down a wide tunnel to a large space where gorgeous Black people were socializing with each other.

A panel of professional judges sat at the end of the makeshift runway. I signed in and received number 76. I was in awe because everything was managed by Black people working for Essence magazine—the premier magazine for Black women. Nonetheless, I was still inspired and impressed as I nervously tried to relax and take it all in. Finally, after forty-five minutes, the organizers called my number. I took a deep breath and walked up the runway toward the judges. I finish my walk, and the men motion me directly toward them. One man with a strong jawline, manicured beard, and regal presence said, "Your outfit is incredible. Bravo, from the hair to the choice of color shirt and tie. Well done." I responded, "Brother, it was all my wife." He continued, "Listen, you would kill in commercial print, television, magazines, and film. I would never put you on the runway because you're a small man." I was deflated after his statement. "Why is height so important?" I asked. "Because the clothes from designers fit better on tall men," He said. I mustered a half smile, turned, and moved a few steps away from the judges. Then, I just walked back and sat down.

I had an internal battle with myself that felt like a championship tennis match. My thoughts volleyed back and forth around taking this rejection, learning from his advice, and moving on. This distinguished gentleman, who was the director of this show, let me down easily. He spent more time talking with me than the other candidates that he had rejected. I connected with him. However, when I decided to take the risk of talking to him, I was obsessed with my thoughts about what or when would be the right time.

I knew it would be a waiting game, but when I had the opportunity, I needed to be short and sweet. I waited for forty-five minutes and watched him accept and reject other candidates. When there was a break, I sprang into action. I approached him and said, "Excuse me, sir, I am new to this area and new to modeling. I know I have the potential. However, I need guidance. Would you be willing to mentor me?" He nodded and said, "Here's my card. I will be in Cuba for a while but stay in touch. When I return, we can get together. And remember, the runway is seasonal. That's child's play. You can make way more money." I danced off the stage and out of the arena, high fiving everyone waiting outside to get in!

CHAPTER 14

Trust Your Instincts

"If I did not work so hard at creating who I am,
then the world would make it what it wants me to be."
Audre Lorde

I picked up my supportive, helpful, assertive, sister-in-law Bekaya from
the Ontario Airport. She volunteered to take care of our children. At the
same time, Venaya began her rigorous first week of school. I ventured
to San Diego, California, to participate in an all-expense paid teacher's
conference for my new job at the Creative Life Charter School. Kaya is
the backbone of the family. She is the oldest of Venaya's siblings. Despite
having no children, Bekaya mothers her nieces and nephews as her own.
She is fun, outgoing, independent, and committed to her values. Of course,
we have that in-law relationship of cracking jokes on each other, but I love
and respect her. She is my sister for life.

Finally, the sweet anticipation of Venaya's first day attending
veterinary school arrived. It always warms my heart to share precious
moments with my love. We got out of bed and planned our morning. I
intentionally scaled down my robust, animated, cartoon character energy
so Venaya had room to concentrate. I put my energy into picking out my
favorite outfit, a burnt orange/reddish collar shirt with plaid pants and
brown dress loafers. My locks were up in a ponytail. The excitement for
this day overflowed like a waterfall. Venaya moved through the morning
efficiently and effectively by putting together a crisp white dress shirt,
cute beige wide-leg trousers, elegant jewelry draped around her neck, and
a beautiful beige and white scarf. We sat in our cramped kitchen, snacking
on fruit and yogurt dressed with strawberries, blueberries, granola, and

a drizzle of honey. Leaving early, we kissed the kids and ventured off toward Western University in Pomona, California. The drive was short and pleasant. When we arrived, we saw a neat and organized campus with students walking, moving in and out of buildings, conversing, and sipping coffee in common spaces. We gently held hands while walking to Venaya's first class. Before we arrived, we talked with one of her fellow students, who snapped a cute picture of us in front of a statue.

Finally, we reached the lecture hall. My charm, smile, and charismatic personality turned up. I saw some students. As I introduced my wife, she tugged on my shirt, pulled me close, and said, "Musa, I can make my friends. I'm great. You can leave now. At that moment, I realized this was the beginning of her path, her moment, so I gracefully backpedaled out of the room so that she could fulfill her destiny.

On my next adventure, I packed my bag, fueled my orange Chevy Aveo, and drove two hours south to spend a week at a teacher's conference. I arrived at the hotel, went to my room, and quickly unpacked my luggage. I returned to the hotel lobby and asked for directions to the nearest beach. I promptly drove to the beach. I couldn't believe I was in San Diego on the beach, just a few hours from Mexico. I strolled along the boardwalk and checked out the restaurants. I noticed there were no other African American men around. As long locks flowed down my shirtless back, I became aware of the stares and smiles. I finished walking on the boardwalk and detoured directly towards the beach. I stepped on the warm sand and walked towards the water, enjoying the sounds of the ocean and the mild temperature.

As I continued to walk, a young White male walked directly toward me and extended his hand to shake mine. In a low tone, he said, "Ahh, bro, do you have some burns?" I responded, "What?" "Burn, bro? Do you have some weed?" He asked. My mood immediately went from sweet to sour. I squinted, stared at him with a menacing gaze, and said, "No." I walked away and tried to find my composure again. Then, four White fraternity-looking guys surrounded me and shouted, "Hey bro, sell us some weed. We got money!" I tensed my body, locked eyes with all four idiots, and sternly said, "I'm a Black man enjoying my time on the beach. Why da fuck would I want to be out here hustling some weed?" I raised my index finger to spew more rage. Then, I stopped before I let out more outrage. They walked away. I tried to shake off being profiled as a dreadlock-wearing drug dealer, but the anger was unbreakable and unshakeable. I knew that exercise and water would remedy my bruised soul, so I jogged into the water. I alternated between pushups and squats, pushing myself with each repetition as the waves provided the resistance I needed to cool down my rage. I focused on my anti-racism workout. After completing my exercise, I laid my towel on the sand and lay on my back to look up at the distant sun. I closed my eyes and listened to the crashing waves. I soon drifted off into a state of consciousness between wakefulness and sleep.

The following day, I arrived at the first session of the conference. At first, I was overwhelmed by the many teachers scattered throughout the hall. I went to the nearest help station for assistance. Eventually, I settled down and surrendered to the beauty and serenity of the campus with its lush palm trees, manicured lawns, and picturesque statues that consumed me. Finally, I joined my first session. I found a desk in the back of the classroom. I pulled out my notebook and listened intently as the facilitators laid out the history of education in ninety minutes. The discussion was lively, and the information was timely as it spurred me to continue researching the history of American education, particularly for African American students. Following lunch, I met with Theodore about the conference and upcoming sessions.

The last session of the day was a keynote address given by an African American woman on a program called AVID. Advancement Via Individual Determination (AVID) is an in-school academic support program for grades seven through twelve. It prepares students for college eligibility and success. AVID places academically average students in advanced classes leveling the playing field for minority, rural, low-income, and other students whose families are not college educated, and targets students in the academic middle, such as B, C, and even D students, who have the desire to attend college and the willingness to work hard. This program was new to me, and I love to learn new ways to help students become successful. The keynote speaker immediately captured my attention with her energy, storytelling abilities, passion for education, and knowledge of the AVID program, which benefited her children. I was inspired by and connected with her resilience and the adversity she overcame to pursue a doctorate while raising a family. Lastly, she entertained the vast crowd of educators with funny jokes, a razor-sharp wit, and a down-to-earth "I made it through the storm, so can you" message.

At the end of the speech, I walked to the back towards the AVID table. I came upon a spirited discussion between some AVID coordinators and AVID teachers. I overheard them share their disappointment with the speaker and how inappropriate it was for her to share that her children had benefited from AVID. I felt a rush of irritation. Her peers should not have dismissed her because she courageously shared her struggles, successes, and accomplishments. My chest tightened as I felt steam flowing through my body and out through the top of my head. I locked eyes with an African American man who also overheard the conversation. We briefly chatted about what we had heard and agreed to confront the AVID facilitator, who spoke against the speaker. However, we were abruptly stopped by an African American woman nearby. I said, "Can you believe the AVID people call the speaker inappropriate and that she does not meet the AVID criteria? Is it because she is——"

The woman stopped me and said with an annoying tone, "Before you guys attack the facilitator, it's not about race. The speaker was inappropriate and braggadocious!" Like a piping hot whistling teapot, I went off inside. With a heated tone, I raised my voice and said, "That's crazy. A Black woman celebrating her accomplishments is braggadocious? She talked about her car to lighten the mood. I heard a Black woman committed to her work. And yes, her kids benefitted from her high level of education because our struggle means much more!" She countered my argument by saying, "You are new to AVID. I've been around for a while. Take a look at the criteria. Please read it and simmer down. You are way too defensive and emotional. She was inappropriate, and her kids do not meet the criteria." I paused and tried to show some respect to this woman as she pointed to information in the AVID handbook. She shared one last point, "Her being

African American is irrelevant. The car she drives does not matter. Her economic status and college education exclude her from the criteria." At this point, I conceded. I concluded that this woman did not see African Americans' more significant struggles beyond economics and class. Any program that does not consider race separates us as Black people. I wanted no part of it. You can't erase generations of racial oppression by ignoring it. Still feeling inner rage, animosity, and heartbreak, I turned and walked toward the dessert table. My feelings from this interaction, like the deep, vast tides of the Pacific Ocean crashing on the San Diego shore, would take time to subside.

The next day during lunch, I saw a group of educators sitting at a round table towards the back of the outdoor patio. The card on the table read, "South Los Angeles High School, Los Angeles, California." Their lively discussion drew me toward their table. To my surprise, the event was a recruitment lunch. Staff from Northern and Southern California attended the event to attract young educators. Before I opened my mouth, a principal and six team members at the table introduced themselves. The principal gave me a summary of the school's history. It was in the heart of Los Angeles at the corner of Martin Luther King Boulevard and Crenshaw. They were undertaking a new and exciting pilot program for male students called Boys Inspired. He did not have to say anything else. At that moment, I knew walking over to that table was destiny. This was where I needed to be. He said, "We are looking for young, educated, energetic men like you. Here is my card and information. Please accept this position now because school will start soon. And what subjects are you certified to teach?" I cheerfully responded, "I'm certified to teach comprehensive Social Studies in grades six through twelve." He raised his glass to take a sip of water and replied, "We have an opening for a Social Studies position, so you need to move fast." Each educator then briefly shared why they loved teaching in South LA. I listened intently, knowing it was a dream come true.

I was enthusiastic at the end of the luncheon. I felt torn about telling Theodore, who had paid my way to the conference, that I would resign my position and work for another school in Crenshaw, South Los Angeles. I decided to walk around the lush campus. Fortunately, the walk to the beach was what I needed. I arrived at the beach with the beautiful palm trees swaying in the wind. The sand was whirling in the air like a perfect typhoon. I dashed towards the edge of the shoreline and began pumping my arms and moving my legs. I continued until my breathing intensified. Afterwards, I found and laid down at the perfect place and space for solitude and rest. Laying on my back close to the water; the water massaged and tickled my feet. I closed my eyes and became relaxed by the symphony of the waves that gently crashed over my feet.

The following day after a healthy breakfast, I decided to call Principal Theodore to request a meeting with him before the first seminar of the day. As I hung up the phone, I felt sweat forming in the palms of my hands and butterflies forming in my stomach. I took a hot shower and inhaled breaths of steam. I also began to obsess about my conversation with Theodore. After my mindful shower, I went to the campus, and with each step, I wanted to retreat, but my feet kept marching forward. Walking through the lobby, past the lush palm trees and picturesque view, I spotted Theodore. He was reading a newspaper and drinking brewed coffee. He hopped up and embraced me with a handshake and hug. "Good morning, Morris. How has this conference been? We are so excited to have you on our team. We have big plans for the opening of this new charter school, and we are itching to get started!" I said, "Theodore, this conference has been meaningful, informative, and transformative for me. The presenters are exceptional. This location is blissful. Thanks again for inviting me." "Yes, I know it was last minute to invite you," he said. "I'm super glad you were able to make it. Now, is there something you need to ask me?" I stumbled over my words as Theodore gently placed his mug on the small oval table. He removed his glasses and leaned across the table to view my discomfort more closely. I finally said, "Man, this is tough. I appreciate you hiring me. I love the idea of your innovative charter school. I, however, met a principal and a team of teachers yesterday that I fell in love with. I have to follow my heart, so I'm resigning from my teacher's position with your school to work at their school." Suddenly everything stood still. I assumed that expressing this would bring a release inside of me.

However, the heaviness in my chest lingered. Theodore stood up and circled the table with his hands on his hips. He removed his glasses, then put them back on. Theodore did this several times. He then sat back in his chair. I wasn't sure if Theodore wanted to yell at me or break down in tears. Looking at the ground, he softly and assertively said, "Morris, I'm crushed and disappointed in you. We invested a lot of time and energy in you in a short time. How could you betray me? How could you betray the kids, the teachers, and the families? You took the position, and now you're backing off. That's a very selfish thing to do." I inhaled slowly, and as I exhaled, all the tension and fear faded. "Theodore," I said. "I understand your shock and disappointment in me. However, I know what's best for me, and where I need to be is in South Los Angeles." He shook his head back and forth like a fifth-grade schoolgirl refusing to accept being rejected by her boyfriend on the playground. He stood up, snatched his newspaper and cup of coffee, and replied, "That's fine, Morris. This is your decision, and I can't change your mind. Be prepared to get a bill for all the expenses incurred at this conference." He pivoted and walked off into the distance.

I arrived home from my San Diego trip exhausted and hopeful about my bold decision to switch from the Creative Charter School to the infamous South Los Angeles High School. Upon entering, Kaya was sprucing up the kitchen and making grilled cheese sandwiches for the kids before they arrived home from school. I'm so thankful that Kaya was with the kids while I was away. It allowed Venaya the freedom to focus on school. Every day Venaya was up early to leave for school. She studied and took classes throughout the day, returning late in the evening just in time to see the kids before they went to sleep.

I playfully stood beside Kaya as she flipped one side of the grilled cheese sandwiches and asked, "How was it with the kids this week? I'm sure they kept you busy?" She responds with laughter, "Musa, I love your crazy kids. I kept them on a schedule. Everything was cool." Then, Naimah marched in the door from school with her backpack attached to her little body. Naimah cuts through the kitchen, and she cannonballs straight onto the couch without saying a word. Lying flat on her stomach with her face buried in the pillow, she began to make deep, weird sounds. Her arms were flailing wildly, and her legs rapidly moved like a swimmer in a pool. I attempted to continue the conversation with Kaya, but she stopped. Spatula in hand, she stared at my daughter with a blank expression. Naimah continued gurgling, grumbling, growling, babbling, and murmuring.

I gently took the spatula from Kaya's hand and flipped the cheese sandwich, now a beautiful golden brown with melted cheese oozing from the sides. Naimah finished her performance and flipped up from the couch. She removed her book bag from her tiny body and placed it beside the dining room table. Calmly, she glided into the kitchen and said, "Hey, Daddy. Hey Auntie Kaya." I pulled her close, hugged her, and said, "Hey, princess. How was your day?" She responded, "It was good," then dashed upstairs and out of our sight. I bite the sandwich as Kaya, still in shock, whispers, "Is she ok?" I ate the delicious crunchy sandwich and said, "Yes. She's cool." With a puzzled look, Kaya responded, "You don't find it odd that your daughter had an exorcism/seizure on your couch?" I laughed and said, "That's her normal routine/ritual when she has a tough day. That's how she lets it out and communicates. Then, she can move on with her evening." Kaya slowly shook her head and said, "My flight is leaving tomorrow. You and these kids are crazy!" We laughed, waiting to see what antics my son would perform when he returned from school.

August 27, 2007, The LA Grind and Shine!

Three times last week, I went to the Los Angeles Unified School District Board building in busy, congested downtown Los Angeles to take a T.B. test, interview with a recruiter, and get fingerprinted. However, I still didn't have my medical exam when I returned today. Therefore, I needed help to move forward with the process. On Thursday, I went to Bobby Ball Model Agency for an open call and quickly got rejected. I delivered headshots to LA Models Agency in downtown Los Angeles on Friday. Currently, I am getting comfortable with being a full-time dad while Venaya is a full-time vet student. Maintaining a daily schoolwork schedule, caring for the kids, cooking meals, cleaning the house, doing

laundry, and purchasing groceries is challenging. Even though I have
had many frustrating days, I'm happy about my progress.

It's a weird feeling of apprehension and excitement as I hear the sound
of my alarm clock and quietly get out of bed. I briefly stare at Venaya as
she peacefully sleeps underneath the covers. Before showering, our cats
walk with me down the hallway and guide me down the stairs to feed
them breakfast. I sit at the table, eating some oatmeal and toast. Then, I
hop up the stairs to take a relaxing shower, pray and put on my uniform.
Uniform! It's convenient to wear one. I have a gray collar shirt, khaki
pants, and comfortable black dress shoes with pointed toes and soft rubber
bottoms. I open the screen door. It was dark and serene outside. I say to
myself it's six in the morning. I have plenty of time to get to work. I jump
in my car and drive towards the highway. I spend twenty-five minutes
on the 60 West Highway until the traffic comes to a complete stop. I was
distraught by the constant stop-and-go motion until I got to Crenshaw
Boulevard. My frustration evaporates as I drive down Crenshaw past
historic streets such as Jefferson, Adams, Rodeo, and King Boulevard. I
stopped at the intersection of King and Crenshaw and became enamored
with the infamous Crenshaw Mall on the corner. Next, I make a left turn
past the Louisiana Chicken restaurant. Everything changed. There are
tidy, neat, and well-manicured homes on both sides of the street. As I
continue driving, I spot the Hollywood sign in the distance, to my shock
and surprise.

Finally, I make a right off King onto the side street where a tall
iron fence like a prison surrounds this huge concrete structure. I pull into
the small parking lot at 8:15 a.m. I was in a panic. My heart exploded. I
realize that my morning commute in traffic and my dream car ride through
Crenshaw was too long. I was exhausted after the two-hour commute. I
dash out of my car and clumsily run inside. I continue down the wide
hallway until I find the secretary's office. She is occupied. Her face is stern
but sweet. She sees my distress and calmly says, "You must be the new
Social Studies teacher. Here is your schedule. Your room is upstairs on the
second floor." I take the schedule, barely having time to say thanks and

go upstairs. I become distracted as I peer through a large hallway window that leads to an enormous outdoor campus. It is filled with many Black and Brown students bustling with noise and energy, ready to barge into the school.

I continue upstairs, turn left, and enter my room. It has desks, a chalkboard, and, surprisingly, no windows. I organize the desks into a neat circle. The school bell rings. It's loud and echoes throughout the room. It reminds me of a bell at a racetrack. I take one last deep breath and stand at my door. Suddenly, the hallway fills up with students. I'm impressed how the kids accessorize their uniforms with colorful sneakers—mostly all different variations of Chuck Taylors—and creative shoelaces.

At last, a few boys walked past me and quietly sat down without questions. Next, two young men walk in, look me up and down, and saunter straight to the back of the room and sit on a ledge. They ignore my attempts to speak to them. More young men with suspicious looks walk in and find seats. They look at each other. One says, "Man, what? You're in here? I'm in here with you? Ah, hell nah!" As this pattern continues, another young man with braces makes a grand entrance. I speak to him, and he laughs in my face. He points at me and yells to everyone, "I'm Maxwell, bitches!" He completes a few laps around the circle, ignoring my directions. He eventually finds a seat next to an athletic, quiet kid and a chubby kid with an Afro. Then, two young men walk inside closer than sardines in a can. One had dark smooth skin with thick brush waves, and the other had brown skin with dusty brush waves.

The latter was sporting cool ocean-blue Chuck Taylors with an LA Dodgers hat in his hand. They give me a quick nod as I welcome them. My circle was made wider to accommodate the growing number of students. The young man with the Dodgers cap had an aura of leadership and a strong presence about him. I wanted to learn more about him. A few more students enter. I leave the door open for any latecomers. Again, the boys continued to react as they looked around the circle at familiar faces. Next, to my astonishment, groups of boys and girls not in my class poke their heads in the door and shout things like "Ha ha! That's the dumbass class. Y'all bad as fuck! We're glad we ain't in there with those bad kids!"

I noticed most young men sinking lower in their seats with each negative comment as the heckling continued. Some fired back with a few derogatory comments. Others tucked their heads between their arms, seeking protection like a turtle going inside its shell. It became apparent to me that the innovative program for which I was recruited was to teach the incorrigible and insolent boys in the school. I gently embraced my rage and made space for my negative thoughts. One boy points his finger across the circle at a student and shouts, "I remember last year when you threw that chair out of the window." The boy fires back, "I remember when you pushed the teacher and ran out of the school."

Another boy jumps in, saying to another boy, "I remember when you started that riot after pulling the fire alarm." The boy responds, "I remember you got suspended for trying to sell kids fake weed with your dumb ass!" Then, another boy shouts, "Don't y'all get it? We are all here because we are bad and dumb as fuck. This school doesn't give a shit about us?" This last response creates an echo of side conversations throughout the circle. I let them talk for a few seconds, then say, "Hey, I need everyone's attention!" They grumble on and on and eventually stop their conversation. I gather the strength of all my ancestors and proclaim, "Let's prove them all wrong! I don't know what happened last year, and I don't care. I see so much anger, hurt, rage, and sadness, but I also see creativity, leadership, and brilliance around this circle. Give me a chance, and I can guarantee that all those kids laughing at you all will be begging to be a part of what we will create together. This will be hard work, however, if you all can find a way to trust me and believe in yourselves, just like that Dr. Seuss book, oh the places we'll go!" I don't care how and why they put you in this "Boys Inspired Program," but we are here. Let's make this an unforgettable year." My chest expands with pride after my first speech while my heart beats at the speed of light. I nod my head and look into the eyes of each boy in the circle in silence and solidarity until the horse track bell rings. And they vanish.

Not yet having enough time to collect my thoughts about the first interaction with my Boys Inspired twelfth grade class, I anticipate what my ninth grade all-male Boys Inspired classroom would look like. Suddenly, I hear loud rumbles from the end of the hallway. In a flash, about twelve or thirteen boys run, scream, jump, twist, turn, and kick lockers as they approach me. I manage to put my hand in the sky, allowing each boy to smack my hand with the palms of their hand. They enter the class wildly and in one disruptive force. Luckily a few sat down at desks, but a few decided to have a karate tournament and wrestling match in front of my bulging eyes. I stepped back and raised my voice with a deep baritone, saying, "Welcome, young men! Before we start, I need everyone to find a seat inside the circle."

I waited, hoping for compliance. Most of the boys, however, ignore my directions. Now, all of them are running around the room in circles or trying new wrestling moves on each other. As I watched, I was not angry, but my body was tense and tight. I felt overwhelmed, stressed, and helpless. Desperate, I raised my voice louder as I tried to usher the boys to their seats and break up each wrestling match like a WWE referee. Finally, they all sat in their seats, not because of me, but because they wanted something else entertaining to do. Visibly shaken on the inside, I am reluctant to take my seat. I choose to lean on my desk, trying to relax, yet react if needed. Then, before I could speak, a frail young man with a nice groomed appearance and crisp uniform looked across the circle and said to another young man, "Boy, look at dem razor-sharp teeth. You look like a piranha!" All the boys burst into laughter except the piranha boy. Then, the piranha boy said, "Shut up, with your little arms, looking like a Tyrannosaurus Rex!" The boys busted into more laughter. I said, "Alright, fellas. That's enough, you two.

"Welcome to my history——" another young man interrupted me and said to the person directly across from him, "Man, I'm about to roast you. Look at your Dragon Ball Z musty ass!" Before I knew it, snaps and jokes were tossed around the circle. All we needed was a campfire and some marshmallows. I'm cringing, sweating, and doing everything to bring order to my class. Nothing I did worked. In addition to the jokes, a kid with a military haircut and devilish smile impressively shows off his krump dancing moves. If I had a white flag, I would raise it and frantically wave it from side to side. I had nothing. The horse bell rang, and in one motion, they vanished.

I sit, then pace back and forth. I practiced pacing my breaths during my first planning period break. I felt desperate and restless as I tried to calm the intensity of my negative thoughts and emotions that continued to crash and collide inside my mind and heart. Lastly, I lowered myself to the floor and did fifty slow pushups before the horse bell rang. It helped. I finished and quickly took position outside my door, relieved that my Boy's Inspired classes were done for the day. Now, I am waiting for my regular ninth and twelfth grade classes. This time, students nodded, smiled, and responded as I greeted them.

As the students entered, I immediately noticed a racial divide between the Black and Latino students. I watched the Black students piled up to one side of the circle while the Latino students took the other. This was the first time I had the opportunity to teach in a school with a significant population of Hispanic/Latino students. I was new to this dynamic but open to learning. A tall, slender young man wearing black high-top Chuck Taylors and a blank expression walked in just as I shut the door. He stared at me for a few seconds, then said seriously, "I don't like teachers. I will not disrespect you if you don't disrespect me." His words were short and painful. I wondered about his experiences as a young Black boy in the public school system. I wondered about his home life and his neighborhood. I was curious and wanted to learn more.

Lastly, the door swung open, and a Latino kid stepped in with a mustache thicker than mine, with a very low haircut. He looked twenty-four years old. His shoulders and chest were broad. I had a hunch his late grand entrance was intentional. He smiled at me and extended his large hand. He squeezed my fingers like a python snake and said, "Hey, teach." He easily picked up a desk from the Black side of the room and placed it between two Latina girls. I wondered about his life, choices, story, and experiences in public school as a young Hispanic man.

I introduced myself by saying, "Welcome to American History. I love to study the people and places that make the past come alive. However, throughout this year, I will be interested in learning about your lives and stories. How about we share something interesting about ourselves?" Not surprisingly, the mood moved from tense to bored as the students sat silently, each waiting for someone to speak or for the bell to ring. We all waited. The time moved slowly, like watching an iceberg melt on a summer day into the Atlantic Ocean. Finally, a thin young man with sharp features opened up and said, "Hello, my name is Martin. I'm happy to be here. I'm an intelligent young Black man who wants to be a lawyer one day." The stale moment began to loosen as the ice continued to melt. A Latina girl with big round eyes, shoulder-length hair, and a smile wider than the Grand Canyon said, "Hi, everyone. I'm Perda Rodriguez. My big dream in life is to be a nurse."

Another Latina with dark eyes spoke rapidly, "Hey, everyone. I'm Didi, and my dream is to be a nurse or a kick-ass lawyer." I was delighted as a few more students reluctantly unmuted and shared. Lastly, the slender young man who expressed his opinion of teachers decided to speak. In a low voice, he said, "I want to run track, play football, go to college, and own a business." I was impressed by his willingness to speak. I, however, was concerned that he did not make eye contact with anyone as he spoke. The older Latino male with the mustache intentionally waited to go last. He placed his arms around the young ladies beside him and said, "Well, getting a trade or being a mechanic. And shit, having a wife and kids is what I want." As he says this, he looks at the ladies to the left and right, gently squeezing them. Everyone laughed except an African American girl who sat with her head resting on her hand and legs shaking underneath the desk. I realized I had a few minutes left, so I asked her, "Young lady, what interests you, or what are your goals?" Now with one leg shaking under the desk, she stared straight back at me without responding. I waited, and her classmates waited. Without speaking, in sync with the ringing of the horse bell, she got up and left. And so did her classmates. Everyone vanished.

After eating lunch and my planning period, I felt rejuvenated and refreshed. I wait for students in my regular ninth grade American History class. The horse bell rang, and I confidently stood at the door to greet my students. They were relatively quiet as they came in. Some were rambunctious. The class was half Hispanic and half African American. One petite young lady with a nose piercing and some sweet dance moves wiggled past me wearing headphones. Before taking my seat, I kindly asked her to put them away. She complied and continued dancing as if listening to the music. Another plump young man with a sheepish grin, and comedic-like persona, naturally began telling jokes and beatboxing in the circle. I liked his improvisation. Next, I tried to get the attention of four Hispanic girls, but they did not respond. After my third attempt, the students yelled in unison, "They don't speak English!" That was a first for me. I panicked slightly and wondered how I could teach non-English speaking students.

I didn't know Spanish, and they didn't know English. Lastly, another tall, slender female student made a grand entrance with her hair in a tiny ponytail and all the confidence of Ru Paul. She immediately shouted, "What is this? Why are we in this stinking circle? I'm not going to like you and this little house on the prairie thing you are trying to do." I was surprised at her 80s television show reference. I kept thinking that the more she talked, the more she reminded me of Sheneneh, a character from *Martin*, the 90s sitcom. I knew she would be a piece of work. And a piece of work she was. Her name was Anastasia. She talked nonstop, like a running faucet. Despite Anastasia's attitude and my chubby comedian's jokes, class time flew by a bit easier. However, it still took lots of effort to redirect a few students to keep them on track. The horse bell rang, and the kids vanished. Reflecting quietly on my tumultuous day, I identified a definite pattern of tension and segregation between my Black and Latino students. I felt the pressure and suppressed hostility from the Latino students towards me. I sat for a while, thinking about this dynamic and how to address this deep-rooted conflict. At last, the first day of teaching at South Los Angeles High School ended.

A few teachers I met at the San Diego conference stopped by to ask me about my first day. My biggest concern was the ninth and twelfth grade all-male classrooms. If I wanted a breakthrough with this group of young men, it would take energy, effort, creativity, and imagination. Just the thought of this daunting task sent apprehension through my body. I was relieved that there would be no school tomorrow. We had a teacher in-service professional development day. I hope to learn new approaches and techniques to enhance my teaching.

The next day I was back on the crowded and congested 10 West highway and the East LA interchange heading towards the LAX Airport. This was the only way to reach the conference center where the professional development was held. Once again, the traffic moved in small spurts, then at a complete stop. Now in the city, I switched to pass the Hollywood Split, the intersection of the 101, 134, and 170 freeways in North Hollywood. Lastly, I made my way onto the most congested freeway, the 405 or San Diego Freeway. My car moved at a lightning pace of 30 mph as cars filled multiple lanes to my left and right. Eventually, I made it to my destination. I found a parking spot and walked inside towards the main conference hall. Immediately, I was overwhelmed by the magnitude of the conference. The main conference hall had round tables with seating for ten. The tables stretched from wall to wall, with a wide stage in front of the room. I scanned the large conference room with its large chandeliers. as I made contact with dozens of educators across the Los Angeles Unified School District, the 2nd largest school district right behind the New York City Public Schools. I was in awe that I was employed in the second-largest school district, thousands of miles from Cleveland, Ohio.

I sat with a big Kool-Aid smile, primed and ready to learn and be inspired by the topic of Culturally Responsive Teaching. As I settled into my seat, I poured a glass of cold water while reading over the main objectives of the pedagogy. The words are as such: "Culture is central to learning. It plays a role in communicating and receiving information and in shaping the thinking process of groups and individuals. A pedagogy that acknowledges, responds to, and celebrates fundamental cultures offers full, equitable access to education for students from all cultures. According to Gloria Ladson-Billings, Culturally Responsive Teaching is a pedagogy that recognizes the importance of including students' cultural references in all aspects of learning. Some characteristics of culturally responsive teaching are positive perspectives on parents and families, communication of high expectations, learning within the context of culture, student-centered instruction, culturally mediated instruction, reshaping the curriculum, and teacher as facilitator.

The speaker stepped to the podium in a tailored plaid suit with a purple tie and matching shirt. His locks flowed down his back in a ponytail. His smile was as smooth as the Nile River. His confidence and self-assurance oozed from the stage into the audience. His name is Dr. Sharroky Hollie. He is a national educator who provides professional development to thousands of educators in cultural responsiveness. Going back twenty-five years, he has been a middle and high school classroom teacher. In 2003, he and two colleagues founded the Culture and Language Academy of Success, a laboratory school that demonstrates the principles of cultural responsiveness in an exemplary school-wide model. He began his talk with a call-and-response technique from West Africa, involving the audience by returning a response from a call he made. I immediately felt involved and energized for the rest of his message. He also spoke profoundly and passionately about validating the culture and experiences of the students you teach. He emphasized incorporating language and multiple learning styles into your curriculum. He challenged us all to re-think curriculum and teaching practices as a vehicle to transport the students into the richness of who they are and into a future for which they see themselves as integral.

As he continued to bless us with his wisdom, I wrote everything that came out of his mouth onto the few notepads on the table. I resonated deeply with his profound message at the perfect time. I thought back to the practices I had already developed to validate the culture and experiences of my students in Ohio. I incorporated the circle, letting students express their feelings and needs and integrating games and movement into my curriculum. I realized that my teaching style fits into the cultural responsiveness model. However, I was now in South LA, experiencing new students with a different cultural frame of reference. I realized I had a lot of learning to do as it related to their lives, neighborhood, and the intergenerational systemic oppression they had faced and are facing. I continued to reflect while Dr. Hollie spoke. I remembered a deep emphasis on the word "oppression" that I had incorporated into a few of my lessons at my old school. I felt compelled to create my first call and response using that word. Oppression is a weight that, no matter where you are from, we have all felt the weight of oppression. I also thought about Dr. Hollie's emphasis on the word "validation" and how I incorporated the diary/journal practice in a few of my old lessons.

In closing his speech, my mind danced like my ancestors, looking for answers with apprehension and excitement. I waited in line to meet him so I could share my appreciation. He gave me his information and invited me to contact him and visit his school in Inglewood, California. I danced out the door with a renewed focus, eager to elevate my self-awareness and cultural responsiveness to a new level of effectiveness. Soon after I had processed and celebrated the day's significance, my triumph turned into tragedy as I slowly nudged myself back on the 405 highways, desperately trying to make it home in the Friday rush hour. Three gut-wrenching hours later, I saw my exit and went home. I thought this commute made me sick. I need an alternative way to get back and forth to work. Someone I met earlier in my townhome complex mentioned catching the train. At this point, I would try anything.

It was pretty late and after my long drive, I was still sitting at the table. I was inspired to keep searching for a way to make students excited about connecting their world and experiences to American History and global history. I wanted to create an awakening in my classroom and the entire school. My mind led me to the word "oppression." Webster's Dictionary defines oppression as "to keep someone in subservience and hardship, especially by unjustly exercising authority. The feeling of being mentally or physically burdened by troubles, anxiety, and adverse conditions. Oppression is a constant weight, or burden pressed against someone, causing them to feel helpless and powerless." Oppressed groups inflict the pain they feel on each other. Inspired, I spent more time searching for various definitions of the word. I obsessively jotted down multiple meanings of the word oppression.

With this word still on my heart, sometime later, I dissected the word until it made one powerful sentence. I searched my notes from Dr. Hollie's speech and found an example of using the call-and-response method to teach cultural competency. Then it hit me like a runaway freight train! Eureka! The call, "Treat me cruel, weigh me down." The response, "Take my freedom, take my crown." I said it a few times, and I loved the sound of it. It would be my call to awareness, responsibility, and action. An affirmation that fully confronts the system of oppression and gives students a choice to use their voice. This affirmation would allow students to recognize when they felt or believed someone was doing something to them that left them powerless, causing them to react out of fear, anger, or hostility.

Because of this, they only saw two choices: submission or rebellion. "Take my freedom" means I have no power to choose. "Take my crown" means I am a powerless, helpless victim who shows my inner suffering to the world. I am overwhelmed with joy as something deep in my spirit knows that this call and response will connect hearts, minds, and souls. Next, as the night progresses, I obsess over a theme song that would help create this awakening in my history classes. I brainstorm Hip Hop music from the 80s and 90s. I remember a classic Hip Hop song that served as political and social commentary on life in the inner city. In addition to powerful lyrics, the beat is iconic, and the hook is catchy and memorable. I hum the melody as I nod my head and tap my feet. "Don't push me 'cause I'm close to the edge. I'm tryin' not to lose my head. Ah-huh-huh-huh. It's like a jungle, sometimes it makes me wonder how I keep from going under," I chanted. "The Message" from Grandmaster Flash and the Furious Five will set the stage and the tempo for infusing Hip Hop into the thread of my classroom. Hip Hop music will open the door and create healthy outlets for my students to express emotions positively. As my eyes grew heavier, I wrote a few more old-school Hip Hop songs on a playlist to introduce them to my students. I then snuck out to the 24-hour Walmart to purchase a mini boom box for my class.

CHAPTER 15

Pressures and Demands
of the Commute

"Difficult roads often lead to beautiful destinations."

Zig Ziglar

My alarm went off. I slithered from underneath the covers and quietly completed my morning routine. I slipped out of my townhome into the crisp night air. I arrived at the Amtrak Union Station, purchased my monthly pass, and waited in the darkness with a few other folks for the train to arrive at four fifty-three in the morning. As I waited for the train, I lowered myself to the ground and completed 100 pushups. I stepped onto the train, weaved between the narrow aisles, and looked for a seat. People had full blankets, pillows, and other accessories to help make their commute as comfy as possible. People also read books, drank coffee, or just gazed out the window into the darkness. I found a seat and pulled out my book by Dr. Francis Cress Welsing, *The Isis Papers: The Keys to the Colors*. I immersed myself in the wisdom of psychiatry and the legacy of racism on the psyche of African Americans. I was revitalized and inspired by each paragraph. As I continued to read, I heard the conductor announce stops in different cities.

I noticed people lining up by the doors as we approached LA's Union Station. The passengers who sat silently on the train were now positioned to race to work. I slowly closed my book and placed my briefcase around my shoulder, still clueless yet cautious. I knew my next journey was finding a 740 or 40 bus to Crenshaw Blvd. Suddenly, the train came to a complete stop. The conductor shouted, "Union Station!" The doors flung open, and everyone collectively sprinted in multiple directions. I struggled to get out of the train car to join the thousands of people moving swiftly upstairs, through tunnels, and towards more trains that released more people who dashed up a large, wide set of stairs.

I was overwhelmed with anxiety and confusion as I helplessly got swept away by the crowd. My goal was to get to the street level and find my bus. There was little to no room on the stairs as people moved swiftly around me. This was organized chaos. Finally, the crowd thrust me onto a platform where buses were aligned in a huge oval. As I looked for my bus, I saw that people filled some buses while others were empty. I searched until I found the 740 bus. I entered the bus, found a seat, and placed my bag on my lap. The smell of fresh bleach tickled my nostrils as I prepared to go over my lesson plan. I heard a commotion coming from the back of the bus. I turned around and saw a Black and Hispanic man cursing and swinging haymakers at each other. Surely, the bus driver could hear the noise but continued to drive like nothing was happening. I stared at the two men and heard, "Get the fuck off me!" "No, you get the fuck off me!"

Just as abruptly as the fight started, it ended. Who knows why the fight started in the first place? Both men ended up sitting in silence. A little shaken by my morning experience, I focused on my lesson plan as the bus rumbled down Main Street. The bus soon stopped at the corner of Crenshaw and Martin Luther King Boulevard. I stepped off the bus and into the surprisingly almost freezing temperatures of the LA morning. I hunched my shoulders and tightened my body as I took long strides past Crenshaw Mall, Louisiana Chicken Spot, and Krispy Kreme toward my destination. I walked past homeless men wrapped tightly in blankets with all their belongings inside shopping carts. I continued walking through streets lined with beautiful homes and manicured lawns. I came upon Connor Boulevard and approached the side entrance of the school. I saw a crowd of well-dressed and well-groomed African American students huddled together.

I graciously said, "Good morning. How are you all doing today? Why are you all standing out here so early?" A young man responded, "We're waiting for the bus. We live in the neighborhood, and our parents don't want us to go to school around here, so we get bussed to Westchester in the Valley." "Do you all like attending schools outside of your community?" I asked. A young lady with a pleasant smile replied, "We hate it. We hate the teachers, and we don't belong there. We know, however, that's what our parents want. It's a better quality school and our best shot at success." My legs and toes were numb at this point, but my heart was warm and tender as I stood and validated their emotions and frustrations. Before I walked away, I shared some encouraging words with them. As I entered the school, Dr. Hollie's word "validation" was still fresh in my mind. The concept of oppression will be the focus as I seek to open young minds. As I walked up the stairs, the school was still empty at six-thirty in the morning. I celebrated the two-hour commute and wondered what adventures awaited me on my two-hour trek home.

The exhaustion from my commute was insane. However, I had enough time to rejuvenate my energy to cultivate the classroom space and prepare for a tumultuous but eye-opening day. My first twelfth grade Boys Inspired class was a struggle. Fortunately, throughout the lesson, I identified some strategies that would work. The young men were distrustful of educators and apathetic to the school environment. Their response to force triggered and stimulated disruptive behavior.

At the beginning of the class, I spread black composition notebooks across my desk and encouraged each young man to take one. Upon receiving the journal, most men slumped down in their chairs and gave a collective chant of grumbles and mumbles to show resistance. Maxwell stood before his desk and proclaimed, "Nobody's gonna write in these girly diaries. We hate writing, and this is history." After Maxwell's speech, I stepped back as more young men expressed disdain for my attempt to get them to record their experiences in the journal. Before responding to any demand or instruction, I remembered the word "validation" along with my NVC training. I took a deep breath and thought, "Hear the needs. Hear the needs." A few other young men shared their frustration while a few gazed off. Another group placed their heads on their desks. I waited a bit longer to gather my thoughts.

I said, "Fellas, I hear the frustration and aggravation around writing. All of you think it's boring and a waste of time. And for once, you would like some choices and freedom in how you learn." There was complete silence in the room. Maxwell sat down, and a few others lifted their heads off their desk. I continued, "This is an American History class, which means we can spend the entire year learning about dead White men, or we can make this class interesting by incorporating your experiences, perceptions, aspirations, and struggles alongside these dead White men. And I promise that, whatever I invite you to do, I will lead by example by sharing my experiences, perceptions, aspirations, and struggles. How about we make journaling optional for now, and those who want to start can, and those who don't, you can do the regular assignments inside the book? How does that sound?" I was impressed with the domino effect of heads nodding in agreement.

I continued, "Now, If we want to begin with history, let's start with a word everyone feels. This word has been passed down for centuries and spans across the world. You experience it daily in your homes and neighborhoods, and it's a big part of your daily frustration and rage. The dead White men and the nations they rule have waged wars over this word, which keeps powerful people at the top and weak or vulnerable people at the bottom." The boys shouted in unison, "What's the fucking word!" I responded, "You all wanna say that again?" They laughed and asked, "What's the word?" I felt strength, flexibility, and harmony in my voice as I shouted, "Repeat after me, 'Oppression, oppression, oppression!'" They mirrored my smoothness and shouted, "Oppression, oppression, oppression!" The bell rang and they vanished.

Immediately, I heard the thundering noise from the high-pitched, screeching incoming ninth grade Boys Inspired students who stormed down the hallway and directly into my room like a wild monsoon. For a brief moment, I tensed up and froze because of the collective chaos created by the boys. I felt woozy. I took a deep breath and remembered my plan. The pace and the boys' horseplay were swift and intense. However, like a Zen master, I focused not on the chaos surrounding me but on the peace from a few boys sitting. I completely ignored the others' misbehavior and placed life and my enthusiasm in validating the behavior that met my needs for cooperation and respect. I told the few cooperative boys, "I appreciate your cooperation and willingness to follow my directions. Let's prepare to discuss how we will learn American History together." It took some time, but like dominoes, each student removed themselves from the chaos, sat in their seats, and requested that I acknowledge their cooperative behavior— everyone except Ricardo, the little krump dancer who continued dancing around the circle, and Hakim, who tried his best wisecracks to distract the class. However, Ricardo and Hakim were ignored by the students. We continued the discussion around the topics we would explore during American History class, and despite a few outbursts, I got through to them. When the bell rang, they vanished from my sight.

I stood in my classroom and thought about my day. I soaked in a moment of brilliance and victory for significantly improving, engaging, and keeping the attention of the wild ninth grade Boys Inspired students. My twelfth grade history class went okay, but I had a few struggles keeping students engaged. Students in my last two classes were uncomfortable opening up and distrustful of other races and cultures. They were numb to writing their emotions and had trouble making personal connections with the history book information.

My school day had ended, and I frantically tossed a few items in my briefcase, hit the lights, and dashed out of the building. I rushed up King Boulevard to wait for the 740 bus to take me back to Union Station. The afternoon breeze was delightful. The sun's rays were bright and mellow, without a cloud in the sky. As I continued to walk, the slender palm trees swayed in the wind. My joy was briefly interrupted by the thick, greasy smell from the Louisiana Chicken Restaurant. I jogged across the street past Crenshaw Mall and reached the bus stop.

I stood against the bus stop shelter and soaked in the energy from the bustling, fast-paced movement of people and cars stopping and going at traffic lights. The bus arrived, and I climbed inside. I looked for a seat and scanned the faces of exhausted, frustrated, indifferent moms with toddlers, hard-working class Latino men, and lots of African American youth. They seemed to all try their best to stay separate even though everyone stood and sat shoulder to shoulder on the cramped bus. Eventually, I could find a seat in the back of the bus after people got off at various stops. I sat next to two girls who I thought looked hard and intimidating. They wore do-rags, baggy jeans, and hard-stone-like glares on their young faces. At first, I sat quietly, but I was very intrigued by the young ladies. To distract myself, I pulled my book out and attempted to read. Something inside of me, however, wanted to spark a conversation with the young ladies. So, I asked one girl, "Have you always lived here?" She immediately responded, "Yeah, but I would love to leave and go somewhere else." Then, the other young lady joined in. We discussed society, schools, careers, growing up in Los Angeles, and setting and reaching goals. One girl said, "I want to counsel and support kids who have to raise themselves without good, strong, Black male role models to guide them. The streets are sucking kids into gang life, not urging kids to go to school." I responded, "Misery loves company." "But the sad part is that they're not telling the little homies how miserable their lives are," one girl continued. Both girls said in unison, "We want to mentor and counsel middle school kids because those kids are still impressionable, and you can guide them away from those gangs."

Both girls graduated from Daybridge High School and said the school had an ineffective principal. I was impressed at their ability to recognize a poorly performing principal. "My friend can also rap and perform spoken word," one girl shared about her friend. I said, "Let me hear a verse!" The girl spat out a strong, confident flow straight from her heart. I acknowledged her flow and the depth of our short conversation. I asked for their contact information before they got off the bus. Inspired and full from the conversation, I closed my eyes and drifted off into a light sleep. Suddenly, I jerked up from my seat when I heard screams and yells from the bus driver! She continued screaming. I gripped the rails on my seat as the bus swerved and weaved in and out of traffic. I lost my grip and fell on the floor as a few other passengers were tossed around the bus. Our bus sideswiped another bus, causing the bus to jump the curb. The bus grazed a fence over a bridge above a major freeway. Sparks could be seen along the fence, and a few windows were shattered. I prayed we didn't bust through the fence, falling to a fiery death. The bus driver swerved back onto the street to avoid hitting pedestrians. She tried her best to avoid parked cars. We spiraled into a busy intersection, scraped a few cars, and crashed onto a sidewalk. The bus screeched to a halt.

Complete silence and relief filled the smoky bus. We were all grateful to be alive. I was in shock, and I am thankful for the bus driver's skillful driving that saved our lives. After we sat for a few minutes, the scared bus driver asked, "Is everyone okay? My brakes went out!" Suddenly, an officer ran onto the bus, escorted us off, and took our statements. I didn't wait for another bus. I started walking towards Union Station. As I walked, I replayed the incident in my head. I felt special that the Creator intervened and saved us from a tragic accident. I thought, "Wow!" There was only a damaged bus, a few damaged cars, and no casualties. We could have easily gone through the fence and off the overpass, crashing onto the freeway below and possibly being killed, injured, and killing many others.

I walked with these intense thoughts in my brain until I got to Union Station. I slowly strolled inside. It was swirling and bustling, with commuters scattered throughout the large building. Some relaxed at the food stands, while others sat on benches reading newspapers and sipping coffee, or others sprinted throughout the vast hall searching for the train to get them to their destination. I continued walking. I was in awe of the massive, elegant, antique structure. The marble tile floors and high ceilings with antique designs took me back to the Depression era in the United States. As I walked along, eager to find the massive stairway leading me to my train, I snatched a brochure off a table. I held it in my hand as I walked through the tunnel of stairs leading me directly to the trains. I found an empty bench and read the brochure. It said, "Union Station is the main train station in Los Angeles and the largest railroad passenger terminal in the Western United States. The station opened in 1939 and has become one of California's busiest transportation hubs, serving over 100 thousand passengers daily." I finished reading the brochure and decided to observe the different ethnic groups and listen to the vast languages spoken by those gathered around me. It was fascinating. Finally, my train arrived, and I delightfully hopped inside and found a seat. Each section of the train had four seats, two sets facing each other. Next, I called my sister-in-law Kaya to check in with her about her flight to Cleveland and shared a few laughs about her adventure taking care of my kids. Surprisingly, as we laughed and chattered, a man sat beside me despite plenty of empty seats throughout the train.

Slightly annoyed and uneasy, I continued my conversation. I attempted to ignore this strange man who leaned closer to me to hear what I was saying. Despite this discomfort, I slightly bend over, contorting my body to get space between us. Kaya asked, "I am planning a surprise get-together for my best friend. Do you think it should be a big party or low scale?" I responded, "If it's your best friend, keep the party intimate. She will appreciate it, and it will be more personable and fun." Shockingly, the stranger interrupted me and said, "No, you need to plan a big party for your friend." In a curious tone, Kaya asked, "Is someone in our conversation?" I whispered a few words, "Kaya, this man is sitting very close to me and is in our conversation." Then, the man tapped me lightly, stood up, and said, "Watch my stuff. I'll be right back." He turns and vanishes, leaving his bag. Kaya shouted, "Musa, get up and leave that fool now. He's crazy!" I quickly took her advice. I jumped up and walked through train cars, ensuring I was far from the strange man. "Kaya, I'm good now," I said. Just as I had spoken those words to Kaya, I saw the man rushing towards me! I tightened up and said, "Kaya, he is following me." Kaya shouted, "What! Oh my God! You see him again? What are you going to do!" The strange man pushes the last door open, darts towards me, and screams in my face, "Hey, didn't I tell you to watch my fucking stuff!" I gently said to Kaya, "Hold on." I slipped the phone into my pocket, threw my bag on the floor, and stepped back. I tightened my fists of fury and placed them directly in front of my torso.

I placed my weight on my legs and stared into this large stranger's eyes. I yelled, "If you don't get your ass out of my face!" Immediately, he did a 360-degree pivot and disappeared through the door he entered. I found a seat. I returned to my call with Kaya. I laughed that we had another crazy story to tell. After my conversation with Kaya, I gently placed my head against the window for the remainder of my adventurous commute. It was quiet and peaceful as I watched the scenery swiftly move with the train's speed. Sadly, the train passed a bunch of tents set up like an internment camp. These tents stretched about a mile, with people, children, and animals together in a homeless or squatter community. I reflected on the extreme disparities of income and wealth of some versus the abject poverty of others. I also reflected on the strange man with mental health issues.

As the train approached my stop, I jumped off and sprinted towards my little orange car waiting in the parking lot. I felt panicked as it was six o'clock in the evening. I had to pick up my kids from after-school care. I anxiously arrived at Grande Ranch Elementary School. I sat in the parking lot briefly, hoping to stay calm and not react if I received any negative news about my son's behavior. I darted inside the mini school trailer to sign my kids out. I felt embarrassed because only a few kids were left. I quickly signed the pad to release my children.

Before walking out the door, the after-school program director said, "Mr. Ervin, I need to share something about Idris." I stopped and attempted to diffuse my initial anger. I said, "Good evening, Ms. Muhammad. I'm listening." She said, "Idris has trouble listening and following instructions from the childcare professionals, and he struggles a lot with keeping his hands to himself. It's early. I'm sure he's adjusting to this new environment. This behavior, however, needs to stop, or I have no choice but to suspend him from the program." "Thanks for letting me know," I responded. "I'll talk with him and let him know there will be consequences." I walked out and dashed down the ramp, heading to the playground area. I waved for the kids to come along. We walked back to the car, jumped in, and headed home.

In the car, I popped in my favorite Ne-Yo CD, *In My Own Words*, to lighten the mood and my frustration with Idris. We arrived home. The kids got out of the car and raced each other inside. I sat for a few minutes, trying to assuage the swirl of emotions and tension from an exhausting, stimulating, and challenging day. I shrugged and sighed, realizing my day was not over. My initial plan was to take up space and not say much.

I knew the stains and residue from my stressful day were fresh in me. Additionally, I needed to address my son's behavior. I slowly trudged inside, struggling to make it to my bedroom. Along the way, I ignored my kids as they fought and wrestled in the living area.

I wiggled past the commotion, chaos, giggles, and screams. I trotted upstairs, went into my bedroom, and shut the door. I sat on the cozy carpet with my back against the wall and closed my eyes. I did some deep breathing, inhaled through my nose, and exhaled through my mouth. I inhaled and exhaled to release all the tension and stress from the day. I wanted to be fully alive and present with my children. As my meditation ended, I heard, "Stop!" "You stop!" "Get off me!" "Quit!" Despite the disruptions, I slowly opened my eyes, did some neck rolls, and took a few deep breaths before exiting my bedroom. I went downstairs and asked, "Who wants to work upstairs, and who will work at the dining room table?" Naimah marched upstairs to her room, turned on her television, and pulled out her homework. Idris stayed downstairs at the kitchen table, shoveling sunflower seeds and grapes in his mouth as the sunflower seeds scattered aimlessly around the table. I did homework with one while the other read. I tried to go back and forth, checking on both of them. We finished homework and ate the dry leftover baked chicken I had prepared the night before with mashed potatoes and peas.

They finished their homework early, so I allowed Naimah to play with her friends and let Idris ride his bike. When they returned from playing, I instructed Idris to bathe while Naimah and I worked on some extra enrichment problems from her math class. When Idris finished with his bath, I smelled him. The staleness remained, so I made him take a quick shower. Naimah prepared her bath while Idris and I discussed his issues and behavior at school. I kept the conversation short and firm. He pouted, crossed his arms, and made some whiny sounds. I told him that if he received a bad report tomorrow, he would be restricted to his room for the weekend. He yelled in a high-pitched voice, "That's not fair!" He ran to his room and slammed the door.

Lastly, I made my ablution for prayer and called both kids into my room for *salat*. Naimah skipped in first, and Idris slowly strolled in like a snail. We made our prayers and finished. We ate some delicious grapes as we sat in a mini circle. Naimah shared how her day went. I shared my day, and Idris whined and complained about our conversation. I ushered them to bed and headed to the dining room table to work on lesson plans for the next day. At the table, I sighed in relief, celebrating that, at least tonight, I did not explode on either of my children. The celebration did not last long, as feelings of self-blame, frustration, and guilt consumed my mind. I took a moment, pulled out a pen, and began to reflect.

"I'm not feeling good as a parent. I have a lot of anxiety, alienation, and exasperation toward my son. Is it fear? Do I project my fears on my son? I'm embarrassed by my hateful, judgmental thoughts towards him, especially when he throws his temper tantrums and becomes disrespectful in his treatment of me, other adults, and children. Idris needs to be punished and suffer the consequences of his actions. I want to use force to teach him a lesson and make him obey. I am tired of dealing with his stubbornness. My real fear is being an inadequate parent. I don't like it because I absorb and internalize everyone who criticizes and judges me based on my son's behavior.

"I would love a free, open relationship with my son built on mutual respect. I need acknowledgment of how hard this is and how much work I am putting in. I need more choices in teaching my son to become a responsible man. I am torn because I want a loving, compassionate relationship, but Idris needs to be respectful. I am torn because it reminds me of the forceful and humiliating way my father taught me to be respectful when I stepped out of line. As a kid, I hated when my dad used physical force and intimidation to "teach me respect." However, I now mirror that strategy and method of oppressive male parenting. In retrospect, my father was afraid and wanted to protect me just like I want to protect my son. I have used it more times than I care to remember, and afterward, I feel disgusted with myself. Do I know who I am as a man, a father, and a parent? Am I still confused? Do I need more clarity and

212

self-confidence? I struggle with this. Although six years old, my son feels attacked, criticized, and sad. He thinks he is a bad kid because people treat him that way. He thinks his father is mean and invalidating when he tries to speak and gets shut down. I see the rage bubbling inside him at the tender age of six. I am guessing he needs understanding and compassion as he develops and grows. He would like me to see his mistakes as opportunities to teach him with gentleness and kindness. Now that I have released my negative jackal thoughts and connected them to my heart, I have clarity.

"I feel poetic now. Something is being born within me. I write. We are reflections of our environment, homes, and neighborhoods. We carry the internalized images of what we learn from our homes into society and the world. All these positive and negative experiences are reflected in our actions. How do we talk? How do we respond? How do we react? How do we treat people? How do we view ourselves? We are the mirrors of oppression. As parents, teachers, and other adults, we must look at our youth and the images they reflect and ask, 'Why don't we like what the mirror is reflecting? How do we own up to and take responsibility for those negative reflections sown in our youth?' When we look in the mirror, it teaches us to look at ourselves. It challenges us to look deeper than what we see and ask what is on the inside. What are your thoughts? What are your fears? How can you change the negative reflections your parents and society have placed on you? How can we change? I realize we all are reflections of each other, individuals, undivided."

A few hours later, I struggled to roll out of bed. It was three-thirty in the morning. I addressed some hygiene matters and took my son to the restroom. In the early morning, I go to the train station for my train that leaves at four fifty-three. While waiting for the train, I dropped to the ground despite the strong Santa Ana winds and completed 100 pushups. The train arrived, and I hopped on. Mostly, everyone was asleep with blankets covering their faces. It was peaceful and serene on the bustling, busy train. At each stop, more and more passengers piled on. The train became lively and congested as passengers battled each other for a position close to the doors. The train stopped at Union Station. The doors open, and an explosive exodus of commuters rush wildly to catch buses and trains to take them to their final destination. I managed to stay calm as I walked up the wide tunnel stairs into the central area where the buses waited. I met a small Filipino woman and a large but gentle African American man who also taught in charter schools. We had some exciting conversations until my 740 bus arrived. As I got off the bus and began to walk, I shivered. There would be a surprise for my students.

The administration combined homerooms for my ninth and twelfth grade Boys Inspired classes. Furthermore, I stood in the middle of flying punches, wrestling moves, and swearing. Amid the chaos, I reflected and then froze. My mind went blank. As the students continued their confusion, I went to where I had placed my boom box, popped in my CD, and the "Message" started thumping through the speakers. Without hesitation, I shouted, "Boys Inspired, push the chairs out, and let's stand in a circle." I noticed the twelfth graders moved when Kelvin, with his LA Dodgers hat, signaled for them to move. They pushed the desks back and formed a circle. Fortunately, my wild ninth graders joined in as well. The circle took shape with all the boys facing each other as, "It's like a jungle sometimes that makes me wonder, how I keep from going under" played. The song mesmerized, distracted, and unified the boys without them knowing its power.

It felt like when Adam in *He-Man and the Masters of the Universe* said, "By the Power of Grayskull, I have the Power!" Or when Lion-O from *Thundercats* pointed his sword to the sky and shouted, "Thunder, thunder, thunder, THUNDERCATS, HOOOOOOOOOOOOO! " It was a wild experience, and I acted quickly by saying, "This is a classic Hip Hop song, and in our classes, we will play Hip Hop songs that have meaning and songs you all can relate to. But we need to break down the meaning. So, we will do something from West Africa called a call and response technique. When I call, you all respond with the same energy, rhythm, and cadence in one voice. Let's try." I belted out as they stood in a stupor. "When I say, 'A child is born with no state of mind,' you respond, 'Blind to the ways of mankind!'" I heard a few whispers, cackles, and curse words.

Kelvin, the self-proclaimed twelfth grade leader, and surprisingly, Lavelle, the loud but sharply dressed ninth grader, said, "Shut up y'all and chill!" I repeated it, and they responded in one voice! The shit gave me goosebumps. Next, I said, "We have 25 minutes in the homeroom together. I know it sucks because the twelfth grade boys want their space, and so do the ninth graders. However, let's make it work." The goal was to have the students come to class, circle up, listen to some Hip Hop music, and do pushups. In a commanding, aggressive voice, Kelvin, and Lavelle said, "Everyone drop down and give me ten!" The boys dropped down like marines, and as they began their pushups. The bell rang, and they vanished. Kelvin was the last to leave. As he left, he gave me a head nod. Exhausted, I briefly sat in my chair to wait for the twelfth grade Boys Inspired students to return.

Surprisingly, after my brief rest, I feel a jolt of energy. I jumped up and replayed the song as the bell rang. The boys glided back into my classroom. As soon as we all sat down, I introduced another call and response to further help them understand the word oppression, which they had so strongly shouted the previous day. "When I say, 'treat me cruel, weigh me down,' you will respond with, 'Take my freedom, take my crown.'" We reviewed the call and response a few times until they started to get into it. It felt good as the boys naturally had a collective rhythm and voice. Geronimo, the self-proclaimed beat maker, improvised different beats on his desk that made the call and response pop. After the call and response, I said, "This call and response defines the word oppression, and we will learn more about oppression in American History.

"We will write about oppression in our lives and communities and analyze the similarities and the differences." After hearing this, Orlando assertively stated, "I don't write. I refuse to write, and I'll never write anything down." I listened to Orlando, sensing there was something behind his defiance. Calmly, I responded, "Orlando, I will not force you to write. However, we need to compromise on another way I can assess if you are learning the material." He quickly nodded as if this response settled his apprehension of writing and allowed us to build trust. I said, "Remember, fellas, this class is our creation, and you are welcome to make suggestions or give me feedback. Now let's explore the beginning of the causes of the Revolutionary War." I gave a quick lecture about the cause and consequences of the Revolutionary War, noticing how the energy deflated in the room. Next, I asked them to answer a few questions from the chapter to see if they had retained the information. It was a challenge to keep them on task. However, I managed to guide them through the questions by supporting them. Before the class ended, I said, "Fellas, journal tonight about any time you see oppression in your neighborhood, your homes, or any time you feel weighed down in your body or spirit." I noticed lots of blank faces. Orlando, my self-proclaimed spokesperson, fearlessly stood up and said, "What he means is write about the crazy shit we see in our hoods and how we react to it." I saw heads nodding around the room. The bell rings, and they vanish.

Right on schedule, the ninth grade Boys Inspired students ran wildly down the hallway, wreaking havoc as they zipped by me and into the classroom. Like most days, they started by verbally hazing each other. They began by hazing "Buck Teeth Bobby." Bobby tried to hold his own. However, like wild sharks who smelled blood, they attacked him from all sides. Ricardo, the dancer with the smile, and Jimmy, who struggled to stay focused and had an anger trigger, were unresponsive to my suggestions and actions. Ricardo initially ignored my directions. He danced and slithered over in front of Bobby's desk. Ricardo hits a slick dance move and simultaneously points at Bobby's shoes, singing, "What are those!" The boys burst out in laughter.

"Ricardo, that's enough," I said. "Have a seat, or you will dance in my detention for your lunch period." Then, Jimmy jumped in and said, "Hey, Bobby. How much wood could a woodchuck chuck if a woodchuck could chuck wood?" Ricardo demonstrated a beaver while pointing at Bobby. The boys burst out in hysterical laughter again. Bobby looked stressed out and irritated. He replied, "Jimmy, at least I have a daddy with your fag bag-looking ass!" The boys all collectively let out one huge sigh. Jimmy was stung. He snapped quickly to hide his devastation, "I'll beat your ass bitch!" He leaped up and tried to lunge at Bobby. I promptly blocked his attempt by gently grabbing his wrists and quickly guided him outside. "Jimmy," I said. "Sit against the wall or walk down the hall. Then, when you feel your anger decrease, slowly count down from 50 and return to the room.

"However, if you return yelling, cursing, or threatening, you will get detention with me, and I will call your mother. Is that clear?" "Is that clear?" I asked again. He shook his head without looking at me, determined to hold back the tears. I returned to class, where the chaos was building. I went to my desk and grabbed two Nerf squishy balls. I said, "Everyone stand up!" As everyone stood, I tossed one ball. The students threw the ball back and forth across the circle. They threw it low and high. The ball dropped many times. They used profanity. They called each other fag bag. They made lewd gestures and threw up gang signs. I continued to watch, not knowing where it would lead. I was inspired to say, "Let's see who can catch and throw with one hand. Ready, go!" Magically, the boys challenged themselves to complete the task. Next, Lavelle said, "Let's see if we can toss underhand and catch with our left hand." The boys challenged themselves to complete this task. Then, Jimmy crept back into the class and rejoined the circle.

I received a few more suggestions from the boys. I asked them to sit at their desks and think of other creative ways to toss the ball. After a few minutes, Hakim, who is mean like a rattlesnake, took the ball, placed his index finger over his lips, and tossed it to Sylvester, the big, oversized, loveable ninth grader with huge hands. Sylvester followed the same motion and passed the ball to Ricardo. Ricardo passed it to Bobby. Bobby passed it to Jimmy, and he passed it to Lavelle, the leader. Finally, Lavelle passed the ball to me. I motioned my index finger in front of my face and did the cutthroat sign to signal completion.

We discussed a few more aspects of our version of the "silent ball." After completing the silent ball, I skillfully turned on "The Message" and led them through my call response on the word oppression. This activity led to a deep conversation on oppression through their eyes and experiences. Surprisingly, they started to write about oppression in their lives until the bell rang. Then they vanished. Soon after, I decided to stroll out to the large courtyard during lunch. The massive courtyard had spacious areas for students to eat and other areas to socialize, play, and dance. As I continued my walk, I noticed a crowd of students who had formed a gladiator-style ring in one spot. More and more students rushed over to engage in the entertainment. I was also curious, so I jogged over to maneuver between a few students to witness krump dancing on another level. One young man with smooth dark skin, short but graceful with every move, had the crowd completely stunned by his performance. The fellas were hyped while the young ladies drooled over him. Lastly, he finished with a perfect backflip while simultaneously removing his shirt to show his physique. The bell rang. He had this perfectly timed. The crowd dispersed. I approached him and said, "Excuse me, young man, that's incredible. What's your name?" He responded with a deep baritone voice, "I'm Benjamin Brash, and this is my first day at South High." "Nice to meet you, Benjamin. I'm Mansa. I'll talk with you later," I said. Benjamin slipped off and trotted over to a few young ladies. They vanished up the big concrete stairs towards the main campus.

Lunch ended. I set up the music for the rest of my classes. My regular twelfth grade students entered with a heaviness that strangled the positive vibe of the music. Despite my flawless seat arrangement, the Hispanic students sat with their group, and the African Americans sat with theirs. To my surprise, two new students entered my classroom. Benjamin, the deep voice, dancing machine, ladies' man, glided in with charm and confidence. And another young man with power that shined through as confidence. He had curly hair, braces, close-set eyes, and a calm demeanor. I walked up and said, "Greetings, young man. What's your name?" In a low voice, he responded, "I'm Jacques." My two new students took their seats as I let the music fade. As I discussed my call-and-response technique with them, Jamela sighed, "UGGHHHHHH!"

Rather than addressing her rude interruption, I paused, realizing how I navigated this storm would determine where each student's attitude went. So, with a shaky voice, I switched gears and said, "What is a weight or a burden that brings you down in life? Let's spend some time writing your responses to this question." The chatter continued as if my instructions were not clear. I stopped to recognize my judgments and self-doubt, then remembered a quote from a book on classroom management called *Champs*. The passage states, "The ratio is always four to one. This means that every time you call out misbehavior or something wrong, look to validate and acknowledge four things that are working well." I scanned the room. It's tough to mentally do this because most students sit, chat, or do nothing. Then, I looked around the room again for something positive. I observed eight students writing thoughts in their journals. With this mindful moment, the energy returned to my spirit. Confidently, while walking throughout my class, I shared, "We have about three minutes left to capture your thoughts about what brings you down." I noticed Didi had joined in the process. Something clicked in her mind. Glenda, my lovable, cheerful Latina, began to move her pain to her pen as she carefully crafted her thoughts. Victor, a disgruntled but exceptional African American male, scratched his temple as he jotted down his thoughts. Analise, my quiet Latina, with a dark eye shadow around her eyes, began writing a few sentences. Her face brightened as she wrote. Then, Jamela shouted, "Ain't nobody even doing this, and nobody gonna talk about these problems?" I ignored her rant. I was determined not to interrupt my positive demeanor.

I used the call and response to get attention when the time was up. I said, "When I say, 'treat me cruel, weigh me down,' you'll say, 'take my freedom, take my crown.' Y'all ready? One, two, three." "Treat me cruel, weigh me down." I get a few mumbles and laughs as a response. However, this does not deter me from my goal of helping my students make a connection to the word oppression. So, I asked, "Would anyone like to share what causes a burden or brings them down in life?" Silence filled the room as the random chatter increased. However, this time, Carlos, the high school O.G., aggressively interrupted and asked, "Can y'all shut the fuck up and say something?" After he spewed this out, he had a devilish look. I was uncertain of his intentions. Was he talking to his fellow Hispanic students? To the African American students? or everyone? I worried about the African American students' response. Surprisingly, they were quiet. Then abruptly and without warning, Jamela flung open her journal, picked it up within an inch of her face, and said, "Watching my father getting murdered in front of me weighs me down every day. I remembered how he looked, his last word, everyone screaming, and blood pouring from him as it ran into the street." She finished. Perda, my sweet Latina, said with a melancholy tone, "What weighs me down every day is when my father got deported to Mexico. It's hard on my family living without him." Her eyes inflated with tears and turned red. Victor read his journal. He emphatically said, "It still weighs me down the way they handcuffed me and treated me like a criminal when I was a little kid in elementary school."

The statements were brief but powerful. You could feel the tension in the room. However, it was a tension that needed to be expressed. With his deep voice, Smooth Dontae interjected, "Man, it hurts not having my pops around. He left me, moms, and my little brother to run the streets. That's why I smoke weed!" He chuckled a bit because he realized that his words rhymed. Then Carlos, with a straight face, said, "It weighed me down watching my pops whoop my mom's ass." I let his words and those of others sit in the room momentarily. Everyone could feel the stillness of emotional tension. I said, "What weighs me down is when kids have to grow up way too fast, losing their innocence and never discovering the beauty of life." I had their attention. I ended by asking those who would like to answer the question at home to do so. This was the beginning of our American History studies. We could tap into the pain and the weight of things felt but not understood. Let's explore history, the past, our present lives, and experiences together. I powerfully said, "Treat me cruel, weigh me down." They chanted, "Take my freedom, take my crown." The bell rang. They vanished.

While waiting for my ninth grade American History students to arrive, I smirked and felt my chest expand as I clicked on the speaker to play "The Message." Like clockwork, Ernestine strolled in with a smile and headphones tucked into her ears. I smiled and signaled for her to take them off. My four Spanish students quietly walked in a tight formation and headed straight to the back of the room. Daquan skipped in, immediately recognizing the song. His old spirit was entertaining and infectious. A few more students slipped in and found their seats. As I prepared to shut the door, Anastasia said, "Uh. Umm. Don't you shut me out. No one shuts me out!" She squeezed her petite frame with long legs around the partially closed door and into the room. Irritated by my choice of music, she shouted, "Turn that off! Nobody wants to hear that old-school rap!" I chuckled and responded, "Anastasia, please have a seat. And don't come for my music! This song is a classic." We continued our banter as the other students observed our dialogue like a tennis match.

Eventually, when she was ready, she stopped, and with a few more comments, she sat down. I began with the call and response. Then, I asked the students to write in their journals for three minutes about their experiences of feeling weighed down in body and mind. When I finished my instructions, most students wrote one or two sentences. I did my best to communicate my question prompt to non-English speaking students. After attempting to explain the instructions for the third time, I reached into my desk for markers and construction paper. I drew a picture. They all smiled and nodded yes as they began to draw pictures of their experiences with the word oppression.

During the last minute of journaling, Anastasia started chattering with Ernestine. I interrupted them and said, "Ladies, I noticed you chose not to write. Would you two like to share your thoughts aloud?" Ernestine pleasantly shook her head while Anastasia shouted, "Stop bothering us. No one wants to do your little diary assignment. Anyway, we need to do some real work." Before I responded, I realized I had given Anastasia enough attention for the day. I replied, "Anastasia, I hear your frustration, and writing about your experiences seems to be a waste of time. However, I'm asking if you can be open and trust my teaching style." Anastasia said, "I'd rather do the bookwork. Ain't that what history teachers are supposed to do? I'm asking you to do your job!" I paused as the students' subtle "oohs" and "ahhs" tickled my ear drums. "Do all teachers make you feel weighed down in your mind?" I asked. "Do you think that teachers put a burden on you? I would say that you have already shared the writing assignment.

"Teachers are oppressors in this system called 'school.' We force students to think and act as we want them to, and if they don't comply, we can punish them. And this makes you angry. Is this why you lash out?" I asked. Anastasia fluttered her eyelids, squinted her eyes, and made a stank face at me. She didn't respond. I continued, "And throughout this American History class, we will explore history from the experiences of the oppressed versus the oppressors. We will also connect history to the daily struggles that young people have in their homes, families, and neighborhoods. I encourage writing down your thoughts and sharing your opinions because they are valuable. This is how we bring the past to life. We have a few minutes left. You can finish writing down your thoughts about the word oppression." Daquean raised his hand and said, "Let's do that. Treat me cruelly, knock me down, brush my teeth, throw me down." The class erupted with laughter. I counted down, "Five, six, seven, eight, 'Treat me cruel, weigh me down,'" they roared back. "Take my freedom, take my crown." Then Daquan set up a beat utilizing his pencil and desk that matched perfectly with the cadence of my voice. We vibed back and forth until the bell rang. Then, they all vanished.

I narrowly made it to the 40 bus. My stomach was upset as I settled into my seat. Like my students, I pulled out my journal to reflect and write what I saw. I saw African Americans and Latino people, no White people. The bus is currently rumbling down Broadway, heading towards Union Station. I stared at a man sleeping with music blaring from his headphones. I wrote, "Too much music and television kills your ability to be creative and think independently. Writing is an escape from reality, like fighting, drinking alcohol, and smoking weed." I am using this man to bring home a larger metaphor about sleep and how it symbolizes a death style. I continue writing, "If violence, drugs, and alcohol represent sleep, any activity that stimulates active thinking and constructive actions is awake. I smiled, realizing I had been inspired to create another way to encourage the students to open up and express themselves. Finally, the bus pulled into Union Station.

I closed my journal and hopped off the bus. As the bus pulled off, I realized I had forgotten to leave a lesson plan for my day off. I wait impatiently for the 740 bus to take me back to Crenshaw. I waited, trying to be patient with myself for being so forgetful. Eventually, the bus pulled up, and the doors flung open. I stepped onto the bus and took a seat. We pulled off. Instantly, the bus driver began yelling at passengers to get off the bus. She also yelled at passengers to get on the bus. One gentleman tried to get on at the middle entrance, and she refused to open the door. "You Black Bitch!" he yelled. As we continued, the bus driver made rude comments when people got off. Finally, I was all alone with the disgruntled bus driver. As the only passenger on the bus, I could hear her grumble and mumble things to herself. Without thinking, I walked directly up to the seat closest to her.

I took a big gulp, let a minute pass, and thought I could offer her my listening ear and full presence. I asked, "How are you doing today?" In a harsh tone, she replied, "Hell. How do you think I'm doing?" I replied, "It seems that you are having a rough day. Is something bothering you?" She responded with less venom. "Yes, people are fucking rude to me all day, and they need manners!" I replied, "Sounds like you value respect and are tired of people who don't value you or your job." She softens more, "Right, and my boss, he's an asshole as well. He gives me the worst routes to drive." I responded, "I hear how frustrated you are and how you would like more appreciation and consideration from your boss." She continued to soften more, "Right. My husband takes me for granted. He never takes me out, and he ignores me." I responded, "Sounds like you're sad and want more connection and quality time with your husband." Then, she burst into tears, "Yes, I'm fat and old. Nobody loves me."

I affectionately responded, "Sounds like you are heartbroken, and you need to love yourself and appreciate your self-worth." Drying her tears, she assertively said, "Right, I care too much about what others think of me, and I need to start doing things that make me happy." I said, "That's what I'm talking about. You're a beautiful woman with lots to offer. Get out there and live the life of your dreams!" With those words, she smiled. It lit up the nighttime sky. The bus arrived at my stop. Before she opened the door, she said, "Young man, I don't know who you are or where you came from, but you have an incredible gift. Keep changing lives." She winked at me. I smiled back and dashed off the bus and into South Los Angeles High School to set up my lesson plan for my substitute teacher.

CHAPTER 16

The Power of Reciprocity

"To Receive with Grace, Is the Greatest Form of Giving."
Ruth Bebermeyer

With all my energy focused on the first month of school, I struggled to keep my dream of acting and modeling alive. Surprisingly, just as he promised, when Davidde, Essence Magazine's Fashion Director, returned from his travels abroad, I scheduled a meeting with him. The first few meetings were exciting as he carefully guided me on how to find auditions and modeling tryouts. Davidde was polished and a brilliant elocutionist. He was tough, no-nonsense, stylish, creative, and generous. I was so thankful he decided to mentor me in the essentials of the modeling and entertainment industries.

At one meeting, Davidde asked, "How did that big modeling audition go in West Hollywood?" I casually responded, "I didn't go." He pushed himself away from the table and sternly asked, "You didn't go? What is your problem?" I shook and clenched my teeth together. I was confused and wondered why Davidde was so upset. I stuttered and said, "I just didn't show up. I have a lot going on right now." Davidde crossed his arms while leaning into the conversation. He said, "We all have a lot going on. That does not mean you blow off a very important opportunity. I had that opportunity specifically set up for you, and you have the audacity to sit here, look me in my face, with the pathetic excuse of 'I have a lot going on.' Listen here. I don't appreciate you wasting my time. I agreed to help you and followed through with my commitments."

I froze. I was flabbergasted and regretful. We sat in silence. I had hoped to think of something good to say in our brief silence. Unfortunately, I was speechless. The silence was deafening, and the tension even thicker. I was not sure if I should apologize or get up and leave. Suddenly, Davidde asked, "What do you want?" I said, "To be a model and actor." He fired back, "That's bullshit, Morris! What do you really want? Stop wasting my time." I felt pretty uneasy. My pupils dilated. My heart began to beat rapidly. My lips trembled. My palms were sweaty. I attempted to speak as tears filled my eyes. Davidde sat silently, waiting for me to continue talking. He sipped his coffee.

Slowly, I said, "I love to mentor youth. I have created this kingdom inside my classroom where kids feel safe expressing themselves. I love to dance and act. I also love fashion. I love to motivate people, so I created a name for this educational, artistic movement. It's called 'Mansa.'" Davidde shook his head. I panicked, assuming his response would be of disgust. For the first time, he smiled and said, "This is what I have been waiting for. I love it! So, tell me more about what Mansa represents." I talked about the real Mansa Musa and why I chose a real African king to model my organization and philosophy after. Davidde quickly jotted down a few things. He slid his notepad across the table with a logo of Mansa. We continued to discuss my mission and vision. By the end of our meeting, I had an action plan to follow through to execute before our next session.

The next day, I woke up tired but made it to the train on time. Monday mornings always seemed to move as slowly as snails. While on the train, I planned my lessons for the day, and while waiting for the bus, I talked with my sister. Unfortunately, because of my tardiness, I arrived later than usual. Despite challenges and setbacks, I stayed on track throughout the day. Each morning, as my students enter my classroom, they expect to hear classic old-school Hip Hop music blaring from my boom box. Before the lesson starts, students have four ways to interact with it before the class formally begins. They would make four squares on a blank sheet of paper and follow the instructions and prompts outlined on the board. They could choose to complete two out of the four tasks. In their journal, they could write on a specific topic, draw a picture, answer basic questions such as who, what, when, where, why, and how, or write a short poem.

It had been a few weeks since working in this format, and all of my students were consistent with the expectations of the learning process. Despite the consistency, some days were rough. Students would explode, especially on Mondays, following the weekend. They would curse each other out and express themselves through passive and physical violence—which was evident throughout the school. Despite this, learning and growth were happening in all my history classes. I also continued to learn from my students. I introduced the concept of sleep and awakeness in all my classes.

Each morning, my ninth grade Boys Inspired, aka B-Inspired students, would rush into my class loud and out of control. They come in, gather in a circle, and toss the "spirit ball." They play a few rounds of the spirit ball to relax and regulate their energy. If foul language is spoken in my room, the boys have to do pushups or use the feelings and words posted around the room to re-phrase their profanity into positive language. Next, we engage in a musical rhythmic activity called choral reading. Choral reading entails one student reading a passage from a chapter in their history text. They pause to leave a word out, and then the class fills in that word like a chorus. When the students are engaged, the process works effectively. This approach to learning keeps everyone focused on reading, and it is fun. Following this, the boys are paired to collaborate by completing a quiz at the end of each section in their text. They can work through challenges and communicate until they find the answer and complete the assignment.

Initially, Lavelle had extreme impulses to speak or misbehave. He regularly used the word "fag bag." Lavelle would yell the word out during games, bell work, choral reading, quizzes, or other times. It always ignited problems in the class on the level of a lit powder keg. Initially, I reacted and harshly reprimanded each boy who used it. I realized it was a symptom of the larger misogynistic culture that the boys inherited. My job was to get them excited about building their vocabulary, expose them to the deeper meaning of their habits, and encourage them to choose another way to express themselves. I empowered Lavelle to keep a tally of how often he said the words and challenged him to set a reasonable goal to control the impulse to say them. This motivation and conscious tracking of the word tremendously decreased his use. I also encouraged the other boys to support Lavelle in reaching his goal.

Lastly, I infused the sleep and awake journal. Journaling allowed students to assess and evaluate their behavior. Before the end of class, each boy contributed definitions of sleep and awake behavior. For sleep behavior, they mentioned illegal drugs, gang violence, theft, and murder. For awake behavior, they struggled to find terminology. This helped me understand how much sleep and negative events occurred around them. I assisted them by saying, "Awake can be many things. More importantly, however, it's about being responsible for your actions and learning from positive and negative life experiences. Awake is being able to clean up the mess you make in life. Awake is when you can turn fear into strength and pain into passion. You can change people's minds, hearts, and souls with your radical actions." To my surprise, the boys hollered and yelled, "That was a dope bar! Can we use this as another call response chant?" I said, "Let's do it. Hakim hit the beat."

Hakim was mean like a rattlesnake, but his instrumentation and artistic skills were top-notch. I shouted, "Repeat after me." "I turn fear into strength and pain into passion. I am changing minds, hearts, and souls with my radical actions." They said, "We turn fear into strength and pain into passion. We change minds, hearts, and souls with our radical actions!" We chanted together a few more times, and the boys went wild with enthusiasm. The bell rang, and they vanished.

I was excited as I wandered down the hallway toward the staff restroom. Walking closer to the room, I saw four young men surrounding another student wearing a blue Dodgers cap hooked on his waist. I sprinted directly toward the mini ambush. One student said with sinister eyes and a heinous tone, "Chris ain't around to protect you nigga. So, catch this fade!" Before Kelvin moved, I pressed my forehead directly against the menacing kid's forehead. I used pressure and pushed him back. I said, "Chris ain't around, but I am! Catch my fade!" I took a small step back and loosened my tie while Kelvin watched in disbelief.

The other young men looked helplessly at their leader. He gave them a nod and said, "This ain't over!" They vanished. I turned and faced Kelvin, who seemed embarrassed by my actions. Kelvin touched my shoulder and said, "Thanks, Mansa. Welcome to my world. Do you know who he was and what you just did? That was a young member of the Rollin 60's Crips. They tried to bang on my friend Chris but banged on me instead. Since your class, I've been thinking about oppression and trying to change my ways." He chuckled and said, "You told him to 'Catch your fade.' That means you called him out for a fight. You're a cool teacher."

We realized we were late to class, and I continued to the restroom, hoping I had not made matters worse for Kelvin and Chris. I, like my students, was now deeply immersed in a gang culture that called for a way to navigate and survive. I returned to my classroom and found the boys doing their bell work assignments while listening to old-school music. They continued with the routine while Orlando, who was cooperative, refused to write anything down. When we finished the assignments, Maxwell asked, "Mansa, you play your music. Why can't we play our music?" Usually, Maxwell could be rude and disruptive. I validated his ability to ask questions without being demanding, pushy, or annoying. I replied, "No problem. I will let you guys play a song, but after it's over, we will discuss whether it is asleep or awake." They all responded, "Ok!" Maxwell popped in a CD, and the boys hooted and hollered as the emcee rapped about Rolling 60s, Grape Street, the drug trade, murder sprees, robberies, and violence. As I listened, I was not impressed with the song, yet I became more intrigued by my student's enthusiasm. Shawn hit every dance move imaginable, wearing his colorful, bleached Chuck Taylors while the boys cheered him on. The song ended, and they acted like the rapper was the best rapper in South LA. Out of curiosity, I let them play a few more songs from different LA underground artists. Many songs continued to glorify gang life. However, some also glorified death. At the end of the songs, we embarked on the discussion of sleep and awake.

Orlando nervously said, "It's because my father was heavily into the gang lifestyle, and I've seen so much violence as a kid, and it got my father locked up." Shawn, with a cunning smile, said, "It's sleep. I live in a Blood's neighborhood. There are shootings all the time. They try to bang on me daily, but my dad ain't having me in no gang. He makes us play football and keep good grades." Jackson said, "It ain't sleep. It's awake. These boys gotta hustle and take care of their families. This is how they make money and take care of me." Maxwell chimed in, "Man, this is life in LA. I play football like Jackson and Shawn, but this gang thing is all we know."

I waited for a few more boys to participate, but they didn't. I was confident they had a solid idea of the difference between sleep and awake behavior. "Gang or no gang fighting," I said, "Killing and selling drugs is sleep behavior, and it's nothing but a destructive path that leads to jail or death. Do you fellas know the history of gangs? How did they start in LA? When and why did they start? What caused them to grow and get popular?" The boys listened intently, hanging on to every word I said. "We have only completed three minutes of journal writing. I want more. We have twenty-five minutes left. Do you all think you can educate me on the history of gangs?" I saw a sea of collective nods. The room was quiet. I turned on some Thelonious Monk. They began to write, and write, and write. There was stillness, peace, and safety emanating throughout the room. A healing culture flowed from their pens to their journals. No one talked. No one laughed or joked. Everyone was writing.

Before the timer went off, I heard a knock at the door. A gentleman with locks tucked underneath a skull cap, smelling like frankincense, enters the room. We embraced. He said, "My name is Deep Red. I'm a poet, activist, and artist. I help facilitate the 'See a Man, Be a Man After-School Program' with the founder and legend himself, Torrence Brannon-Reese, affectionately known as Torrè. We've continuously heard amazing things about the youth culture that you are creating. Come down and check us out." I said, "That's right. I've heard lots of students talk about your programs as well. I would love to support you." Red responded, "Right on. Is that Thelonious Monk playing?" I nodded yes and said, "Absolutely."

He smiled and shook his head with a look of shock and disbelief as he quietly shut the door. The bell went off. The boys calmly stacked their journals on my desk and vanished.

My manic Monday moved on throughout my lunch period. As I prepared for my fifth period, I celebrated how my Boys Inspired students left an indelible stain of honesty and vulnerability with me. They were beginning to understand that life was about showing up. I did a few breathing practices and remembered my purpose. I knew I had my breath to ground and center me. Surprisingly, another new African American male student entered my room. He was huge, at least 6 feet 2 inches tall. I shook his hand. He said, "My name is Raymond." I was leery of adding new students with current students because the current students struggled with change and were slow to adapt to new people and experiences. Initially, Raymond took a seat by the stereo.

I had forgotten that that was Carlos's seat for a split second. Carlos strolled in and saw Raymond in his seat. Carlos snapped and said, "Yo, homie. Get the fuck out of my seat!" Raymond bounced up and shouted, "Fuck you and this punk ass seat!" My students moved the chairs to give them ample space to destroy each other. I wiggled in between them. I realized I had a better chance with Carlos because he knew me. Carlos breathed fire and threatened me, "Get the fuck out of my way Mansa." I had my arms fully extended against Carlos' broad chest. I tried to hold my ground and not be aggressive with him. I, however, was losing my grip as he slowly shoved me toward Raymond. I whipped my head around, and Raymond stood like a giant oak tree. Surprisingly, the class watched in silence.

I inhaled deeply and said, "Carlos, look at me and breathe. Look at me and breathe. Don't go to sleep. Stay awake. Just breathe with me. Just breathe with me. You got this. You got this." Slowly, he allowed me to guide him toward the door. He took space outside of the classroom. I walked up to Raymond, who was sitting down, and said, "Are you ok?" And with a stern voice, he replied, "I'm good now." I breathed to calm my inner chaos and said, "Today, I am adding another style to help you express and analyze yourselves and your actions toward the world around you. We will analyze the world and US history through the lens of sleep and awakeness. As we study the French and American Revolutions, I want you to know there was tension and conflict between groups of people, some with power and some without power. They clashed over political power and resources. Now, let's take a moment to reflect on who lives in your neighborhood and who is sitting in this room."

Victor said, "It's Blacks and Mexicans." Didi said, "Correction, I'm Mexican, but we are not all Mexican." Jorge, who sat in the corner and never said a word, suddenly came alive. "Yes, I'm Colombian, but you have Dominican, Peruvian, and many other ethnic groups that are Spanish speaking." Jamela said, "Well, all y'all speak the same, and y'all are taking over our neighborhoods." Analise responded, "Sweetie, did you not know that California was stolen from us and claimed by the United States? We were here first. Americans call us immigrants and illegal aliens when this is our land."

Benjamin lightened the mood with his charm and said, "I'm an international lover. Ladies love me across the border." Everyone laughed. Little Michael said, "South was Black, and now, with y'all Mexicans and Hispanics moving in, it's creating more oppression because we are fighting each other." Carlos entered the room and nonchalantly said to Raymond, "My bad for coming at you crazy." Raymond replied, "We're good." I asked, "How much do the Black students know about the Hispanic and Mexican students, and vice versa? Did anyone ever realize that both groups have a similar history of oppression? I will ask a few questions. If the answer is yes, I want everyone to stand up. Who struggles with poverty? Who lives in a single-headed household? Who has been affected by gangs and gun violence? Who has lost someone to gangs and gun violence?" Students raised their hands on each question. The reality changed the atmosphere of the room. I asked, "Why do you think we say, 'Treat me cruel, weigh me down. Take my freedom, take my crown'?"

"Historically, Black and Brown people came from a glorious past filled with a rich culture and heritage. Black and Brown people were forced to give up their land or were taken from their ancestral lands. Because of segregation, black people were forced to live in selected areas in LA. When Whites moved out, then Blacks moved in. Eventually, good jobs were lost when factories closed. Communities fell apart due to massive unemployment. Then, the influx of drugs further destroyed communities, giving life to a gang culture of territorial wars. Latinos and Mexicans migrated to the same area as Blacks, forcing each group to experience the same degrading environment. Thus, what do the two groups do in tough circumstances? Blame each other and hate each other. The cycle of oppression begins. Carlos and Raymond almost went to blows over a seat. Their actions represented the endless years of resentment between the two groups. So, take time to be awake. Get to know yourself and your history. Start to realize who the real enemy is. It's not who or what. It's ignorance and lack of knowledge.

"Now, who loves Tupac?" The students threw their hands recklessly in the air. I put on his "Dear Mama" song and let it play. Some students sat still, while others quietly mumbled the words at their desks. I said, "This is a travesty of justice. I know we all know and love this song. Maybe we will be hesitant because we don't know all the words." I passed around copies of the lyrics. Everyone was silent. I said, "I'll start reciting his rap lyrics. I would love for everyone to join in." "When I was young, me and my momma had beef." I pause. Like Hulk Hogan at *WrestleMania*, I placed my fingers around my ears. I waited and waited. They responded, "Seventeen years ago, kicked out on the street." I said, "Though back at the time, I thought I'd never see her face." They flow in. "Ain't a woman alive that could take my momma's place." I turned the music on, and we recited the lyrics together as a class. Before the bell rang, I said, "Tonight, take your journals and write about your observations of oppression, sleep, and awake from your experiences."

Just as I looked at a room filled with warm smiles, an alarm went off. The principal came on the loudspeaker and said, "There is a lockdown in the neighborhood due to gang violence. No buses are coming through Crenshaw, and walking in the neighborhood is unsafe. All students, please report to your designated areas until further instructions." The kids scampered out of the room as I stood with my mouth open, trying to process the news. I walked down the hall to my colleague, Ms. Jimenez's room, for more information. I asked, "What's going on? How long will we be locked in?" She responded, "Sometimes the violence in prisons spills over into the neighborhoods, then schools, as the gang leaders still call the shots from jail. We will be locked in for at least two hours, maybe more. If you try to catch a bus, you will have a serious problem because, during the lockdown, all buses are routed away from Crenshaw." I thanked Ms. Jimenez for the information and returned to my room. Luckily, Venaya had an early day and would be able to pick up the kids from aftercare.

I turned my attention from the current crisis, retreated to my desk, and started reading the journals of my ninth grade Boys Inspired students. I was mesmerized yet frightened at the time and care each boy put into the history of gangs. The information was so well organized, detailed, and intricate. The names of Blood neighborhoods, Crip neighborhoods, and sub-gangs with different names corresponding to specific streets were listed. In addition to their stories, some boys designed fully illustrated street maps of Blood or Crip neighborhoods. Gang culture was deeply embedded in the psyche of the still-growing and developing young men. They each tried to make sense of their lives, identities, and histories.

As I continued to read, I realized sharing their perspective was the greatest gift they could offer me. This was cultural competence at its best. Validating their world as I introduced them to another allowed them absolute freedom to choose. If the boys couldn't decide, then they would most certainly lose. However, they had something to say. Their paradigms, perspectives, and experiences were valid. Whether they realized it or not, many choices had already been made for them based on their families, environments, and neighborhoods. I had offered an opportunity to explore beyond their limited imaginations to a world outside of LA. I had offered them access to beauty and humanity that lived within themselves, a refuge from all the noise, chaos, and uncertainty, a place to be free. Mansa was mentoring lives. It was time to create a sacred space with the boys outside the classroom and Crenshaw. I closed the last journal. I didn't realize that two hours had flown by, and the sun would soon set. I was itching to leave and determined to find a way home. I gathered my bags and headed towards the back exit. Hopefully, I could now walk down Crenshaw until I found a bus that would take me downtown.

Before I exited the building, I heard a voice call my name. I spun around to see the lovely Ms. Alana gliding towards me. She was a charming, brilliant math teacher with a platinum smile and an infectious personality. She brought energy, creativity, and spunk to her profession and colleagues. I said, "Hey, Ms. Alana. Today was crazy, especially with this lockdown." Before she spoke, she pulled me in for an amazing hug. "I know, right," she said. "Mondays are so tragic. But you are working your magic with your Boys Inspired students, who always talk about how much fun they have in your class. They come into my class reciting your chants and bringing positive energy."

"I'm a B-Inspired teacher this year as well. We both know they hand-picked and placed these boys together because they terrorized the school last year. However, you see something in them, and so do I. They love math. They have brilliant minds. It's just keeping them engaged and on a track that's challenging at times. Specifically, I want to mention Kelvin and how he speaks of his relationship with you. I've seen so much growth in his maturity level, and his grades are improving. He's so proud of his A in your class and happy he's learning so much. He's fighting for his education because of you." "Well, I know you," she continued. "It seems like no lockdown will keep you from getting home. See you tomorrow." She pulled me in for another strong hug and walked away.

With a tense stomach, I slipped out of the school. I ventured down Crenshaw in search of a bus. The neighborhood was an enclave within itself. As I kept a steady pace, I slowed down to look at each unique shop. There was bustling activity up and down this historic street. Of course, I walked by a few barbershops, and each barber solicited me for the best deal on a lineup. However, I needed a natural hair care salon to twist my locks. Walking, I smelled different aromas of soul food, Caribbean food, and other creative Black-owned restaurants. Despite my initial fear, I felt alive and connected to the community as I searched for a bus. Soon, a beautiful couple caught my eye. They were standing outside of a natural hair care salon. Their warm smiles compelled me to walk inside and converse with them. We began talking about natural hairstyles for Black folks. Our conversation expanded to issues such as history, government, and public education and how it was designed to create compliance, not critical thinking. We also discussed *The Isis Papers*, the book I was reading. It was delightful to have continuity and synergy around a book with theories and concepts the average person would struggle to understand.

The sister was amazing as we transitioned into the taboo topic of religion. She did a masterful job at linking Judaism, Christianity, and Islam to the lunar calendar of the practices of our ancient African civilizations. Her discussion resonated deeply with my quest to integrate my religious, spiritual, and cultural heritage. Lastly, we discussed communication in romantic relationships. They felt safe discussing their challenges as a couple. I listened and helped them understand the deeper needs they both valued underneath the surface of their judgments of one another. There was a spirit in that room as we talked non-stop for two hours. We exchanged information and embraced each other. I then continued down Crenshaw in search of a bus.

Further along, on my walk, I stopped to talk with an older African American gentleman who was a community leader. He briefly shared information about a cultural safe haven for African Americans in the heart of Crenshaw. It was called Leimert Park. He said, "Here's my information, and I'm willing to sit down over some hot tea and tell you all the history of this area." Before we finished our delightful talk, he pointed his finger towards a few blocks down Crenshaw. "Cross the street, and you're in Leimert Park," he said. "You can cut through Leimert Park, back onto King, and the buses should run over there." He gave me a firm handshake, and I continued my trek through the palm trees, urban sights, sounds, and vibes along Crenshaw.

As I walked along, I saw a park. I crossed over Vernon Avenue, just past Starbucks, and there I was. I watched a few older men play chess at a table. I saw some brothers and sisters jamming in a drum circle. I cut across the grass along a smaller street where many stores, shops, restaurants, and theaters were open. I was in awe as I viewed all the stores. Each was Black-owned, and each store had something positive to contribute to our culture. I saw healthy soul food restaurants, African clothing stores, shops, and Black-owned bookstores. Outside the bookstore, I grabbed a pamphlet with the words *Leimert Park* printed on it. I was compelled to read some of it. I stopped in a small coffee shop to purchase a slice of pound cake. I took my dessert outside, found a seat, and read through the pamphlet. I skipped to the section outlining the brief history of Crenshaw and Leimert Park.

"Leimert Park is named for its developer, Walter H. Leimert, who began the subdivision business center project in 1928. He had the master plan designed by the landscape architecture firm of the Olmstead Brothers company, which was managed by the sons of Frederick Law Olmsted (1822-1903), the landscape designer known for Central Park in New York City and other major projects. Elderly Japanese American residents still live in the area, and some Japanese gardens still exist. The Crenshaw Square Shopping Center was inspired and designed in the style of Japanese architecture. The center was a retail hub in the mid-1950s. The core of Leimert Park is Leimert Park Village, which consists of Leimert Plaza Park, two blocks of 43rd Street, and one block of Degnan Boulevard. In Los Angeles, Leimert Park Village has historically been a hub of African American art and culture. It has been compared to Harlem and Greenwich Village, and in 1998, it was seen as "the cultural heartbeat of Black Los Angeles. Leimert Plaza Park was designed by the Olmsted Brothers to serve as the public hub of the master-planned community. The park has been a go-to community space for the African American community since the 1980s, hosting art walks, a regular drum circle, annual celebrations, rallies, protests, and memorials. The village has blues and jazz nightclubs, theaters for musicals, dramatic performances, award ceremonies, comedy specials, poetry readings, and venues for Hip Hop. Project Blowed is the world's longest-running Hip Hop open mic, started

in 1994 by rapper Aceyalone and friends. It is hosted by Kaos Network and held every Thursday night at 43rd Place and Leimert Boulevard.

"Crenshaw and neighboring Leimert Park are the largest middle-class Black neighborhoods in the United States, despite heavy damage from the 1992 riots and the 1994 earthquake. However, the growth of the gang-dominated crack cocaine trade in the 1980s made Crenshaw district one of the most violent neighborhoods in Los Angeles, with the stretch of Crenshaw Boulevard between Slauson Avenue and Adams Boulevard remaining a virtual free-fire zone for years. The majority of Crenshaw is just another unremarkable South Central thoroughfare. It runs from Long Beach in the South to Wilshire Boulevard, where it ends. The fact that Crenshaw stops dead at the northern edge of South Central, at the point where the racial mix starts to change rapidly, gives the street its significance. Since the fifties, Crenshaw has been a street African Americans can think of as their own. Other than that, the only other notable peculiarity of Crenshaw's geography comes around the junction with Slauson; at this point, it becomes the widest street in Los Angeles, divided by a central reservation laid out long ago with grand ambition that somehow hasn't materialized, except once a week, on Sundays, when the street comes alive with the Sunday-night cruise."

"From Adams, past the Crenshaw-Baldwin Hills Mall, through Leimert Park, and down Imperial, Black and Mexican youths come out flossing their chromes and motors. It's the time when African American and Latino youth get to rule three miles of tarmac. The Crenshaw Cruise is a carnival that anyone can join, and it's free. There are so few places in South Central where young men and women can hang out together without trouble. There is little public space, and local parks routinely become territories of individual gangs. The more prominent streets, like Crenshaw, often form the borderlands between gang turfs, are neutral ground as long as you stick to the street—the lack of safe space for people to meet feeds into gang animosities. If more situations like the Crenshaw Cruise were available, in which members of different gangs could socialize, there would be less mutual fear and hatred on the street"

I closed the pamphlet, dropped it into my satchel, and continued past Leimert Park, cutting through the side streets heading towards King Avenue. As the sun began to set, ushering in the night, the lush palm trees swayed back and forth in the wind. I found King Avenue and felt relief as at least half of my adventure was over. I quickly jogged across the busy street. As soon as I got to the other side of the street, an LAPD cruiser sped toward me and rested on the curb. A Black and a White officer sprinted towards me. The Black officer took the lead as he walked within two inches of my face. Screaming, "Boy! You just broke the damn law by jaywalking. I should arrest your ass!" I stared directly into his eyes and withheld the rage, disgust, and pain I felt toward cops. I was disheartened because the Black cop took the lead as an attack dog while the White cop patiently waited to take aggressive force, if needed, in the background. I took a deep gulp and responded in a low tone, "My apologies, officer. It's been a long day, and I am trying to get home." The officer replied. "You better be sorry it's a lockdown. We are weeding out all suspicious individuals involved in drug or gang activity." He continued to lecture me, knowing I didn't fit the description of a drug dealer or gang member. Lastly, he said, "I'll let you go with a warning this time." They both jumped back into the squad car, pulled off the curb, and recklessly accelerated down King Avenue. I took a moment to shake off the crazy experience and continued walking toward the bus stop. Fortunately, the bus arrived within minutes, just as darkness had set in. I was too happy to take the bus to Union Station.

The next day, in my ninth grade Boys Inspired class, we began with a game of silent ball. We placed the desks in a circle, and they all pulled out their journals. I said, "You will have all the time you need to write about the history of Los Angeles gangs. As you write, think about the concepts of oppression and being asleep or awake. Go." Complete silence filled the room until I slipped on another jazz CD. They wrote with the intensity of a best-selling novelist or a student writing their essay for the SAT or ACT exam. My twelfth grade Boys Inspired class was the same. The only interruption to their stream of consciousness was the sound of the bell. They confidently placed their journals on my desk and disappeared.

Later in my planning period, I visited the school suspension classroom. The sea of desks was filled with Latino students. Their faces and actions illustrated apathy, resentment, resistance, and combative and disruptive behaviors. Clearly, it was too much for the overwhelmed, stressed-out teacher. I stepped in, and all the students said, "Hey, it's the cool teacher, Mansa!" Instinctively, there was a warm connection between me and the students, something new to me. I saw my student, Analise, sitting beside her boyfriend, Rigo, and walked over to her. I knew Rigo was affiliated with the 18th Street Gang, the rival Mexican gang to the Bloods and Crips. Analise, who rarely smiled and had an air of sadness surrounding her, brightened up when she saw me. She said, "Hey Mansa, I'm sorry I'm going to miss your amazing class today. However, I'm here because I'm always late to school and missed the first period." I smiled and said, "It's cool. You know parent-teacher conferences are today, and I expect to see your parents." Before she responded, "Rigo jumped in and said, "I'm the only family she has. She lives with people who don't care about her."

Analise affirmed what her boyfriend said. "Yes, he's right. I live with my mom, a few uncles, aunts, and cousins in a crappy two-bedroom apartment. We use sheets to divide the place into a few more sections. All the adults, including my mom, work hard labor and odd jobs to make ends meet. They're never home. I feel like I live in a shelter. I love your class, Mansa. You make us feel at peace with ourselves." I responded, "Ana, you're tremendously courageous, and you have a brilliant mind. Building trust isn't easy for you, and I validate that. So, I want you to use my class as inspiration to stay awake and graduate." Ana's sad face brightened up. She smiled and said, "Thank you, Mansa. Treat me cruel, weigh me down. Take my freedom, take my crown. How about we try this call-and-response thing in Spanish?" I said, "Wow, Ana, that never occurred to me. Let's go for it!"

All of the Latino students were now fully engaged in our conversation. They all moved their chairs closer to Ana, Rigo, and me. They spent ten minutes laughing, chanting, and teaching me a little Spanish until we agreed on "*Somos una familia chingonas.*" They roughly translated it as

"We are a kick-ass family." We ended our impromptu session. The Latino kids were happy that I spent time with them. They were sad to see me leave. The day flew by as the evening ushered in my first parent-teacher conference. As I set up materials for the parents to read, I felt calm and serene as the parents, primarily African American, slowly walked into my circle. With each group of parents, my warm words, incorporation of music, and unique teaching style created a genuine, safe atmosphere of caring.

Each parent listened and connected with the principles of my class. Despite being warned, it still felt odd as my Spanish-speaking parents smiled and nodded gleefully without speaking one word of English. I felt sad for the non-speaking English-Latino parents. The inability to speak English created a huge barrier that blocked them from advocating for their children. My African American parents came deep, mostly mothers, who were frustrated with the Boys Inspired Program's lack of information. I discovered that most parents were unaware their sons had been placed in a special program. I provided a warm, safe atmosphere and offered them empathy while reassuring them that their sons were in the best hands with me. Most moms expressed delight and joy that their sons were learning and having fun in my class. I felt supported and accountable by the sea of Black moms who only wanted the best for their precious sons. In between my sessions, I had a few conversations with moms who needed more time and attention.

Little Mike was in my twelfth grade American History class and had a proud mother with a charming Southern accent. She was straightforward with me concerning her son. She inspired me to learn more. I listened to her concerns about the school's lack of structure and organization. I realized she could assist me in building my mentoring program. I also connected with the fear and concern in her eyes as she worried about little Mike's future. As the night progressed, I spoke with other mothers who wanted more for their sons and were willing to give and sacrifice more. I sensed the overwhelming stress in their personal lives being compounded by their suspicions of the intentions and practices of the school. I felt the tremendous pressure of being a single mom in LA and was impressed with the grit, passion, and resilience I heard in each conversation. I believed I represented the hope they yearned for.

As the successful, eye-opening, and insightful conference ended, I replaced chairs and tables in preparation for the next day. My ninth grade Boys Inspired leader, Lavelle, dashed in with his mom. She had an aura of irritation, consternation, and frustration. I watched as she complained about the images in my room. She looked straight at me and asked, "Where is the teacher?" I was in awe at such a gorgeous woman with such a horrible disposition. In her eyes, I saw the beauty of LA deeply hidden beneath the smog of oppression. She represented the beautiful palm trees, gunshots, despair, and creativity. Los Angeles' high elevation, the beautiful stars, and the mountains were all tucked into her hateful stare and ugly glare. I sensed she was waiting for something which I could not provide. Lavelle, visibly excited, attempted to play "The Message." She immediately said, "No, cut that off!" She was fuming and asked, "Where is his textbook?" I started to explain, but Lavelle gracefully interrupted me. He pulled out his acrostic poem and skillfully related the concepts of American History and the oppression he felt living in Los Angeles.

Suddenly and surprisingly, the veil of disgust lifted from her face. She said, "Wow! Lavelle, that's great. I love it!" Seeing how engaged his mother had become and the entry of his beautiful grandmother, Lavelle decided to go for it. Lavelle looked at his mom and said, "I love you, Mom, but sometimes you're why I'm 'sleep' in school. Sometimes, you are evil, and I feel you don't want me. It hurts me more because I don't know my father." Lavelle's mom stepped back, placed her face between her hands, and began crying. Lavelle slowly approached her and wrapped his skinny arms around her waist. His grandmother stepped up and said, "Mr. Mansa, you have changed Lavelle's life in such a short time. He walks differently, talks like he has sense, and he's not getting into trouble. He's learning about himself and his history. I'm raising my grandson and feel humiliated that my son has chosen not to be a part of Lavelle's life.

"It's truly tragic, and it's all my fault." "Grandma," I said. "I feel your pain and determination to raise Lavelle correctly. You are trying to give him what he needs to succeed. I'm willing to step in and provide what I can." Lavelle's mom interrupted and brusquely said, "This conference is over!" I was clueless as to what caused her outburst. With my eyebrows scrunched together and flailing my arms, I said, "I would love to support your family, especially Lavelle, because——" She interrupted me and shouted, "You're not a therapist, counselor, or psychologist, so it's not your place to pry into my business." I fire back, "Listen, I understand Lavelle is your son, and he needs you. I sense your pain and rage. However, Lavelle needs a male mentor in his life. I care about you, Grandma, and Lavelle's well-being. I feel honored to be a part of his life." She shook her head as tears filled her eyes. "Again, it's not your place!" I extended my hand, hoping this last gesture would keep us connected. She ignored my gesture and shouted, "Come on, Mama! Come on, Lavelle!" Lavelle reluctantly left with tears running down his face. I inhaled the deep mist of tension as Lavelle's grandmother gently shook my hand and left.

CHAPTER 17

Cultural Swag

*"Students must have initiative; they should not
be mere imitators. They must learn to think and act
for themselves—and be free."*
Cesar Chavez

The next day, while riding on the train at dawn, I reflected deeply and critically on how much Hip Hop music had impacted my life. I smiled as I remembered how obsessed my friends were with watching Hip Hop videos as they dreamed of emulating the latest styles and trends. I remember watching Hip Hop artists like Big Daddy Kane and Special Ed with high-top fades, jewelry, expensive suits, and dope lyrics. I was also introduced to Public Enemy, a group with a fierce, provocative, unapologetic style that introduced me to Black History, power, and politics, all through the art form of music and videos. KRS-One was a lyricist, emcee, and storyteller who embraced his people and culture. His lyrics are filled with wisdom and substance. They labeled it "conscious rap." We also embraced West Coast rappers and groups like Ice-T and N.W.A. In addition to the dope male emcees and groups, I was equally impressed with the lady legends of rap, such as Queen Latifah and MC Lyte. They mesmerized me with their lyrics that promoted 100% respect for Black women. Their lyrics were powerful. Of course, we all fantasized about living in New York City because that was the mecca and birthplace of Hip Hop.

Rightfully so, my parents' generation needed help understanding Hip Hop, and they failed to see how Hip Hop music connected us to their generation of music through sampling. We were introduced to old-school artists such as George Clinton, Roger Troutman, James Brown, Bootsy

Collins, and many more through hip songs that sampled old beats and hooks from soul, funk, and blues music. Later on, when I was a teenager, Hip Hop spread from the East Coast to the West Coast, the Midwest, and the Dirty South. Groups and artists like Snoop Dogg, Wu-Tang Clan, the Fugees, and Outkast bumped through my speakers.

Through diverse styles of Hip Hop, we learned our history, received advice on relationships, got terrific fashion tips, and learned about violence and street and gang life. We also had fun music to party to and express ourselves. Youth culture and all movements are influenced by music. As I chose to become an educator, I realized how Hip Hop of my generation was similar to the 60s and 70s Black Power movement of my parents' generation. Fascinatingly, the music continued to evolve into the 2000s. I intended to constantly educate myself on my students' music, fashion, and style. I did not necessarily have to like it, but educating myself and giving space to their music kept me relevant. I have always revered Hip Hop. Even though I am a writer and love to read and write poetry, I have only dabbled in writing a few rhymes. Many of my close friends were Hip Hop artists and activists in college. I focused more on Hip Hop's style, militancy, and activism. I shied away from writing and performing.

Before the train pulled into Union Station, I felt a spark to share the first complete rap story I wrote. Even as the thought freely meandered in my mind, I wanted to shut it down and push it away. However, in case I got froggy today with the boys, I shuffled through an old folder and pulled out the rap appropriately titled "Treat Me Cruel, Weigh Me Down." I arrived at school, set up my classroom, and looked forward to a smooth day. My emotions and excitement from the Parent Teacher Conference were ever-present. Today, during my Boys Inspired twelfth grade class, I split the young men into three groups. Their job was to study the Preamble to the Constitution, interpret the meaning in their own words, and construct a call/response to integrate their learning authentically. My job was to facilitate their learning while clarifying questions about the Preamble or the Constitution. The group with the most creative and catchy call/response would be used for the week.

Surprisingly, Victor, my twelfth grade student, entered my room with the Boys Inspired crew. Victor loved being in my regular history class, but his heart resided in Boys Inspired. I had developed a strong affinity and bond with Victor despite our rocky beginning when he threatened me on the first day of class. I chuckled and said to Victor as he happily and sheepishly sat with one of my groups, "Vic, you are not supposed to be in here, so if you get in trouble, that's on you." He smiled and responded, "Whatever, Mansa, I got you." He knew I supported him. We had an understanding. We rocked out through the Preamble to the Constitution. I clarified some words, and we listened to all the calls and responses. Of course, Victor's group performed last and skillfully chanted in a deep harmony accompanied by his percussion. "Sovereignty. Sovereignty. People have the right to rule! People have the right to rule!" The boys, including myself, joined in as we all said in unison, "People have the right to rule!" The laughter was infectious. We all knew who the unanimous winner was! While the laughter subsided, I peeked at the clock. I only had a few precious moments left. My body tensed and tightened as I squeezed my fists together while leaning on the desk.

I belted out, "Treat me cruel, weigh me down." They collectively respond, "Take my freedom, take my crown!" Despite the robust response from my boys, my brain went blank. I was speechless. The boys sat quietly with perplexed looks on their faces. I paused, summoned Hip Hop legends from Rakim to Slick Rick to André 3000, and said, "Treat me cruel, weigh me down. Take my freedom, take my crown. Li'l boy growing up in the streets with a frown, exploited by sex at an early age, felt frustrated and animated in a world of pain. Confusion and delusion were my earlier thoughts. I was living life automatically without feelings and thoughts. Adolescence hit me hard like a heavyweight fight, jabbing, punching, and swinging. I was wasting my time. I was searching for my soul. It was hard to find. Testing my limits with my father figure was like climbing a rope without arms and legs and going to battle without ammunition. Conditions are like unbreakable chains: stay calm, relax, and listen, and you can ease your pain. But rage made its way to the front of my mind. Sanity and peace were hard to find. I was going down on a ship. I could not save until self-reflection and knowledge of self-revived my heart and spiritual wealth. It opened my eyes from my sleepwalk and reawakened my soul to my feelings and thoughts. I found purpose. It fits like a glove. I got the spiritual power to fly away like a dove. Alive and strong, I can reclaim my throne. Mansa Musa is the name I can call my own. I was still searching through my past to enhance my present. Adolescence came and went. I'm finally learning new lessons. It took a long time for me to welcome my pain. I turned it into a passion with my radical actions."

Everyone leaped from their seats with howls and deafening, thundering applause. They surrounded me with hugs and high-fives. We soaked in the moment. Amid the cheers, we gazed towards the doorway as a group of five co-ed students said in unison with disgust, "That shit ain't fair why we didn't get Mansa as our teacher." We laughed. I nodded at Victor. He was right on cue, tapping the pencils, producing an infectious rhythm. I shouted, "I turn fear into strength and pain into passion. I'm changing hearts and souls with my radical actions." They shouted, "We turn fear into strength and pain into passion. We change minds, hearts, and souls with our radical actions!" The bell rang, and they vanished.

Soon after my boys left, my classroom phone rang. I picked it up. The school secretary asked me to meet with the principal in his office immediately. I ran down a few stairs, trying to understand why the principal wanted to meet. I was obsessed with every step as I tried to figure out what he wanted. The one thing my gut told me was, "I'm in trouble." Finally, I was at the main office. The secretary said, "Hey, Mr. Ervin. He's waiting for you. Just walk right in." I walked in and sat in the spacious yet cluttered office. Shuffling papers on his messy desk, the principal got to the point. "Mr. Ervin, we value your work at South High School, especially what you do with the Boys Inspired program. Unfortunately, we have to make some budget cuts and lay off teachers. Since you're new and have no tenure, we have no choice but to lay you off." My whole body tightened. I had a sour look, like I had just tasted a lemon. I said, "You're going to lay me off? The kids are going to be devastated." He attempted to soothe me with some encouraging words while I tried to loosen the grip that my rage had over me. I was thinking of how I would break the news to my beloved students. The principal finished his comments and wished me well. I reluctantly shook his hand, pivoted, and quickly left his office and headed to the courtyard.

I stood with my hands on my hips as I looked at the palm trees and the beautiful sun perched in the sky. My tear ducts were full as I tried to suppress the tears from flowing, knowing I needed to control my emotions. I took a few deep belly breaths. I inhaled and exhaled as I tried to regulate my nervous system. I counted backward from ten as I returned to my classroom. I waited for my regular twelfth grade History class. I quickly attempted to arrange the desks in a circle before they arrived. While placing the desks, my inner thoughts of rage and sadness were deafening and made it a challenge to stay in the moment. However, I mustered the strength to stand by the door, smile, and greet the students as they entered my classroom. Surprisingly, as each student filed in, all my tension and rage dissipated. Lightness and power settled in my mind, body, and spirit. Ironically, the lesson was on the beginnings of the French Revolution. As students settled in, I began the class by saying, "Treat me cruel. weigh me down." They collectively responded, "Take my freedom, take my crown." I sang the call and response and added a new inflection and intonation, "Treat me cruel, and weigh me down!" They sang back, "Take my freedom, and take my crownnnnn!"

Before I shared the news, I scanned each of their beautiful faces and soaked in all the tremendous progress we had made as a class. I briefly recalled the intense moments while celebrating my accomplishments of creating a community of diverse learners who learned to observe and think critically about the world around them. I took a deep breath and said, "Life is unpredictable, and change is the only constant thing. However, remember that you have everything you need as long as you have the will and spirit to achieve at all costs." As I continued to deliver my last speech, I could see the perplexed look on each face. Carlos interrupted, "Mansa, what's going on? Are you dying or something?" Whispering engulfed the circle. Then, with a razor-sharp tone, Didi intuitively said, "Mansa is about to leave us. I know it, and I can feel it!" The chorus and powder keg of whispers brewed into a total explosion. "Mansa, is it true?

Mansa, is it true? Are you leaving us? This isn't fair!" My heart melted and stopped beating as the tension in my chest overwhelmed me into silence. My students stewed in anger and helplessness.

With his baritone voice, Smooth Benjamin spoke, "Mansa, you need to say something. Is it true? These kids are about to burn this bitch down like the French Revolution." As Benjamin finished, I used my breathing techniques to reduce the intense emotions that were building within me. My sense of peace was returning. Then, Victor, with rage in one pupil and tears gathering in the other, shouted, "This is bullshit! I hate this school! How they gonna take the best teacher we've ever had away from us?" Carlos stood up and declared, "We gonna tear this bitch down if they fire Mansa."

As the collective rage from Victor and Carlos' inciting words ignited more outrage and thoughts of mutiny, I spoke, "Everybody is mad or angry that I'm getting laid off. Everyone wants to destroy or tear things apart to cover their grief, sadness, and shock. This feels like yet another blow of devastation in your lives. And look at what's happening. Look around the circle. Please take a moment to notice how you all are united by rage and more united around the value of this class. You are united around the relationships you have built with me and each other. So, all the emotions, from rage to powerlessness, sadness, grief, and helplessness, are all valid. Emotions are messengers from above that stimulate action. We are now in our emotions.

"The whole point of this circle is to give space to express your emotions, not to suppress or hide them or let them drive you to do destructive things. Remember, we always have a choice. You all can continue to express rage around this circle. The next step is to——" Perda, who often smiles, interrupted me, and sternly said, "Turn fear into strength and pain into passion. We're changing minds, hearts, and souls with our radical actions. Let's be awake now and figure out how to use our communication skills that Mansa has taught us to make the principal keep him." Perda's words helped to evaporate the rage that was in the room. Everyone calmed down. I said, "Like the revolution, people mobilized to accomplish a goal through organized action. As we will study, people often use violence to overthrow the oppressive monarchy that rules over them. However, we can use words as ammunition and weapons to convince or persuade your monarch to change their mind."

Little Michael added, "We can role-play with Mansa how we will speak up for our rights. We have power because the principal or no one would have a job without us in these seats!" Then, Analise said, "Y'all think that blockheaded principal is going to listen to a bunch of Black and Latino kids? Well, who cares? It's worth a try because we are *Somos Una Familia Chingonas!*" The class burst out in laughter. I said, "Analise, tell everyone what that means." Analise noted with the other Latino students, "We are one kick-ass family!!"

Surprisingly Jamela said, "Well, I'm in for this protest, but if the principal pops off, I'm going to cuss his SpongeBob head ass clean out!" I was relieved that the kids felt confident and empowered to act. I said, "Let's offer empathy to the principal. Remember, he is in charge, and you want to soften and deactivate his defense mechanism by offering him empathy first." Jacques, who was often silent, interrupted and said, "You would guess that he's probably overwhelmed and needs us to understand the pressure he feels from the people who order him around." Carlos added, "He doesn't want to look soft and fire those lame-ass teachers that have been here forever. But Mansa, you're new, so you're easiest to lay off." I responded, "Yes, I know it's hard, but we must humanize Principal Blockhead. He has feelings, too. So, look at the feelings and needs lists around the room. Guess what he might feel and need and use that to express your feelings and needs about why it's important to keep me." The students worked in pairs, jotting down ideas about what the principal felt and needed while clarifying their feelings and needs. We did a role play where I was the principal, and they walked into my office to express why they wanted to meet with him about laying me off. However, they were prepared first to offer empathy to the principal and second to soften him enough to express their feelings, needs, and requests. The bell rang, and they all vanished.

Emotionally drained, defeated, and heavyhearted, I managed to keep it all together by sharing the devastating news with my students throughout the day. As the school day ended, I quickly gathered my briefcase, headed towards the door, and soaked up the sun as I solemnly walked toward the bus station. The sun was bright. Despite the smog, the palm trees swayed gently from the breeze. On the bus, I jotted down my feelings. However, my mind was vacant as I attempted to recall my reactions to the day's events. Eventually, I made my way from the bus to Union Station. I trotted down the narrow stairs until I reached the section to wait for my train. I sat on a bench, just settling in to observe my surroundings, anything to get my mind off being laid off. A few feet down the landing, I spotted a middle-aged African American man with excellent workout equipment and bands placed neatly around him.

I immediately walked towards him, curious to spark a conversation about his profession. I said, "Afternoon, brother. Are you a personal trainer?" He replied, "Yes, young brother. I'm Roj. I have my fitness boot camp called Blackshear Fitness. You're in good shape. You want me to show you some exercises?" I dropped my satchel beside his equipment and said, "Let's go for it." Roj demonstrated a squat, bicep curl, and triceps extension with these long elastic stretch workout bands. I fixated on his every move as he effortlessly and flawlessly showed each exercise. He finished, politely handed me the elastic bands, and instructed me to begin. I took the bands and placed my feet in them while I attempted to pull them with both hands to perform bicep curls. I struggled to pull them while balancing my weight on the concrete floor. Roj smirked and said, "It's harder than it looks. Keep trying." I twisted and turned, pulling, and extending the bands as sweat beads formed on my forehead. I managed to complete one full yet shaky repetition. Next, I positioned myself for the triceps extensions. I stepped in the bands with both feet, stretched the bands behind me, and leaned forward to do a repetition. When Roj walked away to answer a phone call, the band snapped from behind and struck my back. The pain was sharp and persistent. I felt humiliated as strangers passed by, watching me whip myself. Roj finished his call and returned. I acted as if nothing had happened. He assisted me in the next band position for the squats. I also struggled with the squats. I struggled to balance myself while pulling the bands and stretching muscles I had never used. Despite the harrowing but enlightening experience, I quickly finished and handed Roj his bands. He said, "Here's my card. Since we ride the same train, I can give you a free workout. It's great publicity for my boot camp." The massive train pulled up before us, and we exchanged a handshake. I waited for Roj to hop on. I followed him and found a seat.

I plopped down in a seat and decided to pull out my book, *The Isis Papers*, to soothe my aching bones and distract me from the shock of being laid off. I read a few pages. Suddenly, an African American woman in a stylish outfit with long jet black hair and piercing green eyes decided to sit next to me. She immediately introduced herself by saying, "Hi, my name is Tammy. How are you today?" I warmly responded, "It's been an emotional day for me. I have just been laid off from my teaching position." She reacted with shock, "That's terrible news! I'm sad to hear that." I responded, "I'm sure I will recover from this setback. But it was tough because I was making a difference with my African American and Latino students. They need as many strong, educated Black male role models to help them navigate the harsh system of oppression." Her eyes brightened, not expecting that type of militant response from me. She wanted a pleasant conversation, and I was the wrong person to sit next to.

Tammy said, "Oh, I see. You're one of those 'Power to the People' brothers who blames the system and slavery on the White man." I calmly responded, "I'm a brother who seeks to enlighten my people about the patterns and conditions we have suffered and continue to suffer from a historical lens. I also help us embrace critical thinking, resourcefulness, and resilience to choose a path of freedom." Her curiosity peaked a bit more. Playing the devil's advocate, she fired back, "Slavery ended 400 long years ago. We, as Black people, make excuses. That was then, and this is now. We have choices now!" I briefly considered her comment and responded, "The past is a thread that connects to everything we do today. Intergenerational trauma can be passed down through generations long after the initial traumatizing experience. The horrific incident of the Trans-Atlantic Slave Trade and its impact on our people manifests itself in our experiences today. For example, do you notice how obsessed we, as Black Americans, are over hair texture and skin color? We determine our standard of beauty based on the European standard of beauty.

"We believe that Black people with lighter skin and straighter hair are more attractive and superior to Black people with darker skin and coarse kinky hair. Tragically, this class of lighter skin Blacks was created by the sexual exploitation, objectification, and rape of our women by White enslavers. Within the caste system of slavery, lighter-skinned Blacks received more privileges and benefits than darker-skinned Blacks, creating inner conflict and hatred toward each other. Do you not see that this pattern of colorism between Blacks exists today?" She shook her head and nodded in agreement. Then, she clapped back, saying, "Well, Black men are still affected by slavery, not Black women. We are strong. We are independent. At least we don't make excuses. We do what we have to do to take care of our kids with or without Black men." Her eyes protruded from their sockets as she twisted her neck sideways like a pretzel and stared at me triumphantly. I paused a bit, giving her a moment to gloat, and then I assertively said, "Why are Black women independent, and why are Black men dependent? Why are Black men struggling to secure jobs, and why are we struggling to grow up and be men?

"This failed relationship dynamic between Black men and women has a historical cause. It began with both groups being negatively socialized and conditioned during slavery. The whole concept of a strong Black family was counterintuitive to the financial institution called slavery. Black men and women were bred like horses to produce the strongest offspring for hard labor. Black men were forced to breed with different women on different plantations, and the institution of marriage between Black people was forbidden.

"If Black men attempted to rebel against the system by marrying the woman of their choice or by escaping various plantations to be with their wives and children, they would risk being publicly flogged, mutilated, or worse, lynched and left for everyone to see. White enslavers forcibly raped Black women and forced them to rear their children and also the children of White mistresses on the plantation. Despite this loyalty and commitment, at any moment, Black women feared having their children sold to another plantation. Black men and women lived in constant fear. As slavery eventually ended, the anxiety, trauma, and failed relationship dynamic continued and perpetuated through later generations until this very day.

"The destruction of the Black family and the healthy relationship between Black men and women evolved from oppression into internalized abuse and dysfunction. The chains are still there but invisible. Today, if you look clearly at Black single-parent households, Black women are forced to raise their daughters to be strong and independent while spoiling their sons in hopes of shielding them from the harsh realities and pressures to which they will ultimately succumb. This further perpetuates the cycle, making it easier for Black men to leave the family unit, and Black women struggle to fulfill both mom and dad roles. If people fail to study the history of this traumatic experience and seek counseling, we will never heal and will continue to victimize ourselves. In my family, on my mother's side, she is the only one married. Single moms raised all my cousins. And yes, despite being raised by both parents, generational trauma, fear, and dysfunction still exist in my household. I could only imagine what it was like for my cousins. A cycle of mental, physical, and sexual abuse runs rampant throughout my family. From generation to generation, the many secrets that continue to torture souls are swept under the rug, covered up with a euphemism, or 'don't tell our family business.'

"Therefore, suffering, suffocation, and misery continue as individual and collective wounds never heal. As a family, our coordinated response is to self-medicate, escape through abusive relationships, engage in risky street behavior, and use drugs as a maladaptive coping mechanism." I finished. I notice a softness in her eyes. Tears formed in the corners of her eyelids as she softly said, "You have made the connection. I get how everything from our past connects to what we do today." She asked, "What is your last name? You briefly shared your family's intergenerational pain and suffering, which sounded exactly like my family story! I did not realize that this story is part of the Black experience in America by design."

253

Tammy shared a few more stories about her pain, emotional history, and her family's inability to let go of the past. Eventually, my stop arrived. We wrapped up the conversation and exchanged appreciation and respect for each other.

I hopped off the bus and headed toward the ticket station to purchase another monthly pass. With my emotional vibration higher than the clouds, I poured my soul into a Nigerian Union Station worker by saying, "We want our culture. I want my heritage. As African Americans, we were ripped from our ancestral homelands and stripped of our identities!" As I repeated my sentiments, I felt a deep connection with my Nigerian brother as his eyes began to water softly. I will never forget his words, as he assertively said, "Once you start finding your history and culture, you open yourself up to a world of rich possibilities in the past, present, and future. You move beyond space and time. When you decide to visit the Motherland, it's like God." We touched each other's souls in that brief but rich moment. I spoke with another beautiful Black couple about melanin and energy. Of course, I quoted a few lines from Dr. Welsing's book. The brother responded with a warm embrace and said, "You're the only Black man I have ever met who has read Dr. Welsing's masterpiece."

Overwhelmed with joy, I jumped in my car. I gently touched the steering wheel and felt my heart beating rapidly. My heartbeat felt like an ancient tribal rhythm. I sat quietly and just listened. As I prepared to pull off, I recited words that had manifested in my spirit, "'Those who cannot remember the past are doomed to repeat it.' We have a rich, creative, unique culture that goes beyond the traumatic experience of slavery. Unfortunately, we fail to realize that our individual and collective responses tend to be traumatic survival responses caused by slavery. We are so much more if we would only take the time to dig beneath the surface. If you fail to learn your history, life remains a mystery."

The following day, like clockwork, I began my daily ritual. I was on my way to the train at four fifty-three. In the darkness, I stood a few feet from the train tracks. I glared at the lights in the distance as the train lumbered directly toward me. Upon entering the train, I twisted my narrow body between the aisles and sleeping commuters whose legs and feet dangled in the aisle. Luckily, I found an empty seat and sat by the window. The train moved along in the darkness. Fortunately, my anger and rage from yesterday's news had fully subsided. I accepted it and planned to make the best of my last days at school. Then, as I sat quietly gathering my thoughts, a large, stocky man with broad shoulders and a bald head approached the empty seat next to me. His huge biceps pushed my body toward the window as he sat down. I readjusted my body until I had enough space to breathe. I rode with my face plastered against the cold window while the big man fell asleep. Suddenly, we heard a loud noise, a colossal screech, as the whole train began to shake back and forth. People were jolted from their seats as the train instantly went from silence to complete chaos. I pivoted my head around to the big man and asked, "What's happening?" He responded, "I'm not sure, but it sounds like we hit something on the tracks. Let's hope it wasn't a car sitting on the tracks. Some people have committed suicide by driving their cars onto the tracks." I immediately raise my hands to the ceiling with concern and disgust. I said, "Man. What? That's a crazy way to go. You must be in a pretty miserable state of mind to do that." He responded, "Nothing surprises me living in Los Angeles. I moved east to the Inland Empire to escape the city's madness." I said, "I hear you. My name is Morris. I recently moved here from Cleveland, Ohio. I teach in South Los Angeles." The big man responded, "My name is Big Marvin. I grew up in South Los Angeles. I played baseball and graduated from Crenshaw High School. Nice to meet you." Big Marvin continued, "Well, whatever happened, I have a hunch we will be sitting here for a long time."

The train had come to a complete stop. People were still in a frenzy, although the initial chaos had subsided. We sat and sat. I felt cramped as I waited impatiently for news or information about the accident. After forty-five minutes of anxiety and torture, the conductor said, "There has been an accident. The train hit a car that was sitting on the tracks. More information will be provided as we get it. However, the train will be delayed for a few hours. We will not move until an investigation is completed." Chaos ensued as commuters shouted, screamed, and released profanity. Their complaints echoed from the front to the back of the train. Big Marvin was stoic and emotionless. He was chill and did not react to our current circumstances. I closed my eyes and placed my hands gently across my stomach. I inhaled deeply, then blew out as much frustration as possible. I repeated what I called the vacuum breath five more times. I finished, then raised my head over my seat to watch people frantically call employers on their cell phones. Big Marvin was still as I dialed my school to share the news with them. Time slowly inched along like a snail. I was impressed by the gentle, serene nature of the giant next to me. I curiously asked, "Bro. How do you stay so calm and unnerved by this shit? Somebody could be dead, and we could sit on this hot-ass, overcrowded train for hours." Marvin calmly responded, "I see you doing your meditation."

"Meditation is accepting your reality without judgment. So, the moment I realized what happened, I also started meditating. Growing up in South Los Angeles, I have learned how to survive through many crises." I excitedly said, "I've been teaching at South High School. It's been an experience learning and educating myself about the many complex neighborhoods, cultures, and worlds that interact outside of my classroom that my students bring inside my classroom. I know about the Jungles, that housing project where many of my students live, and that it is only a few blocks from the 'Black Beverly Hills,' Baldwin Hills, a rich, prominent area for African Americans. I have also learned and experienced the flavor of Leimert Park, a rich cultural footprint for Black heritage, art, and culture. Despite all the complexities and history around me, I am fascinated by the gang culture and the tight hold gangs have over our youth." Marvin loosened the tie around his thick neck. He cracked his knuckles and rotated his neck a couple of times. I wasn't sure if he wanted to talk or fight me! With a blank face, he said, "South was an elite school in the 70s and 80s."

"The Jungles was an exclusive place to live up until the 1980s. Ladera Heights was also considered the Black Beverly Hills. Dorsey High School, the rival school to Crenshaw High, was a top exclusive place to get an education." He stopped to ask, "Are you following me, young brother?" I nodded, staying enthralled and glued to the conversation. Big Marvin continues, "Black people lived affluent lives in the Jungles during the 60s and 70s. In the late 1960s, Blacks migrated from the South to work in factories like McDonnell Douglas. These were good-paying jobs that employed a lot of Blacks, allowing them to make money and buy houses. Surprisingly, during this time, Compton was a White neighborhood until 1976, and no Blacks were allowed on that side of town."

"When Blacks tried to move into Compton, there was a lot of racial violence between Blacks and Whites. I mention this because the first gangs established by Blacks served as a means to protect themselves against racist White mobs." Marvin asked, "Are you still following me, young brother?" I responded, "Yes, I teach history, and I'm familiar with this pattern called invasion, succession, stimulated by 'White flight.' An area is deemed of no significance and value for White people. They move out when they fear Black people are moving in. I'm from Cleveland, Ohio, and I have seen this shift in communities that were once White and affluent. They are now predominantly Black with tons of abandoned factories, houses, liquor stores, churches, and under-resourced, underperforming schools."

Big Marvin returned to the conversation and asked, "You got it? Historically, Locke High School in Watts and Crenshaw High School were high-performing schools with a great reputation for sports and academic excellence. However, as you mentioned, White flight and redlining, which redirected resources such as bank loans away from specific communities of color, massive closing of factories, and the migration of Black people to California, made these once prosperous communities cesspools for violence and drugs. Black men, like my uncle, could no longer provide for their families, and things started to fall apart."

"Unfortunately, Black men like my uncle lost their jobs. Marriages fell apart, so they turned to drugs like cocaine. The drug trade fueled the turf/gang wars because drugs were the only means to make money in places that local governments strategically abandoned. Black people were blamed for using this as a means to survive. Similar patterns of oppression occurred with Mexican and Latino immigrants. They were forced to live in certain areas like 18th Street, Florence, and Huntington Park, with no jobs and real opportunities. The underlying factor for Blacks and Latinos in these segregated but very close communities was the drug trade to make money. This fueled more violence between Black and Mexican gangs. These catastrophic trends started in the late 70s and early 80s, but segregation began the day Blacks got off the trains and landed on Main Street. Main Street divides east and west Los Angeles. South and Southeast Los Angeles are Black and Mexican neighborhoods, including Watts and South Central LA. Whites moved further west into the San Fernando Valley."

"I was fortunate enough to go to Crenshaw when it was a step above neighborhoods like Inglewood. I used athletics to channel the frustration and despair I witnessed through loved ones in communities around me. I saw the destruction of drugs and gangs and how they destroyed Black communities when economic opportunities dried up. I was lucky to play on one of the best high school baseball teams. I played and grew up with the superstar Darryl Strawberry, who had a complex life of tragedy and triumph. Our team, the Crenshaw Five, was among the greatest in history. I wrote a book about my story. I would love for you to read it." Happy, we continued an enlightening conversation throughout the investigation as police and emergency services arrived on the scene. We were uncertain if anyone had died inside the car that interrupted our commute.

Eventually, the train began to move. I felt relief as I had time to teach my afternoon classes. When the train arrived at Union Station, I exchanged information with Big Marvin. Before we parted ways, he said, "If you want to change that community, start with one and change their mentality. Start educating and working with the concerned parents with low skills who want to be involved in their children's lives. They will support you, and you can build your movement from there." I hustled up the stairs, through the tunnel, and into the main area to wait for my bus. I arrived at school and entered through the side doors.

I had the weight and pressure of being late, feeling depleted, and wondering how my afternoon classes would go. My emotions were thin as I walked down the dull hallway to check in with the secretary. I entered the office. She immediately said, "Hey, Mr. Ervin. I bet that was a crazy experience. You look tired. Why don't you rest before your next class? Let me tell you something. I was so proud of how your twelfth grade History class, I mean your entire class, marched in this office this morning. They were quiet and respectful. I noticed two young men, Black and Hispanic, take the lead as they politely asked to speak with the principal. I told them to knock at the door to see if he had time to meet with them. They did. The principal quickly answered the door and said, 'Hey, kids, I'm busy and do not have time to meet.' Then, the tall, skinny one said, 'You seem frustrated and pressed for time. However, we are also frustrated and need to speak with you about Mr. Ervin. May we return after this period is over?'" Principal B was shocked and pleasantly surprised at the eloquent response and quickly said, 'Yes, next period,' as he slammed the door. Then, all the students quietly and respectfully exited the office without a sound. Next period arrived, and right on time, all your students silently marched back into the office. The same young men politely said, 'Excuse me, my name is Victor, and I'm Carlos. We have a meeting with Principal B about our teacher, Mr. Ervin.' I chuckled inside. However, I felt power and purpose from those students I've never seen displayed in my entire career - and I've seen plenty! I responded, 'He's waiting. Please knock on his door.' They knocked. The door swung open, and the Principal snarled and said, 'I can't fit an entire class in my office!' He pointed at Victor and Carlos and said, 'I'll only take you two!' So, while the rest of the class stayed quiet and polite outside, the two young men strolled into the office."

"The meeting lasted about fifteen minutes, and your class sat quietly. Then, the door swung open, and the two young men triumphantly shouted, 'We did it! We did it. Mansa gets to keep his job!' The rest of the students cheerfully whispered, high-fived each other, and hugged as they proudly walked out of the office." I stood speechless as I listened to the secretary share this heartfelt story. I said, "I appreciate you taking the time to share this with me." Then, I slowly turned and walked out of the office. Overcome with joy and delight. I detoured outside to the courtyard to soak up the soothing, warm, nourishing LA sunshine. I softly closed my eyes as the gentle breeze tickled my face, sending chills throughout my body. I made it up the backstairs to the third floor and turned the corner to a sea of radiant, smiling faces sticking out of my doorway. I triumphantly glided down the hall to greet my students. I hugged Carlos and Victor before walking into the room.

As I entered, all the students rushed towards me, almost knocking me to the dusty floor. We clapped, smiled, cheered, and hugged each other. I chanted, "Treat me cruel. Weigh me down!" They responded, "Take my freedom. Take my crown." Ana stood up and chanted, *"Somos Una!"* We all responded, *"Familia Chingonas!"* We settled in our seats, and I said, "Words will never be able to express how proud I am of this entire class. You all united despite differences and took destiny into your own hands to achieve a common goal." Benjamin interrupted, "We did that thing! Principal Blockhead was so surprised at how organized we were. He just knew he would send us little Black and Brown kids away. He thought wrong. We would have protested in that office for the rest of the year until he hired you back!"

Jamela said, "Mansa, you will be proud of me because I wanted to curse him out so bad!" The class shouted, "Yes, she did!" We all burst into laughter. Perda shared. "Mansa, we all decided to prepare Victor and Carlos to be the voice. We knew we couldn't speak, so we trusted Victor and Carlos." Then little Michael added, "Yeah, Mansa, we all met up early in the courtyard to do role play. I played Principal Blockhead, and I deserve an Oscar!" The joyful, exuberant conversation continued throughout the period. Before the bell rang, Glenda, the lovable Latina with a smile that could heal the world, perfectly summed up their protest by saying to the class, "We were awake. We fought for something that we all love, and that's Mansa. Nobody will ever be able to take this moment away from us! This is our moment!" The bell rang, and they all vanished.

While soaking in the joy and happiness, I wondered how my morning B-Inspired classes went. Then suddenly, Orlando and Jackson burst into the room! They stood in front of me with hearts pounding from their chest. I quickly jumped to my feet and said, "Fellas, what's up? What happened?" They both stuttered and interrupted each other. I struggled to decipher what was being said. Orlando said, "Mansa. It's Kelvin. His rivals were trying to gang-bang on him today. They confronted him in the bathroom. We heard lots of arguing and commotion. There were three of them. We ran into the bathroom just as the principal came in. Kelvin was tired of being intimidated and knew he had to take matters into his own hands. He wanted to protect his homie, Chris, too. So, he told us last night that he would bring a machete to school and end all this drama. Jackson interrupted and said, "It was incredible. The kid pushed Kelvin. I tensed my whole body because I knew he would grab the machete wrapped in newspaper behind the third stall that nobody uses. I was wrong. He stood there, taking intense breaths, and said, 'Treat me cruel. Weigh me down. Take my freedom. Take my crown.' He did not flinch."

"It's like he turned into you or something!" Orlando jumped, saying, "Yeah, we had his back, but he rose above it all. Then, Principal Blockhead and his team grabbed us by the necks and took us to the office. They let us go with a warning, but I'm unsure what happened to Kelvin and the rest." Flabbergasted and relieved, I asked, "Is the machete still there?" Jackson and Orlando looked at each other, and then Orlando reached into his bag and pulled out the machete wrapped in newspaper. I said, "I'm impressed, Orlando and Jackson, with your tremendous courage to do the right thing. I'm grateful we have a bond, and you all came right to me. Please share this with no one else. I want to see what happened with Kelvin." We all quickly embraced, and both boys left.

I dashed down the two flights of stairs like an Olympic athlete. I rushed into the main office, looking for Principal Blockhead. He was gone. Then, I sprinted down the hallway toward the Dean of Discipline's Office. I slowed down before walking inside. The dean was a pleasant, plump, nicely dressed man with a great sense of humor. The dean sipped coffee from a large mug and said, "Mr. Ervin, take a seat. What can I help you with?" I said, "Dean, my student Kelvin Keystone was involved in an incident with a few other young men this morning. What happened?" The dean stretched his arms and said, "What happened to all those hooligans that led them to a life of gang activity will take a lifetime to explain. However, if you're referring to what happened after the incident, we gave them all an opportunity to transfer." The muscles in my face tightened, and my stomach had a burning sensation. I asked, "What exactly is an opportunity to transfer?" "Well, Mr. Ervin," the dean said, "It means either they agree to be transferred to another school or they get expelled for the rest of the year." My heart sank like I was trapped in quicksand. I fired back, "Those are young men who tried to bang on Kelvin. You do realize that he did not lay one punch on them. You realize Kelvin has improved his grades and behavior significantly since last year. You do realize that Kelvin has transformed himself into the leader he's meant to be. If I'm not mistaken, the Boys Inspired Program is intended to give these young men a second chance to prove themselves. This is his first incident this school year, and you all expelled him?" My tone had an aura of seriousness that flirted with rage and hostility as I attempted not to turn my sadness into madness. With each word, alarms went off inside of me. I felt that my inner Bill Bixby was about to unleash. My respect and admiration for the dean somehow interrupted my full-on explosion. I stopped. The dean said, "Mr. Ervin, the process was signed off by the principal and me this morning. It's over. Kelvin no longer attends South Los Angeles High School."

CHAPTER 18

Learning From Loss

"My hurt is my greatest heartbreak and my greatest gift.
Be still. Something higher communicates through pain."
Morris H. Ervin, Jr.

The devastating news about Kelvin felt like a sucker punch to my gut. Momentarily speechless, I placed my head in my hands. Backing up the chair to stand, I turned and left the dean's office. As days came and went, the next month flew by. My lessons seemed to flop. Each day, the behavior of my students, particularly my B-Inspired twelfth grade boys, went down. My twelfth grade B-Inspired class turned into a dumping ground as a few more disrespectful boys from schools around the city were transferred into my room. One boy named Demond joined my class. It appeared his goal was to destroy everything I stood for. Demond tormented me with his sarcastic remarks and used divisive tactics to pit the boys against each other. He was a genius at causing chaos as he sat back with his hands behind his head and a sinister laugh. Every student became a problem. Jackson was caught doing inappropriate things with a young girl in the courtyard. Upon his return to class, all the boys hollered and clapped, co-signing his misogynistic behavior. Carter, the charismatic kid whose energy and positivity had the potential to take him far in life, came to class wreaking of marijuana. Unfortunately, most of my boys diminished themselves into followers. Chubby Scooter, Maxwell, Roland, and Shawn constantly heckled my teaching with wisecracks and refused to complete any assignments. Every day, Orlando's emotional outbursts became worse. I had to remove him from class to avert a potential fight.

Jerry wore his headphones and went to sleep in class. Chris, Kelvin's best friend, started to cut school, and I rarely saw him. Edward, my most well-behaved B-Inspired kid, tried so hard to stay on task, but with all the chaos and drama, he occasionally messed up. Lastly, my youngest B-Inspired boy, Geronimo, who used to crack jokes, took a back seat to Demond. Geronimo ignored my directives while retreating to his scratch pad of sketches and drawings as a form of isolation and self-protection. I struggled to maintain control of this class. Before each class began, I ruminated about Kelvin's fateful day and how the school gave up on him and sabotaged my class.

I struggled to get through the last two weeks before winter break. Usually, students are out of control and rebellious before a holiday. I thought it would be the perfect opportunity to challenge the AVID accelerated classes to a dance performance. The AVID teacher was young, cheerful, and outgoing. I knew she would be open to this idea. Plus, it would allow my B-Inspired boys to interact with other students in the school. We set a date for a Thursday afternoon before Winter break. The AVID accelerated kids would compete against my ninth- and twelfth grade B-Inspired classes. After completing all the work, the boys and I agreed to rehearse each day during the last ten minutes of class.

The rehearsals were so much fun. Over dope beats and instrumentals in the background, we practiced our call responses while synchronizing our movements. We practiced different steps as we recited our chants and formations in unison. We added the Soulja Boy Dance to spice up our chants and movements, as this dance had become a worldwide sensation. Each rehearsal filled my heart with joy. The new boys were trying to cooperate. Some days, practicing with the ninth grade boys was aggravating and hilarious. We began with pushing and shoving, then running and playing until eventually everyone was ready. A beautiful transformation of power, brilliance, energy, tenacity, and focus united the ninth grade B-Inspired boys. After our last rehearsal, I was convinced beyond a shadow of a doubt that we were ready to take down the AVID Accelerated Program.

Finally, the day arrived, and visions of a B-Inspired victory danced wildly in my head. I gathered the boys in a circle one last time for a pep talk. As we stood shoulder to shoulder, I said, "We got this! Let's go out there and show them our power and, more importantly, have fun." We turned in a single line and proudly marched through the hallway. However, as the AVID door grew closer, the line started disheveling. It fell apart like a bad marriage. I heard many arguments as the boys began losing their confidence. Sadly, like dominoes, the tension went from the front to the back of the line.

I took a deep breath and went to the front of the line. I peeked into the room to see the AVID students relaxed and ready to take the stage. I mustered some courage and said, "Treat me cruel, weigh me down!" I waited, but there was no response from my students. The boys all froze in a quicksand of terror. I strolled into the room as the boys quietly followed behind me. Ms. P., the AVID teacher, kindly said, "Mr. Ervin and the B-Inspired boys, I am glad to see you all. My kids have been salivating for this performance all week."

I smirked and said, "We are ready. Right, fellas?" No response. Ms. P. then smirked and said, "The stage is all yours." I immediately walked towards the stage. I jumped on it and turned around. The boys were still plastered against the back wall. The AVID kids mimicked them and laughed, shouting, "What's up with B-Inspired? What's up with B-Inspired?" Their booming voices and chants shook the walls. Standing alone on stage with the spotlight shining in my eyes, I desperately and frantically waved my arms for the boys to join me on stage. No response. No movement. Nothing.

They stood frozen in fear. They stood frozen in their past criticisms and labels placed on them. They stood frozen with no belief in themselves or their abilities. In their minds, they were saving face and keeping cool by guarding themselves against humiliation or being roasted. In my eyes, the hurt and betrayal stung like a police taser. I stood on stage with the pressure of holding back the tears filling my eyes. I trudged through the calls, responses, and choreographed movements alone. I finished and hopped off the stage. I joined the boys and helped them hold up the wall as we witnessed the magical performance of the AVID kids. Dejected, we turned and walked back to our room. Disgusted, I softly told Ms. P., "It's hard motivating a group that continues to defeat themselves, but I'm not done yet. My ninth grade B-Inspired boys will deliver."

Back in my classroom, my ninth graders blew in like tumbleweed in a deserted town. I quickly gathered them in a circle. We huddled together like a quarterback giving calls in the final drive to win the Superbowl. I ferociously said, "I am hurt and disappointed at what happened with the twelfth graders who left me alone on the stage. I need each of you like never before! Say yeah if you're all ready, like I'm ready!" The boys fired back with a "Yeah!" We went over a few moves and our calls and responses. We stomped loudly, proudly, enthusiastically, and passionately. Right before our performance, Ricky led us in prayer. The prayer revealed our nervousness and tenderness. After the prayer, we turned and made two lines outside my classroom. I walked ahead of them as they followed in military-style formation. We marched as I shouted, "Treat me cruel. weigh me down!" They marched and responded, "Take my freedom, take my crown!"

We all were one, in harmony and unity. As we slowly worked our way down the hallway. I felt proud, and for the first time, the ninth grade B-Inspired was showing up and showing out! As we continued our trek toward AVID, fright hit them. The boys started squabbling. They dropped out of the line as the pressure mounted. As we passed Mrs. Bright's classroom, her delicate, soothing voice encouraged the boys to continue. She shared how well they were doing and inspired them with a story about her sorority. "Show time! Go time!" Hearing the commotion, the AVID kids stuck their heads out of the doorway. They were still laughing and giggling from our earlier fiasco. AVID kids were experts at intimidation.

The boys were shaking as my frustration grew like vines on the side of an abandoned house. I felt helpless as the boys completely took their focus off of me and onto the tricks and tactics of the sinister AVID students. Desperately, I darted straight onto the stage. I hoped my ninth grade B-Inspired boys were preparing to stand behind me. Rightfully so, my prayers were answered as they strolled past the AVID kids and joined me on the stage. I let out a deep sigh and looked left to right, getting nods and confirmations from the boys. They were scared yet determined to get through the performance. Ricardo flew across the stage with flips and somersaults as the music dropped. We made all of our calls, responses, and affirmations. Lastly, we did the Soulja Boy Dance. Slightly impressed, the AVID students let out a thunderous roar of claps, cheers, and encouragement. We looked at each other with a tremendous sigh of relief and jumped off the stage.

We waited patiently for the AVID kids' performance. I hugged my students, who were smiling and relieved of tension. After the AVID kids performed, Ms. P. and I let both groups mingle and socialize before returning to our classroom. I said, "It's easy to clown, roast, fight, and disrespect kids and adults. But the challenge is to create something you love and trust. The challenge is to use your gifts and dig deep within yourself to find that inner courage and strength. Being a Mansa is not running away from adversity, giving up, or passively sitting afraid in the back of the stands. Being a Mansa is accepting, believing, and loving yourself. As you work to eliminate the fear of criticism and approval from others, the world will embrace you."

As I sat on the train reflecting on our performances with AVID, I felt torn between the awful twelfth grade performance and the celebration of the ninth grade performance. I realized I had placed more expectations and pressure on the twelfth grade B-Inspired boys for selfish reasons. My competition with the AVID kids and teachers had become personal. I wanted to prove something to those teachers and students. In my blind rage, I did not see the lack of commitment by the twelfth grade boys. In my blind rage, I missed how uncomfortable they felt outside my class-room. My classroom was their safe space. Lastly, in my anger, I realized I needed a break. This new world had me on an emotional roller coaster. I felt depleted and exhausted. I barely made it to Winter break. Before closing my eyes, I wrote in my journal, "We need more space for manhood preparation and practice."

December 2, 2007, Sad Anniversary

I woke up on Sunday morning with a strange feeling. I felt a charge of negative emotions swallowing me. Eventually, my painful emotions made me yell at my wife and children. I jumped into my orange bucket and drove away to escape the unbearable pain. With each twist and turn, my thoughts made me wild. Seeking clarity for my anger, I drove several miles to cover up my unbearable sadness. Finally, the negative thoughts and painful emotions subsided, and I turned around on Highway 10, heading home. I arrived home a bit more tender and sorrowful. Without exchanging words or eye contact, Venaya left, as I assumed she needed to study. She called me at the exact time she discovered little Emmanuel one year ago. I held the phone as she sobbed. This connection softened my heart and freed me from any expectations. We were still mourning Emmanuel.

To lighten my mood, I took the kids grocery shopping. It was enjoyable. I decided to eliminate my children's Sunday chores. We visited a stable and went to the local library. The library is my second favorite place besides nature. A particular book caught my eye. It had a Black man walking in water with a ship far off in the distance. The title was The Old African. Before I checked out the books, I had to pay a considerable fine. As we returned home after a pleasant afternoon on the anniversary of Emmanuel's death, I was reminded to cherish myself and my loved ones. It is important to spread love, respect, and understanding everywhere.

Later that evening, my family created the ritual called "Bath, Foot, Massage, and Gratitude." In candlelight, we put our feet in warm, soapy bath water and freely spoke while sharing our appreciation for family members. Naimah said, "I like Dad because he uses his feelings and needs." Idris said, "I like it when Daddy plays sports with me." Venaya shared, "I like it when Dad performs the household duties. It makes my life easier." Naimah added, "I appreciate it when Mommy does my hair and buys me nice things." Idris shared, "I like when Naimah lets me play with her and gives me respect." Naimah replied, "I like it when Idris stands up for me and protects me." Finally, I said, "I like it when Mom advises me. She is my advocate, friend, and life consultant."

On the last Sunday of Winter break, I awakened the family bright and early for our adventure to the Kwanzaa festival at Leimert Park. I surprised my family by purchasing four train and bus tickets to Los Angeles. Waiting for the train, my children could barely contain their excitement as they intently watched the train bustling into the station. We stepped inside and let our kids select the seats. As the train slowly chugged along, Naimah and Idris pressed their small faces against the window, taking in the sights and sounds. Venaya and I enjoyed some peace and quiet. Finally, we reached Union Station. My family cheerfully followed me out of the bustling train, up the steep flight of stairs, and onto the street to wait for the 740 or 40 bus. While riding on the bus, the excitement and curiosity of this new city percolated inside my children and within me.

I was grateful to show them the community and neighborhood I worked in. My children were in awe of the sights and distinct smells of the city. Finally, we arrived at the corner of Crenshaw Boulevard and King Avenue. The colossal Crenshaw Mall covered the entire block directly across from us. We dashed across the street into the huge mall and immediately went to the food court for lunch. We explored some shops and stores in the spacious, densely populated mall. My wife was drawn to the African jewelry on the second floor. Inspired by her love for African adornment, I quickly seized the opportunity to purchase a necklace and a stunningly colorful matching bracelet for her.

Not a moment too soon because our children were restless as we exited the mall and headed to the cultural oasis, Leimert Park. Not surprisingly, as we drew closer, the delicious smells tickled our nostrils while the pulsating drums awakened the rhythm within our souls. We felt like we were in Mother Africa as we approached the park. Beautiful, gorgeous Black people, adorned in African garments and colorful head wraps, glided by us with various natural hairstyles of locks, Afros, and braids. We gazed in all directions at food trucks, vendors selling fresh fruit and vegetables, clothes, African art, books, and an assortment of pro-Black tee shirts and sweatshirts. My spirit was open, and my smile was big. My heart was filled with pride as I experienced this richness alongside my family. I was mesmerized that I was standing in the epicenter of Black culture, directly in the heart of Crenshaw. And although I am a transplant from the Midwest, I couldn't feel more at home. We let the children purchase their favorite tee shirts and necklaces while Venaya and I bought two matching African dashikis. Satisfied from investing our dollars with Black businesses, we continued down the crowded sidewalk as the Reggae tunes blasted loudly from under a white tent at the end of the street. Impulsively, I jogged excitedly towards the music, waving for my family to follow.

Finally, inside the tent, I was placed in a spiritual trance as I was transported through time and space to Jamaica. I joyfully gave my family a nod. They understood how contagious and infectious live Reggae music was to my entire being. They cheerfully waved at me as I shimmied, shook, and slowly pulsated my way onto the dance floor as the Reggae band cultivated the meaning and vibration of life through incredible music. They jammed, and we jammed with them. I moved every muscle in my body while the band continued to play. We all sweated in unity inside the tent. Song after song, I discovered new ways to express the life flowing within me through dance. My big, fixated smile never changed as sweat poured down my brow.

I inhaled deeply and exhaled, basking in pure joy and freedom. A feeling of pure refreshment washed over my mind and heart. As the music faded, people gave out high fives and hugs. The musicians thanked me for bringing so much energy and enthusiasm into the jam session. Walking towards the train, I thought, "This was a spiritual cleansing that met my needs for beauty, life, vitality, and connection. The Kwanzaa celebration left a deep cultural impression on me. It was so beautiful to spend this sacred time with my family." On the train ride home, the children slept while Venaya and I cuddled and held hands until we reached our destination.

Now, at home, as soon as I carried the children to their rooms and placed them in their beds, my phone rang. I was concerned because it was late. "Hello," I said. I heard heavy breathing and chatter as multiple voices said, "Mansa, Chris is dead. He was shot and killed tonight by the Crips." I squeezed and tightened my abdomen as my head nearly exploded. In shock, I rambled a few words. Someone said, "Mansa, it's Orlando, Shawn, and Maxwell. Sorry to bother you, but we thought you should know what happened to him. School's gonna be crazy on Monday. We need you!"

The surprise and alarm still loomed in my chest and nostrils as I commuted to South Los Angeles High School the next day. My mind was obsessed with images of Chris dying tragically. I arrived at school early to mentally prepare myself for the shock, grief, and devastation this tragedy would bring our students. Before the first bell, my twelfth grade Boys Inspired crew rushed inside my classroom. After we embraced, they quickly set their desks into a circle, intending to hold space for something larger lurking in the tense atmosphere. Suddenly, with the second bell ringing, a wave of restless, heavyhearted, despondent students of all racial and ethnic backgrounds camped out in my room.

I purposely let the chatter go on as long as needed, watching my young Mansa men give hugs, receive hugs, grab tissues, and attempt to help with this makeshift mourning ceremony for Chris. Eventually, when everyone settled, Roland entered the classroom with puffy red eyes. Roland told us firsthand how he and Chris were hanging out at a park, notoriously known as a Bloods hangout. They and a few other members were repping their set. Then, as they left the park, a car sped up, and shots rang out. Chris was hit and fell to the ground while the other members ran away. He took a total of eight bullets. In an instant, he was gone. Everyone sobbed and held each other as even more students took refuge in my room for the impromptu memorial service for Chris.

Throughout the morning, I foolishly waited for an announcement from the principal or administration acknowledging his death and offering some emotional support for the students. Nothing happened. Outrage and resentment grew within me. I decided to cancel my classes for the rest of the day. I held space for Chris and the many students who needed a safe place to process his untimely death. As the tough day moved on, I managed to push my emotions aside to be present for the students. However, as I held a circle for students throughout the day, this seemed to cause chaos and disdain for teachers and administrators. During one of my classes after lunch, the door swung open, and Principal Blockhead strolled in with a few administrators from the School Board.

My students stiffened as he and others stood awkwardly outside the circle as tension built inside the room. Principal Blockhead whispered a few words to his administrators while they jotted down notes on dusty clipboards. I decided to break the tension by saying, "Listen, South students. Today has been rough, coming to school to discover that one of your beloved classmates has passed away. What makes matters worse is that the principal and his team are more concerned with pretending to assess teachers' performance rather than supporting them during a time of need. I want you to remember authority and power are only perceptions. You have the right to listen or reject them."

As my words reverberated throughout the room, Principal Blockhead screamed, "Mr. Ervin, get outside right now!" I slowly stood in the circle as students made a few painful moans and groans. I walked outside and propped myself against the wall. The fury that had engulfed my inside flowed throughout my body and swirled around my head like a typhoon. It was challenging to articulate a thought, feeling, or worry about my future at South High. With a disgruntled demeanor, I looked like a troubled teenager in high school. I smirked and thought about how satisfying it felt to provoke and embarrass Principal Blockhead in front of School Board administrators. The smirk vanished like my childhood memories when Principal Blockhead opened the door. With no eye contact and a loud tone, he said, "Ervin, meet me in my office now!" Unconsciously, I wandered through the hallways from one floor to the next, hoping to shake this righteous trepidation and indignant feeling trapped inside me.

I knew I needed to loosen up with each step. However, there was so much inner rage and resentment about many things. I was afraid I could not escape the enormous mess I had made. Eventually, I made it to the principal's office. His door was cracked just enough for me to ease in, sit, and wait for my fate. I was weary. I sat with my head in my hands and my knees tucked tightly into my chest. Finally, Blockhead pushed the door open and walked behind his huge, messy desk. Sitting down, he said, "The stunt you pulled upstairs was a disgrace! Who do you think you are, trying to challenge my authority and humiliate me like that in front of my bosses? Your level of insubordination and disrespect was off the charts! Listen to me, hot shot from Ohio. This is my school, not yours. I really should fire your narrow ass!"

The animosity, contempt, and disgust reached a boiling point in his cramped office. Fortunately, after his rant, rather than respond, I intentionally stayed quiet. In this silence and space, the tension that engulfed me cooled off. My tough shell began to evaporate like steam coming from a vaporizer. I connected to Principal Blockhead in this silent space for the first time. I waited for an opportunity to speak. I wanted to be absolutely sure he had finished speaking. Principal Blockhead loosened his tie, then placed both hands on his forehead and asked less aggressively, "Ervin, do you want your job?"

Initially, my gut said no. I quit. However, flashes of a train ride home, knowing I was jobless with a family in California, enabled me to think sensibly. I answered, "Yes." He responded, "Good. I trust that we will not have this type of conversation ever again. Also, since you failed your classroom evaluation today, I'm assigning you a classroom coach to work with you for a few days." I sat in silence, knowing my principal had punished me. He continued, "Listen, Ervin, you're a great young teacher with great potential. Hell, I see a lot of my younger self in you, especially that fire that you have to make a difference. However, you can't make it in this system by being defiant, disrespectful, and pissing off your colleagues and superiors. Now, please leave my office. I have work to do."

I watched him shuffle some papers and pick up his phone. I walked out of his office happy. I had a bruised ego, but at least I was still employed. I circled back to my class and found some of my boys lingering around my classroom even though the school day was over. Their faces brightened like the sunrise when I trotted back inside the room. They all shouted in unison, "Mansa, did you get fired?" I responded, "Naw, fellas, but it was a close call!" Roland, whose eyes were still red, walked up to me and said, "Mansa, as you know, Chris was my homey. The funeral is tomorrow. My moms don't have a car. Can you take us?" Without hesitation, I responded, "Yes!" Roland continued, "Another thing, Kelvin, Chris's best friend, also wants to come with us. Here is my address. Kelvin said he would meet you in front of the school tomorrow morning." The boys left.

Before I could sit and reflect on my day of grief and indignation, a few teachers casually walked into my room. One of the teachers said, "Mr. Ervin. I hope you don't plan to attend Chris's funeral tomorrow. He was in a gang. Gang funerals can be dangerous as retaliations happen, and there could be a shootout." I casually acknowledged their concern for my safety. "I'm not afraid," I responded. "My goal is to pay my respects to Chris and his family. He was a student of mine. I'll be there, and it's a shame that I'll probably be the only teacher representing this school." They gave me a sinister look as they turned and left my class.

The next day, I woke up at four in the morning. I intentionally pulled out my funeral garment, which I wore for Emmanuel's funeral. I kissed my wife and children on the forehead and left the house, determined to beat the rush hour traffic. On the highway, despite Chris's tragic death, I joyfully anticipated reconnecting with Kelvin. I wondered if he was going to school and staying out of trouble. My exit approached, and my headlights lit the dark street en route to Crenshaw Avenue. I pulled up on a side road by South and anxiously waited for Kelvin to appear. I closed my eyes to rest as I anticipated a stressful day. I attempted to center my breathing and body sensations to anchor my conscious and unconscious emotions. Each repetition of deep breathing and the gentle breeze blowing through my car window enabled me to find my flow. Suddenly, I heard a knock on the window. I slowly opened my eyes. It was Kelvin.

Excited, I gathered my senses and reached over to unlock the passenger door. He plopped down in the seat as we dapped each other up. "Kel, how have you been? It's been a while since I've seen you," I said. Kel calmly responded, "Mansa, I've been okay. I'm staying out of the way, and everything is alright." We continued our conversation as we drove to Victor's home. Immediately as we pulled up on the curb of 6th Ave and Vernon, Victor, with his skinny legs, leaped over his porch and dashed to the car. He slipped in the back seat and said, "What's good, Mansa? What's up, Kel? Great to see you, bro." We ventured down Crenshaw and turned down a side street. The neighborhood changed. It felt like a dark, evil veil, and despair surrounded us. I slowed my car to a complete stop. I cautiously scanned the graffiti and trash that covered the shabby, rundown tenements. The scenery pierced my soul. I became frightened about how living, surviving, and growing up in such a poverty-stricken neighborhood would feel. I was petrified. Suddenly, I heard, "Mansa, we comin'." I looked across the street and saw Roland and a thin woman I assumed was his mom. Roland jogged towards the car as his mom slowly followed him. Roland's eyes were still puffy and red. We embraced.

"Mansa, sorry for not letting you know, but my mom wanted to come with us. And don't be trippin' on her because she only knows a little English because we are from Belize," Roland said. Astonished, I thought, here is a young man raised by a single immigrant mother in a gang-infested community. No wonder Roland acts so silly and wild in school. That's the only place where he feels comfortable and safe. I walked around the car and greeted his mom. She nodded her head and smiled. Kelvin moved to the back seat so Roland's mom could sit up front. He squeezed into the back seat with Victor and Roland. As we pulled off, I was slightly afraid about the funeral. Fortunately, my faith, conviction, concern, and care as an educator for my students and those in my car overrode any feelings of fear. After that brief moment of anxiety, I drove with inspiration and purpose. I was confident that we would be protected.

We arrived at the funeral home. We got out of the car and followed people walking toward the entrance. We walked inside. The room was filled. People were standing around the walls. We stood in the receiving line to view Chris's body and greet his family. I intentionally walked behind the young men and Roland's mom. We gathered around Chris's casket. He wore a nice Black suit and had a fresh haircut. We were overwhelmed with grief. As tears streamed down their faces, I placed my hands around Victor, Kelvin, and Roland. I tried to hold back my tears, but I couldn't. After we paid our respects, we hugged Chris's mother and family members. Despite all her pain and devastation, his mom told me, "Thank you for teaching my son and being here today. He loved your class."

Luckily, we found a few seats in the back. Before the family viewed Chris's body for the last time, twenty young men boldly walked into the funeral home dressed in red with pictures of Chris airbrushed on the back of their tee shirts. They threw up gang signs while viewing his body. As they walked away from the casket, one said, "We gonna get them niggas." Chills of uneasiness ran through my veins. I couldn't believe Chris's gang members dared to attend his funeral and threatened revenge. I had never experienced anything like this in my entire life. The minister officiating the ceremony struggled to maintain control of the crowd as the gang members exited. He asked those who wanted to say something about Chris to come forward.

A woman who identified herself as a good Christian criticized Chris for not being a Christian. Chris's mom stood up and started screaming and yelling at her. She shouted, "You don't know shit about him or us! How dare you stand here at my baby's funeral talking crazy!" Oblivious to Chris's mother's response, the woman left the podium as Chris's mom and others continued criticizing her. Dozens of people began shouting profanity at the woman. People also started screaming and yelling at people across the aisle. Helplessly, the minister attempted to regain control over the loud noise and hostile crowd. He flapped his arms like a seal as his multiple cries for calmness were ignored. "I need everyone to settle down, please, for the sake of Chris and his family. If this continues, we must shut this down and remove everyone except the family," he yelled. Slowly, I rose from my seat and gingerly walked toward the preacher. With each step, I inhaled deeply and exhaled deeply. Frantic, the minister was unaware of my presence until I stood directly before him. We were inches apart as I watched sweat beads drip down his nose. I firmly said, "Pastor, I need to speak. I need to speak right now." Rattled, desperate, and hopeless, he begrudgingly handed me the microphone and stepped to the side.

Confident as an Olympic skater, I stood directly in front of everyone. I gazed around the room. Suddenly, a deep sense of peace and purpose flowed inside of me. It felt like a rush of waves during the morning tide on a sandy beach. With this rush of waves flowing through me, I said, "I would like to start with the African greeting of 'Hotep,' which means, 'I come in peace.' I'm Mansa Musa, which means 'West African king.' I have a simple but powerful request before I start. Would everyone with a heart make a fist and put it in the air to show unity?" Silence filled the room. Like dominoes, a sea of fists rose through the room as an immediate expression of solidarity.

"First, I want to give my sincere condolences to Chris's siblings and his parents. Words nor actions can express or describe the pain, devastation, and loss you're experiencing. However, as you see the fist still held proudly in the air, know we are with you. I enjoyed teaching your son in my history class at South Los Angeles High School. Chris was a quiet and pleasant young man who led by keeping his voice low. He listened and completed every activity and assignment without complaining. He had a strong foundation and family to support him. Obviously, he was influenced and raised right by two strong, dedicated parents. Every day, Chris wrote in his journal, and I encouraged all the Mansas in my class to reflect on their struggles and achievements.

"The Mansas and I spent time analyzing, reflecting, and applying words and their deeper meanings into our lives. One phrase goes like this, 'Treat me cruel, weigh me down. Take my freedom, take my crown.' I emphasized the importance of the word oppression and how deeply it impacted our lives, families, and communities. I told the Mansas that, ultimately, their actions would determine if they kept or lost their crown. Chris's crown was taken. He was assassinated, and that's part of a bigger picture of what's happening in our community. Young men like Chris get gunned down in the streets way too often. The minds of our young people are being held captive by a lifestyle that leads them down a path of suffering and misery. Our young men are being cheated, tricked, and fooled by a way of life that disconnects them from their humanity. As I look around this room and when I'm in Los Angeles, I see beautiful Black and Brown faces kissed by a shining sun and pretty scenery. This is natural. However, the stress from trying to make ends meet, keep a job, protect your family, and survive destroys the beauty within. This creates a fertile ground for violence to creep in and slowly take us away from what it means to be spiritual beings connected with the heart. Violence kills the finer emotions of the heart. It's a slow death. However, our creator gave us minds to think and hearts to love. Together, this makes our spirits strong! African Americans are the original people of light and energy!"

"That's right! Say it, brother!" someone said. I noticed Brother Torrè with his fist still up, looking proud! "Look around you." I continued. "When you look in the mirror, you see a connection with God. Our collective purpose is to absorb God's energy from the sun, or God's natural light, and use this light and energy to bring our families and communities together. Everyone's natural purpose is to bring life together, not destroy it. We can start by shining the light on ourselves, then our children, spouses, neighbors, and even other races. As Black people, we have the power to heal, understand, think, love, and share our natural gifts with the world. The first step is to open our hearts and let the sunshine in! Mansa Chris, may you rest in peace."

I finished and calmly returned to my seat. Shortly after a few more speakers, the service ended. We filtered outside into the sun. Folks embraced and hugged me. One gentleman squeezed me tightly like a python and said, "Who are you, and where did you come from? I have never met anyone like you!" I gracefully bow to him. I was grateful to him and others who could see my gifts. Immediately following that exchange, Brother Torrè, with his powerful presence, walked up to me and said, "Brother Mansa, you're a powerful brother. We need to link up. I have an upcoming event I organized called the "Man Child Conference. I would be honored if you would present two workshops for me." Graciously, I said, "Sure, brother. I would be happy to do so." Torrè responded in a deep Paul Robeson-type voice, "Excellent, brother. We will talk about the details. Be easy now." I gathered the boys and Roland's mom. We stopped to get something to eat before I took them all home.

CHAPTER 19

Discover the M.A.P.
(Make Awareness Personal)

"When we relate to ourselves and others violently,
we diminish or suppress the divine energy
that connects us in each moment."
Morris H. Ervin, Jr.

The next day, I struggled to contain my emotions and harmony in my classes. I asked my students to evaluate my teaching effectiveness in my first-period class. I needed positive feedback to help me change the months of feeling inadequate, helpless, and unmotivated. As I regurgitated the question, I knew I was taking a considerable risk. I slowly took a few deep breaths, tightened my stomach, and asked, "Who feels free when they come into this class?" A chorus of hands were lifted.

However, I noticed a small section of disgruntled students with sour expressions. I stared at them until some said, "We want education." "We don't do anything here." "This class is stupid!" I was stung! Their words set off an explosive reaction from the rest of the class. I asked everyone to calm down and asked those who spoke to elaborate. With squinty eyes, Carter said, "We always have discussions, play games, and write in our journals. We barely ever do any bookwork like other kids in their classes. I don't care about expressing my feelings. I'm not learning anything!" This set off an argument between the majority of the class, who understood and appreciated my teaching style, and a minority of students who weren't feeling me. I attempted to intervene as the chaos increased into more arguing and, eventually, threats. I continued encouraging everyone to calm down, sit, and take deep breaths. I reminded them to create space to listen to one another. When the dust settled, one student passionately shouted, "Mansa is taking a chance on us, and he is doing what we love. I'm a better student because of it!" Many in the class agreed with thunderous shouts and claps. Then, Geniqwa, who agreed with Carter, said, "We like Mansa too, but we have standardized tests coming up, and I want to be prepared."

At that moment, I realized each group had valid concerns. Now, speaking in a calmer atmosphere, I said, "I understand your concerns about my approach to teaching and preparing you to take tests. A traditional teaching style is safe and easier for some students to comprehend. However, I strongly believe the educational system has fooled and tricked you. Education should not be about standardized tests and random facts irrelevant to your lives. Nor should it demand that you be complacent and obedient, rewarding those who do good and punishing those who are bad. It's about cultivating trust and building community while helping you become independent critical thinkers. It's tough for me to teach lessons straight from the book when no one is engaged. In that type of learning, keeping everyone focused is a real struggle. I value interactive and reflective learning that will benefit you all over your lifetime. I'm planting the seeds for your long-term development."

After my speech, I encouraged students to record their reactions in journals. The bell rang, and the students vanished. Before the rest of my day continued, I sat down to reflect and write about what had occurred. I tried to relieve myself from the intensity of my last class, knowing my twelfth grade B-Inspired boys would soon arrive. My journaling was interrupted. A tall, White man with a thick grayish-white beard appeared before me. I immediately took a defensive stance. Surprisingly, he put his hand out for me to shake it. I was reluctant. He said, "Good afternoon, I'm Jim Fire, and I'll observe your class while offering feedback on areas needing improvement."

My class generally begins as soon as my students are seated. Jim politely positioned himself in the back of the classroom while I started my lesson. During my lesson, a few young men decided to leave the circle.

They went to the windowsill and began conversing as Mr. Fire quietly observed every action. He politely walked over to the windowsill to speak with the young men and returned to his seat. I became frustrated and bitter as I encouraged the class to answer the focus questions in the chapter. Some students ignored my request and began talking, while others placed their heads on the desk. A small group attempted to answer the questions. Again, Mr. Fire walked around the room and spoke with a few students. I didn't particularly appreciate being judged and hassled by this stranger who had invaded my space. I looked around the class and saw that Orlando had checked out and was planted against the windowsill. Mr. Fire approached him. I chose to remain at my desk. Mr. Fire spoke to him. Orlando stood up and said, "I don't write anything down, and I don't talk to adults I don't know." Mr. Fire made a non-verbal gesture and returned to his seat in the back of the room. The talking and socializing increased as more students ignored the lesson. I reluctantly stood up and tried to connect the meaning of the content with the ideas whirling in my head while Mr. Fire watched.

The bell rang. I and the students were out of misery as they jumped up and quickly left my classroom. Nervously waiting to hear Mr. Fire's assessment of my class, I sat on my desk swinging my legs restlessly back and forth, hoping that this giant White man would disappear like Houdini. I closed my eyes. When I opened them, his large frame stood before me. I sighed to settle the uneasy, aggravated feeling within me. He said, "The structure of the class and your enthusiasm seemed distant today. I've heard great things about your exceptional ability to motivate students, especially students as challenging as the B-Inspired boys." "You can't come here and judge me off of one class," I snapped back. "You have no idea who I am or who these boys are." Mr. Fire responded, "It was challenging to see any parameters set or expectations around what you wanted them to produce for the day. A few young men were off to the side, and you did not invite them to join the lesson." I shouted, "I've been through a lot this year. I've given so much to this school and these young men. The administration has dumped new boys into my classroom who have no idea about the culture I've built. My class has turned into a dumping ground. I don't have the strength to continue to manage these extreme behaviors every single day. It's exhausting. These boys need to be in a free environment, not in chaos, but they must learn how to cooperate and respect each other, which takes time. They are angry, scared, and have created a culture of resistance thicker, longer, and deeper than the Great Wall of China! They live in fear. Fear is a slow process that kills the finer emotions of the heart."

"Likewise, creating environments of love is also a slow process. No institution or school will ever teach them that. This school took away a real leader, a kid trying to change himself. They didn't care about the positive impact he was making. He was kicked out of this school. This is deeper than this program. This is about life! Lives are at stake! Another one of my boys was murdered, and the school didn't care. So, sending you here to teach me won't change anything!" I exclaimed. As I ended my fiery rant, I felt a burning in my chest. My face felt tight.

Mr. Fire took a moment and calmly said," I'm sensing some conflict and imbalance between the teacher and relationship roles. Traditional teachers lean heavily on providing order and structure, while you rely heavily on creating connection and healing. I can see why this imbalance has caused you to feel inadequate and frustrated about the demands you've placed on yourself from a place of healing and connection. That daunting, never-ending task will burn you out and leave you with resentment, rage, cynicism, and apathy. Please focus on rebuilding a healthy balance between the teacher and relationship roles and not on the administration and your anger around things you can't change. I've taken some notes and have some suggestions to help you integrate the two roles. I'm confident that this integration of functions will decrease your burnout and increase your motivation, commitment, and effectiveness to be that master teacher."

"I recommend you use a process called 'Consistency Management.' I've developed a system that helps you manage and regulate your teaching abilities and provide structure while building deep relationships. Lastly, take my workbook and read over some of my best practices. Try them out and let me know what you think." Mr. Fire shook my hand, picked up his briefcase, and left my classroom. I was stunned and also motivated to make some changes. I didn't realize how badly I was suffering in silence. I closed my door, loosened my tie, and turned on my favorite jazz musician, Thelonious Monk. I sat with my feelings and began to write.

January 7, 2008, Energy and Epiphanies

I understand that my real strengths are healing, creating connections, and building relationships. Healing is my form of consistency management. However, without a consistent plan of the structure and a plan to embrace the role of the teacher, it is counterintuitive to focus solely on healing as a focal part of learning. The school as a system operates on a different paradigm. I now realize I have been fighting that paradigm. I never realized this until a few moments ago. I have felt out of place in my teaching career because I was unwilling to embrace my role. How can I be in the teaching profession and refuse to accept the teacher's role? The order and structure of teaching are inherently bad, wrong, or punitive. Thus, I avoid it. I realize I am no different than the rebellious boys I teach. I thought my only option as a teacher was to act out or rebel against it. This is why I am so quick to lash out and defend myself. I had labeled myself a rebel inside a system I didn't trust. I resist the system to which I am loyal and committed. I am a walking contradiction. I am conflicted inside the system.

I harbor pain and a lot of resentment. I am a rebel, and my students are my co-conspirators. That's a lot of pressure to put on them and me. Now I understand why, at times, they have resisted my intensity. Today, after speaking with Mr. Fire, I realize I had judged myself a failure when Kelvin got kicked out of school. For the entire semester, I had mentally shut down. I became a victim, blaming myself and everyone around me. I was stuck in misery and the past. I did not fully mourn the loss of Kelvin. I had become a victim of circumstance. Upon deep introspection, I shut down to meet my needs for safety and protection. However, I am a healer - and that's exceptional. Therefore, I need to balance the healing and relationship aspect of my teaching with the structured production aspect of it. I now understand I must take my desire to heal beyond the walls of a school and into the larger community. I need space and freedom to work with the boys, and I know who to start with first.

Without hesitation, I scramble through my briefcase, desperately looking for Kelvin's number. Eureka! I found it. I dialed the number. It rings four or five times and then goes directly to voicemail. I confidently say, "Greetings Ms. Keystone. This is Mansa, Kelvin's old teacher from South Los Angeles High. I have started a new mentoring program focusing on manhood preparation, emotional intelligence, leadership development, and cultural arts competence. We will meet on Saturdays at 10 a.m. I would love for Kelvin to participate in this life-changing experience. Please call me back at your earliest convenience."

Happy, as a kid at Toys "R" Us, I ended the call. Later, I spent a few hours reviewing Mr. Fire's curriculum manual. Turning each page, I am more intrigued by the simplicity of his ideas and eager to try them in the classroom. A few weeks passed, and I attended some of Mr. Fire's after-school staff development training. I feel confident because I incorporate his "Consistent Management" techniques in my classes. It has revived my teaching and anchored my emotional stability. I love his concept of the "praise word note card." I ask students to write on a note card what word or phrase excites and motivates them. When I call on students to answer a question, I can enthusiastically read their praise word or have the class read it in the call-and-response format. This process allows me to easily track who's participating in class and ensure everyone is learning.

Most importantly, Mr. Fire has this revolutionary idea called "Consistency Management Positions." Teachers juggle many assignments. We keep records, take attendance, develop lessons, pass out materials, keep track of time, and discipline and reward students. We struggle, get overwhelmed, and stressed out. However, Mr. Fire's Consistency Management Program helps identify different positions we need in class. It creates real job opportunities for our students to contribute to the class's functioning, productivity, and environment. Furthermore, this program doesn't randomly hand out duties. Mr. Fire's system prints out job descriptions and applications and encourages students to dress up and interview for the job of their choice. The applications must be neat and complete, with references from three people. Additionally, students can be fired from jobs for disruptive behavior or poor job performance.

Without a doubt, if this isn't preparing our students for real life, I'm not sure what is. Above all, his radical techniques completely transformed the most challenging, poorly behaved student into a real empathetic leader.

One day, during a staff meeting, the ninth grade teaching staff spent forty minutes complaining and venting about six-foot-one drama queen, chaos creator, and teacher slayer Anastasia. I listened and thought that girl was relentless and incorrigible, and nothing could be done. Then it struck me like a rod of lightning! I was going to introduce the Classroom Management Positions to my ninth graders. I would do my best used car salesman approach to get the students, especially Anastasia, to buy into what I was selling. Later that evening, I sat in my dining room thinking about what positions would best serve my needs and those of my ninth graders. I needed a greeter with positive energy to welcome the kids entering my class. I needed a materials manager to pass out and collect materials. I needed an attendance/tardy manager to take attendance and direct students to sign in if they were late. I needed a time manager to keep track of time during class to let me know when to switch to new activities or to wrap up the lesson for the day. Certainly, I needed someone with positive energy to lighten the mood and lead the class in the call responses we created.

Most importantly, I kept a miscellaneous position open that would be unique to each class. I was confident the position would reveal itself to me in real time. Immediately after brainstorming the positions, I needed, I gathered sample interview questions for students to answer and created a job application. Proudly, I sat at the table feeling empowered and energized as I joyfully anticipated my introduction of the Classroom Management Positions to my ninth graders. Lastly, before retiring to bed, I wrote a quick note in my journal to channel the warm feelings percolating inside my spirit.

January 28, 2008, The Essence of Being a Human Being

Without the enduring principles of love and trust, which is a long-term process, your entire being, existence, or system will collapse because there is nothing of substance in your heart and mind. Love and trust are vital principles for survival. They are like breathing in oxygen, eating healthy food, and drinking water. Water is essential to life, just as building a culture of love and trust is essential to life. Love and trust are a part of human nature and go with the natural flow of life. Sadly, the public education system contradicts the natural flow of human nature. Schools are filled with unnatural, temporary, quick strategies that destroy young peoples' genuine spirit and willingness to give and receive. I believe everyone is of value and has something to contribute. Everyone contributes something inside a system, right, wrong, good, or bad. Systems at home and in school tragically miseducate youth into the little world of punishment, reward, submission, or rebellion. "Mansa, your main objective and mission was to create a connection," I told myself. "Your task is to challenge families, schools, neighborhoods, and communities to examine their cultural paradigms and maps of how they perceive and experience the world around them. Your main objective as an educator, Mansa, is first to understand and second to be understood.

When we sincerely and honestly reflect on our lives and experiences, we ask ourselves, 'Am I happy? Am I suffering? Am I miserable? Is my life working? or Am I worthy?' Mansa, your objective is to offer respect and kindness to the world. Your purpose is not to play the blame game. Mansa, you have a vision of families, schools, and communities learning skills to connect with nature. You want people to live in harmony and interdependence, where everyone can trust that all needs matter while acknowledging that some peoples' needs of power and privilege are met at the expense of other peoples' needs.

Let's build a world that acknowledges power differentials. However, those in power can use their influence to lift those with less power and create a greater good for all. Let's learn to speak the language of love, respect, and compassion for our children and youth. Children need to know and feel that they are essential to us. They need to know they influence the relationship. Children need influence and voice in their lives. Adult guidance can build mutual trust, respect, and understanding. Children trust and believe adults have their best interests at heart. As *they grow into adolescence, they can avoid the power struggles with adults who can hinder their development and stunt their growth. This is the essence of a relationship. We, as adults, need to listen to the wisdom of our children and take and use their ideas. The result will be children who can blossom with grace, courage, and confidence. They have roots and wings to accomplish amazing things. The foundation of positive character traits that have been created will be valued. They will pass their knowledge and values to the next generation.*

While helping our children plan for their future, we must value them as precious gems. There are two key challenges when engaging our youth. First, is learning how to maintain a healthy balance when cultivating a mutual relationship as we encourage them to achieve and produce positive results and outcomes. Second, is helping them see the value in their lives and the benefits of achieving goals from internal commitment and motivation, not from a place of force, coercion, and external control. When everyone invests in a relationship, we will find the desire, motivation, skill, and capacity to work together. Mansa envisions an orchestra, a sweet, mellifluous sound of multiple ethnicities, identities, beliefs, interests, and lifestyles blending into the sweetness of one community. A place where we all live with compassion as we shout from the rooftops, "Where there is unity, there is strength!"

Today, I introduced the Classroom Management Positions to my ninth grade American History class. As I explained the entire process with excitement and zeal, the students absorbed every word. After I had shared every position, nearly every student was eager to fill out an application. Daquan, my speaker, entertainer, beatmaker, and rapper, applied for the greeter position. Daquan was thrilled. He could barely contain himself. Ernestine, my alpha female who loves to be in control by inserting her attitude and opinions as freely as the oceans are vast, jumped on the attendance/tardy manager positions, which fit her personality perfectly. Despite the overall buy-in from the class, Anastasia complained. She ranted and said, "I mean, who wants a silly little job anyway? This is stupid. Y'all are all dummies for filling out applications. I mean, they are not even real jobs."

Anastasia's comments irritated me. However, my irritation quickly faded when I realized Anastasia loved the freedom to choose. In that brief moment, I offered Anastasia a position highlighting and showcasing what was important to her. At that moment, I saw a young lady who loved attention. She loves a captive audience. She wants to be seen, heard, and, most importantly, contribute. I saw a young lady who liked to control the class's emotional energy, mood, and climate. However, no teacher or adult can see beneath or beyond her rants, attacks, and disruptions. She wanted value and self-worth. Anastasia wanted to have influence and be a leader. I knew it would be risky.

I, however, needed to offer her an idea in a non-threatening way and co-create the position with her. "Anastasia, I noticed you're frustrated with these management positions. Is there a position you want to create for yourself?" I asked with a cheerful tone. She snarled, "I mean. I don't know. Everybody acting all fake like they love these little stupid positions. I don't care." I paused and softly said, "Anastasia, it's not about everyone else. Are you upset because you think you don't fit in or belong anywhere, so you keep your guard up to protect yourself?" She softened a bit and said, "Well, yeah. My momma doesn't like me. Teachers don't like me, and kids are afraid of me." I noticed the conversation had shifted as the class tuned into our talk like a tennis match at Wimbledon. "Your honesty touches me," I said. "I want to reassure you that you are, and always will be, safe in this class. I also want to offer you a special position called 'Empathy Manager.' Your job is to assess the mood of the class and offer advice to any student having a rough day. You can provide motivation and positivity to the class as well. Lastly, for this to happen, you need to——" Anastasia interrupted me and said, "I need to stay out of trouble in other classes, watch my smart mouth, and show up early to your class, ready to offer my peers the emotional support they need." I was astonished! Her transformation left me speechless.

It was as if a cocoon had just hatched before my eyes. "Tomorrow, I will hold interviews for each position, I announced. "Be aware you might not get your first choice. Manager positions switch every three weeks. You can reapply for a position if you don't get the job. Take a few minutes to fill out your applications now, and when you leave for your next class, find a few teachers and ask them for a reference." The bell rang, and they all left. I jumped around the room and danced a little, feeling refreshed and accomplished. The manager's idea suggested by Mr. Fire was a complete success.

I was in awe as I witnessed the management system in full effect. It worked like a well-oiled machine, especially with my Boys Inspired twelfth grade class. Maxwell, who began the year as an immature, annoying, and verbally belligerent student, patiently waited by the door and greeted everyone with a smile and welcome as he flashed his blinding silver braces. Chubby Scooter, who began the year as a wise cracking, horseplaying kid, never taking anything seriously, patiently passed out the materials, pens, and books and prepped the class before we began. Shawn, my cool, mellow kid, stepped over to the computer, ready to take attendance. He started as a quiet kid who distanced himself from everyone.

Edward, who was also quiet, had become outspoken in my class. He grabbed the sign-in sheet and waited for any latecomers to arrive. He offered a smile while quickly signing them in. Orlando, who began the year with an abrasive attitude, blossomed in class and became outspoken. Preparing the timer for a five-minute countdown, Orlando signaled me to see if I was ready to start the bell work activity we always complete before the school bell rings. He protected that timer like it was gold in Fort Knox. Carter, the energetic, wild, rebellious ladies' man, began with no motivation or focus. He positioned his string bean body before the class and belted out with a yodel-like silly tone, "Treat me cruel, weigh me down." The boys responded in unison, "Take my freedom, take my crown." We began the lesson. It ran smoothly.

We had time before the school bell rang, so I read an African folktale called "The Talking Skulls," a fable originated in Cameroon. "The story is about a talkative man living in a small village. He, however, never had anything positive to say. He had a bad habit of distracting villagers as they worked with idle chatter. One day, when he was walking, he found a talking skull. He ran back to his village to show the chief and the villagers." The boys were attentive as my dramatic reading matched the colorful images and depictions of Africa—everyone except Geronimo, who seemed preoccupied with something other than my master storytelling abilities. I was getting impatient and bitter about his rudeness and disrespect. "In conclusion, the man was kicked out of the village because the skull did not talk when he presented it to the villagers and chief. The moral of the story is, 'Talking is easy. However, having something to say that is worthwhile is not.'" I finished, and without question, I had instilled the art of storytelling in these boys—the oldest, most ancient form of teaching.

My irritation with Geronimo persisted like a paper cut at the tip of your finger. Mindless, I jetted over to Geronimo's desk and angrily said, "I'm tired of the disrespect and erratic behavior, Geronimo! You're laughing, cracking jokes, being distant, and shutting off. Today, you began joking, then, when I started telling the story, you completely ignored it and began scribbling or doodling on this pad." Geronimo sat for a moment. Without a word, he opened his scratch pad. Ultimately, I had to eat my words. Geronimo showed me the most beautiful regal images and sketches of emperor-like figures wearing lavish robes and jewelry. The stunning background was filled with kingdoms colored in gold and camels. In addition to portraits of kings, I saw the word "Mansa" painted in graffiti block letters with rich, vivid colors highlighting each letter.

Flabbergasted, I extended my hand to shake his hand. My brief tirade and egregious assumptions about how Geronimo spent his time embarrassed me. He communicated his appreciation of the story through his creative art. I said, "Geronimo, please accept my apology for reprimanding you. I was completely wrong. If you're willing, I want to add a new position to our classroom managers." Turning to the class, I said, "Everyone, we now have a graphic artist position." Geronimo sheepishly smiled and grinned as he awkwardly accepted applause from his peers. The bell rang, and everyone left except Geronimo. Reluctantly, Geronimo said, "Mansa, I forgot my bus tickets this morning. Would you be able to take me home today?" Cheerfully, I responded, "Absolutely, G. I'm glad I drove today. Let me gather my belongings, and we can leave." We quickly exited the building. While driving, I noticed a change in Geronimo's personality. He became reserved, soft-spoken, dry, sort of like a robot.

It seemed he was preparing himself for something. Eventually, we arrived at a big old house on the corner. Before he tried to leave my car, I said, "I want to meet your parents. At least I can introduce myself and tell them I drove you home." Geronimo kept his mouth shut as he turned towards the narrow door leading up some stairs. I follow him. He knocked on the door. We waited a minute. Finally, the door opened. An older Black woman said in a deep voice, "Geronimo, you know the deal. Go wash your hands and join us in the living room." After she gave him her firm instructions, Geronimo vanished into the small but tidy apartment. The woman turned her attention to me. She looked me up and down with a mistrustful glare and asked, "Young man, who are you, and why did you drop my foster kid off?" I swallowed saliva and nervously said, "Greetings, I am Morris Ervin. I teach your son, oops, I mean your foster son, at South Los Angeles High. He forgot his bus tickets, so it was no trouble for me to drop him off." She took a moment, adjusted her head bonnet, and gave me approval. "Well, I appreciate that," she said. "Come inside for a second. Would you like some coffee?" I graciously declined. However, as I walked through the apartment, it looked like a mausoleum. There was no speck of dirt anywhere, and everything was flawlessly placed in order.

As I peered into the living room, I was surprised to see four more boys, including Geronimo, carefully spaced out on two couches, waiting for instructions. The woman was braggadocious and scoffed, "Listen, I run a business here. These boys have to follow my lead. I'm the captain of this ship. We have a regimented schedule of chores, homework, dinner, recreation time, then bed. Nobody wanted them, so I'm here to give them the accountability, structure, and discipline they need to survive in these streets." I gazed at each boy, including Geronimo. They all seemed lifeless. After she finished her rant, I said, "I appreciate the time, ma'am. I'll leave now because traffic on my commute home will be monstrous." I nodded at Geronimo. He barely nodded back, and I exited his world, galloped back down the stairs, and walked to my car. Gripping the wheel tightly before I pulled off, I screamed with pure frustration at my helplessness to influence change at that moment. I yelled and screamed. I was ignorant about the worlds my B-Inspired young men face beyond the classroom. I screamed and screamed. I yearned to make a place outside of school for them where freedom, creativity, confidence, meaning, and dreams could come to life. As I drove away, I concluded that my first Mansa mentoring outing would be on Saturday.

CHAPTER 20

Power through Mentoring, Healing, and Building Community

"If I have seen further, it is by standing
on the shoulders of giants."
Sir Isaac Newton

Frustration quickly mounted as I finally merged my orange vehicle onto Highway 10, heading east. Cars moved at a snail's pace while the sun beamed over Los Angeles. Luckily, I had many ideas around my first Mansa outing to distract me from the irritation of being stuck in traffic. I pulled out my journal and began jotting down key principles and ideas about the program. Meetings would be held on Saturday mornings from 10 a.m. until noon, and I considered hosting sessions on the University of Southern Los Angeles campus. I wanted the young men to sacrifice time on Saturdays so I could instill discipline and focus in a creative and fun way. I also wanted them to wear dress shirts and ties to distinguish themselves as reputable young men.

I discovered the University was only a few minutes from South High. The value of being on a college campus would immerse each mentee in an environment that would hopefully and intentionally plant seeds of what's possible in their future. I envisioned sessions in public spaces and inside the campus library. Saturday sessions would include enrichment field trips that would expose the young men to a world outside of Los Angeles. The main principles of the Mansa Saturday Experience would focus on manhood preparation, emotional intelligence, leadership development, and cultural competence. Activities would also center around the self-reflection process of journal writing, discussion, music, movement, and storytelling. The Saturday sessions would also allow them to learn and practice their skills for healthy social development.

Participation of their mother or guardian would be essential to the program's success. I understood the difficulties of one-parent families raising young men in the savage streets of Los Angeles. Therefore, providing single mothers with emotional, social, and spiritual support would be crucial to the development of their sons. So, mentoring young men, mothers, and families creates that sense of connection, wholeness, and community. Eager to kick things off in an exciting way, I decided to invite the boys to a movie for our first outing. I selected a film based on the real-life events of an African American debate team called *The Great Debaters*. Relieved and satisfied about moving forward with my Mansa vision, my mind returned to LA's terrible rush hour traffic. For a brief moment, I sat seething in traffic, and then I became inspired to play music and tap into my creative side. As the instrumental CD pumped beats through my speaker, I nodded with the stop and start of my tiny wheels as I continued to inch along the highway. Occasionally, I rhymed a few words or laughed aloud. I felt my confidence grow like a newborn as I began to put a few bars together. I was flowing and riding with the beat like a surfer rides a wave. When I switched to another beat, my mind naturally shifted to LA gangs and all my experiences teaching young men.

The beat was serious and melancholy, which matched my current mood. I paused and allowed something special to nourish inside of me. I spat out, "The streets is my father, so why even bother, because the homey in these streets keep raisin' me." Immediately, the sadness and rage from Chris's murder fueled and stimulated my determination to create a rap. Motivated by the moment, I reached across my front seat and pulled out my tiny silver voice recorder. Ironically, just as I pressed record, the traffic opened up, as my flow opened, and a cornucopia of rhymes poured out of my larynx. I unleashed so many rhymes around Chris's tragic death and how it paralleled the tragic lifestyle of LA gangs. I was overwhelmed as this creativity allowed me to release tension and grief around what happened to Chris. This creative release also enabled me to express myself by channeling my fear into strength and pain into passion through music. Finally, I arrived home as the sun faded into the evening sky. I slowly pulled into the garage. Still, in full songwriting mode, I jotted down a few notes and recorded more verses for my rap. I relished the creative juices that began because of my long car ride. I dashed inside the house, eager to share a rough version of my new rap with my family.

I was anxious and had a restless night. I couldn't contain my energy and enthusiasm to share the Mansa Saturday Experience outing and my tribute rap to Chris with my class. The following day slowly arrived. I skillfully removed the covers from my side of the bed and somersaulted like a ninja into the restroom, being careful not to wake my queen. I quietly finished my morning rituals and scampered out of the house with the moon peering in the frigid distance, making my way to the train. Excited about the day ahead, I rode impatiently to work until I reached Union Station. I sprinted up the steep walkway like Jesse Owens, heading for the buses. Eventually, after the brisk jog down King Avenue, I walked into South High, making it to my comfy classroom.

Cheerfully, I invited all the young men in each class to participate in the official start of the Mansa program. Specifically, my B-Inspired classes took a special interest in my invitation. Rightfully so, as we had bonded in a way that had left an indelible mark on their hearts and how they perceived themselves and their challenges. In each class, I explained what the Mansa Saturday Experience would entail and my expectations of them. I passed out permission slips that needed to be signed and returned, especially if they wanted to attend the first movie outing. During seventh-period class, the students zoomed in with high energy and drama. Everyone set up their classroom management positions, although the room felt chaotic and unsettled. However, Anastasia skillfully went up and down each row confidently, peacefully, and cheerfully. During the first few minutes of class, she checked in with each student while helping them identify strategies and needs to move forward with their day. Anastasia single-handedly brought peace and stability into my class with grace and ease. Her complete makeover developed out of our creating an opportunity for her to share her gifts in an authentic and fulfilling way. The disruptive, snarling, growling girl had disappeared. She had blossomed into a mature young lady with meaning and purpose. I remembered one of my most outstanding mantras about the essence of teaching. Through Anastasia's transformation, I saw the Latin word *educere*, meaning to draw forth from within.

Later that day, Victor and Smooth Benjamin Brash entered my classroom during my lunch break. They asked, "Mansa, what's good? What are you into?" Before responding, my fear and self-doubt attempted to hold me hostage. I was reluctant to share my rap about Chris. The boys could sense my unease. They looked at each other and laughed. Victor said, "Mansa, you've been writing something. We know it. Let's hear it. Let those bars go!" I grinned. He added, "Better yet, let's get you warmed up. It's a nice day in LA. Let's go to the courtyard and see what happens!" My insides shook. However, my pride and reputation were on the line, so I followed them out of the door and down the back stairs directly into the massive courtyard.

Students were flipping on the grass, eating their lunch, as small guerilla pockets of cliques formed at each table. The energy was all over the place. It was wild, rebellious, and potent. Immediately, we let Benjamin lead the way. As we followed him, he hugged and winked at every girl until we strategically set up a table in the chaos. Victor pulled out his pens and pencils disguised as percussion sticks and forcefully laid down a nice, steady beat. We let Victor ride that beat like an old-school Cadillac as Benjamin and me, like in Double Dutch, took turns doing freestyle rapping. With each round, I grew more comfortable, relaxed, and fully engaged with my self-expression.

Shockingly, exceptionally talented Victor maintained a steady beat while joining our freestyle session. It was unbelievable. We immediately noticed dozens of students flocking around us like seagulls as we continued to freestyle. Engaging the crowd, Victor switched to various rhythms without missing a beat. I took a few full breaths and inhaled the beauty and creativity as we celebrated the power of music together. Simultaneously, I jumped back in as Victor switched to his last beat. I said, "Let's always remember Chris. He will always be in our hearts. I wrote something special for him, so I'm going to spit this rap. I need everyone to join in. Every time I say, 'The streets is my father, so why even bother because the homies in these streets keep.' Then I want y'all to respond ferociously with, 'raisin' me.' Y'all ready?" I asked. The colossal crowd uniformly responded with, "Yeah!" I dove in. "The streets is my father, so why even bother because the homies in the streets keep raisin' me!"

"A young life is taken by the pull of a trigger in the blink of an eye. Somebody tell me why I put in work just like a machine cause I'm down for my set, just like a basketball team. My dreams and ambitions resonate like Tupac's. I was that rider, and I pulled that Glock. Let's take a look, just like a crystal ball, back into the past, trace the bullet and all. To the homie that pulled it, what kind of stuff was he thinking? Was his heart kind of pumping? Did he really mean it? I'm thinking, if he was drinking, it was just an illusion, a fantasy world created from pain, living life in these streets to escape the pain and maintain this gangsta swag. That's all I need because the homies in these streets keep raisin' me.

"My moment of truth, my rites of passage becoming a savage or maybe a slave controlled by my rage, immediate praise. I feel the ultimate pleasure. I feel the ultimate pain. Blood stains remain cause death is all around me; that's all I see because the homies in the streets keep raisin' me. Am I looking for death? Is it looking for me like the scent of our ancestors hanging from a tree? I'm free. I pulled the trigger. That's what I did. Did I do it for me, or did I do it for them? Wait. My mind freezes like I'm living in Cleveland. Standing in silence, situational violence. Who is the victim? The boy on the ground, or the one who took his freedom and took his crown? Can I still be down? As I sit on the curb, feeling very disturbed. My moment of truth is finally here, I clearly realized. I was living in fear. Love was taken from me at an early age and replaced with guns, violence, and lots of rage. I tried to numb the pain with drugs and sex, obliterate my mind with violent crimes, serving time, selling dope, living life with no hope. Serving time, selling dope, living life with no hope.

Cause the streets is my father, so why even bother, because the homies in these streets keep raisin' me!"

The students jumped all around, slapping high fives with us. Of course, the girls hugged Benjamin. He gave them his final stamp by doing a backflip. We received lots of compliments and praise from the students. Suddenly, the bell rang, and everyone went to class. Victor, Benjamin, and I embraced each other. Benjamin and I said, "Wow, Vic, you held that beat for like 20 minutes." Vic gave his signature cheek-to-cheek smile as he responded, "I know, dog. We were all feelin' it. I couldn't stop the cipher." Then, Benjamin and Vic said, "Mansa, you were killin' it with the freestyle, and that tribute rap to Chris was tough!" I responded, "Wow, fellas. Do you all realize we just put on a concert entertaining the entire school?" We all laughed. We left the courtyard and went inside the school to finish the day.

I had a busy day at school and had to prepare for an even busier weekend. In addition to the outing, I needed to prepare for my workshop at Torrè's Manchild Conference at LA's Community College. As I entered my classroom, I was happy to see the permission slips scattered across my desk for the first Mansa outing. Before I left the building, I checked my voicemail. Kelvin's mom had left a message giving Kelvin permission to join the Mansa outing and become a part of the Mansa Experience. I ecstatically jumped three times in the air and clicked my heels together. I quickly gathered my things, rushed out the door, and hurried up King Avenue to hop on the 740 bus to Union Station.

March 17, 2008, Spring Break: Mansa's Historical Outing

Venaya ironed my blue jeans and black collar shirt while helping me with the red and yellow tie I would wear with my black leather vest. On Friday, I told all the moms about dropping off their sons at South Los Angeles High School. I arrived early, eager to embark on this special outing with my young mentees. I wore a smile on my face brighter and shinier than my leather vest while my heart sang out with passion. I blasted KRS-One's old-school single, "Black Cop," while waiting for everyone to arrive. Kelvin's mom pulled up. Venaya called to tell me that

Jackson's mom called to say he couldn't attend because of financial reasons. I immediately called her and encouraged her to allow Jackson to participate in the event and not to worry about money. Jacques arrived with his mom, who always had a cheerful smile and delightful personality. His younger male siblings were in the car. Their faces were glued to the window. They looked like they desperately wanted to attend the outing with their brother. Jacques was relieved to get some time away from them. Smooth Benjamin's mom finally pulled up to drop him off.

We were now on our way to the theater to see The Great Debaters. All the young men looked distinguished in their ties and button-down shirts as we walked towards Crenshaw Mall and into the movie theater. We arrived a little late but glued our eyes to the big screen the entire time. At the end of the movie, we engaged in a lively discussion. The young actors in the film used their words and intellect against racism and the brutal oppression they experienced in the South. All the boys loved the character James Farmer, a 14-year-old who had the opportunity to debate college students on a national platform.

As we left the theater, they recited his memorable line, "You better hope we choose the latter, civil disobedience over violent acts of rebellion." The boys discussed their longing to be successful but only saw limited options through sports. We explored our greatest fear because that topic had surfaced in the movie. Jackson said his greatest fear was getting hit by a car. Benjamin kindly corrected him and said his fear was not getting hit by a car. His fear is death. Jacques added that he fears going to new places and seeing new things. Again, Benjamin chimed in and said his fear was of the unknown. I marveled at our lively and spirited Saturday afternoon conversation. We continued our conversation as I drove back to the High School so Kelvin's mom could pick him up. I reiterated the purpose of the group and the expectations. All of my students agreed to participate.

We explored the difference between the "Jungles," the dangerous, low-income housing developments where many kids lived, versus "Black Beverly Hills," the nickname for an affluent neighborhood of wealthy African Americans. Benjamin said, "The worlds are so, so close. You can walk from the Jungles to Black Beverly Hills in minutes. We are just that close, yet so far apart." I was curious to see the disparity between these two worlds. Kelvin's mom arrived, and he expressed his thanks for the opportunity.

We returned to Crenshaw Mall for lunch. My mentees flirted with girls, and we window-shopped while enjoying each other's company. The young men agreed on a uniform. They decided to rock a shirt, tie, tapered jeans, and sneakers as a uniform dress code for Mansa. Immediately after our conversation about sneakers, we walked by an urban sneaker store. A pair of patent leather high-top Puma sneakers with Jamaican flag colors was strategically displayed in the window. They spoke my language. The boys encouraged me to buy them, and I did.

As the sun began to set, we took a drive through the Jungles. I am amazed at so much poverty and despair juxtaposed with the lush shrubbery and big, beautiful palm trees. Eventually, we drove through the streets, laying out the prosperity of Black Beverly Hills. As I drove slowly, I marveled at each mansion. They sparkled like stars in the night sky. Luckily, to end the epic day, we discovered a space high in the hills where we could see the beauty and brightness of Los Angeles. We all sat on the hood of my car, entrenched in the beauty and the majesty of the City of Angels.

The following day, I roared out of bed. I completed my early morning routine before driving to LA to attend the "Strategies for the Development of the African American Manchild" conference, a program hosted by Torrence Brannon-Reese, affectionately known as Torrè. I arrived at seven-thirty in the morning and wandered across the spacious campus, following signs until I reached my destination. Energized and eager, I arranged my classroom in a big circle and went over some music as I jotted down an outline of my workshop. Next, I played some Marvin Gaye and Al Greene music to set the tone and tempo for my workshop. As I jammed to the music and continued to write a few notes, I felt thankful for my relationship with Torrè.

Torrè is a tall, slender, handsome older gentleman who perfectly represents an activist, leader, healer, father, grandfather, entertainer, and so much more. Torrè is a rock, a beacon of light and support for the people of Crenshaw and the surrounding areas. He is firm and speaks his mind. His voice is deep, and he is a prolific poet, as each word or syllable is delivered from a deep cultural, intellectual, and spiritual place. Torrè knows his roots, as he often speaks of his migration to Los Angeles from New Orleans. He says everyone should visit New Orleans and experience its history and culture. He speaks highly of his mom, his upbringing, and all his experiences serving in the military. I love his absolute love for soul music. His favorite artist of all time is Sam Cook, and his obsession with soul music reminds me of my father's love for soul music. Torrè is in a singing group called Street Corner Renaissance. They travel across the country and world, harmonizing and revitalizing street corner music from back in the day.

Suddenly, I was distracted by footsteps coming from the hallway. It was Torrè. He entered the room wearing neatly pressed dress slacks and an African print dashiki. In his deep baritone voice, he said, "Brother Mansa. I appreciate you presenting at my conference. I dig your style and how you get down with the kids at South. You are a breath of fresh air to South High. Your gifts, talents, and abilities will advance the cause as you are part of the younger generation of leaders." I was touched, moved, and inspired by his words. I was curious about something and asked him a question. "Brother Torrè, you have done so much in South LA with your activism, community development, and music. How would you like to be remembered?" Without hesitation, Torrè shared, "Well, I'm most proud of being a father and a grandfather. I'm an authentic person who cares about my people and my community. The sacrifices I have made to better my people are genuine acts of my labor of love. It takes more than money to change. It takes real commitment and dedication to do whatever it takes. As Curtis Mayfield says, 'Keep on pushin'.'" I repeatedly nodded my head as his words nourished my soul. Torrè continued, "Cool, my brother. Well, have fun. I know your workshop will be out of sight!" As Torrè left, my mind drifted to other significant men who had deeply impacted me. I looked at my watch. I had fifteen minutes before the beginning of my workshop.

It was my second experience at the masjid after becoming a Muslim the weekend before. Today, I am at the masjid for the late afternoon prayer with a few brothers. A tall brother with a strong presence and hearty laugh entered the prayer room. He sensed I was new and said, "As-salamu Alaykum, brother. I'm Luqman Abdullah. What's your name?" "Musa," I said. He greets the other brothers and engages in a brief conversation with them. Luqman turned to me and another brother and said, "I have a community event at a church on 79th and Woodland that I think you both would benefit from. Put on your shoes. I'll be waiting in my car." The younger brother and I looked at each other, shrugged our shoulders, and followed Luqman. My eyes widened as I walked towards a mint condition, sky blue Lincoln Continental that looked like a tank with wheels. We joined Luqman and made our way to the event. People were packed like sardines inside the church. We followed Luqman as he gracefully greeted folks with his broad smile, energy, and stylish appearance. We found a few seats and joined in a political community rally. I listened to men and women share ideas and strategies to uplift Black communities.

Throughout the night, Luqman explained what some speakers were talking about because, as teenagers, we did not understand everything. Eventually, the rally ended. We waited for Luqman to interact with people in the church and parking lot before he took us home. Luqman said, "As Muslims, we are not isolated from the rest of the world. We are part of what's happening at the community, local, state, national, and international levels. Don't let brothers fool you into a limited, small-minded way of thinking. Learn to think for yourself in this religion. Learn the beauty and the brotherhood of this religion. Don't be afraid to explore and discover new things." His words shook me to my core. His intensity left an indelible mark on me that night. Unfortunately, I only had that one interaction with him. He was kicked out of the masjid, and I never saw him again. Brothers at the masjid tried to throw shade on him. Luqman, however, had impacted me on a deep level.

Surprisingly, I ran into Luqman at Kent State University some years later. It was a brief but powerful interaction. I still remember what he told me. Luqman shared that after graduating from Cleveland State, he had fulfilled his desire to travel worldwide. He started visiting African and Middle Eastern countries. Impressed, I shared I had met many Muslims from around the world in college. I was involved with the campus Muslim Student Association and continued to attend political, cultural, and social rallies. He was pleased to learn about what I was doing. We said goodbye, and he drove away in his mint-conditioned Lincoln.

Over the years, I learned Luqman had made his pilgrimage to Mecca, the obligatory trip Muslims must make once in a lifetime. I also heard about Luqman's travels throughout the Middle East and Africa. Luqman had a special love for Morocco, where he began teaching English. While Luqman traveled the world, I married during college, graduated, started a family, and began my teaching career. Despite these accomplishments, I still struggle with my faith, confidence, and manhood. Fortunately, exercise and flag football are the panacea that help me channel my emotions and release built-up testosterone. On a flag football team I played for, one of our quarterbacks quit before starting a new season. Desperate for a quarterback, I thought of Luqman as he had returned to Cleveland. Luqman was tall and a great basketball player. I asked him if he would be our quarterback, and he agreed.

We began intensely training together. We would meet at the crack of dawn and run sprints on the track of a local community college. Luqman was impressed by my blazing speed. I was impressed with his long strides. Following each grueling workout, we would discuss marriage, fatherhood, religion, politics, sports, and international travel. Our talks energized my spirit. He became my mentor. I was willing to talk to him about my struggles. Luqman had an uncanny way of linking sports with his advice. I once shared my frustration with marriage and thoughts about walking away. He listened intensely, then related my situation to sports by saying, "Why, after having a star player with you for all these years, would you want to trade her in just to get back on the market and look for a rookie player? You are taking a chance on someone with no experience and no time invested in the game." Initially, I struggled with his analogy. I grappled with it for a while, and since it related to sports, it *stuck on me like a bad suit. Luqman also spoke with my wife. He listened to her concerns about my immaturity, neglectfulness, and carefree attitude. I love Luqman's spirit and the skillful and refreshing way he uses his knowledge to make us feel safe expressing ourselves. I was in awe of his non-threatening ability to challenge my wife while giving her space to share fully. Most importantly, he related it to Islam and spirituality.*

Before we played our first game with Luqman as a quarterback, he watched a few of my games and played with us. He had hands like the great football receiver, Chris Carter. His basketball experience and tall frame taught him to position his body between the defender and the ball. He wasn't fast, but he had long legs and long strides, so he always ended up in the end zone. On our first game together, everyone had their eyes glued to us. This was the four-by-four league, with a 60-yard field, two eligible receivers, one center qualified to run routes and catch the ball, and no blocking. The game was about speed, quickness, and creating advantages for your team. In addition to Luqman, we had Reg, a crafty veteran who played the center position with an uncanny ability to find openings and run to the end zone against younger defenders. We had Katari, an ex-college receiver who ran precise routes with savvy and confidence, and me. I created match-up nightmares for the opposing teams with my speed and quickness.

So here we are at the first game with Luqman as our quarterback. This was his first flag football game. Before he snaps the ball, he dismisses a rule that all quarterbacks live by in the league. All quarterbacks play from the shotgun position or stand about seven yards behind the center. This position enables the defense and rusher to run directly toward the quarterback and attempt to pull his flag at a longer distance. As we prepare to run our routes, Luqman steps behind Reg, refusing to honor the shotgun position. All the teams were whispering, gawking, and laughing in anticipation of a complete meltdown from our team as we were playing the best in the league.

Luqman quickly said, "Hike." He threw quick, perfectly positioned passes to all his receivers within three seconds. The other team and spectators were amazed at how he quickly snapped and released the ball. *The person rushing him did not have a chance. Five touchdowns later, we gracefully shook hands with the opposing team and victoriously walked off the field, shocking the entire league. We steamrolled through the season with Luqman as the quarterback. In one game, we were up big, 35-7. I casually told Luqman, "Let's take it easy on them." With a lighthearted, assertive tone and signature laugh, Luqman, towering over me, said, "They're competing just like we're competing. We're not going to disgrace them or ourselves by letting up. They know what they signed up for. This is bigger than football. In life, you always keep the pedal on the gas and give everything you've got. You hear me? You hear me? Now, run a deep pattern. I will throw it as far as possible, and you go get it!" Luqman said, "Hike!" He tosses that ball to the heavens while I dash down the field, running under it as it gently lands in my hands like a blessing. We did not let up. As we dominantly continued to win games, more and more teams and spectators crowded the sidelines to watch us. They wanted to see us win and also hoped we would lose at the same time. However, the league, team, and spectators respected us because we won with dignity, grace, and class.*

Near the start of one game, Reg and I began to worry as there were no signs of Luqman or Katari. Reg and I warmed up by stretching as we watched the crowd grow. It was the biggest game of our undefeated season, and we were facing the number one team in the league with a ferocious, tough player called Leviticus. As the clock ticked closer to the start time, our anxieties grew like a teenager's warts. The ref looked at Reg and asked, "Where's the rest of your team? The game starts in one minute!" Reg and I discouragingly walked on the field as Leviticus and his football thugs salivated. We got the ball. Reg flipped me the ball. I turned on the afterburners and dazzled the crowd with a 60-yard touchdown. It was all downhill after that as Leviticus put together a few drives, torturing our team of two. We were helpless. His team, as well as the crowd, heckled us. They scored touchdown after touchdown. A few seconds before halftime, my eyes drifted toward the parking lot.

I saw Katari, Faroq, a new player, and Luqman casually jogging toward the field. I screamed, "Man, hurry up! Y'all late, and we're down 28-7." The second half began. Immediately, Leviticus threw an interception, and Faroq took it to the house. The crowd went wild. We played tough defense as we kept them out of the end zone. Luqman, who is always calm, said, "We got 'em on their heels now." He then picked their defense apart as we ran down the field. He tossed a sweet pass to Katari. Touch down! We denied them every opportunity to score. Leviticus was livid! He was yelling and cursing at the refs. Luqman said, "We got to score quickly to tie because we have only two minutes left." He laughed ferociously and said, "I call this the Musa special." The Musa special is when I go isolation on the opposite side of the field with their best defender. Everyone floods the other side of the field when Luqman says, "Go!" I delay for a second, then turn on a burst of speed while my teammates drag over the top of me. Luqman threw the pass at an angle as I sprinted to catch it in full stride, leaving the defender in the dust. Touchdown! The crowd hooted and hollered as Luqman raised his finger in the air, symbolizing one stop. Surprisingly, Luqman switched with our pass rusher and decided to harass Leviticus. They completed a few passes downfield as the time quickly ticked away.

During the fourth down, as Luqman's large frame made it difficult for Leviticus to see, he tossed the ball to the corner just short of the end zone. Katari snatches it out of the air and takes it down the sideline. We all watch as Leviticus desperately tries to leap and grab Katari's flag, but Katari puts a slick move on Leviticus, who misses and crashes hard into the ground. Unfortunately, Leviticus separated his shoulder in his attempt to stop Katari. Katari, however, skipped into the end zone. Touch down! The crowd went wild! We quickly shook hands with the other team but were concerned about Leviticus. Everyone congratulated us and shook our hands. Although we had a crazy comeback victory from the jaws of defeat, we maintained our undefeated record. We knew the ultimate goal was to win the championship. The season progressed, and we continued to win games. We had a perfect 15-0 record and were heading into the playoffs. Not surprisingly, we knew we would face Leviticus and his thugs in the championship game.

The championship began. You had to beat a team two out of three times to win it all. The first game started as a tough, grueling battle and went down to the last play. We were driving down the field as the final seconds ticked away. On fourth down, Leviticus decided to line his big frame against me to bully and intimidate me. Luqman and I locked eyes. I automatically knew what route to run. Leviticus had fire in his eyes, and I had a smirk on my face. Luqman said, "Hike!" I did a jab step towards the left of the field, then cut back to the right corner. Leviticus had positioned his hips wrong, and I sprinted toward the back corner. Luqman let the ball go later than expected, and it floated in the air longer than he wanted.

Helpless with my momentum carrying me toward the back of the end zone, Leviticus recovered from his mistake, leaped up, and snatched the ball out of the sky. He took it down the sideline and scored a touchdown! We all dropped our heads in deep disappointment. Luqman immediately approached me and said, "Brother, that was me. You had him beat. It was my fault." While Luqman talked, I felt his sincerity and profound disappointment in himself. I did not say a word. I gently caressed his broad shoulders and shook my head, indicating my support and confidence in him and our team. We would redeem ourselves. It stung us all. It was our first championship loss. The sting, however, was temporary. The loss ignited a fire that extinguished Leviticus and his thugs for the next two consecutive games. We destroyed them as Luqman lit up the scoreboard. He terrorized their defense. We won the championship, and I'm sure Leviticus has nightmares about us until this day. Luqman continued traveling abroad, and I stayed in Cleveland, a changed man.

In my first year of college, I met Kareem Abdul Azeez, a strong, physically imposing man with a sweet, tender spirit. Kareem adored a few things: family, Islam, wrestling, and love. We met at a Friday prayer service at the masjid just a few blocks from Pearl State University. He immediately became the mentor I needed. He saw my innocence and wanted to protect me from the evils of college life while building a healthy relationship around brotherhood, friendship, leadership, and service to the community. After we met, we exchanged numbers. Kareem gave me a ride to my college dorm and said, "I'll be back to pick you up for the Friday prayer next week." He did not ask or wait for my reply, as it wasn't an option. In addition to being my spiritual mentor, we did fun things like playing video games and traveling. I instantly thought he was the coolest dude on the planet because this muscle-headed man, who practices Islam, had a softness and charisma that attracted people. I watched how he interacted with friends and strangers. His big smile and laugh endeared people to him. He made people feel accepted and seen when in his presence.

I remember the first time he invited me into his apartment for dinner. Like clockwork, he picked me up. I was awed that he always pulled up in a new sporty car. Later, I found out he worked at a car dealership. While driving to his apartment, he mentioned his wife wanted to meet the college kid her husband had been cheating on her with. I was shocked because I had no idea he was married. We pull up to his apartment complex and walk inside to his apartment. It smelled delicious as the sauces and spices tickled my nostrils. Kareem and his wife lived in a small yet cozy apartment. Kareem walked me into the kitchen connected to the living room and said, "Mariam, this is Musa, and Musa, this is Mariam." Mariam greeted me with a traditional greeting, "As-salamu Alaykum." I responded, "Wa Alaikum Assalaam." She had a light complexion and piercing eyes and wore the traditional covering for women, a hijab. She had a little mole on the right side of her face.

She seemed sweet, but I knew not to mess with her. We ate dinner and chatted. Kareem and I did my favorite thing: prayed, then hopped in front of the television to play my favorite game, Streetfighter. After a few rounds, Mariam called Kareem. He paused the game and disappeared into the back room. As I sat with the controller in my hand, I heard raised voices pierce the tiny apartment. I was clueless and in shock. Kareem emerged from the room, with Mariam quickly following him. She was pointing her finger at the back of his thick neck. Kareem refused to turn around. Softly and silently, he made his way toward me and said, "Come on, Musa, let's go." Mariam continued her rants and threats. I hesitantly slid past her and followed Kareem to his car. We rode in silence back to my dorm. As we rode to my dorm, I realized Muslims have real problems like everyone else. I also realized that, as a man, Kareem did something really stupid to make his wife so mad.

A few weeks went by without any contact with Kareem. I assumed he got busy with his job and marriage. However, a mutual friend, Katari, transferred to my college. It was exciting to know that Katari wanted to become a Muslim. At the Friday prayer meeting, I met with Katari and his Muslim roommate, Burundi. Kareem also attended. Katari took his Shahada, the process of becoming a Muslim. Following the ceremony, Kareem graciously took us to lunch. During lunch, Burundi and Kareem bonded because they were both all-state high school wrestlers and competed in college. Katari and I reflected on our days in high school. We shared our experiences converting to a new religion different from our families and how it impacted them. Burundi and Katari had a shared interest in Islam. It was Burundi who taught Katari about Islam. Just before we finished our lunch, with his bulging and bright white teeth, Kareem said with a firm tone, "We all are athletes, and staying in shape is vital to our spirituality.

"So, Thursday through Sunday, I will pick everyone up at five a.m. sharp so we can pray our morning prayer at the mosque. We will work out at my gym, run on the track, and watch the sunrise." We all sat stunned and nodded our heads in unison. Kareem sat back with his trademark smile and said, "I knew y'all would see it my way." The following day, I rolled out of my bunk bed and stumbled down the frigid hallway into the restroom to freshen up and make wudu daily ablution. I went downstairs, out the door, and into Kareem's new Black Jeep. We scooped up Katari and Burundi and made it to the mosque for the morning fajr prayer. We stood in one row with brothers from Africa, Asia, the Middle East, and Australia. The brother who leads the prayer recited a verse from the Quran as we prayed in unison. We finished the prayer and went to the gym. It was only six in the morning. We worked out. I was amazed as Kareem did multiple presses of 225 pounds over his head. He lifted the weights like a broomstick. Burundi was equally as strong. The workout was intense, and it felt good to strengthen my body right after my spirit was lifted in prayer. We completed our exercise in the dungeon gym and walked up the rusty basement stairs into the bright sun beaming down on us. We hopped back into the Jeep.

Our camaraderie expanded my heart. I enjoyed this intense morning. There was no tightness or tension in me. I felt a lightness and liberation in my spirit. Our last stop was the college track, where we ran a mile. Wearing what resembled a giant plastic trash bag, Kareem jogged at his own pace. Briskly, I, along with Katari and Burundi, took off. As we jogged, I decided to raise the stakes a bit by accelerating my speed. Burundi chose to match my pace. I raised the stakes again and said, "It's time to separate the professionals from the amateurs." Boom!

Like a cannon, I turned a jet booster on and sprinted like Jesse Owens in the 1936 Olympics. My heart was racing, legs and arms churning as the resistance from the wind blew against my face. Surprisingly, Burundi, the bigger, muscular wrestler, was right on my hip! I moved into light-speed gear! I was churning my legs, pumping my arms, and running like my life depended on it. Burundi silently stayed right with me! We blazed the first two laps and zoomed past Kareem, who was still running at the same pace. We bent the corner, leaning shoulder to shoulder through the third lap. We were racing. The only sound was the air gasping from our lungs. We continued this grueling sprint through the last lap. I tried desperately to leave him, but he was determined to stay right with me. Finally, we ran even faster as we approached the last two hundred yards. My heart, chest, and lungs were on fire. Burundi was quiet, but I knew he was also hurting. We both zoomed through the finish line. A tie! I walked a few feet down the track while Burundi dropped down with his hands covering his face. I stopped, raised my hands over my head, then placed them back on my knees.

It took about four minutes to catch my breath. I heard Kareem's sinister laugh as he finished his fourth lap. "You all are some fools trying to kill yourselves like that," he said. "And since you all have so much energy and so much to prove, let's go to my wrestling practice at the high school," he continued. Katari appeared out of nowhere and said, "You all look like you were about to die on the last lap. It was funny to watch!" Burundi and I slowly gathered ourselves and stammered back to the Jeep while Kareem and Katari waited. I grabbed Burundi's shoulder and said, "Let me know when you want a rematch!" Later, after that early morning workout, grueling wrestling practice, and a full day's worth of classes, Kareem and I decided to get some pizza and wings from a local pizzeria. As we drove to the pizzeria, we heard a loud boom! A large boulder hit the car! We both turned and looked through the rearview window. About eight White fraternity boys scattered through a path of shrubs and trees. As calm and serene as a Buddhist monk, Kareem gently turned the wheel and went down a few side streets. He cut down a narrow pathway and pulled up to a rocky driveway.

It was perfect timing as we saw one of the frat boys shutting the door behind him. We both exited the vehicle without a word and went to the door. I turned the doorknob, not expecting it to be unlocked. Voila, the door opened. I rushed inside as Kareem followed right beside me. I yelled, "Who threw that boulder at our vehicle? Are y'all crazy? Y'all could have killed my brother and me!" I circled the living room as the frat boys stood pale and frozen as igloos. Kareem stood strong yet silent, his muscles popping and bulging from his dingy gray long-john T-shirt. I raised my voice as I strolled around the living room and into the kitchen. "Was it you? You? Who was it?" I raced back into the living room. My blood was boiling as I took a swing, barely grazing the fragile jaw of a frat boy sitting on a couch.

Then, Kareem roared, "My brother asked which one of y'all did it!" The whole house shook with his thundering words. Silence. Whimpering. I heard a few fake apologies. Eventually, Kareem and I both decided we had made our point. We turned around and left. I shut the door behind us. We continued along our journey and got our pizza and wings. I reflected on Kareem's influence on me. I realized he was the biggest, baddest dude—with a gentle spirit—I had ever met. Someday, I hoped to be the biggest and baddest dude for the young men I would mentor.

One day, while attending Friday prayers at the mosque, I noticed a tall, slender man with a bronze complexion, wearing circular glasses and high water slacks. He was around 40 years old. I had never seen him in the mosque before. He listened to the sermon, prayed, politely shook hands with a few brothers, and vanished. The following week, I saw him again. Later that night, we had a community dinner at the mosque. Community dinners were the best, especially for broke college students. I called Burundi and Katari so they could meet me at the mosque at seven in the evening. We arrived at the small, cozy mosque, removed our shoes, and went down the narrow hallway and up the stairs to the spacious prayer room. On Friday nights, the mosque had an informational talk called a Holoca. Lots of brothers from the Middle East gathered in a huge circle as someone led the discussion on a topic related to Islam, the Prophet Muhammad's life, etiquette, conduct, things that are lawful and forbidden, and other issues. During these talks, I tried to stay focused. However, the pace of the conversation could have been faster.

I often daydreamed about random topics until it was time to feast on the community dinner. Today, however, was different. Mubarak Hussein, a guest speaker from Egypt who had moved to the area for an engineering job, would lead the discussion. Quietly, Mubarak walked to the front of the circle, took the microphone, and graciously greeted everyone. As he began his talk, he immediately engaged Burundi, Katari, and me by asking thought-provoking questions. By including everyone in his topic, he captivated the entire room with his speaking ability. To our surprise, and for the first time, we felt seen and heard at the mosque. Each Friday after that, we camped ourselves and our minds on that illustrious green carpet and engaged in Mubarak's lesson that filled us with spiritual wisdom and life skills. Eventually, Mubarak was replaced with a new leader. To our amazement, Mubarak opened up his home to continue his teachings on Friday nights. I remembered the first night that Burundi, Kahari, and I entered Mubarak's home. He opened the door with a big smile. He embraced us all while guiding us upstairs to a small, cozy room with a cushy, lush green carpet.

I immediately began to make judgmental comments about other Muslim brothers at the mosque, who looked wealthy, and my disgruntled feelings towards them for not spending more time and investing in the mosque. Mubarak listened politely until I finished. He then gently admonished me about my lack of empathy, compassion, and ignorance *surrounding other people's circumstances. He said, "It's wrong to condemn anyone as we don't know their heart or intentions. God is our judge. That's not where the focus of our energy should be. Let's focus on appreciating our Muslim brothers for showing up to the Mosque for whatever reason. There is no place for criticism in this religion. It's toxic and a narrow-minded way to approach life." I sat motionless. We all sat and listened to Mubarak as he nurtured our young souls and firmly corrected us when we needed it. His place served as a refuge for young African American men who needed to belong and sort out their spiritual identities. He also helped us gain clarity and perspective on racism, ethnocentrism, and other acts of human ignorance in the community beyond our control. He was humble about his scholarship. He held the space for conversations about complex issues in religion and complex issues in our lives from a broad context of spirituality, guidance, wisdom, and brotherhood. We experienced so much growth in our Friday night sessions with Mubarak. He sacrificed time with his wife, six children, and the demands of his grueling schedule as an engineer to be with us.*

Most importantly, he spent his money every Friday ordering pizza! His generosity, compassion, spiritual wisdom, and guidance will always be part of me. The greatest gift Mubarak gave us was life's most precious resource that can't be recycled. Once it's gone, it's gone. The resource is time. I learned that if you want to impact people profoundly—especially young, impressionable men like me who bear heavy wounds and scars from society—spend time getting to know them and showing them genuine respect. It will make all the difference in the world.

I awakened from my memories with a sharp, piercing pain in my gut. Desperate, I stood up from the desk, attempting to move around to get some relief from the shrieking pain. I doubled over with aching and cramping pain. I realized I had earlier signs of this before. I managed to calm myself and took a few deep breaths while readjusting my posture. Luckily, just as folks started to walk in for my workshop, the pain diminished from a ten to a three. I played the CD, and the dope beat pulsated through the speakers. Of course, the circle was primed and ready, with the chairs pushed to the furthest perimeter. I started with a clap and welcomed an intergenerational group consisting primarily of females into the space.

I was somewhat disappointed as I wanted more Black men in attendance. I, however, quickly accepted it as I recited the first bar to a rap classic by Grandmaster Flash and the Furious Five. "Broken glass everywhere, people pissin' on the stairs--you know they just don't care. I can't take the smell, can't take the noise, got no money to move out. I guess I got no choice. Rats in the front room, roaches in the back, junkies in the alley with a baseball bat. I tried to get away, but I couldn't get far 'cause a man with a tow truck repossessed my car. Don't push me 'cause I'm close to the edge. I'm tryin' not to lose my head. Ah-huh-huh-huh. It's like a jungle sometimes. It makes me wonder how I keep from going under."

I let the song play to the end. When it finished, I introduced myself and said, "Today, we will discuss Black men and Black families. Today will be an opportunity to share grief, sorrow, accomplishments, and celebrations as we explore the complex phenomenon of Black men and Black families. I'm here because I believe in Black men and Black families. I am a father and husband who loves to teach Black culture. However, I'm not blind to all the issues surrounding us in our homes and communities. Also, I can see that most people in this room are Black women and children. Let me start with an analogy. The lion is the king of the jungle. However, if he receives a wound, emotional or physical, he will go into a catastrophic condition, and then weaker animals can attack him.

"The lion becomes the victim. The hunter becomes the hunted. Roles can reverse in nature. This is not natural. The lion's power is gone. He is useless, kicked out of the pride, humiliated, confused, embarrassed, and left to die alone, only to vaguely remember his great past. This is our state, so let's take small but progressive measures to build our kings up again. This process starts in the home with all the pain we are dealing with. As I gaze around the room at all the single moms raising children, my seething anger is wrapped in silence. The pain and rage I see in children's eyes who have to face the harsh realities of the world without their fathers." As I finish my initial talk, the raw emotion and tension immediately fester in the space like an open wound or scab. I carefully ask, "Would anyone like to talk about their fathers, the good, the bad, and the ugly?" A young lady, who was shaking with emotion, abruptly shared. "I hate everybody. I hate my dad. I have low self-esteem, and I cut myself." Her brutally honest and open words echoed across the room. A young man shared, "My dad is a drug dealer. I used to hate my dad. I love him and can't understand why he would jeopardize our lives. It's hard for me to visit him because it's unsafe. He will do drugs right in front of me. It's like he doesn't care." A few more youths speak as adults listen. Another young man, who had been quiet, jumped up and screamed, "My dad died two years ago!" as he ran out of the room. I motioned for one of the room assistants to go out and provide support.

A mother took a moment and said, "My husband of fifteen years just left me. Now, I have to raise my son alone. I struggle daily because my son has become a liar and cannot be trusted, just like his dad. I spend so much time I don't have at his school because he constantly lies about his grades and everything else. I did not ask to be a single parent. I had dreams. I'm an artist. I gave them up to marry my husband and have a child, and then the wounded lion, as you say, leaves. What about us women? We don't have a choice, but he gets to leave. It's not fair!" I let the tension release. I held space for the hurt shared in the room and unspoken pain. Forty minutes is not enough time to address generations of stress and abandonment. However, it was all the time I had. I wanted to put context and perspective on what was shared and provide action steps before ending the workshop. I wanted the participants to feel empowered and hopeful despite their circumstances and harsh realities.

I encouraged everyone to get on their feet and make a large circle. Looking around, I took a deep breath and said, "There's a lot of hurt in this room. No one is a victim. Looking around, I see strength, courage, beauty, and resilience. Despite absent fathers, current circumstances, and realities, I recommend regularly having these conversations with our children. Give them space to express their feelings and sort out their troubles with you. The simplicity of having conversations with our kids is transformational. Despite it all, they know you are there to listen to them. More importantly, for the single parents in the room, you must have a support system when conversing with your children on these deep topics. It would help if you also had a place to vent your frustrations and a place to help regulate your emotions. When possible, you will be prepared to have healthy conversations with your children from a place of healing rather than resentment or victimization. Specifically for the mothers raising boys, it's unfortunate when fathers leave.

"You can't control this. However, to identify healthy male role models, find mentoring organizations, sports teams, counselors, and clergy as positive options. Finally, as parents struggling to raise children, we can work to improve ourselves, get counseling, learn about our past, and build coping mechanisms to deal with stress. Oppression, survival, and trauma make you feel isolated and alone. There's always a community. It starts with your willingness to reach out. Parents, single moms, and single dads, I salute you. Continue to build your self-esteem, and your children's self-esteem will increase."

I played the song "Optimistic," sung by the Sounds of Blackness, and encouraged everyone to clap to the beat of the infectious soulful music. The clap grew stronger. I saw smiles circulating the crowded space. The lyrics played, "When in the midst of sorrow, you can't see up when looking down. A brighter day tomorrow will bring. You hear the voice of reason. Telling you this can never be done. No matter how hard reality seems, just hold on to your dreams. Don't give up, and don't give in. Although it seems you never win. You will always pass the test as long as you keep your head to the sky. You can win as long as you keep your head to the sky. Be optimistic." We all repeat the chorus, "As long as you keep your head to the sky, you can win. Be optimistic!" The session ended, and people departed. Victorious and exhausted, I wrote a few notes after everyone had left the room. I wandered into another room to participate in a workshop by a man with a complex history.

The gentleman speaking had a fierce aura. He had a deep, robust, and militant-sounding voice. He immediately captured everyone's attention when he shared his father was Stanley "Tookie" Williams, the infamous leader and co-founder of the Crips gang. He spoke candidly about how his father had utterly transformed and redeemed himself in jail. His father had written a memoir, several children's books, and books deterring people from gang life. Despite his father's literature, nomination for the Nobel Peace Prize, changing the lives of thousands, and protests by celebrities and influential leaders for his death penalty to be commuted to a life sentence, his father was executed on December 13, 2005.

He said, "There were a lot of rumors about my dad having lots of kids. All lies. He only had two children, me and my brother. Yes, my dad did a lot of destructive things in life. However, he redeemed himself in prison and tried to make it right! This gang life is still powerful and alive in LA. You have men in their 50s still out here in the streets gangbanging. Now, I gangbang for Christ!" As he spoke, everyone in the room was still, silent, and zoned into every word he said. In a fiery tone, he said, "Put your hands up if you're banging for Christ!" I looked around the room as a dozen hands went up. He continued sharing how he worked to get young men out of gangs and off the streets into more productive things. I sat in awe and remembered the controversy around Stanley "Tookie" Williams' last days on death row. His story gained worldwide attention. I had never thought I would be in the heart of South Los Angeles teaching and learning so much about the history of gangs. Nor did I ever think I would attend a workshop led by the son of a legendary, controversial, and complicated individual such as Stanley "Tookie" Williams. The workshop ended. I briefly spoke with Mr. Williams and shared my appreciation for who he is and his efforts to prevent gang violence. Later that evening, I researched Stanley "Tookie" Williams' entire life.

I learned he grew up as a scared little boy raised by a single mom who had moved from New Orleans to Los Angeles. After his father abandoned the family, she wanted to improve her son's life. I learned that "Tookie," who found himself in a tough, dangerous street environment, became a product of his environment. Like my rap, "The streets is my father, so why even bother because the homies in these streets keep raising me." His initial response to violence was to ally with other young men to protect himself, his friends, and families from bullies. However, he refused to be a victim

317

after being kicked out of multiple schools and a few vicious beatings. While in juvenile detention from age 15 to 17, he had a manifestation. He said, "I will be the leader of the biggest gang in the world!" Upon release, he carried out his plans. He became a bodybuilder and a vicious street fighter. He unified many smaller gangs under his leadership. He partnered with Raymond Washington, who founded the Crips. Tookie, however, became known as the Crip King. Rather than protecting and defending people against bullies, Tookie eventually became the bully.

He terrorized communities and glorified and perpetuated violence. As Tookie's appetite for violence and destruction grew, his life spiraled out of control with the excessive use of drugs and women, leading to his arrest and conviction of multiple murders. Ironically, during six years in solitary confinement, Tookie started reading and studying. He discovered his true self and true purpose in life. His complex story as a gang lord, prisoner, bestselling children's book author, Pulitzer prize nominee, Nobel Award Prize nominee, and national hero is a tragic cautionary tale. It inspires me to continue creating environments that serve as sanctuaries for thousands of young men in neighborhoods nationwide who are born into circumstances similar to Stanley "Tookie" Williams'. Young men need environments that challenge them to know their gifts while helping them discover constructive and alternative ways to belong, be accepted, and become productive leaders who can impact social change.

CHAPTER 21

Troubled Black Man

"Owning our story can be hard but not nearly
as difficult as spending our lives running from it."
Brené Brown

Following the conference, I drove to the emergency room because the pain in my stomach had become unbearable. Sitting in the emergency room, I worried about my kids being off for Spring Break, my need to work on the Mansa Mentoring Program, and parental workshops. At the same time, Venaya completed her first year of veterinary school. I felt that our relationship had become mechanical or stale. Sometimes, I was clueless and confused about spending quality time together. I worried about my inability to treat her like she deserved. I love Venaya to the moon and back, but in the words of Tina Turner, "What's love got to do with it?" I know my actions or inactions impact my marriage. Using my work and children as an excuse not to work on my marriage is very easy. I have had rough moments with my children. However, I feel connected to fatherhood. There's no actual loss of self-esteem. When I have rough moments in my marriage, I plummet into negative, self-defeating thoughts. I experience a heavy heart and a loss of self-esteem. My core beliefs about my marriage are that it is hard, I'm incompetent, and I can't get it right!

My parents are coming to visit us. With each thought of their arrival, my stomach and lung muscles tightened. My stomach was cramped, and I had shortness of breath. However, my thoughts faded away when Venaya arrived at the hospital. I know she will be annoyed with me for waiting until the pain rushed me to the emergency room. Venaya was very concerned about my physical condition. Doctors performed a series of tests, and

319

blood was taken. Finally, after a long wait, the doctor walked in and said, "Mr. Ervin, you have developed an H. pylori infection. This infection occurs when H. pylori bacteria infects your stomach. H. pylori bacteria are usually passed from person to person through direct contact with saliva, vomit, or stool. H. pylori may also be spread through contaminated food or water. A positive H. pylori stool antigen, breath test, or biopsy indicates that a peptic ulcer likely causes your signs and symptoms due to these bacteria. It is treated with antibiotics and other prescribed medications to kill the bacteria and stop the pain and the ulceration."

Nervously, I gulped because I realized this was serious. My wife asked, "Can this lead to cancer?" The doctor responded, "The infection won't cause problems for most people. But in some, H. pylori can cause long-lasting irritation, swelling, and pain in the stomach, known as severe chronic atrophic gastritis or SCAG, and stomach ulcers. This can lead to cancer. Millions of people worldwide are infected with these bacteria. Very few, between one and three out of 100, develop stomach cancer. Researchers think this is because some types of H. pylori are more likely to cause problems than others. Smoking and what we eat can also increase the risk of H. pylori infection, leading to cancer. Mr. Ervin, you will need to take eight pills a day, and over time, the bacteria will be treated," the doctor continued. Venaya said, "I knew something was wrong because you have lost substantial weight since last year. You had to give away all your clothes, especially your suits because you looked like a toddler in them. I'm still worried about this. And please go to the doctor when you have any symptoms rather than wait another year." I nodded in agreement and gathered my belongings, ready to leave the emergency room.

My parents safely arrived in California. It was exciting we could fly them to California for the first time. When my mother got in the car, she asked, "Can you take us on a tour, especially of Crenshaw?" "Ma and Dad, we don't live too far from the airport, so let's drop the luggage off, then we can tour Los Angeles," I said. Upon arriving at our townhome, my parents hugged Venaya and the kids. Venaya escorted them to our room. She had cleaned and prepared everything to make it comfortable for them. After unpacking the luggage, we returned to the car and headed to Los Angeles.

While driving on Highway 101, they saw the famous Hollywood sign and Dodgers stadium. We went to Rodeo Drive in Beverly Hills, Venice Beach, and our last stop was Crenshaw. "Drive slow so I can look at all the scenery and interesting people," my mom said. We slowly drove past Crenshaw Mall, through the Jungles, and to Black Beverly Hills. We went down Slauson Ave and made our way toward the location of the LA Riots on Florence and Normandie Avenue. Throughout the tour, the conversation with my parents was lively and animated as I talked about the sights, history, and popular culture of Los Angeles. My parents were in awe at every location and experienced the energy from the people in the City of Angels. Lastly, my mom said, "I want some chicken from Popeyes. Can we stop at the one on Crenshaw?" My dad said, "Yes, chicken with some iced cold Pepsi!" I thought to myself, "Popeyes chicken? Really? On Crenshaw?"

Then, without hesitation, we swerved through a few back streets, and within a few minutes, I pulled up into the drive-through at Popeyes Chicken & Biscuits. We waited in a long line. When we pulled to the window, my parents were startled to see a bulletproof, steel-looking window. We couldn't see the employees. We just heard them speak into the microphone. "May I take your order?" I chuckled and said, "This is Crenshaw! This is South LA." I placed my parents' order and put the money into a contraption on the steel window. The window rotated, and we got the hot, greasy chicken and biscuits. We cruised Crenshaw Avenue as my parents voraciously scarfed down those chicken and biscuits. I zipped onto the highway, and we drove back to Ontario, California.

My parents' visit helped us tremendously. They cared for the kids while Venaya and I worked and managed our busy lives. We, however, quickly paid the price with my mother's passive-aggressive behavior. One evening, we came home to a spotless kitchen. However, we promptly piled dirty dishes into the sink without washing them. When I went to check on my parents the following day, my mom barely responded to anything I said. My wife pulled me aside with frustration and said, "Your mom has been making little comments about our home and our leaving dirty dishes in the sink. I'm so fucking annoyed. This is our home, and I refuse to be uncomfortable in my own home. Musa, I'm really tired of holding my tongue with your mother. I need you to address her passive-aggressive behavior. Yes, we appreciate them watching their grandkids. We bought their plane tickets and flew them here to vacation, but we don't owe your mother anything."

As she continued talking, my brain felt like spaghetti noodles. Like Hurricane Katrina, anxiousness, insecurity, and self-condemning thoughts flooded my body. It was tough not to internalize Venaya's words because I received them as criticism of my mom and manhood. Like a captain navigating his ship in a vicious thunderstorm, I tried to stay above the water and navigate the colossal waves coming at me. I fought against shutting down. Finally, she stopped talking and looked at me with those gigantic, almond-shaped eyes that were wider and brighter than the moon. Hearing nothing from me, she asked, "When will you talk with her?" She waited and waited.

I mumbled and stuttered. I responded with some gibberish and nonsense, hoping it would distract her so I could escape. Nope. "Musa, you're not making any sense. Do you even care about my feelings?" I struggled, then responded, "I know my mom is a lot, but we only have a few more weeks. Can we ignore her?" Venaya paused and allowed her rage to subside. But she glared at me like a mom chastising her son. In a harsh and teachable tone, she said, "Musa, you avoid any challenges in your life, from technology to fixing things, and what's most hurtful, you avoid our marriage. I feel avoided because of your inadequacy. I don't doubt that you love and take care of our kids. I have no worries there. My biggest worry and concern, however, is how you don't care for me. It's been eleven years, and you keep hiding behind the same excuse of 'I don't know what to do.' You're afraid of growing up and taking on real challenges, especially regarding your relationship with your parents and me." My whole body hardened and stiffened like stale toast. I barked back, "Marriage has never felt natural to me. It feels procedural. It feels mechanical. It——!" Venaya skillfully interrupted me and continued.

"You are a dedicated, very skilled, and passionate teacher who will sacrifice everything for the development of your students and the families you spend so much time with. I often wonder, are you using your work in the community as an escape from our relationship?" I squeezed my fists and tightened my abdominal muscles and shoulders as I said, "It's hard working in Crenshaw and working with Black and Latino boys and families who have no hope, are marginalized, displaced, and alienated from themselves. I have a mission and a vision to help them turn fear into strength and pain into passion. You know how those kids and families treat me, yet I still show up with an open heart!"

Venaya clapped back, "You did not answer my question. I listen to you vent about the kids taking your kindness for a weakness and how you feel hurt, disappointed, hostile, and resentful. You judge them as being so ungrateful. You don't understand why they don't appreciate you or how they reject the beautiful gift you have offered them. However, what you fail to realize is how you treat me is the way those kids treat you! You are just like the people who live in Crenshaw. You have taken advantage of my vulnerabilities, kindness, compassion, unconditional love, and undying loyalty to us and our relationship. Similarly, I'm working harder than you, but you're stuck in your head and unwilling to change. This is the source of our tension and resistance. Likewise, this is the tension and resistance you receive from your students. You take me for granted, but you know I will always stay and try to make things work because that's who I am! I make things work! I won't quit! However, instead of taking advantage of my attributes, you use them to walk all over me and treat me disrespectfully!" She finished and walked out of the room.

After she left, I staggered over to the small table in the kitchen and sat down. I sat for some time as my mind was in a chaotic frenzy. I was paralyzed by what had happened. I slowly opened my composition notebook and attempted to write what was on my mind. I finally wrote the phrase "A Troubled Black Man." I realized Troy was coming over to share his music and self-published poetry book. I appreciated our potent, reflective, and deeply profound conversations. We were different yet cut from the same cloth. As Leos, we struggle to measure up to the potential that others see in us and that we see in ourselves.

Troy arrived and looked fit and dapper. He enthusiastically asked, "Musa, what's good, boi?" He noticed that I was sad and distressed. He asked, "Man, did you and my sister argue?" I slowly shook my head to confirm his guess. I went on a rant expressing my frustrations and challenges of trying to meet the expectations of my mom, wife, and students. Additionally, dealing with these pressures and demands made me feel empty and incomplete. Troy listened for a while, then stopped my pity party. He leaned across the table with a serious-looking face and asked, "What's most important to you?" I paused and thought about his question. I felt butterflies in my stomach as I struggled to find the correct answer.

Troy watched me. He observed my dilemma and said, "Musa, it's straightforward, don't make it complicated. What's important to you?" I slowly opened my mouth and said, "My family, my career, my community, and my love for humanity." Troy belted out a gut-belly laugh and assertively asked, "What about yourself? What about caring for you? Because you taught me about connecting with my emotions and my needs. If you don't work, nothing works. You, like me, are a recovering people pleaser. When we people please, no one is ever happy. We lose. I know you want to be that guy for my sister. I know how important change is to you. However, change is an inside job. I can only imagine your position in managing those dynamics between your wife and your mom—the stress of that. However, if you let outside influences inside your marriage, it will never work.

"Start coming from your heart, not your head. Close your eyes and disconnect from the world. All the answers and all the wisdom are within you. Meditate, and you will find your truth. My sister is a strong woman, and she married a strong man. I've been watching your growth for years. You're it. You're the one. You're special! You're struggling with your marriage because you haven't accepted that this marriage is a part of your legacy. You're different. My sister is the only woman for you, so honor and cherish that. It's okay to be afraid and make mistakes. Know that your legacy is part of this beautiful love story that you've created with my sister. You found your love at a young age, and that's what great men like Gandhi and King did! So, admit your weaknesses, check yourself, and realize you're the person you're looking for when you look in the mirror. It's you! You owe God because he has given you these gifts and blessed you with a woman to share them with on life's journey."

When Troy finished speaking, I experienced a flow, a current of energy rushing through my body. I took a moment to fully take in Troy's wisdom and made space to receive his poems and celebrate his artistic accomplishments. After Troy left, I returned to the small kitchen table, thrilled to unleash the thoughts and reflections that were bubbling inside me after his transformational words.

April 7, 2008, Self-awareness

Okay, I will admit it. I have avoided the tough conversations about marriage, and I do not fundamentally understand how to confront my deeper fears about marriage or myself. My focus has been on my children rather than building intimacy, trust, and a committed relationship with my wife. My focus has been on the quantity of my marriage, eleven years rather than the quality of the marriage, like taking time to care for my wife's real authentic needs and my own. I view marriage as an outside process where I allow external influences to shape my attitude about it. I surrender my agency in my marriage and put all the responsibility on my wife. I see the error of my ways. However, what will I do to repair and restore the integrity of my relationship?

My wife sees me as a hypocrite who pretends to be a happily married man because of our children and for the approval of others. I have to put my ego aside and accept that I have not put forth any effort in the relationship for six years. My wife gives of herself. She is caring, supportive, and understanding. She is clueless as to why I am so numb and insensitive in our relationship, and I am not honest enough to admit it. She feels hurt, sad, and not deserving of this treatment. Her fundamental questions are: why are you resisting me? Why are you taking advantage of me? Likewise, I question my relationship with my students and other students. I give my students the gifts I have as a strong, sensitive Black man. I bring a radical revolutionary approach to teaching that helps them love themselves and think critically and deeply while breaking out from generational patterns and curses of inferiority and learned helplessness. So why are they resisting me? Why do they make it so hard, and how could they not appreciate a teacher like me?

Despite the pain and the suffering, I know I have, as Victor Frankl, a Jewish holocaust survivor says, "an awareness of the last of human freedoms." The Nazis could control his environment and violate his body. Frankl, however, was self-aware. His identity was intact. He could decide whether his situation would affect him negatively or positively. He had the freedom and the power to choose the response. Similar to Frankl, I have a sense of self-awareness. I know my strengths and weaknesses. I can think, evaluate, and learn from others' experiences and my own. I can break bad habits. I am not my feelings, moods, or thoughts.

My self-awareness separates me from them. My journaling and meditation practices are essential because they separate thoughts and reality. Therefore, this allows me to integrate from a place of wholeness and soulfulness, not victimization and brokenness. Self-awareness enables me to examine how I see myself, the most fundamental paradigm for effectiveness. It affects not only my attitude and behaviors but also how I see other people. It's my basic map. I can examine my paradigms to determine whether they are a reality, principle-based, or a function of my conditioning and conditions. I can choose to see rebellious, disruptive, defiant boys or students struggling to navigate in a complex, frustrating society. They need me to see their beauty and worth at their worst.

My wife can choose to see me as a disrespectful, irresponsible, hypocritical, inconsiderate man. On the other hand, she can see a man struggling to understand his role in a committed relationship with a woman who is determined to love and challenge him to be and do better. I am sharing these lessons of self-awareness with my students. However, I am not applying them to my relationship. We don't see with our eyes. We see with our consciousness. Often, the only vision of ourselves comes from the social mirror of opinions, perceptions, and paradigms of people around us. Our view of self is like the reflections seen in a room of mirrors at a carnival. We must realize we are more than the projections of loved ones and society that often causes more harm than good.

I finished journaling and took a deep breath. I had an awareness of what to do. Later that evening, I patiently waited for Venaya to return home from studying. When she arrived, I gently pulled her close, embraced her, and softly said, "I have been detached from the relationship. I was wrong. I want to make it better. I have taken your gifts for granted, and I want to receive the ways you give to me in fullness. I want you to know you are my rock, and my job is to protect you from harm. Tomorrow evening, I will let my parents know we will discuss our concerns about my mom's treatment of you during dinner." With a skeptical, surprised expression, Venaya said, "Are you sure this is a good idea?" I responded, "I am not sure how it will turn out, but it's to confront this situation with my mom, stand by your side, and assert myself as the leader of my family. During dinner, I will begin by sharing my concerns, and then you can share your concerns." Venaya nodded and said, "I'll be ready because I have plenty to get off my chest." She went into the bathroom to take a hot shower.

While Venaya slept, I drafted my talking points for the difficult conversation with my parents as if I were preparing for a seminar. I wanted to be careful how I began the conversation to ensure I spoke truthfully and from my heart. After I had completed my writing, I went to my parents' room. I saw the light under the door and was relieved they were still awake. I ignored my fears, turned the doorknob with sweaty palms, walked in, and sat at the edge of the bed. "Ma and Dad," I said. "I am buying dinner for us tomorrow night, and I want to have a 'clear the air' discussion between us. Mom, I know you were annoyed about the kitchen situation, and while we appreciate you and Dad being here to help take care of the kids, we have concerns we would like to share." I finished. My dad was silent. My mom responded, "We don't have any concerns. People need to clean up after themselves. We will be there." I stood with some trepidation, yet relief, and shut the door.

The next evening arrived quickly. I prepared plates for the kids and allowed them to eat in their rooms. Venaya came home from school and immediately sat at the dining room table. I took a moment to review my questions. Delighted and surprised, likewise, Venaya wrote down her thoughts. She said, "I will be careful and take my time. I am not trying to be nasty. I want to share how I have felt for years." I was nervous and jittery. When I heard my parents walk down the stairs, I put my jitters aside and went for it. My parents quietly sat down. My dad made a few jokes in an attempt to hide his discomfort. My mom's face was tight, heavy, and emotionless.

Venaya looked cautious and ready. I began, "Ma and Dad, I have been married to Venaya for eleven years and have never dared to speak up for her. There has been disrespect towards her for years that I refused to acknowledge and address. For years, I have pleaded with her to let it go. I minimized the situation and invalidated her feelings. I don't like conflict. Mom, I did not want to hurt your feelings. However, Venaya is my wife. Her feelings also matter. I intend to have a productive conversation where everyone has the space to say what they want without being critical, judgmental, or aggressive. I began the conversation. Now Venaya will speak about her experiences." Looking at my parents' expressionless faces, I hoped they would truly understand the importance and need for the conversation.

In a soft tone, Venaya said, "Mrs. Ervin, I have always wanted a mother-in-law and a sister-in-law, but from the day Musa and I shared our plans to get married, you criticized me, put me down, and excluded me from the family. I want to share a few things about——" Before Venaya could finish speaking, my mother lost it and screamed, "I don't give a damn! You and your uppity sisters think you're better than us, and you have no place to try to come for me like this! Keep your house in order! Learn how to stay in your place and care for your man!" Venaya said, "Mrs. Ervin, let me finish." I raised my voice, "Ma, ma, ma! Listen, Venaya did not finish what she had to say!"

The conversation was out of control. My mom stood up, pulled out some paper from her purse, and ripped it up in front of us. She continued, "Venaya has truly disrespected me, and I won't tolerate it! I hate myself sometimes. I've written plenty of letters to give to Venaya, but I tore them apart! For years, I wanted to ask both of you why you treat us like this. Why did I get a daughter-in-law and son that don't care about us? I don't have the best personality, but I pitch in because I'm helpful. Venaya is so inconsiderate! She did not even thank me for cleaning that messy ass kitchen! Morris, I'm not like you or your father. People judge me as standoffish! I don't need your fake love! I have never felt pretty or any real love for myself! Come on, Mo, let's go!" She rushed towards the door, and I ran behind her just as I saw Naimah and Idris standing at the top of the stairs! Naimah's eyes were filled with tears! Venaya sat calmly at the dining room table. I tried to reason with my mother by saying, "Ma, sit down. How can we have a relationship and work things out? When I talked, you listened. When Venaya talked, you exploded!" My dad said, "Morris, it hurts coming from her. You're our son. Maybe you can tell us what we have done so that we can change!" Then my mom interjected. "I ripped up my letter to Venaya because she was so disrespectful. She doesn't deserve it!"

My mom tried to fight back the tears while demanding that I immediately take them to the airport. Distraught, defeated, and appalled, I helplessly watched my mom storm up the stairs as my dad followed closely behind her. Their suitcases were packed within minutes. They went to the car and waited for me to take them to the airport. I hurried down the sidewalk and opened the car doors as they squeezed their suitcases into my little car. On the ride to the airport, I was depleted as my mom continued to throw shade at my wife to justify her case. She continued to rant but eventually stopped as we approached the airport. I pulled into Ontario Airport, hopped out, and removed their bags from the car. I wrapped my arms around my mom, shook my dad's hand, and watched them enter the airport.

When I arrived home, Venaya immediately greeted me at the door with a hug and said, "Naimah was pretty worked up about your mom. I finally got her relaxed and calm. She fell asleep. Idris is a little too young to understand what happened." Holding hands as we sat in the kitchen, I said, "That was wild. I ruffled their feathers when I spoke, but they did not respond angrily. As soon as you started talking, my mom went ballistic!" Venaya said, "I had a bad feeling. Well, I am over it. I am glad I will not have to deal with her again. Her whole vibe frustrates me. It was so much stuff with the kids that I tried to ignore.

"It's like she is trying to compete with me. I told the kids no when they asked for something a few times. Then your mom turned around and gave it to them—yet your mom called me rude and inconsiderate. Your mom puts people on eggshells. She has treated you and your sister like this for years. Your mom has hated on my mom and my sisters ever since the wedding shower when she and Maya isolated themselves from us the entire time! Naimah's baby shower was an even worse disaster with their shitty attitudes! They think all the decisions we have made together were my decisions. They believe all the times we missed your family events were because of me. Truthfully, you were unorganized and forgot to tell me. Sadly, things would be different if she wanted a relationship with me. This situation sucks for you, but I'm happy I don't have to see them again." Venaya finished some things while I sat in the kitchen to write a reflection.

April 8, 2008, Momma's Wound

My mom is good at convincing people that she is the victim. It is hard to feel sorry for a wounded dog if it continues to attack people viciously. No one understands why the dog is so bitter because it won't let anyone get close to assess their wound. I get mixed messages from my mom. When she is hurting, she spews so much venom it is hard not to believe she is in control. However, I realize my mother is out of control on the inside, so she tries everything to control her family on the outside. My decision to marry an independent, successful, educated woman eleven years ago directly threatened her control. My mom is unaware of the gravity of her actions, making it so hard to understand her. She appears confident and assertive, but underneath, she is fragile and insecure. Despite it all, I love her. I respect and understand if my wife never talks with my family again. I am confident my mother will spin this situation in her favor so people can rally around her, "the victim." Sensitive people are so insensitive!

Despite the disaster with my parents, I firmly believe time will possibly heal those wounds. Spring Break ended, and I returned to work sharper, wiser, more self-aware, and eager to continue integrating my role as teacher and healer. My self-awareness improved my relationship with Venaya. I continued to slow down and notice my actions with my students. In addition to my school and home life, I found tremendous joy and fulfillment in creating the Mansa Mentoring Program. I led meetings at local LA libraries and recruited young men with supportive single moms who bought into my vision. It was great to consistently meet with Jacques, the quiet, intelligent young man from my eighth-grade class. Benjamin, the super smooth man-child, convinced his mother to allow him to be a member of Mansa. Likewise, Little Martin, the brilliant ninth grader with the gift of gab and loads of potential, attended. His mom, Katrina, was a super involved, dedicated, and driven woman who wanted only the best life for her son. Kelvin continued to participate in my Mansa Saturday Workshops even though it was a challenge to communicate with his mom. Lastly, Victor, my innovator, beatmaker, and savant student who threatened me in our first encounter, has blossomed into a well-rounded young man.

Although Victor was not a part of Boys Inspired, he snuck into my room during the B-Inspired time to make my lessons musical and magical. His single mother, Shanice, had positive energy and the necessary grit to raise boys in Crenshaw. Shanice persuaded me to take Victor's younger brother, Ezekiel, into the group. I had other young men who attended a few Mansa outings. However, my B-Inspired students were my foundation. I intended to build a relationship with the boys while providing emotional support to their mothers. I invited mothers to separate workshops that helped them develop self-awareness skills and how to provide their sons with a well-rounded life.

I required the moms to journal their experiences with their sons to help create a shared reality and make communication easier. I directed the boys and their mothers to sign a pledge. Mothers recited the pledge at the end of each parent workshop, *"I promise to support my son in his transition into manhood. I promise to help implement the daily activities required in this arduous process. I promise to consistently transport my son to sessions, workshops, or field trips. I promise to attend meetings and provide honest feedback on the program. I promise to have faith and trust in this program. I promise to contact Mansa for assistance, support, and coaching during any difficult situation with my son."*

Daily tasks outside of my Saturday program required the young men to read for thirty minutes, journal in a quiet place for ten to twenty minutes, study vocabulary words from our Saturday sessions and be able to spell and recite them at the meeting, drink water, and exercise thirty minutes a day. They also had to practice speeches and poems created during our Saturday sessions before family and friends.

During the end of one parent session, Shanice, Victor's mom, was excited to share a few lines of her journal with me. She recited words from her composition notebook. "I am a woman who is the head of my household, raising four Black males. I make a way out of no way and am proud of all my boys. I see the value of the Mansa Program. This is why I have my 17 and 14-year-old sons involved. Mansa provides my two sons with exposure to manhood development, leadership skills, emotional intelligence, and critical knowledge about their history and culture that will give them a competitive advantage in this world. However, I'm concerned about Victor. I don't want him to fall through the cracks. Victor is too dependent on me. I want Victor to be an independent man with exceptional self-development skills. I want the house to flow when I am not there. Sometimes, I'm beaten up because being a single parent is tough. However, I believe God will protect us and keep powerful men like Mansa in our lives. Getting moms and sons to clarify their thoughts and feelings is the first step to a sustainable relationship." All the moms appreciate how I push them and their boys to turn fear into strength and pain into passion.

The final days of the school year approached. It was time to give my Boys Inspired class my final message before their twelfth grade graduation ceremony. I carefully and intentionally typed my last journal entry with my best life advice for young Black men. I planned to give the letters to them at graduation. Sadly, I will not see these boys again. However, I implanted deep awareness and consciousness practices that will last a lifetime.

"I see the MAN-sa in you. Do You see it in yourself? You know you have received an inadequate education. You resist home. You resist school because you know it's not right, healthy, or suitable for you. You resist because no one has taken the time to see your strength or help you find your voice. You pretend to enjoy this wild, rebellious behavior because you don't see any other way. You gloat because the reaction from adults and peers gives you a temporary thrill. The streets provide a quick escape. However, no matter what, you're left feeling lost and empty. You have valid reasons to be furious with the world, your environment, and your circumstances.

"Society and everyone in it has failed you. They have not initiated you into a meaningful, productive, and purposeful life. Instead, you are left to seek toxic masculinity from the streets. I suggest you channel your pain into passion. I suggest you overcome your fears and show the world the gifts that live within you. You should find ways to express the hurt, disappointment, and betrayal you feel towards adults in healthy, creative ways. Remember, you always have a choice. You can continue to resist, rebel, and act out at home and school. You can continue to stay asleep, hanging out in the streets, wasting your potential trying to escape reality. Or you can stay awake, find creative outlets, and spend some time in quiet reflection. Don't be a victim or a statistic to the system.

"You have gifts, so set goals as you grow. Let your lives express the love and community we built this year in Boys Inspired. Remember, I promised to make Boys Inspired a meaningful, powerful program. Those who stayed with me are graduating and moving on to life after high school—hopefully, post-secondary education. We created a culture of success together! It is your turn to deliver on your promise by pursuing your dreams. My next dream is to leave public education to establish a natural holistic education process for marginalized youth, especially

Black boys. Let us always remember Chris! "Treat me cruel, weigh me down. Take my freedom, take my crown."

It is graduation day. I feel excited and nervous about today's graduation. I wore my tan suit with a light blue shirt and tie combination. I drove my orange tangerine car to Trade Tech College to participate in the ceremony. I quickly called Venaya before I walked into the empty college auditorium. I said, "Hello" to Ms. Jones, the administrator who immediately put me to work. She asked me to organize the programs and certificates that were on stage. I felt calm, relaxed, and happy. After setting up for forty minutes, I darted outside just in time to meet all the buses carrying twelfth grade students.

Another administrator, who drove an expensive Audi truck, asked me to get the special pens for my Boys Inspired program from her vehicle. I returned with the pens and put them on all my boys. They looked fly in their colorful suits, slacks, and dress shirts. They had a scared yet confident aura about them. So, did I. We socialized with other graduate classes and took pictures with each other. All the classes wanted to take photos with us. As time passed, the students started getting anxious and bored, standing in single file as they waited to walk in. Finally, we got the nod from a teacher to proceed into the auditorium. My B-Inspired boys were the last to walk in. We were greeted with cheers and screams as cameras flashed and the boys nervously smiled. We sat through a painful speech from Principal Blockhead and some student performances and speeches.

The ceremony began. We were the last group called. Each teacher was responsible for calling their student's name as they received their certificate. We waited and waited. The boys were on point, keeping their composure through this excruciatingly long process. I anticipated our names being called next, so I quickly slid my letters to Orlando, who took one and passed them down the line. I secretly motioned for them to open and read the letters. Finally, the principal said, "It's time for the Boys Inspired program students to walk to the stage." The parents and students went into a frenzy with excitement. I jumped onto the stage and walked to the podium. When I touched the microphone, the emcee in me took over. I shouted, "Okay, we have the Boys Inspired in the building, and they have been sitting for a while. Now, it is time to make them smile. First up, give it up for the kid with the golden smile. He's not from Florida, but he's got the juice! Please give it up for Orlando. Next, give it up for the rain man who loves to dance. Show some love for Shawn! Next is the man with the million-dollar smile and the crazy flipping skills, Maxwell!

"Okay, coming to the stage is the one who puts in work on the field. Could you give it up for Action Jackson? Next, this man needs no introduction. On the count of three, everybody says, Scooter!!! Next, we have Edward, the B-Inspired boy with more bounce to the ounce! Next, we have 'picture me' Roland. I know his momma is proud! Man, what! Can I get a yodel for the best artist in LA? Please give it up for Geronimo!!!! Ladies, he needs no introduction. Man, when he applies himself, ain't nobody smarter. Please give it up for Carter!"

Fascinatingly, as I gave each boy a personalized introduction, the auditorium went wild with admiration and cheered for each student. My powerful voice gave my students the confidence, space, and time to own their moment. After introducing the last B-Inspired boy, I removed the microphone from the podium, walked to the center of the stage, and said, "We lost a group member. Everybody, please take a moment of silence for Chris and put your fists in the air for solidarity." I gazed at hundreds of families and students with their fists in the air. I shared a few precious words of remembrance.

"So, you know what's next, B-Inspired. Wait for it!" I said, "Treat me cruel, weigh me down." To my shock, the entire twelfth grade class of Black, Hispanic, honors, regular students, and Boys Inspired students responded with a thunderous reply that shook the stage and the whole auditorium. In unison, "Take my freedom, take my crown!" I dramatically stepped back and smiled with joy. I repeated it a few more times. The whole twelfth grade class responded with one voice. They roared, "Take my freedom and take my crown!" I was so energized I forgot where I was. I turned and looked at all the administrators, including Principal Blockhead and the superintendent, staring at me with tight, tense bodies. I dropped the mic and clapped my way off stage as the auditorium clapped with *me. The ceremony ended. My B-Inspired boys and I rushed outside to a barrage of hugs from parents, friends, and teachers. I was overwhelmed with joy as my enthusiastic parents formed a line to hug me. All the parents surrounded me with their boys and asked in unison, "Why were my sons not in your class?"*

CHAPTER 22

Epilogue

I am sitting in my favorite room, adjacent to the kitchen in Solon, Ohio. I love being in this room because it has gigantic windows allowing natural light to flow in, and I can look out over the massive deck into nature. Twenty minutes before sitting in my favorite room on the comfy gray couch with a pen in my hand, I felt depressed, rattled, and unsettled.

Now that I have taken the time to journal after washing the dishes, I feel balance and equanimity have returned to me. Journaling is my number one spiritual radical self-care practice. Last night, I got an abrupt call from my sister, letting me know my parents were in town to see her new place. I immediately felt the pressure, the disconnect from my body, and the deep sadness and deep perplexity around what was wrong with them or what was wrong with me. Venaya, my soul mate, immediately went into protection mode in reaction to my dismay. She vehemently roars, "They can visit Maya whenever she moves but fail to drive up to visit their grandkids! I'm still over them!" At the moment, I feel perpetual loneliness, and I am torn and angry about the sting of my wife's truth. I am overwhelmed with continual grief and agony over the whole situation. I burst into tears. Venaya moves next to me and, with a touch, comforts and consoles me.

I sigh and say, "A beautiful day interrupted; isn't that life?" I pulled myself together and decided to visit my parents at my sister's new place. In the darkness of night, I arrive at my sister's home and park on a side street. I walk towards the two-story house, where I see my nephew, nieces, and parents grabbing items from my sister's SUV to take inside. Nervously, I say, "Hey, Maya. I didn't know you were moving. Why didn't you ask me to help?" Without missing a beat, Maya responds, "Morris, it's no big deal. I called you, didn't I? Stop being so dramatic." Disappointed, I buried my emotions as I walked upstairs to greet my parents. Desperate for their response, I gently plopped between my parents and asked, "I'm so confused. You all live in Orlando now. Why didn't you let me know you were visiting Maya?" My dad was on his phone. Surprisingly, he had discovered YouTube. He doesn't respond. My mom says, "Morris, we're here to help Maya settle into her new place. It just happened. It was the spur of the moment. Hopefully, my response was good enough for you?" I paused and swallowed my disgust like it was vomit. I stayed for two hours. Like always, we entertained ourselves by listening to oldie-but-goodie records. I put my pain aside and convinced myself that this unscheduled connection was better than no connection. I left with a heavy heart, feeling like an unwelcome guest.

Nevertheless, I felt peace and rejuvenation as I reflected on the troubles I had experienced. Before that uneventful call from Maya, my wife and I had had an epic day. We traveled to animal shelters all over the city to introduce Dr. Venaya Jones and announce the opening of her hospital, the Cleveland Veterinary Clinic. Surprisingly, most of the clinics and hospitals already knew about my wife and the grand opening of her clinic. Next, we stopped at a local market to eat lunch. To our surprise and excitement, Venaya and her veterinary hospital were featured in a local newspaper article titled "Women Bosses!" We were both thrilled, even though Venaya was concerned if the final construction of her hospital would be ready in time for the grand opening.

I sat in awe of my wife. Venaya envisioned owning a veterinary hospital and what it would look like. She worked closely with the builder, helping him design and tailor the blueprints to her specifications. She is a boss. While eating lunch, we discussed my role as her marketing guru, mindfulness teacher, and empathy coach. Throughout my wife's journey, graduating from vet school, landing a position working with a vet, and now venturing off on her own to make history as the first African American to own and operate a veterinary hospital in the City of Cleveland comes with tremendous stress. Plus, she is driven to provide exemplary, innovative, stress-free care to her beloved four-legged companions. I see how the community, including young people, admire her accomplishments. I know the potential burden and expectation that comes with public recognition. So, we willingly practice mindfulness and self-care. I also support her in developing a meditation practice. To promote and market her hospital, I created a marketing team consisting of some family members. We disseminated flyers at events throughout Cleveland, developed a press kit with information about the hospital's grand opening, and used our connections to schedule interviews for Venaya on local television stations. More importantly, my path to becoming a certified Nonviolent Communication trainer celebrates my commitment to nonviolence in my marriage, parenting, and the work I have been doing in schools, organizations, and communities nationwide. Despite my reservations and hesitations about getting this certification, it will expand my reach while exposing me to an international community as the first African American male trainer in history.

I am at a crossroads with my NVC work. I have integrated it into my personal and professional life since meeting Marshall Rosenberg, NVC's founder, in 2006. However, there is a void. Something feels incomplete. Despite the decades of work, I have done implementing NVC into my household, in schools, and at mindfulness retreats with educators across the country and globe, I don't think I am enough. I pause. I am afraid. I have often told myself that becoming part of the formal NVC community is unimportant. I don't need them. I have been innovating, expressing, transforming, and inspiring many folks without them. I pause. I reflect. I ask myself, "Why do you feel lonely?" I pause. I reflect.

There is an open wound from the past. I have been avoiding it. Many moons ago, when I was invited to my second NVC intensive retreat, I was asked to co-lead a few breakout sessions. At that time, my practice was solid, and I had taught NVC to a few hundred high school students in my history classes. However, during the workshops, I quickly realized it was not an opportunity to co-lead. It was someone else's decision for me to do manual labor while certified trainers led the workshops. I wanted to add value to a session, so I shared some insights. After I spoke, the lead trainer shut down my offering as if it wasn't wanted, needed, and destructive to the training.

I cringed. Everything inside of me tightened and constricted. I did my best to subdue my "Black Boy Rage." We made it through the session. After the event, I felt like a boy wearing a dunce hat as the trainer scolded me for interrupting the workshop. I was told what I said was detrimental and did not fit the NVC process. I immediately put up a protective barrier. I was convinced I was not entirely welcome to express myself in "White NVC" spaces. So, after that retreat, I disappeared from the NVC community. My dream of becoming a certified trainer dried up like a raisin in the sun.

Now, ten years later, I have decided to revisit my dream. In the past ten years, I have developed more complexity, confidence, and depth of who I am and who I am determined to become. By revisiting that painful event, I realized it would be a catalyst to break through my limitations and fears. It revealed a more significant purpose that would usher in healing, reconciliation, and interdependence—for me and the masses.

I said, "Yes!" I found an NVC assessor I recognized from my first NVC retreat and cultivated a relationship. I respected how she held NVC and Marshall's work to the highest standards. It generally takes five years to become certified. Unfortunately, despite the depth of my conviction for NVC work, my passion, truth, wisdom, and work would not allow me to give five years.

Legacy awaited me, but more trouble was on the way. The path to becoming a certified trainer did not pay the bills. Although I had success as a motivational speaker, educator, and wellness coach, my bank account rarely showed it. I had this denial around my cash flow and refused to accept the reality of my situation. I did great professional development seminars at schools, and during the summer, I led powerful mindfulness retreats for educators at places such as the Omega and Esalen Institutes. However, while remaining confident, my cash flow stayed intermittent. Add the financial pressure of my two children, who were now college students. As a result of my financial instability, we were forced to sell our beautiful, spacious retreat-style home. The stress from this juggling act of my immaturity, selfishness, and denial led to more significant troubles.

Fortunately, the grand opening of my wife's hospital was a huge success. The district's council member joined my family to do the ribbon cutting. Venaya had a great turnout from the community. She had a doggie fashion show, entertainment, and vendors. She took everyone on a clinic tour, and a reporter interviewed her for a local television station. The interview went viral, and the publicity gave her many supporters who brought their pets to the clinic. Following the grand opening, my wife battled the pressures of running a new clinic, training new staff, seeing all the patients, and managing her finances. Phew! She *is* a *boss*! I did my best to support her mentally and emotionally with NVC and mindfulness meditation.

Unfortunately, our house did not sell as fast as we would have liked. We took it off of the market to make repairs. I had a few contracts working with school districts, but the money still was funny and did not flow. I lost my enthusiasm for my journey to become a certified trainer. I distanced myself from actively taking steps to move through the process. I retreated into my narrative that "I am not a good fit to be an NVC certified trainer." Additionally, I integrated conversations about anti-racism, privilege, and power into my professional work. All of which is unpopular or unwelcome in many NVC spaces.

Without any warning, the world stopped. Suddenly, everything shut down, and we were thrust into a global pandemic caused by the deadly COVID-19 virus. Instantly, the life we knew had vanished. I could not share my light, energy, education, or message. There were no schools to speak in, no communities to mentor, and nowhere to travel. My identity, my zest, and my purpose were gone. Even my beloved summer meditation retreats were canceled. I worried about what to do, where to go, and how to be of service. Someone told me about being an online educator teaching English to Chinese students. I failed at that. I attempted a few other online teaching gigs. They either failed, or I lacked follow-through. As time passed, my thoughts of insecurity, fear, worthlessness, and hopelessness remained. In my efforts to find work, I realized I had a good college friend who worked at a huge residential campus called NextCare. NextCare provides outpatient services, behavioral health counseling, after-school programming, and residential treatment for traumatized and neglected youth between the ages of 11 and 17.

I had worked in residential environments for 20 years before becoming a teacher. I have done plenty of speaking and workshops within juvenile settings. This job, however, was different, complex, and mentally challenging. It wasn't my best choice. It was my only choice. I applied, interviewed, and became a Cottage Supervisor. The hours were long. The pay was low, and the work was dangerously unpredictable. I supervised a crisis unit that had clients who had been severely abused, neglected, abandoned, and experienced sex trafficking. My days consisted of stopping fights and restraining kids who attempted to harm themselves, others, and staff. I arrived at work feeling cheated, overwhelmed, overworked, and unhappy. COVID-19, which everyone dreaded, infected several staff members. Within 30 days of employment, I contracted this mysterious virus. To make matters worse, I infected my wife and daughter.

My wife was outraged because she had to close her clinic! I seethed with fury and rage, looking to blame everyone. Underneath the mask I wore, I had lost my purpose. I was lost. I did not want to eat or shower. I only wanted to lay in bed. Yuck! I had given up. Fortunately, my wife made me realize I was depressed. I believed to my core I was not worthy. I was a victim. Regretfully, I lived with that core belief and self-defeating thoughts even after my long road to recovery and return to work. I had tough days at work. I was merely surviving and felt stuck, trapped, and unhappy.

Life went on until I finally became aware I had abandoned my journaling, my mindfulness, and my NVC practices. I had buried my values underneath thoughts and beliefs that were detrimental to me. One day, following a rough shift, the kids at NextCare conspired to take over the unit. Surprisingly, I had noticed something brewing in their behavior and mentioned it to a staff member. She said, "Morris, you're overreacting and hovering over the kids." Her statement bothered me. I watched the mutiny as the kids became more unruly and rebellious throughout the day. Finally, when it was time for bed, all the kids refused to go to their rooms.

My patience had worn thin as a young man rushed towards me, screaming, "We hate you, and we're tired of you telling us what to do." He lunged at me. I grabbed him and pulled him to the ground. Then, I told my staff to call for assistance from other units. When more staff arrived, kids threw punches at all the adults. This melee lasted about thirty minutes until a few kids were removed from the unit. Following that situation, the kids told my supervisor I had choked a girl into unconsciousness. Depleted, exhausted, and infuriated, my supervisor informed me I had to be investigated. I struggled to listen to her without lashing out. Equally important, my supervisor's last words were, "Morris, you don't operate in a vacuum. If you felt something brewing early on, you could have reached out for help. You don't have to do this alone." Those words stuck with me like sweat on my body.

The following day, I went for an extra-long walk with my dogs. As I walked, I had several epiphanies. I rushed home. I meditated, and when I opened my eyes, I grabbed a pen and started to journal. I wrote one of my favorite quotes at the top of my notebook. *"Action springs not from thought, but from a readiness for responsibility," by Dietrich Bonhoeffer. I wrote that "readiness is a willingness to do something. There is power in stillness. Something is always brewing underneath the surface. If you act prematurely, you miss the beauty of the volcanic eruption flowing inside you. Not rage. Not blame or ego. But profound clarity, wisdom, and guidance from beyond. Today, my ideas are more integrated and fluid as they flow from an eternal spring of hope. The gift of a practice reduces or relieves the tension between thoughts and actions. We all have thoughts, opinions, and beliefs. However, not everyone is ready or prepared to take the time to allow the pause or the space that will metabolize their troubles into joy."*

It never occurred to me I had abandoned my ability to turn pain and suffering into something worthy and profound. I got comfortable in my shame and sorrow. Renewed and invigorated, I revisited the practice of self-empathy and self-forgiveness. I scrambled to find my feelings and needs sheets. Equally important, I acknowledged and verbalized that my life, which included a global pandemic, losing my consulting contracts, accepting a job I hated, contracting COVID-19, and infecting my family, had not gone according to my plans. Despite all the self-judgment, shame, and guilt, I asked myself, what needs were I trying to meet? I was trying to address the need for self-compassion. To allow myself compassion, I needed space. When I have space, I can discern and make better choices. When I am in true discernment, I realize that learning to accept my circumstances creates an opportunity or an opening for something new to emerge. But taking radical responsibility for my life is the best place to start. I could breathe freely and felt the expansion in my chest and abdomen.

Ultimately, I had a freedom within my reality I never imagined. I became aware that the freedom to choose lies within me. Soon after this realization, I had a new purpose. My creativity and imagination blossomed like a beautiful rose. I walked into that residential treatment facility with a sense of adventure, discovery, innovation, and a determination to grow, learn, and lead. I learned everything about the kids' treatment and practiced the skills with them. I started bringing my years of experience with mindfulness, NVC, and youth development into the facility. I learned how to integrate my experience within the context of the treatment facility. Slowly, I challenged myself to move my workshops, seminars, and motivational talks to the Zoom platform. I reconnected with my assessor and continued on the path to becoming a certified NVC trainer. I transformed that residential environment within two years with my teachings and practices. I recreated my speaking organization on Zoom by teaching and leading many racial and social justice workshops. Equally important, the last few months of pursuing my NVC certification pushed me beyond my limit.

Of course, my wife stood beside me as she offered timely words of wisdom when I tried to overthink the process, which led to many unnecessary distractions. She kept me focused on the task at hand. Despite it all, my journey to become a certified trainer helped me turn my wounds into significant healing. My journey, once filled with fear, self-protection, and isolation, became my road to healing and reconciliation. When I walked away from NVC ten years ago, I realized I wanted to contribute and be loved and valued. Besides all those things, I am confidently and fully self-expressed in who I am. I am the first African American male NVC certified trainer and deeply connected to my mission of creating a world where we truly see beneath and beyond the surface.

Above all, I had the opportunity of a lifetime to join a team of NVC trainers to support the construction of a school on Rusinga Island in Kenya. This facility is dedicated to the sustainability of youth empowerment, peace, and nonviolence. I close with the words of Patrick Overton, "When you come to the edge of all the light you have and must take a step into the darkness of the unknown, believe that one of two things will happen. Either there will be something solid for you to stand on, or you will be taught to fly."